Constructing an Avant-Garde

Constructing an Avant-Garde

Art in Brazil

1949–1979

Sérgio B. Martins

The MIT Press
Cambridge, Massachusetts
London, England

This book was set in Helvetica Neue Pro by
The MIT Press.

Library of Congress Cataloging-in-Publication Data
Martins, Sérgio B., 1977–
Constructing an avant-garde : art in Brazil, 1949–1979 /
Sérgio B. Martins.
pages cm
Includes bibliographical references and index.
ISBN 978-0-262-01926-2 (hardcover : alk. paper)
978-0-262-54410-8 (paperback)
1. Art, Brazilian—20th century. 2. Arts—Experimental
methods—History—20th century. I. Title.
N6655.M378 2013
709.81´09045—dc23
2012046924

Para Nina

Contents

Acknowledgments ix

Introduction 1

(Non-)Objects 17

The Constructive 51

Taking Positions 81

Enigmages 119

White on White 161

Coda: Radical Present 183

Notes 197

Index 229

Acknowledgments

My research would not have been possible without the financial support I have received ix throughout my graduate studies at University College London. Therefore, I would like to thank the Higher Education Funding Council for England, the Graduate School of University College London, and the University College London Department of History of Art.

I also thank these individuals and institutions who have helped my research in various essential ways: César Oiticica Filho and Ariane Figueiredo at the Projeto Hélio Oiticica; Elizabeth Varella at the Museum of Modern Art in Rio de Janeiro; the staff at Daros Latinamerica and Casa Daros, in particular Melanie Zgraggen; Guilherme Bueno and Marcia Muller at the Museum of Contemporary Art in Niterói; the library staff at the Museum of Modern Art in São Paulo; and Ana Paula Marques at the Arquivo Histórico Wanda Svevo (Fundação Bienal de São Paulo). I am especially grateful to Antonio Dias, Cildo Meireles, Ferreira Gullar, Antonio Manuel, and Renata Lucas for their generosity and availability.

I am thrilled to work with the MIT Press. I am thankful to Justin Kehoe, Matthew Abbate, Julia Collins, and Margarita Encomienda for their work, and especially to Roger Conover for his enthusiasm about my project and for his thoughtful suggestions.

An abridged version of chapter 5 was published in *Object* 11. I am thankful to the journal editors and to my anonymous reviewers for their thorough and very useful comments on my draft. Parts of chapters 1 and 2 were published respectively in numbers 105 and 114 of *Third Text*. The latter was a special issue on Brazilian art that I had the honor of guest-editing. This experience has informed my book in many meaningful ways, and I am thankful to Rasheed Araeen and Richard Appignanesi for giving me this unique opportunity.

My thanks to Michael Newman and Dawn Ades for having been thorough and critical examiners; their response was a first and important step in the process of transforming my dissertation into a book. I then benefited from the patience and insight of Michael Asbury, Ed Krcma, Steven Gambardella, Frederico Coelho, Milena Tomic, and Kaira Cabañas, who offered to read parts of my manuscript and whose brilliant feedback was simply invaluable. These were not random choices of readers, for they are also friends on whose sincerity and intellectual sharpness I felt I could always count; and so are Rafael Cardoso, Felipe Scovino, Luisa Duarte, Miguel Conde, Pedro Duarte, and Isobel Whitelegg.

Mark Edwards, Phillipa Kaina, Klara Kemp-Welch, Linzi Stauvers, Denise Frimer, Thomas Morgan Evans, Cadence Kinsey, Gil Pasternak, Paul Fox, Paolo Magagnoli, Cliff Lauson, Sanjukta Sunderason, Warren Carter, Sue Walker, Patricia Lee, Wenny Teo, Bryony Berry, and Maggie Gray are just some of my friends and colleagues at the UCL History of Art Department whom I'd like to thank; I wish I could name them all, for I feel privileged to have spent time and shared thoughts with them. I am deeply grateful to the department's faculty for nurturing and inspiring such a challenging intellectual environment. I would also like to thank friends and colleagues from elsewhere who have supported me in many different ways or discussed important ideas with me over the years, or both: Mariana Cunha, Roberta Barros, Marcela Oliveira, Guilherme Wisnik, Luke Skrebowski, Matheus Rocha Pitta, Erika Tambke, Daniel Steegman, Paula Braga, Max Jorge Hinderer Cruz, Tatiana Leiner, Leandro Gejfinbein, Ana Beatriz da Rocha, Rodrigo Nunes, Tamar Guimarães, Adrian Anagnost, Melissa Geppert, Paloma Carvalho, Joana Bergman, Heleno Bernardi, Stuart Davis, Irene Small, Elizabeth Torrance, Hugo Houayek, Bianca Tomaselli, Gustavo Motta, Clarissa Diniz, Erica Papernik, Paulo Venâncio Filho, Victoria H. F. Scott, Leo Phillips, Tania Rivera, Maria Iñigo Clavo, Ana Holck, Reme Perni, Leon Garcia, Daniela Gomes Pinto, Ana Cândida de Avelar, Nina Galanternik, and Suzana Vaz.

Paulo Sergio Duarte's unparalleled generosity and passionate intellectual engagement prompted me to take the first serious steps on the path I now tread. I cannot thank Tamar Garb enough: without her singular openness to students coming from different backgrounds I simply wouldn't be doing any of this. Her inspired teaching, guidance, and supervision have marked my work in more ways than I can account for. Above all, I feel immensely privileged to have worked with Briony Fer as my supervisor during my Ph.D. program. I never ceased to be amazed by her combination of intellectual sharpness and originality, demanding generosity, and profound interest in every aspect of my work. My ways of thinking and writing about art are profoundly indebted to her, and so is this book.

I thank my family for their support and regret that my parents, Lúcia Amélia and Rogério, are not here to celebrate with us.

Finally—and thankfully—there is Ana Wambier, not only in these pages and my thoughts, but also by my side. I'm lucky enough to dedicate this book to her.

Introduction

The events discussed in this book happened between 1949 and 1979, but the best way to elucidate its historical approach to the art produced in Brazil in this period may be to start with two exhibitions that took place ten years later, in 1989. The first one, in Belgium, displayed works by Brazilian artists Tunga and Cildo Meireles. In his introductory essay, Brazilian critic Paulo Venâncio Filho suggests that the European spectator would simultaneously sense "that the works are very familiar, from the perspective of contemporary European art" and "that Brazil, or whatever one thinks of Brazil, is at a remove."[1] Roughly at the same time, British critic Guy Brett expressed his worries about a supposedly incipient "'boom' in Latin American art."[2] For Brett, overexposure in the art market would not undo the interpretive segregation enforced by problematic curatorial strategies. His examples are "the survey, with its inevitable over-simplification and homogenization of another reality" and the "myth of the odyssey, a report of the exploration of a far-off unknown land in search of art." Thus his effort to situate "Transcontinental: Nine Latin American Artists" (1989), which he curated, critically beyond "a polarized relationship between 'there' and 'here,' between 'they' and 'we.'"[3] After all, these were works that belong "to an international urban practice of art and can therefore be more easily translated to a European gallery."[4]

Taken together, both situations configure an experience of uncanniness, in that the unexpected familiarity of the works on display is precisely what makes them *un*familiar. Geographic distance as a pretext for all sorts of mediations (such as the survey and the "odyssey") is bypassed; as Brett puts it, these are works that "burst on the scene." This is not simply a matter of criticizing and deconstructing a Eurocentric view of Latin America. For, as Venâncio Filho adds, the situation of the European spectator is surprisingly akin to what Brazilian artists themselves experience, leading to a fundamental but productive out-of-jointness, an "obliqueness" in relation to oneself that "represents a structural position and not properly an identity."[5] This is an odd solidarity, to say the least. It is not, then, that those works stand as tokens of "otherness," but rather that their uneasy closeness puts modernism as whole, or whatever one thinks of modernism, at a remove—even in the eyes of its "natural heirs." A negative solidarity, then: Brazilian artist and European spectator are joined together in their being displaced. Both are equally out of joint in relation to modernism.

The aim of this book is to acknowledge this obliqueness fully, to turn it into the basis of a renewed critical vocabulary and a reconfigured account of defining moments in the recent history of the Brazilian avant-garde. It departs from the assumption that a proper engagement with this avant-garde must resist the imperative of filling gaps in current art historical knowledge (although it does involve unearthing new information and establishing new connections). Instead, it must stem from the recognition of the urgency of such historiographical engagement. If the Brazilian avant-garde is culturally and geographically displaced, it is so also from a historical point of view. This means that attempts to fit it into more familiar pigeonholes are intrinsically problematic. For critic Paulo Sergio Duarte, the "formation of art in Brazil" cannot be properly addressed without taking into consideration the fact that modernism could not simply be imported without having to contradictorily negotiate its processes and repertoires with the uneven Brazilian cultural landscape.[6] By the same token, any art historical approach to this modernism "on the margins" must undergo a similar negotiation.[7] Taking Duarte's and Venâncio Filho's arguments one step further, I would suggest that this obliqueness of the Brazilian avant-garde can be tentatively broadened into a critical reappraisal of modernism as a whole—of its impasses and dead ends, and of alternative critical possibilities it may still offer (even if the name "modernism" no longer applies). This book, then, aims to contribute to making the Brazilian avant-garde "burst on the scene" rather than "boom."

One of the reasons there is no proper place for this history is because it did not simply take modernism on a detour—it actually *hijacked* it. In this process, not only were its projects and utopias continued and renewed, but also the historical understanding of European modernism was radically shifted. This gained further complexity as artists began to face the work of their pop, minimalist, and conceptualist contemporaries later in the 1960s and 1970s. "In a society where set artistic paradigms lack density," Venâncio Filho continues, "it is up to the artist to create a history for himself, and to establish references for dialog. Therefore, this mythology that appears in Cildo and Tunga is by no means subjective; it is an objective reality."[8] By hijacking and reconfiguring their past, I will argue, Brazilian avant-gardists were able to face their present challenges from a unique—and, more important, an oblique—standpoint.

LEFTOVER

This brief description of the historical efficacy of the Brazilian avant-garde cannot fail to recall Hal Foster's famous critique of Peter Bürger.[9] Foster's text, or rather the historical and conceptual differences between his argument and mine, provides a starting point for addressing my choice to frame my discussion within the scope of avant-gardism, since it already raises the question of the historiographical relevance of redefining it.

Let us review the basic coordinates of Foster's argument. Against Bürger's indictment of the neo-avant-garde as a farcical repetition of avant-gardist transgression, Foster invokes the Freudian notion of *Nachträglichkeit*, usually translated as "deferred action." This involves shifting the register of the first avant-garde from *shock* to *trauma*; that is, from a tragic and somewhat intentional revolt against established norms to a hole in the Symbolic order, a disruption in signification. Foster takes this shift to reveal the fact that the achievements of the avant-garde were not circumscribed by the ultimate failure of its explicit project (or projects). And the reason they were not circumscribed is because they were as yet unelaborated, which is logical if they can reasonably be assumed to have perforated the symbolic mesh of their epoch. If their program had indeed failed, their formal inventions—such as the monochrome and the readymade—persisted as a sort of dormant residue. In fact, these strategies would only be recognized as the true (and thus traumatic) core of the avant-garde in retrospection, as they were worked through once again in the context of the neo-avant-garde. So the readymade, for example, could no longer be regarded as a historically finished form upon which one could pass a final verdict. Just as the reception of Duchamp was not monolithic, the actual meaning of the readymade was dependent on a complex relay among production, circulation, and reception.

Of course, for this logic to work, there must be a structure of repression in play that will justify discontinuity and return. For Foster, the agency of the "institutional repression" of the avant-garde is "the disciplinary order of late modernism."[10] As his narrative goes, the attacks on artistic *conventions* by the historical avant-garde (as in the readymade or the monochrome) were then *institutionally* repressed (one cannot help thinking here of a relay between Alfred H. Barr Jr.'s chronological diagram of modernism and Clement Greenberg's teleological celebration of high modernism). But this was due in part to the historical impossibility of the avant-garde articulating its critique in institutional terms. This failure would be thus redressed in its reception by a neo-avant-garde for whom the institution of art was finally at issue.

As far as Bürger's theory is concerned, Foster's critique is well aimed. It is also indebted, as he acknowledges, to Benjamin Buchloh's work on the monochrome.[11] Both authors conceive the historicity of the avant-garde in Freudian terms, opening up to a temporality that puts Bürger's ultimate reliance on originality and authenticity in check, and Foster's recourse to deferred action is a sophisticated twist in this respect. Indeed, the difficulty of historically reconsidering the supposed authenticity of experience is an important part of this book (especially when I discuss Hélio Oiticica's *Parangolés*), making such concerns all the more relevant.

However, when it comes to undermining continuity and linearity, the success of Foster's critique is less sure. Or, to put it another way, he does succeed in dismantling Bürger's progressive account, thus questioning the way modernist criticism has used a similarly linear conception of history to further more conservative aims, but ends up puzzlingly replacing those accounts with a sort of teleology in disguise. The problematic core of this operation becomes adamantly clear from the perspective of the Brazilian avant-garde. For, as art historian Michael Asbury has forcefully argued, Foster's account depends on accepting a fundamental estrangement between high modernism and the theoretical apparatuses of phenomenology and structural linguistics, so that minimalism can be posited as that crucial moment when both are finally confronted under the guise of a decisive break with modernist discourse.[12] However, Asbury continues:

> [The Brazilian poet Ferreira] Gullar's reading of Merleau-Ponty (an indirect route to Husserl) and [the Brazilian poet] Haroldo de Campos' discussion of semiotic categories in relation to concrete art seem to question the decisive character of minimalism in Foster's account.... The fact that dada's deferred action upon minimalism cannot be considered as an exclusive historical relationship seems to escape Foster whose linear narrative could be interpreted as a product of his own provincialism.[13]

But how does Foster, armed as he is with a conceptual apparatus that insistently refuses linearity, fall into this trap? There are historical and conceptual ways of answering this question. On the historical side, my suggestion is that the agency of repression he names, in other words, "the disciplinary order of late modernism," is excessively narrow in its scope. He is right, of course, in seeing the modernist narrative as an agent of inclusion and exclusion whose domain is the canon. But he fails to perceive that, for all its power, this is but a local operation (thus Asbury's damning "provincialism"). In the context Foster writes from, the linearity of the modernist canon is hardly separable from the geopolitical, economic, and cultural shift that pulls the center of gravity of modern art across the North Atlantic in the postwar period. It is not that his critique of Greenberg is fundamentally wrong, but that he doesn't recognize how much his own critical position bears the stamp of that of the senior critic.

Uncannily, then, his rupture with modernism swaps Duchamp for Mondrian and Rauschenberg for Pollock, but the vertical and exclusive link between the most advanced North American art of its time and its European predecessors is left untouched. For Foster, the "first neo-avant-garde," whose major emblem is Rauschenberg, hysterically acts out the "anarchistic attacks of the historical avant-garde."[14] Indeed, the paradigm of passivity that informs Rauschenberg's *White Paintings* ultimately reflects New York's newly inherited position of mastery.[15] To put it simply, both the "disciplinary order of late modernism" and the supposedly "hysterical" rupture with it were not so opposed when it came to standing for the newly acquired hegemony of the US art world.

As I mentioned, Foster argues that the main route for understanding the relay between historical and neo-avant-garde is the latter's updating of a critique of conventionality into one of the institutions of art. As he puts it, "the so-called *failure* of both historical and first neo-avant-gardes to destroy the institution of art has *enabled* the deconstructive testing of this institution by the second neo-avant-garde—a testing that, again, is now extended to other institutions and discourses in the ambitious art of the present."[16] What made the neo-avant-garde still radical is that it was able to come up with an agenda of institutional critique in ways that had been previously unavailable. However, provincialism may be at play here as well, since this sweeping institutionalization of modern art is ultimately specific to the US and European context. The Brazilian situation was quite different: the few institutions that supported modern art emerged alongside the geometric abstract avant-garde in the late 1940s and 1950s, and were mostly regarded as laboratories for new explorations, and even more as allies against the larger backdrop of unsympathetic and anachronistic museums and art schools.[17] A telling comparison can be made between the role of MoMA in institutionalizing modern art (and, bearing Barr in mind once more, in contributing to a teleological view of modernism) and of the Museums of Modern Art in Rio and in São Paulo (MAM-Rio and MAM-SP), whose histories were often precarious and whose grounds served as catalysts for avant-garde groupings. In Rio, for example, future members of the neoconcrete group attended Ivan Serpa's workshop at MAM-Rio when it still operated in the Ministry of Education and Health building, and later witnessed firsthand the protracted construction of the museum's own building. MAM-Rio would remain a central stage even after the decline of constructive tendencies, hosting several avant-garde exhibitions and events during the 1960s (Cildo Meireles, another artist whose work I will discuss, would eventually teach there in the early 1970s).

The limitations of Foster's account can be conceptually accounted for if we turn to the structure of repression he sets in place. If his argument against linearity results not so much in the latter's demise as in a more sophisticated version of it, this may well be due to a problematic rendering of the repressive operation. This seems to be historically the case, further confirming Asbury's suspicions about Foster's ultimate dependence on Greenbergianism as "the culmination of modernism as a whole."[18] By implicitly universalizing a version of modernism as the agency of repression, Foster actually inflates its mastery so as to later undermine it. When he reaches this point, however, historiographical damage is already done, for the subversive position of the neo-avant-garde becomes paradoxically dependent on canonizing that which it is taken to rebel against. What is more, Foster's model boils down to a somewhat overstated polarity between modernism and antimodernism, which vaguely correspond to the "Oedipal narratives" that he attributes to two "generations" of art historians: one which reaches "Picasso by way of Pollock" and the other which goes back to "Duchamp by way of Andy Warhol."[19] If we pick central conceptions of the art object in the Brazilian avant-garde, especially the idea of the non-object—which is clearly a non-Greenbergian link to modernism— things get more complicated than this. One could ask, for example, to what extent the surrealist object plays a part in these formulations, especially considering how attentive or sympathetic key Brazilian critics were to the movement. While this particular question falls beyond the scope of the present study, it nevertheless illustrates the difficulties of a too-schematic conception of such relays with the past.[20]

Like Foster, Buchloh also criticizes Bürger for his excessive reliance on notions of originality and authenticity, going on to argue for "the Freudian concept of repetition that originates in repression and disavowal." Buchloh's emphasis nevertheless suggests a broader interpretive scope in that he adds: "This would entail clarifying the peculiar dynamics of selection and disavowal, of repression and 'simple' omission that resulted from the particular dispositions and investments that the various audiences brought to their involvement with the avant-garde after the Second World War."

There are two main reasons why I find this passage particularly suggestive. First, because its more pronounced historical tone resonates with my suggestion that Foster's agency of repression is too narrowly defined in that it fails to account for wider cultural shifts. Second, because if we were to expand this notion of "particular dispositions and investments" of "various audiences" in the postwar period a little bit, then we would admit the relevance of investigating other developments of modernism, such as the Brazilian avant-garde. What is still needed, then, is to further flesh out a model of "repression and disavowal" that can question the limits of Foster's account.

Since what is ultimately at stake here is narration and interpretation (i.e., historiography), the modernism/antimodernism polarity can be speculatively rendered, after Slovenian philosopher Alenka Zupančič, as that between "the conscious, manifest content or interpretive narration" and "the unconscious as the nondigested/nondigestible piece of the other's message."[21] However, Zupančič quickly dispels this duality by arguing that it overlooks the fact that "the unconscious itself is also always-already an interpretation." What is crucial about this insight, and about Zupančič's essay in general, is that it engages with the *ethics* of interpretation from the psychoanalytic viewpoint, trying to wrest it away from the status of a mere regime of knowledge (over)production. It is worth quoting her at some length:

> If the constitution of the unconscious does in fact coincide with a certain ("conscious") interpretation taking place, i.e. with a certain solution that is given to the enigmatic message of the other, this does not mean that the unconscious is simply what is left outside (and is not included in our interpretation); rather, the unconscious is that which *continues to interpret* (after conscious interpretation is done). Even more precisely: it is that which only starts to interpret after some understanding of the enigmatic message is produced. For what it interprets is, to put it bluntly, precisely the relationship between the given interpretation and its leftover. And it interprets from the point of view of this leftover.[22]

There are two initial points to consider in relation to this passage. First, it clearly refuses to embrace an inclusion-exclusion duality by stressing that the unconscious's relation to conscious content is not one of exteriority. The unconscious is not simply "what is left outside." This already prompts us to rethink modernism's repressive structures less as the product of a "disciplinary order" than, to borrow Rosalind Krauss's definition, as a "self-contained space of ideology."[23] In other words, and this is my second point, the unconscious becomes the effect of a surplus that constantly displaces that which it exceeds. This is why the unconscious is so often referred to as the locus of a *work*—as in the dream work—rather than a fixed site.[24] Any critique of modernism should thus avoid the temptation of "exteriorizing" it so as to make it an easier, wholesale critical target. In Krauss's words, it would be less a matter of searching for "an 'outside' of the system" than of figuring forth "the 'beneath' of the system."[25] This beneath, of course, is that which is produced as a sort of "internal excess" by the very logic of the system. It is the "leftover."

This is crucial, for the problem as I see it is that Foster's conception of the neo-avant-garde cannot supply the "point of view of this leftover." This is due both to the implicit duality in his account, which installs a relation of exteriority, and also, as I have been insisting, to the fact that the rupture it is taken to mark vis-à-vis modernist discourse does not make it less a legacy, in a broader cultural and geopolitical sense, of modern art. The interpretive tools may change, but the position of the interpreter remains the same, so that Foster has it both ways: Dada subversiveness is invisibly coupled with Greenbergian authority. The linearity that creeps back into his account not only disavows other lineages of modernism, but also renders the critical effectiveness of its *Nachträglichkeit* significantly flawed.

Now, as we have seen, the situation of the avant-garde in Brazil problematizes Foster's model both because it bypasses the Greenbergian paradigm and because of the different and precarious relationship between modern art and artistic institutions in that context. Another factor is the latter's peripheral position: Brazil was by no means the natural heir of modernism. A proper engagement with modernism in that context called for more than passivity—in fact, and quite on the contrary, it required (and effectively gave rise to) a language of enthusiasm. Examples are manifold, but none is perhaps as stunning as Lygia Clark's 1959 personal "Letter to Mondrian," in which she resuscitates him to be her interlocutor as she confesses both her allegiance to him and her doubts about neoconcretism, finishing with a poignant declaration: "Today I am crying—crying covers me, it follows me, comforts me and warms, in a certain manner, this hard and cold surface of fidelity toward an idea. Mondrian: Today I love you."[26]

My point is not that the art of the Brazilian avant-garde is intrinsically "better" than that of the North American neo-avant-garde. Nor am I trying to forge yet another arbitrary and linear link with the past. I do believe, however, that the emerging historiography of Brazilian art currently poses a challenge. Is it to become smoothly integrated into the symbolic machinery of art history and of the international curatorial circuit as yet another novelty in the service of the art market and of specialist academic authorities, thus confirming Brett's fears about a "boom"? The way Brazilian art tends to be "fielded" (or "subfielded" as part of another problematic field, that of Latin American art), especially in US academia, tends to preclude its interventional power vis-à-vis the general historiography of modernism. This is why it is so important to create a dialogue between the Brazilian avant-garde and certain aspects of the European and North American critical debate without simply letting the former be subsumed by the latter.

This problem is also relevant to whatever contemporary perspective on avant-gardism this book can propose. As art historians Taina Caragol and Isobel Whitelegg have argued, this geography-specific conception of Latin American art as a field is less prevalent in the United Kingdom than in the United States.[27] It is not, of course, that overdetermining interpretations are utterly absent from UK exhibitions. However, and significantly, the authors highlight the singular trajectory of Brett, whose personal experience in the Signals Gallery and his subsequent and pioneering exchanges with various Latin American artists since the 1960s provided the blueprint for the "artist-by-artist" approach of landmark exhibitions such as "Transcontinental." With its "constellation-like" nature, "Transcontinental" would thus exemplify an approach to Latin American artists based in historical connections and collaborations between artists rather than in a conception of the avant-garde as "a shared and consistent project."[28]

This latter premise, in turn, is Caragol and Whitelegg's critical target in their approach to "Inverted Utopias: Avant-Garde Art in Latin America" (2004, Museum of Fine Arts in Houston):[29]

> In choosing to continue to widely "field" Latin American art, the large-scale exhibition necessitates a prescribed narrative to foster immediate comprehension. In the case of *Inverted Utopias* the project of the avant-garde structures that narrative. This project is traced over a series of discrete historical moments. Conveying the passage of time as an unfolding totality, the exhibition replicates the survey model from which it desires to break away in terms of display.[30]

So, the authors claim, the avant-garde becomes a "Modernist *deus ex machina*" that ties the exhibition to a progressive model of history. Geographic circumscription is neatly coupled with linear and coherent narrative. If we compare this state of things to the problems in Foster's argument, it becomes clear that the historiographical function of continuity and linearity is conveniently malleable. In Foster's case, it guarantees a "provincialist" defense of an inherited position of mastery, whereas in "Inverted Utopias" a similar position is installed alongside the constitution of a "field," as narrative is deployed in order to demarcate the latter's boundaries. In both cases, the risk of horizontal slippages is disavowed, leaving the stable positions of enunciation of the curator and the art historian undisturbed.

Now, one crucial question remains: is it possible (and desirable) to rescue the notion of the avant-garde from this impasse, from this exclusive but mutually supportive polarity that turns this very notion into a historical *cordon sanitaire*? If this polarity poses what I took as a risk to the emergent historiography of Brazilian art, then the stakes are very high indeed. Simply to jettison the notion of avant-garde may be a poor way out. Even if one agrees with Caragol and Whitelegg's call for a model of reception that can account for the discontinuities and contextual displacements so as to question smooth, overarching narratives, the fact is that the critical power of discontinuity per se only goes so far. To abandon *history* in favor of fragmented *histories* (after, say, a micropolitical model) is not without its own risks. The work of Oiticica is a fine case in point: it can be argued that a piecemeal understanding of his trajectory actually contributes to curatorial selections of his work that favor extraneous arguments or totalizing narratives. His early geometric abstractions fit easily into exhibitions of Latin American art (especially when they emphasize geometric abstraction on a cross-country basis), while his 1960s practice can be more conveniently posited as a predecessor to more recent developments in participatory art. The *name* Hélio Oiticica, almost like a brand, unproblematically bridges these two registers without taking into account that their actual relation offers a potentially disruptive alternative to conventionally established limits between modernism and postmodernism.

8

The problem thus becomes how to create historiographical hinges that make trajectories coalesce into important contemporary critical stances without letting them lapse into either overdetermining narratives or free-floating fragments that can be indiscriminately appropriated with little or no resistance. It is clear, then, that the polarity between continuity and discontinuity must be overcome somehow. My own suggestion in this regard, returning to Zupančič's formulation, is that the Brazilian avant-garde currently offers art historians the opportunity to engage with interpretation from the point of view of the leftover (it is telling that in her account the leftover is something that is "out of order," which is also a more straightforward connotation of Duarte's "on the margins" formulation in its Portuguese original).[31]

As a matter of fact, it is precisely by noting that difference between the position of the Brazilian avant-garde and that of the neo-avant-garde in Foster's model that the former's potential of supplying this viewpoint becomes all the more evident.[32] It is because it lies at such an unstable and risky threshold that it is so *necessary* to consider its potential impact in the history of art, and not simply in order to award it a long-overdue place in the canon. "The constitution of the unconscious," Zupančič continues, "coincides with the *presupposition* of meaning, with the forced choice of meaning (which only makes interpretation possible) and not simply with the repression of the first representation that eludes this interpretation."[33] Once again, this immanent model confirms that perhaps the most radical kind of difference there can be (and also the most difficult one to address) is *self-difference*—a reminder that positions of enunciation are not necessarily identity positions, to return to Venâncio Filho's description of an "obliqueness" in relation to oneself that is "not properly an identity." The uncanny belatedness of the Brazilian avant-garde, not only in terms of its actual reception but also of the projections it attracts from audiences informed by canonical narratives, can be thus regarded as a paradoxically productive drawback. It is what makes Brazilian art not simply one of many competing narratives that could arbitrarily replace Foster's. What makes it a leftover is a real historical configuration that needs to be urgently addressed—and if this makes it a "compromise formation" then it also inscribes it, as Zupančič puts it, "in the dimension of truth."[34] It is this dimension that can ultimately submit the reconfiguration of the past to the articulation of present necessities. Or, in a particularly striking passage where Jacques Lacan mobilizes the Platonic concept of anamnesis (a radical form of reminiscence that transcends ordinary recollections and points straight to truth):[35] "Let's be categorical: in psychoanalysis anamnesis, what is at stake is not reality, but truth, because the effect of full speech is to reorder past contingencies by conferring on them the sense of necessities to come, such as they are constituted by the scant freedom through which the subject makes them present."[36]

PASSAGES

I would like to envisage my own position of enunciation as the author of the present study as a "compromise formation" in this particular sense. The experience of dealing with two different languages, and particularly of thinking about your own language from the perspective of another one, is conflictive in the sense that it is not simply a matter of translation, but also of bringing different ways of thinking about art into an often unre-solvable friction. As Beatriz Colomina beautifully puts it (with the proviso, of course, that my own case is about Portuguese rather than Spanish):

> It was as if, with language, I was also leaving behind a whole way of looking at things, of writing them. Even when we think we know what we are about to write, the moment we start writing, language takes us on an excursion of its own. And if that language is not ours, we are definitely in foreign territory. Lately, I have started to feel that way about Spanish. I have managed to become a foreigner in both languages, moving somewhat nomadically through the discourse on an unofficial territory.[37]

Colomina's territorial metaphor suggestively resonates with a number of works and writings I will discuss, such as Antonio Dias's *Anywhere Is My Land* (1968). The words are in English, but this would probably be a rather one-dimensional painting had it been made by an English-speaking artist. Linguistic displacement is at least as important as physical displacement here, especially in that it unsettles the authorial position, enacting an ironic and enigmatic stance of self-awareness. These strategies are nothing but ways of navigating through "unofficial territory," or perhaps of establishing such territory in the course of the navigation. This can be a subtle but forceful critical operation, I think, in that it rejects essentialisms and set positions, and one of my modest hopes is that this kind of self-reflexive uneasiness can somehow disturb art historical writing as well. I am not suggesting, of course, that native English-speaking scholars have necessarily *less* access to Brazilian art. In fact, the coexistence of different perspectives has been and will continue to be crucial in this respect, since different writerly and intellectual trajectories demand different accounts of one's art historical stance qua "compromise formation."

As a matter of fact, certain stumbling blocks in translation have often shed light on the thought of the artists and critics I address. As a consequence, the footnotes that resulted from these difficulties were no doubt the most laborious ones to write. These minute episodes may offer snapshots of the "obliqueness" Venâncio Filho talks about, or better yet, of how this obliqueness can also inflect one's position as an art historian writing about the Brazilian avant-garde. Therefore, it is not simply a matter of translation

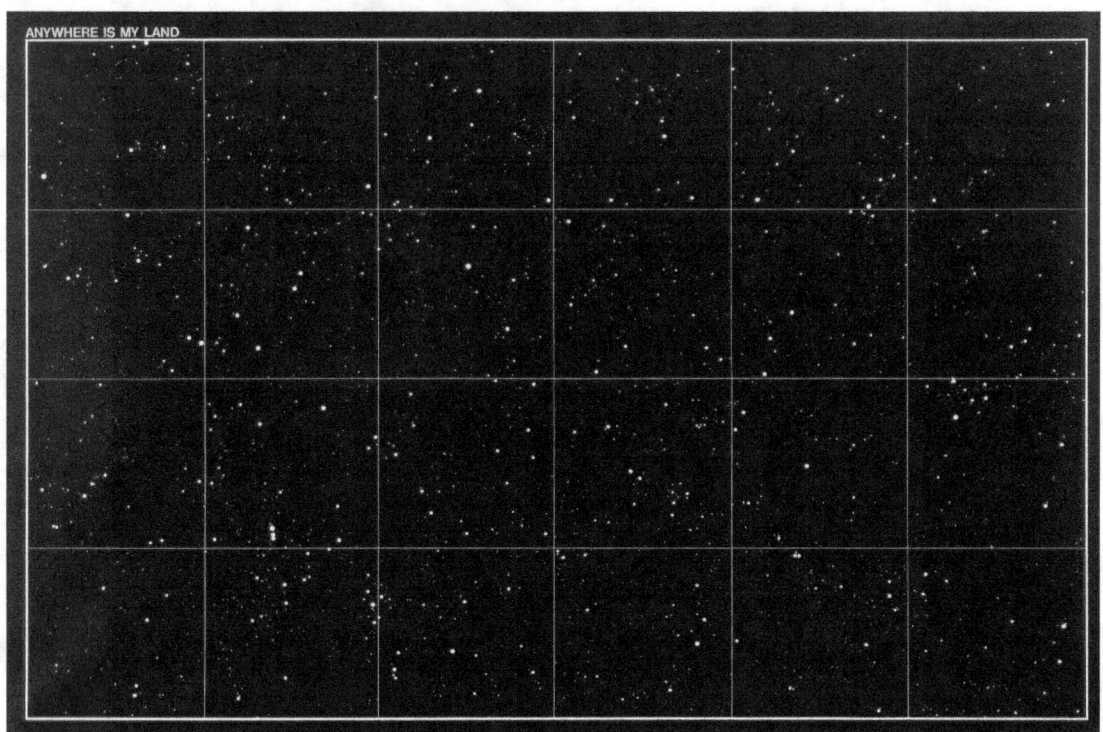

I.1

Antonio Dias, *Anywhere Is My Land*, 1968.
Acrylic on canvas, 130 × 195 cm.
Private collection. Courtesy of the artist.

INTRODUCTION

in the sense of producing clear meaning so that linguistic exchanges can be envisaged as a "sharpening of consciousness," but rather, and once again, a matter of letting a certain *work* take place.[38] Likewise, my aim as a Brazilian art historian writing in English is not simply to synthetically translate a supposed treasure trove of art historical knowledge to the English-speaking world. On the one hand, this knowledge does not exist, in the sense that there is not a systematic edifice of Brazilian art history hiding behind the language barrier.[39] On the other, such an attempt would miss the more fundamental shift from *knowledge* to *truth* that I have been trying to advance as the very interventional value of the Brazilian avant-garde within the contemporary field of art history (for truth is precisely what redefines one's relation—cognitive or otherwise—to reality and history).

This is why I conceive this book as a series of *passages*. This unavoidably echoes the title of Krauss's fundamental study *Passages in Modern Sculpture*. Although my project differs from Krauss's both in focus and scope (with the exception perhaps of my discussion on medium specificity in relation to the non-object in chapter 1), it does follow hers in at least one methodological aspect, namely the choice to dwell on case studies. As Krauss puts it, the hope is that "the gains to be derived from a detailed examination of a single work, or of a group of related sculptures, will offset the losses this has meant for a wholly inclusive historical survey."[40] Likewise, my own hope is that there is more to be gained from an outright confrontation with fundamental "passages" of modern and contemporary Brazilian art than from trying to come up with a sweeping, linear narrative of the Brazilian avant-garde as a whole. But these passages do hinge the history I propose—in the sense that they allow me to speak of such a thing as a Brazilian avant-garde—in a way that isolated case studies might not. The prominence of (and the different positions assumed by) key figures like Hélio Oiticica, Ferreira Gullar, Mário Pedrosa, Antonio Dias, and others throughout this book is telling in this respect. I believe these agents, with the partial understanding we still have of their practices, can be mobilized in order to rethink the articulation of the avant-garde. So the term "passages" stands for, so to speak, a kind of nonlinear consistency that can be asserted only from the present standpoint.

That said, the artists and works I address are not necessarily to be taken as a definitive selection. Granted, I have chosen artists who are central in many ways, but mostly because their interventions somehow elucidate the importance of the historical passages I want to rethink. Like Krauss, I do aim at developing useful concepts out of my chosen case studies that can be "generalized to apply to [a] wider body of objects," but I also aim at constructing a historiographical viewpoint that will enable a more productive appreciation of the highly original set of artistic concerns that I will attempt to isolate.

Therefore, one of my concerns is to avoid positing "foundational" moments of Brazilian art. But how can one ignore this risk when the very first chapter of this book focuses on concretism and neoconcretism? In a way, my solution is to recognize the mythical status of the latter. In brief, neoconcretism is not consistent enough to be manipulated as an autonomous signifier, that is, as a name, without generating a good deal of mystification. Neoconcretism is more properly the name of a provisional "aesthetic commitment": as a "movement" it is nothing but the stitching together of a few manifestos and exhibitions of more or less disparate works and of some initial retrospective accounts of it (like Oiticica's in 1967 and, more important, Ronaldo Brito's in 1975).[41] So I pick this one particular and crucial thread—Ferreira Gullar's "Theory of the Non-object"—and pull it to open up a retrospective line of inquiry about the conceptual origins of Gullar's thought. This is why a great deal of chapter 1 is concerned with a close reading of crucial texts not only by Gullar but also by a number of his interlocutors, especially with senior critic Mário Pedrosa's thesis on Gestalt theory. My aim is to reveal how much the efficacy of the non-object—Gullar's theoretical attempt to account for the phenomenological effect of neoconcrete artworks—was staked on a teleological reading of modernism as the overcoming of medium specificity, and how problematic was the ensuing interpretation of some artworks. I cast the sculptures of Amilcar de Castro not as privileged examples of the non-object, but as an internal limit of the interpretive strategies advanced in that context. The whole breakdown of constructive tendencies in Brazilian art can be thus mapped onto the tensions among historiography, theory, and visual production. To historicize neoconcretism is to make it less an *agent* of this crisis than its *site*.

This will also involve detaching neoconcretism from a hackneyed zeitgeist view of its indebtedness to 1950s developmentalism (in fact, my emphasis on *passages* is at odds with the notion of the zeitgeist as a whole).[42] Such an operation runs the risk of pulling neoconcretism too closely into the orbit of Hélio Oiticica and Lygia Clark, as if it belonged to yet another zeitgeist, that of 1960s experimentalism. One of my aims in chapter 2 is thus to avoid the facile distinction between Oiticica before and after his encounter with the Mangueira samba school in 1964.[43] By following his visual and discursive commitment to the idea of constructivity, and more specifically to the work of Mondrian, I read this passage as an uncompromising heightening of the contradictions of the constructive avant-garde rather than a simple "turn" away from it. This is not to say that his experimentalism in the 1960s is fully indebted to his neoconcrete period. Oiticica's notion of the constructive is, among other things, a historiographical concept that updates and criticizes the non-object, discarding its teleological historicism (although the artist's own account of overcoming painting remains relatively unchanged). My point is that the relay between the non-object and the constructive mediates the passage from the 1950s to the 1960s within avant-gardist circles in a more complex way than if this passage were a mechanical consequence of a change of context. Crucially, the concept was able to guide Oiticica's avant-gardism through a period of crisis when organized concrete movements virtually disappeared. His faith in the "constructive will" throughout the 1960s was an attempt to make avant-gardism face its generative contradictions. This would lead him through uncharted territory, thus paving the way for a modus operandi he would later term "the experimental" (and which will play an important role in chapter 5).

Chapter 3 will depart from the consistent engagement of artists active in the 1960s, such as Antonio Dias and Rubens Gerchman, with portraiture and more specifically self-portraiture. On the one hand, this will be seen as a head-on confrontation with the tightrope the avant-garde then walked in its attempt to position itself within broader cultural struggles, especially vis-à-vis the formulaic aesthetics often advanced by representatives of the student left. On the other hand, and more importantly, I will try to retrospectively account for the dilemmas facing the construction of artistic positions since the 1950s, mostly apropos of the construction of Brasília. Seen from another angle, this chapter will also make explicit a subnarrative that informs chapters 1 and 2, namely that of the avant-garde as identity crisis. Moreover, this process takes place alongside the skeptical reception of pop art, prompting this "crisis" to become mobilized as a strategic response. In other words, what will become clear is the heightened sense in which the "formalization of experiences of non-identity," to borrow the striking formulation by Brazilian psychoanalysis theorist Vladimir Safatle, would become a driving force in the hands of those artists.[44]

In chapter 4, this tensioning of identity and of the image is shown to give way, in the passage from the 1960s to the 1970s, to an antivisual turn (albeit one that retained an important phenomenological component). As some artists moved abroad and entered into direct contact with different artistic contexts, their projection of Brazil and of their own position as Brazilian artists underwent a new twist. This was hardly a matter of trying to assert national identities (in fact, Oiticica's and Meireles's statements in the catalog of MoMA's 1970 show "Information" clearly state otherwise) but of using their own missed encounters abroad—mainly with conceptual art—as ways of further displacing their own linguistic, cultural, and geographic certainties.[45] As Brett remarks, Oiticica's definition of Brazil in "Information" as "the country that simply doesn't exist" points to the "simultaneously real and chimerical nature of 'cultural identities'" (this is especially crucial considering how invested the Brazilian dictatorship was in nationalist slogans and pantomimes).[46] The practices emerging in this moment involved increasingly shifting paradigms of value and the assimilation of a whole new vocabulary; more specifically, the questioning of the visual register went hand in hand with the assimilation of other codes, such as the cartographic and the economic, which were played out in Meireles's theatrical installations and through Dias's insistence on painting. This is not to say that these codes became new subgenres. Rather, they became ways of articulating a radical disjunction of representational registers—it is in this sense that Oiticica at one point termed Dias's works "enigmages"—that responds to the perceived failure of the 1960s renewed figurative production to sustain its criticality.

In chapter 5 I take advantage of a hiatus in Oiticica's trajectory, apropos of which he develops his crucial dialogue with Malevich first in the passage from the 1950s to the 1960s and then in his 1970s experiments with cinema. The very suggestion that a hiatus is particularly significant to the trajectory it interrupts exemplifies how notions of continuity and discontinuity can be pitted against each other without resulting in the kind of impasse I discussed earlier. This chapter condenses and puts in play some of the key motifs that appear throughout the book—linguistic displacement, enthusiastic engagement, historiography, and self-inscription. As a matter of fact, Oiticica expands his early, pictorial interest in the monochrome into a full-fledged conception of engagement, or so I will argue. More importantly, I will distinguish this updated version of the monochrome from the one Rauschenberg developed by introducing John Cage—whom Oiticica much admired—as a way of setting up a comparative study. Since the vast majority of Oiticica's work in the 1970s takes the form of writing, I will also propose that his insistence on the manifesto as a *form of writing* relies on an immanent position of enunciation, which is one striking way of approaching, once again, the point of view of the leftover.[47]

As this introduction already evidences, my account is often informed by Lacanian psychoanalytic theory. Despite the fact that psychoanalysis is traditionally strong in Brazil, I do not wish to argue for its relevance on historicist grounds, although such a case could be made. The most telling evidence is surely that of Lygia Clark, who was an analysand of Pierre Fédida and an avid reader of the work of the British psychoanalyst Donald Winnicott to the point of naming her own therapeutic practice, started in 1976, "Structuration of the Self." Also, as Brazilian psychoanalyst Tânia Rivera stresses, if Pedrosa's critical vocabulary was not particularly inflected by psychoanalysis, he was nevertheless interested in the broader cultural relevance of the latter and was clearly acquainted with the writings of Freud.[48] Not to mention, of course, his personal and intellectual affinity with the French surrealists (his wife was the sister-in-law of the poet Benjamin Péret) and his keen involvement in the workshop of the Engenho de Dentro psychiatric hospital. The latter, which I will address in chapter 1, was certainly a sign of his awareness of a psychoanalytic approach to culture, but the main theoretical background against which the work of the mentally ill acquired relevance for Pedrosa was undoubtedly Gestalt theory.

Rivera calls for the recognition of psychoanalysis's share in the formation of the intellectual framework of artists and critics in postwar Brazil, questioning the exclusive attention that is more often paid to the direct influence of theories such as phenomenology (and semiotics, one might add). My own thought on this matter follows a few different paths. First, I believe it is important to impose certain restrictions on the extent to which theoretical apparatuses can be said to have determined artistic practices. So, for example, my own discussion of phenomenology is initially restricted to its role in Gullar's writings. It is precisely because of this mediation that certain problematic interpretations arise once his formulations are projected in turn onto neoconcretist artworks. Second, such problematic interpretations expose deadlocks in the dialogue between theory and artistic practice that have, in some cases, given rise to enduring misconceptions (as in the case of Amilcar de Castro). I have found psychoanalytic concepts particularly helpful in confronting these deadlocks; they act, so to speak, as dialectical catalysts. Third, it seems plausible in retrospect to propose that the insistence on concepts derived from the notion of the object (non-object, transobject, new objectivity, probject, etc.) in the works I discuss are indeed attempts at "experiences of non-identity" in that they consistently (though often implicitly) reject what Safatle describes as "an ontological link between the subject and the identity principle."[49] What psychoanalysis offers, in this case, to echo Freud's claim for dreamwork, is a royal road for such a retrospective glance.

In short, I deploy psychoanalysis mostly in order to work through historiographical impasses and phenomenological closures rather than as a constant vocabulary. This is why it appears somewhat unevenly throughout the text. There are moments when I follow relatively long historical accounts that will eventually lead to an impasse. Elsewhere, I borrow certain concepts in order to rethink the very way a work can be described (as in a relatively long discussion of Antonio Dias's *The Hardest Way* in chapter 4). But even in those cases when psychoanalysis appears as a sort of alternative phenomenology (or a phenomenology of the lost object), I have tried to avoid casting works as mere illustrations of concepts (a sin committed by many a psychoanalyst).[50]

My ultimate aim was thus to instill this coupling of *history* and *historiography* with a sense of urgency. In this sense, to *construct* an avant-garde is not simply an effort to describe what those artists and critics were doing, but also to engage in ongoing reflection about ways of addressing it from our present perspective. Such a construction is a practice of art historical anamnesis, with the self-reflective charge that this particular kind of recollection brings. As a matter of fact, the very idea of belatedness, along with its difficulties and prospects, is somehow inscribed in the title I have chosen. For while the period between 1949 and 1979 comprises most of the practices I address, it also marks the gap between the writing of Pedrosa's thesis on Gestalt and its publication thirty years later. Considering the effects of this delay (to which I will soon turn), this may well be an emblem of the temporal complexity of the Brazilian avant-garde. Fredric Jameson once wrote that "only a genuine philosophy of history is capable of respecting the specificity and radical difference of the social and cultural past while disclosing the solidarity of its polemics and passions, its forms, structures, experiences, and struggles, with those of the present day."[51] In dealing with such temporal complexity, this book will attempt to respond, however modestly, to this provocation, which has lost none of its pertinence since it first appeared — coincidentally enough — in the year of Pedrosa's death.

(Non-)Objects

Questioning the concept of the *non-object* should be less a matter of asking what it is than how it comes into being. For much of the significance of Ferreira Gullar's radical formulation lies in what it responds to, in the kind of historical space it carves in order to enact its sophisticated conceptual operation. I take the cue here from Gullar himself: after three or four brief opening sentences, mostly dedicated to saying what the non-object is *not*, the "Theory of the Non-object"—the now famous essay he wrote in 1959—suddenly turns to a reappraisal of modern art through the lens of the newfound concept (and under the subtitle "Death of Painting"). For the "issue," the poet remarked, "requires restrospection."[1]

It did, and still does—in more than one sense, perhaps. First, it does require that we review the kind of retrospection Gullar had in mind. As artist and art historian Carlos Zilio wrote in 1982, the constructive avant-garde elaborated, for the first time in Brazil, "a systematic reading of the history of [artistic] forms."[2] What is crucial about this insight is the historical consciousness it ascribes to the avant-garde. As the theoretical backbone of neoconcretism, the non-object would test its ground against the very history it claimed for itself. In other words, it would have to establish its legitimacy not only in the here and now of artistic production (through the phenomenological cogency of non-objects themselves), but also across the terrain of history; this, in turn, meant engaging in a dispute over the meaning of modernism as it can be traced through the debates of the 1950s within geometric abstraction circles in Brazil.

If we read Zilio's statement from another perspective, a second kind of retrospection comes into play. For the context of his commentary is a broader discussion of Hélio Oiticica's sense of history, which was published in 1982, little more than a year after the artist's untimely death. This points to a significant aspect of the international (and also of the local) reception of the Brazilian avant-garde. As these histories emerge in a fragmented manner, oriented by a somewhat selective retrospective look, our grasp of the issues that informed this avant-garde becomes overdetermined and therefore distorted. The fact that neoconcretism has "gained international notoriety while remaining contextually obscure," as art historian Michael Asbury puts it, has lent it a "quasi-mythical status" as the "origin of contemporary Brazilian art."[3] More specifically, neoconcretism becomes generally known as the origin of Oiticica's and Lygia Clark's production, and thus of the avant-garde as a whole. What is more, it is subtly assumed to belong to a certain 1960s zeitgeist (conforming not only to the best-known work by Clark and Oiticica, but also to well-established accounts of the limits of modernism).[4] Despite its notorious lack of unity, neoconcretism is made to assume the role of an influential style: the more narrowly understood it is, the more vaguely and broadly its influence can be claimed. I would supplement Asbury's diagnosis by arguing that neoconcretism has also remained *conceptually* obscure, at least in terms of the dynamics of its theoretical constitution. In questioning the conceptual matrix of the non-object—as opposed to dealing with neoconcretism as a historical given—my aim is thus to avoid both a myth of originality (by stressing the way the concept arose from a series of dialogues and polemical responses) and simplistic assumptions of historical continuation in terms of influence.

I have already mentioned that the historical assertion of the non-object involved not only its legitimization *within* modernism, but also a dispute over the meaning (or rather the *telos*) of modernism. This leads to a third and final type of retrospection, the one I am mostly concerned with. To put it bluntly, there is no way of understanding the non-object without addressing its strategic value. Again, the non-object was above all a *response*, and a multifaceted one at that. As an idea, it sprawls way beyond the paragraphs of the "Theory of the Non-object" (hereafter referred to as the "Theory") and occupies a number of manifestos, reviews, essays, and even a strikingly Mondrianesque dialogue. The "Theory" assumes this role as a consequence of the theoretical stage Gullar had at his disposal at that time, the Sunday supplement of the Rio de Janeiro-based newspaper *Jornal do Brasil* (hereafter abbreviated *SDJB*). It was through the *SDJB* that he could address, either directly or indirectly, a variety of interlocutors: poets and visual artists from São Paulo (initially his allies, then his adversaries); his fellow artists at the Grupo Frente, and then at the neoconcrete group; a more generic art public still in a stage of formation; and finally other agents (a most important one, as we will see, was the senior critic Mário Pedrosa). It is essential to reconstruct the trajectory of the non-object—even and especially before it gets crystallized under this name—as it conceptually emerges from these debates.

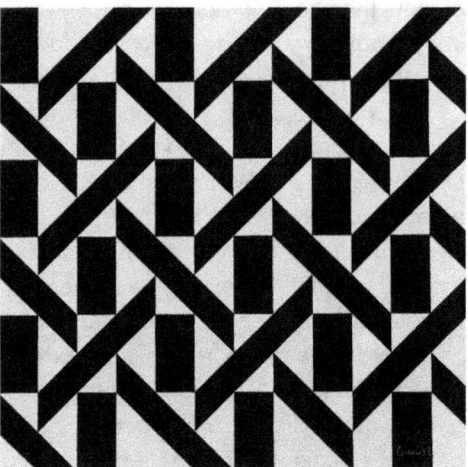

1.1
Waldemar Cordeiro, *Untitled*, 1958. Enamel on plywood, 51 × 51 cm. Private collection. Photo: Romulo Fialdini.

What I want to avoid is a facile opposition between an earlier concretism characterized as too "rationalistic" and its more "intuitive" adversary, neoconcretism; or at least, the internalization of these adjectives as essential attributes of well-defined movements. This comparative cliché can be traced back to an article by Pedrosa, in which he singles out the discrepancies between the São Paulo and Rio de Janeiro representations in the 1956–1957 "National Exhibition of Concrete Art" that took place in each city successively.[5] As is well known, the exhibition brought the two groups together for the first time and ended up stirring their differences rather than strengthening their affinities; two years later, members of the Rio de Janeiro group made their opposition to São Paulo concretism public by signing the "Neoconcrete Manifesto." One of my aims, however, is to place this schism, to which I will return in due time, in a different historical perspective. It is far too easy to compare certain paintings by Waldemar Cordeiro with Oiticica's *Metaesquemas* (see figure 2.3), and see the programmatic repetition of forms in the former opposing the intuitive articulation of planes in the latter. It is equally easy to see a vast number of concretist artworks, such as Hermelindo Fiaminghi's *Circles with Alternated Movement* (see figure 1.4) as a (literally) circular play on Gestalt principles. What is less easy—but necessary—is to bear in mind the strategic value all of these terms and theories had, and the way this value shifted over time.

AUTONOMY

In some ways, the non-object *is* indeed a myth. Gullar's anecdote about the origin of the concept is well known. He describes being invited, alongside Pedrosa and others, to a dinner at the home of Lygia Clark, where she meant to show them a recent piece of work. Gullar's many later descriptions of the latter are far from consistent, but they commonly portray a diagonal construction of interlocked painted wooden plaques, connected at the edges. An impromptu debate followed about a proper way of defining the piece. Pedrosa would have suggested calling it a relief, to which Gullar objected on the grounds that a relief "presupposes a surface" against which it would stand. Gullar recalls spending some time alone with the work before finally announcing his proposed definition: non-object. It would now be Pedrosa's turn to object (no pun intended), stating that "the word object means an 'object of knowledge,' and thus a non-object would be something that is not an object of knowledge, and therefore it is nothing." Gullar's retort was to clarify that he meant the word "object" strictly in the sense of an ordinary thing, an item of "personal use" like "a pen, a table, a chair, a book"—the prefix was meant to detach the artwork from that kind of ordinariness. So the non-object is, according to this account (and in keeping with a number of statements Gullar made in his articles and manifestos at that time), the product of a double negation: on the one hand, the choice of the word "object" itself denies medium-specificity; on the other, the prefix "non-" denies the immediate consequence of that first denial, namely the perceptual leveling of the artwork to the ensemble of ordinary objects in the world (a consequence analogous to what Michael Fried would term a few years later "literalism").

There is something odd about this anecdote, namely the fact that it is incredibly hard retrospectively to pinpoint that particular work by Lygia Clark. It is fair to assume that the meeting *did* take place, and approximately *when*, but Gullar never refers to the work by its title and his descriptions find no exact match in Clark's oeuvre.[6] It is occasion-

1.2
Lygia Clark, *Bicho-Máquina*, 1962. Aluminum,
20 × 19 × 25 cm. Photographer Marcelo Ribeiro
Alvares Correa. Courtesy of The World of Lygia
Clark Cultural Association, ref. no. 00391.

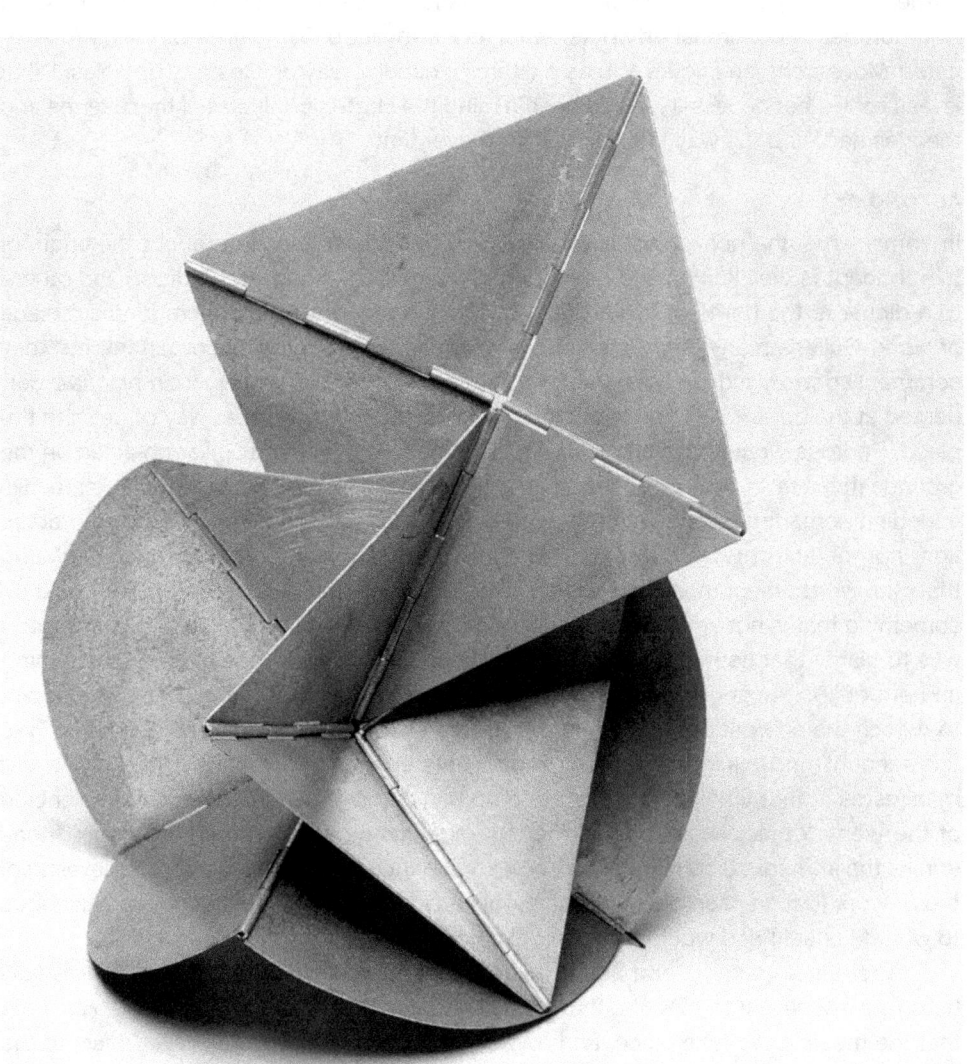

ally said to stand on its own, in contrast to her works so far and like the famous *Bichos* (Beasts/Creatures) she would soon start making (and that Gullar would often refer to as quintessential non-objects); but, then again, the latter are not wooden. The poet also refers to different sets of colors: sometimes it is "avocado green" and gray, sometimes black and white—colors Clark often employed in different works. Given all that, my somewhat Lévi-Straussian suggestion is that there is less to be gained by trying to establish whether any one of the poet's descriptions is factually accurate than by assuming that we are dealing with a mnemonic mix (or myth) of whatever Gullar had seen that one night and other roughly contemporary works by Clark. In short, only one thing is certain about this elusive and primordial non-object: it is built of at least as many layers of memory as it is of wood.

Considering how fiercely invested Gullar has been in his many intellectual disputes ever since the 1950s, and the pivotal role neoconcretism often played in them, it may be rather obvious that his thirty-, forty-, and fifty-year-old memories should be taken as layered constructions rather than as documentary evidence. In other words, the content of such disputes is the "stuff" some of those layers are made of, meaning that the very terms of Gullar's descriptions are highly charged, to the point of indicating his stakes in certain debates. More specifically, I want to regard the non-object anecdote as a key for understanding the poet's complex and also layered relationship to Pedrosa's precedence as a critic (Clark's work being a particular site of conflict).[7] For the story is not simply about the non-object itself, but is also a tale of succession: the younger critic, armed with the theoretical apparatus bestowed on him by his senior (Gullar often acknowledges his critical, theoretical, and art historical debt to Pedrosa), takes the master's place and becomes the legitimate spokesperson of a redefined avant-garde.[8] Which is to say that Gullar's own critical coming-of-age is tantamount to the rise of neoconcretism itself. More than a movement's name, "neoconcretism" was also a sign that that particular group of avant-garde artists was now drawn to the poet's critical orbit (for good or bad, since allies and detractors alike have often suggested that, to a great extent, "neoconcretism" named a set of Gullar's personal investments rather than a proper collective movement).[9]

It is here that one telling detail of Gullar's anecdote should be singled out: his alleged disagreement with Pedrosa in defining Clark's new work as a relief. There can be little doubt that her 1959 *Counter-Reliefs*—which are precisely constructions of painted, wooden plates, albeit wall-mounted rather than freestanding—are a pivotal ingredient in the mnemonic mix of the primordial non-object, especially considering that, according to Clark, the *Bichos* were "born" from those works.[10] As for the historical pertinence of the term, suffice to say that one of the few images chosen by Gullar to illustrate the newspaper publishing of the "Theory" was also a *Counter-Relief*—not Clark's, but Tatlin's.[11] But it is from a theoretical perspective that this persistence of the "defeated" term both in the 1950s and in later interviews becomes truly remarkable. For it is tempting to see in Gullar's objection that a relief always presupposes a surface on which it is constructed an implicit reference to Pedrosa's theoretical field of expertise, Gestalt theory, with its own emphasis on forms differentiating themselves from a ground.

This adds some complexity to the way Gestalt theory is usually accounted for in the context of 1950s Brazilian art. In his groundbreaking and influential study, critic Ronaldo Brito goes as far as seeing Merleau-Ponty's critique of Gestalt theory as analo-

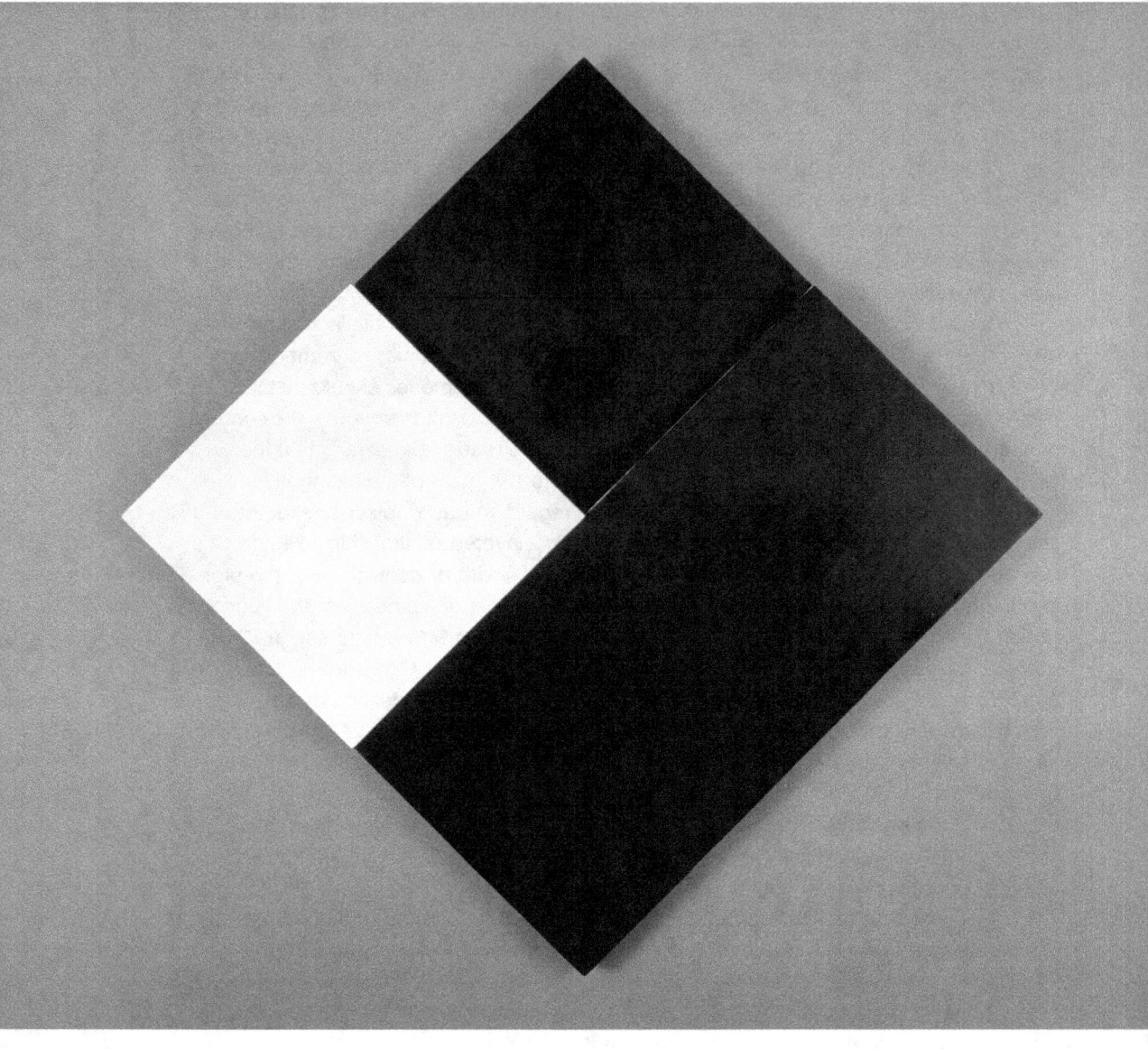

1.3
Lygia Clark, *Counter-Relief*, 1958/1960. Industrial
paint on wood, 56 × 56 × 1.5 cm. Photo: Mark Morosse.
Courtesy of The World of Lygia Clark Cultural
Association, ref. no. 00649.

gous to neoconcretism's critique of earlier concretism.[12] This is an important point I shall return to, and Brito is right to an extent, as Gullar's writings confirm. But it is worth noting the problem of restricting Gestalt theory in Brazil solely to the role of an overdetermining theoretical dogma that was "imported" alongside other international concretist tenets; for this is to ignore the key role Gestalt played as a theoretical intervention in the hands of Pedrosa, its earlier local advocate. Brito can perhaps be excused for his oversight, since Pedrosa's 1949 thesis on Gestalt, *On the Affective Nature of Form*, was published only thirty years later, in 1979—that is, a few years *after* Brito had finished writing his study—at a time when the elder critic was no longer keen on it.[13] It is well known, however, that the thesis, or at least its central ideas, had circulated among artists and critics close to Pedrosa and to his positions in the late 1940s and 1950s.[14] Gullar, for one, claims to have read it even before moving to Rio de Janeiro and meeting Pedrosa in person for the first time.[15] And there is no question about the nature of those positions in 1949. As abstraction gradually ceased to be the domain of a few isolated practitioners and started to gain institutional backing (for example with the Belgian curator Léon Degand's 1949 show "From Figurativism to Abstractionism," in the recently inaugurated Museum of Modern Art of São Paulo), a fiery polemic ensued, with Pedrosa and others fiercely defending it against attacks from artists and critics associated with the earlier generation of figurative modernism.[16] In this context, Pedrosa's engagement with Gestalt theory must be seen as strategic rather than dogmatic (which partly explains his faded interest in it in the 1970s). It is worthy of notice that it was a former Trotskyist militant who came to inaugurate a full-fledged discussion of Gestalt theory in Brazil. If, on the one hand, Pedrosa was committed to political transformation, on the other he was also convinced that the role of art in this process was not simply illustrative. As Brazilian theoretician Otília Arantes has put it, he was consistently obsessed with "determining the specific modality of knowledge in art and its objectivity, that is, its power to communicate."[17]

Evoking Gestalt then would first of all counter a common criticism of abstraction, namely its supposed solipsism. For example, in a particularly virulent attack, in 1948, painter Emiliano Di Cavalcanti had branded abstraction a "sterile specialization."[18] Of course, Pedrosa's thesis is not about abstraction—not explicitly, that is. It starts with a rejection of the notion that "perception is preceded by a virtual act of recognition," which would amount to the recognition of *useful* objects.[19] But if we understand these statements as analogous to the figuration/abstraction debate, we can see how Di Cavalcanti's terms are virtually reversed. Implicit in the Gestalt principles as Pedrosa exposes them is the sense that figuration comes always *after* form. In short, what Pedrosa is initially seeking is to question the determination of form: "If certain forms remind us of objects more directly connected to our practical activities, this fact is a consequence, an effect, and not a cause of the organization [of the form]."[20] Or, making the reversal even clearer, and in terms that point to the core of the present discussion: "If we grant affective signification to these figurations [i.e., if we recognize certain appearing forms as things pertaining to us], this is the result of a preceding fact: their preliminary existence as *sensible objects*."[21]

I would go as far as to argue that Pedrosa himself provides the key for reading the Gestalt debate as a potential analogy to that of abstraction in Brazil. In a crucial part of the thesis, he advocates a comparison between the universality of recognizing a face and that of an artwork, rejecting the theory that the child protractedly labors toward distinguishing the human face piece by piece from the chaos of primordial sensation. On the contrary, he sides with Gestalt in defending the spontaneous, meaningful emergence of the face as a universally recognizable "good form." He compares this to the recognition of art in the universal guise of form: "[The art object] is endowed precisely with this physiognomic power that we grasp so well, that the animal grasps, and that the child grasps in a face."[22] How striking can this be, if one just thinks of how abstraction was attacked for being little more than a chaotic sea of meaninglessness? This is Di Cavalcanti again: "[Abstract artists] construct expanded little worlds out of free-floating fragments of real things: these are monstrous visions of amoebic or atomic residues, microscopically revealed by sick minds. For me, whenever an artist nurtures his imagination on those obscure fissures [desvãos] of the world, then reason is not at work."[23] An earlier attack, published in 1947 by art historian Quirino Campofiorito, also targeted art produced by "live instincts uncontrolled by reason."[24] However, this was not directed against abstraction in the context of modern art, but against a show of works produced at the painting workshop of the Engenho de Dentro psychiatric hospital, in Rio de Janeiro. This is no casual coincidence, since Pedrosa and three artists who would eventually play key roles in the emerging constructive movement—Almir Mavignier, Ivan Serpa, and Abraham Palatnik—were enthusiastically involved in the workshop, which became a sort of institutional refuge.[25] It was in this context—and with the help of discussions generated by the daily experience of the workshop—that much of Pedrosa's thesis was conceived. Pedrosa, of course, reacted strongly to commentaries such as Campofiorito's; as sociologist Glaucia Villas Boas argues, the polemic involving the art of the mentally ill went hand in hand, for a while, with the figuration/abstraction debate.[26] This is to say that if Pedrosa's interest in Gestalt allowed him to theorize the artistic validity of the workshop, it also allowed him to mobilize the production of the mentally ill itself—especially their production of geometric abstraction—in order to legitimate the universality of abstract forms.

The intelligibility of abstraction was thus a major issue in the debate. Practically at the same time that Pedrosa finished his thesis, Waldemar Cordeiro published an article turning verdicts such as Di Cavalcanti's against themselves: "Only by objectivizing, by depersonalizing a form can one make it a matter of reflection, determining the intelligibility of a work." For Cordeiro, to "objectivize" meant getting rid of the "hidden zone"—a term strikingly analogous to Di Cavalcanti's "fissures of the world"—of the represented three-dimensional form. He would argue, in line with Theo van Doesburg's manifesto "Art concret," for a "real language of painting" based on "color and lines that are color and lines and do not aspire to be pears or men."[27] As a rhetorical coup de grace, Cordeiro made a point of emphasizing the reversal of the charges against abstractionism: "we, the abstractionists, denounce the unsociability and the solipsism of figurative art."[28]

Moving beyond analogies, it is important to understand how Pedrosa accounts for art in this scheme of perception. In his definition, the work of art is "relatively objective"; that is, it is both "phenomenologically objective" and "functionally subjective."[29] It is precisely on this two-tiered definition, which complicates traditional subject-object relations, that Pedrosa's commitment to artistic autonomy is staked. The most important consequence of this definition lies perhaps in what it *denies*. First and foremost, it denies any level of *determination* of the art object that is extrinsic to its formal appearance (such as, say, the artist's inner feelings, iconic resemblance, or a political agenda). The argument here runs in parallel with what I described earlier: whatever the effects the art object produces, it does so in the first place by its "phenomenologically objective" appearance as a form. Or, in Pedrosa's words: "In art, [form] is definitely the chief, *independent* element, which forces subjects to go no further, to refrain from crossing it in search of extrinsic elements, a practical intention, an abstract concept, the satisfaction of an interest etc."[30]

It is because form is capable of preempting all of these virtual determinants while still *appearing* to the subject that it becomes universal (the arbitrary ring of such reasoning was not missed by Merleau-Ponty, for whom Gestalt had the "good fortune of encountering constants" in perception rather than laws referring the perceived form back to intrinsic characteristics of objects).[31] This amounts to a sort of spontaneous availability of form to each and every subject, with special emphasis to the "each" part. For this universality implies no subjective closure; what is special about the art object, Pedrosa maintains, is that it offers an "incomparable mediation" between "us and the other," a privileged relation between "an expressive form and an affective phenomenon."[32] This is where art leaps into becoming "functionally subjective," or, as Pedrosa claims, "The realized object is the point of arrival in the artist's action, but [also] the viewer's starting point."[33] As we shall see, reworkings of this particular conclusion triggered a great deal of polemic in the mid-1950s debates.

But if this universality of art is not meant to communicate the artist's psychological interiority—as Pedrosa repeatedly clarifies—or any other "extrinsic" content, what kind of content does it communicate? And how can it articulate a politically progressive notion of artistic autonomy? Leaving aside for the moment the problematic aspects of the Gestalt theory (to which I will return in the context of Gullar's later formulations), the answer, as Otília Arantes summarizes it, is startlingly simple: "The critical dimension of art is [for Pedrosa] one of defamiliarization."[34] Pedrosa's Trotskyism is once again key here. Just as form would do without a predetermining function, art would simply communicate the potential of a renewed perception (based on the "good form"), one that contained, in its turn, the potential of breaking with the established, utilitarian relations that structured capitalist society.[35] Pedrosa regarded Gestalt as an authoritative theoretical validation for an optimistic belief in the autonomy of art that found its perfect translation in abstraction—or, more specifically, in *constructive* abstraction.

(NON-)DETERMINATION

I want to go back to that striking formulation by Pedrosa: "The realized object is the point of arrival in the artist's action, but [also] the viewer's starting point." This question of the temporal articulation of the subject-object relation is decisive in the ensuing debates over geometric abstraction in the 1950s. Some years later, in a 1956 manifesto entitled simply "The Object," Cordeiro would cast his earlier concerns about the intelligibility of art in very similar terms. For him, the latter would be staked on the "universality of the object," leading to the radical conclusion that "content [in art] is not a starting point, but an arrival point."[36] Viewed in comparison with Pedrosa, this statement is perhaps less a disagreement than a qualification—one meant to steer the pertinence of Gestalt toward a clear-cut conception of subject-object relation. This involved a passage from the intrinsic *meaningfulness* of art to art as the producer of unequivocal *meanings*. In such conception, the "product" (as opposed, in Cordeiro's lexicon, to "expression") of artistic activity would be a universally translatable object.

A brief but important aside is due here: the corresponding subject of this kind of object was supposed to be ideologically exempt—even when an explicit ideological position was invoked.[37] Cordeiro believed, after Gramsci, that "culture only comes into historical existence when it creates a unity of thinking between the 'simple' people and the artists and intellectuals."[38] His argument, however, never reaches the point of diagnosing hegemonic culture, or of explaining a potential working-class basis for counterhegemonic strategy. On the one hand, like most of the historical constructive avant-gardes, the concretists assumed that their formal repertoire had an intrinsic, universal emancipatory character (being "crystal-clear"). On the other, as Brito remarks, significantly, they naïvely welcomed the mass media as an "instrument of cultural penetration pertinent to the 'spiritual needs' of the modern man," thus ignoring their role as "ideological apparatuses of capitalist states."[39]

In a sense, this sort of political self-reflexivity was strategically unavailable to artists and critics at that time. The passage from Pedrosa's conception of the artistic object to Cordeiro's must be understood against the grain of a broader one, from the relatively marginal fight for the acceptance of abstraction within their artistic milieu to the confident identification of geometric abstraction with a national, progressive project. In the 1952 manifesto that launched his Ruptura group, Cordeiro no longer assumed the general position of "we, the abstractionists"; quite on the contrary, he made a point of distinguishing "those who create new forms from old principles" from "those who create new forms from new principles."[40] His target was abstraction understood as a "non-figurative hedonism" rather than a program. From Cordeiro's viewpoint, a general abstractionist alliance had become unnecessary and even undesirable. Unnecessary because abstraction in Brazil was already standing on its own feet: the newly inaugurated museums of modern art in São Paulo and Rio de Janeiro were joined in 1951 by the São Paulo Biennial in guaranteeing a receptive institutional framework for modern art in general, and for abstraction in particular.[41] For example, in 1954 Pedrosa would be able to reverse the terms and polemically declare that the second Biennial could have done well without painters Candido Portinari and Lasar Segall—major representatives of the earlier, figurative generation. And undesirable because the acceptance of "hedonist" trends within abstractionism threatened to prevent art from achieving programmatic efficiency, as Cordeiro would put it elsewhere: "Art can participate in the contemporary spiritual work when endowed with its proper principles. The question is to consider art a means of knowledge as important as the positive sciences."[42] Dispersion was the enemy that Cordeiro sought to counter by proposing a collective and focused endeavor to disseminate formal rigor, for, as critic Lorenzo Mammì has pointed out, concretist aesthetics favored "a continuous exercise of the eye, and not a singular and intense experience."[43]

Hence the growing tendency of Ruptura-aligned painters to distribute their repertoire sparingly throughout a number of works, restricting the pictorial procedure of each individual work to one or very few clear organizing principles. It was less a matter of dogmatism than a statement of the programmatic coming of age of abstraction in Brazil under the guise of what Mammì terms "argumentative reasoning."[44] The unequivocal (and cumulative) clarity of these works, often reinforced in the titles, elevated artistic production one level beyond simple intelligibility, namely into the articulation of a stance that would be personified, in Brito's words, by the figure of the artist qua "superior designer."[45] It is easy to see how this deeply positivistic stance could be confidently posed as progressive at that time. As Cordeiro published "The Object," industrialization would be gaining momentum under the popular (or rather populist) and optimistic presidency of Juscelino Kubitschek, whose "fifty years in five" slogan, coupled with the promise of a new, modernist capital—Brasília—would provide the cue for a widespread understanding of modernization as a sweeping force against a provincial and archaic past. In São Paulo, particularly, the successful luring—via fiscal incentives—of multinational automobile manufacturers such as Ford, Volkswagen, and General Motors suddenly turned the city's outskirts into a veritable industrial landscape.[46] This confirmed and lent a considerable boost to a process that was already under way, that of São Paulo becoming the industrial core of the country, a process that further gained visibility as the city's boom—between 1940 and 1960 its population grew from approximately 1.3 to 4.3 million inhabitants[47]—quickly saturated it with the distinct, concrete color of modernist architecture.

That said, I don't want to partake in the hackneyed view that posits a relation of expressive causality between modernization in Brazil and the local rise of constructive tendencies.[48] I would rather see modernization as a *bonding* force, in the sense that the enthusiasm it provoked across the social strata and the political spectrum smoothed over numerous social and cultural contradictions.[49] Much less visible, of course, were the social and economic costs of Kubitschek's ventures, which increasingly took their toll toward the end of the government, in the form of a soaring public deficit and an inflation rate that reached, in 1959, the alarming figure of 39.5 percent. Kubitschek's momentum was in fact a complex construct, due in part to his ability to fashion himself into an emblem of a new era—he was nicknamed "the bossa-nova president." But it was also sustained by an intricate political arrangement that issued ambivalent—and often contradictory—nods to parts of the country's bourgeoisie, to government bureaucrats, and also to the worker's unions, which were becoming a rising political force in the wake of fast industrialization.

My point here is that, considering the complex matrix of contradictions underlying the supposed unanimity of the 1950s modernizing ethos, the very fact that enthusiasm was able to sustain itself is worthy of notice.[50] For now, let me just stress that Cordeiro and others unproblematically identified their own stance with the broader forces they saw in action in the economic and cultural fields (a number of artists and poets at this time actually experimented with graphic design and advertising, courting the mass media in a way Brito would retrospectively find naïve). The specificity of art, from that viewpoint, would be its privileged position for tackling form at its purest—by means, for example, of the insistent "concretions" of guiding principles—and subsequently inform other spheres of activity from a "spiritually" elevated viewpoint. Thus the striking title of a number of Cordeiro's works: *Visible Idea*.

28

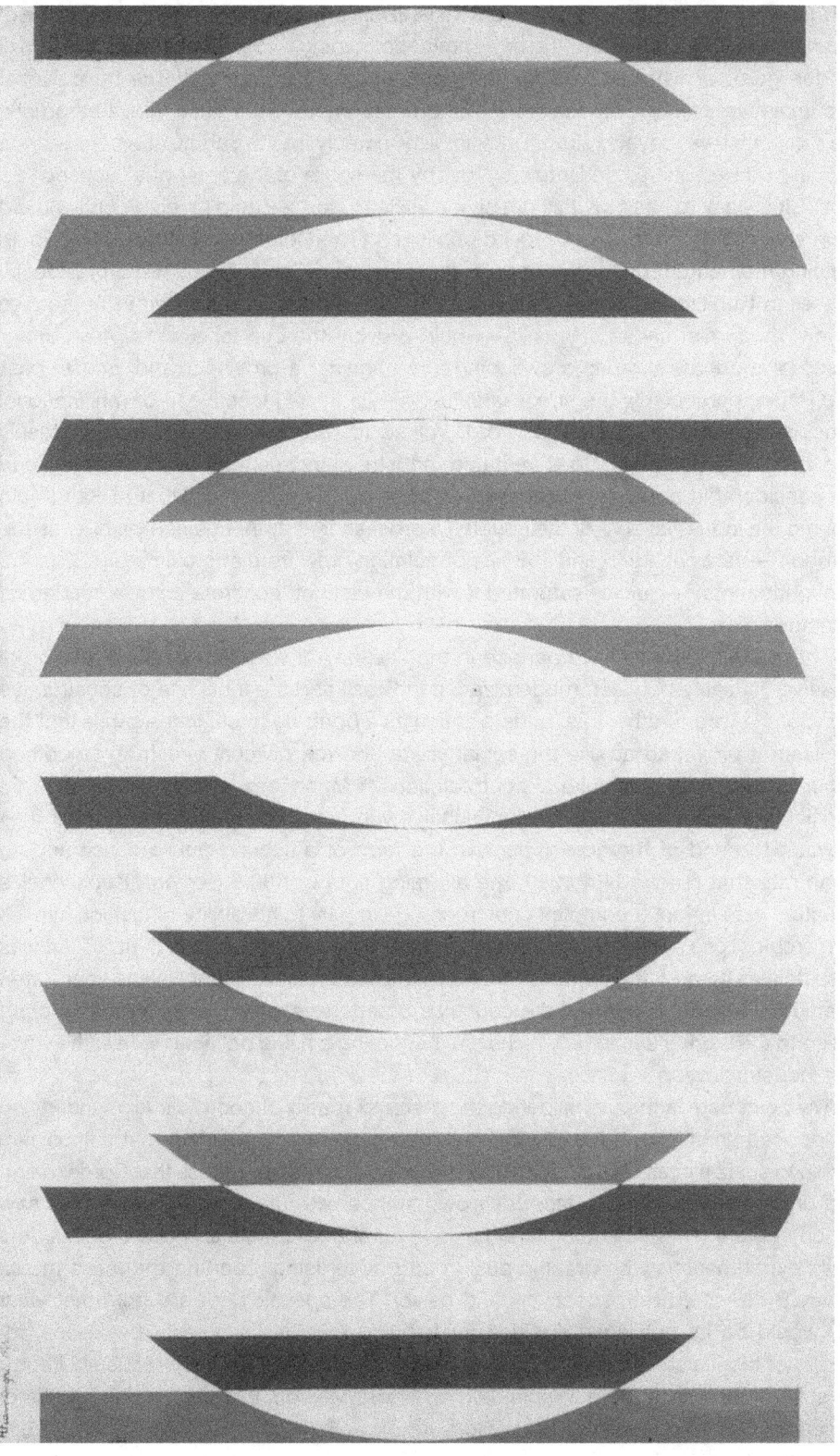

CHAPTER 1

1.4
Hermelindo Fiaminghi, *Circles with Alternated Movement*, 1956. Enamel on plywood, 60 × 35 cm. Coleção Museu de Arte Moderna de São Paulo. Photo: Romulo Fialdini.

This is not to say that São Paulo concretism was devoid of inventiveness. The sculptural *Concretions* of Luís Sacilotto, for example, are unequivocally driven by Gestaltian principles (most specifically by the law of closure) and by the logic of "continuous exercises" Mammì describes—thus their titles, always accompanied by a four-digit chronological index. Works like *Concretion 5942* (1959) and *Concretion 6045* (1960) depart from an original, square metal plane. It is this original form—the square—that is kept and multiplied throughout an intricate series of cut-and-fold operations. These are designed to create even intervals between the metal strips that are equivalent in width to the strips themselves. Most importantly, the opposition between opaque matter and empty space becomes secondary in that both strip and interval cooperate in forming the positive gestalt of the resultant squares. To put it briefly, these pieces prompt the viewer's perception to complete the lines and contours of the virtual squares they propose. In art historian Ana Maria Belluzo's words, Sacilotto's aim was to "update a permanent figure and reveal the complexity of simple things."[51]

Can we still think of such a procedure within the rigorous concretist aesthetic and ideological framework? As an answer, it is possible to say that Sacilotto's inventiveness was meant to affirm the elasticity of the concretist visual repertoire, and thus its overall validity and versatility.[52] The limit of Sacilotto's multiplication remains strict: it lies precisely in the threshold of the resulting planes remaining intelligibly traceable back to their originating figure. As Belluzzo has pointed out, Sacilotto "started from a single surface, which is definitely square, to create various planes." *Definitely square*, Belluzzo says, proceeding to stress that he "never loses sight of the original form."[53] The success of Sacilotto's work is thus staked on how effectively he draws a multiplicity of shapes out of a first, single one, while keeping this initial reference intact and unequivocally referring the viewer back to it—shapes that are furthermore securely aligned in planes. This is the *magic* of his operation, to borrow another term by Belluzzo, a very apt one indeed: we are meant to follow his cuts and folds backward, in the same way we would follow a stage magician revealing his sleight of hand in order to understand and marvel at the simplicity of the operation. If proliferation were somehow stretched beyond this exercise, the sculptures would risk their status as (intelligible) "products" and quickly collapse into (arbitrary or intuitive) "expressions"—at least according to Cordeiro's rigorous terminology.

Such inventiveness nevertheless leads Belluzzo to protest that the "plural forms that characterize Concrete production reveal an organic, functional structure every time they are folded and unfolded," at odds with the neoconcrete characterization of them as "mechanical serial forms."[54] It is wrong, however, to see the neoconcrete criticism of the "mechanical" only in terms of seriality. As a matter of fact, Gullar's vocabulary in this case was borrowed straight from his main theoretical reference at the time, Maurice Merleau-Ponty's *The Structure of Behavior*, from which I want to quote a particularly elucidating passage:

> A mechanical action, whether the word is taken in a restricted or looser sense, is one in which the cause and the effect are decomposable into real elements which have a one-to-one correspondence. In elementary actions, the dependence is uni-directional; the cause is the necessary and sufficient condition of the effect considered in its existence and its nature; and, even when one speaks of reciprocal action between two terms, it can be reduced to a series of uni-directional determinations.[55]

What is key here, of course, is the idea of *determination*. Irrespective of how much these forms are "folded and unfolded," they never lose sight of a given set of generative principles (in fact, they strive not to).[56] The temporality of experiencing phenomena implicit in Merleau-Ponty's passage is thus akin to that of the concretist artwork: an analytical inventory of "one-to-one correspondences," of causes and effects; it is a temporality that, in short, folds the moment of experience onto that of production, the latter understood as a "series of uni-directional determinations." It is in this sense that the object can be seen as something else than a "starting point": there is no "beyond" it; experiencing it means engaging in the exercise of decoding it rather than giving it continuation through subjective experience. Thus we reach Gullar's 1957 critical reversion of Cordeiro's notion of the object, again in dialogue with the sense of nondetermination that motivates Pedrosa's earlier formulation: "the poem starts when the reading is over … thus, in the concrete poem, the reader is brought into encountering a *durable* object — that puts the poem in opposition to the advert and to advertising processes in general — where language aims only at precipitating an action by the reader, not to create an object for him."[57] By further advancing that the poem "must count as a quotidian experience," but one that aims at a "*transcendental totality*," Gullar was already introducing what would become a major topic in the "Theory": the uneasy matrix of an artwork whose experience bypasses the specialized, privileged space of the fine arts, but which nevertheless refuses to remain simply as an ordinary object among other, utilitarian ones. This is the precise meaning of the word "transcendence" in his writings (incidentally, this is also a major point of differentiation between the non-object and the later minimalist object).

Of course, in the passages I have just quoted, Gullar is referring to poetry rather than visual arts. As a matter of fact — and this is a crucial formative feature of Gullar's thought — the schism between concretists and future neoconcretists happened on both fronts, with Gullar engaging in polemical dialogues and exchanges both with Cordeiro and with the founders of the São Paulo poetry group Noigandres: Haroldo de Campos, Augusto de Campos, and Décio Pignatari. Such an intense interpenetration of poetry and visual arts was a distinctive characteristic of Brazilian concretism, to the point that poems were exhibited alongside paintings and sculptures in enlarged, wall-mounted, poster-like pages at the "National Exhibition of Concrete Art" — the show that first sparked major divergences between the Rio and São Paulo groups.[58] This juxtaposition allowed the direct comparison between both sets of practices and, in some crucial cases, prompted a radicalization of positions akin to the one that was already taking course in painting (shortly after the show, Cordeiro famously denounced what he saw with shock as a lack of rigor in Ivan Serpa's paintings: "there is even brown in these paintings").[59] As the show opened in Rio, still before the polemic ensued, Pedrosa published two critical articles about the internal differences in the concrete avant-garde. One, as I have already mentioned, took note of the different inflections of the Rio and São Paulo groups, while the other, which is the one I am interested in here, had the sole aim of distinguishing the opposing ways concretist poets and painters structured their practices.[60] For Pedrosa, whereas the concretist painter "wants to get rid of all direct phenomenological experience" so as "to realize a pure and perfect mental operation, like the calculation of an engineer" the activity of their fellow poets "is always and passionately phenom-

1.5
Luis Sacilotto, *Concretion 5942*, 1959.
Painted aluminum, 30 × 30 × 17 cm. Photo:
Sergio Guerini. Courtesy Arquivo Sacilotto.

1.6
Luis Sacilotto, *Concretion 6045*, 1960. Painted
iron, 31.1 × 90.2 × 39.4 cm. The Museum
of Fine Arts Houston; The Adolpho Leirner
Collection of Brazilian Constructive Art,
museum purchase with funds provided by
the Caroline Wiess Law Accessions
Endowment Fund.

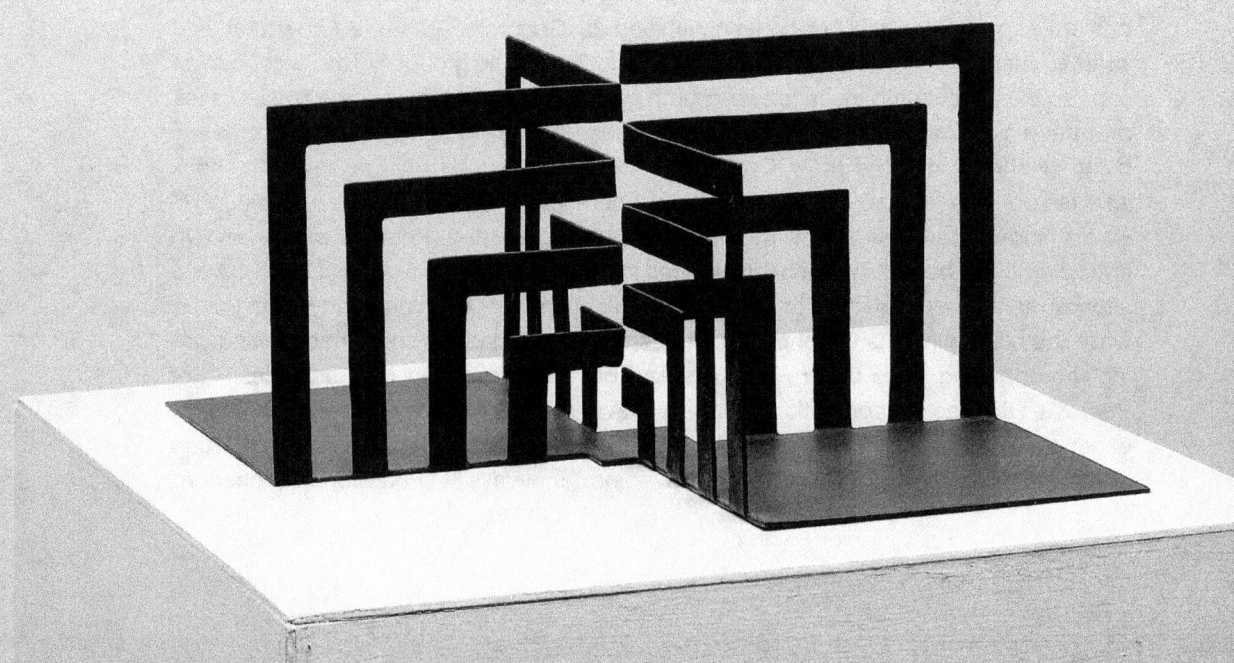

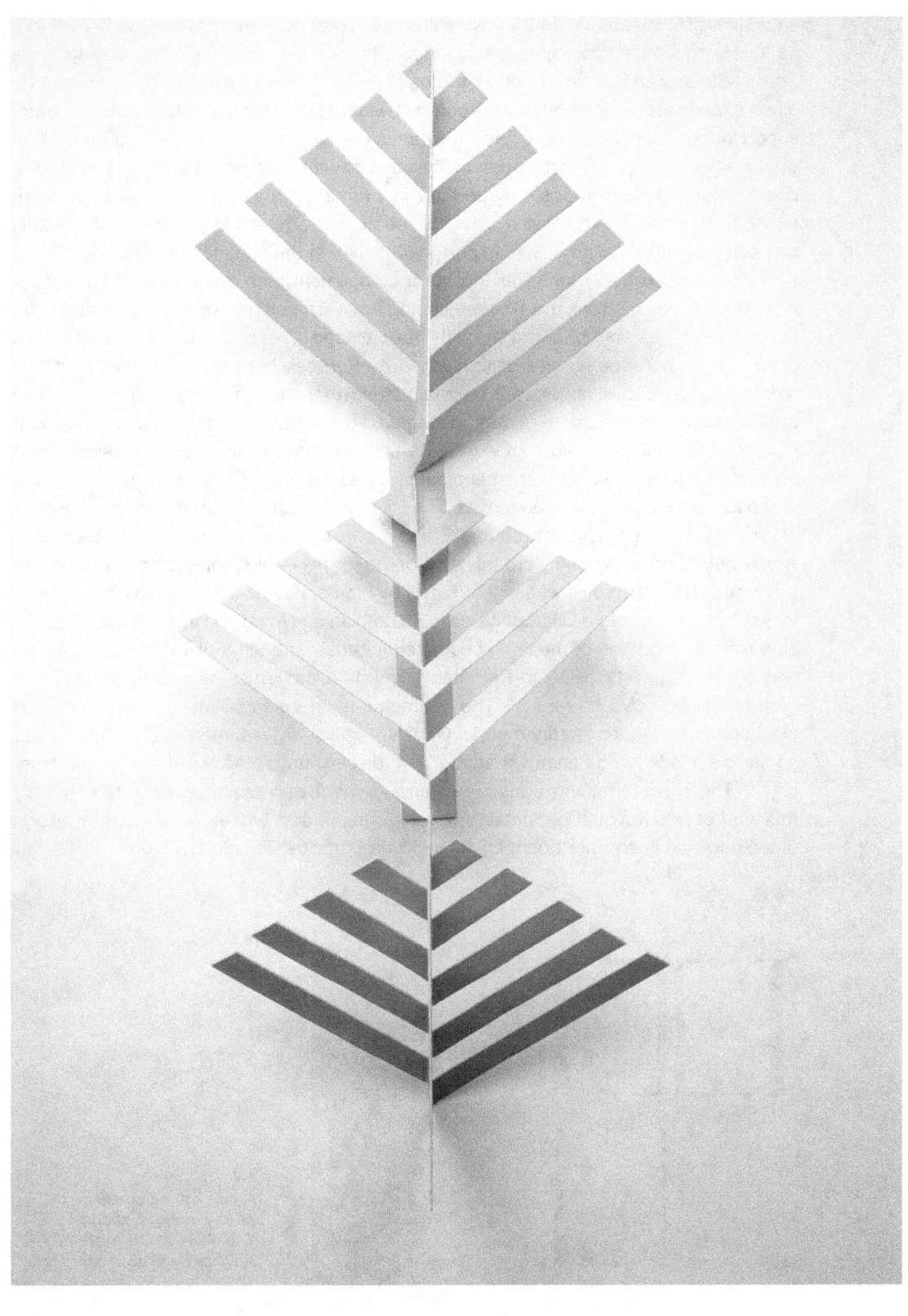

enological."[61] He explains that by wrestling the word away from syntax and keeping it as a nonconceptual "combine of sounds and letters, phonemes and diphthongs," the poet ends up with "a mere phenomenological object, immediate and primary data for direct experience."[62] In short, and in contrast with the mechanical efficiency of a painter supposed to transfer his "idea" onto the canvas, the poet retained the word itself as an object—one whose irreducible materiality was not without a say in the final form of the poem: "Haroldo de Campos, maybe the most romantic of concretists, sees his poem taking form while hearing, like a constant refrain, the sound of the words, which pays him company and maybe which, in part, directs him in their spatial distribution."[63]

Campos probably took this less as a compliment than as criticism. In a famous manifesto entitled "From the Phenomenology of Composition to the Mathematics of Composition," he announced that, with the passage already explicit in the title, "the difference of attitudes so well distinguished by Pedrosa between concretist poet and painter will tend to disappear."[64] He maintained that the "exact moment of creative option" would be the mathematical definition of a structure that would *precede* and *determine* the ultimate choice of words. Campos effectively aimed at bypassing the encounter with the word qua phenomenological object, at least insofar as the structuration of the concrete poem was concerned. The São Paulo poets would further theorize this self-critical passage as one from the "*organic-physiognomic*" poem to the "*geometric-isomorphic*" one. The spatial organization of the former—take, for example, *Ovonovelo*, by Augusto de Campos—was still dictated by iconic resemblance to the actual object in question (in Augusto de Campos's case, to both an egg [*ovo*] and a ball of yarn [*novelo*], alongside connotation of meaning being continuously spun in a dialectic of new [*novo*] and old [*velho*]), which Décio Pignatari termed "a movement that imitates the real [*movimento imitativo do real*]."[65] The geometric-isomorphic poem, on the other hand, would be arranged, as literary theorist Gonzalo Aguilar argues, more like an "ideogram," so as to achieve "simultaneity in space" and discard any residue of "syntactical ordering."[66] The predetermining principle of arrangement that would eventually dominate this kind of poem would be, unsurprisingly perhaps, that archetypical modernist form of the *grid*—as in another poem by Augusto de Campos, *Tensão* (Tension).

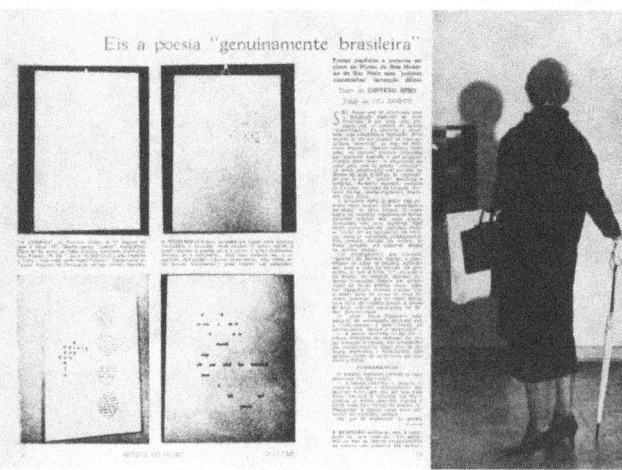

1.7
Article on the presence of poetry in the "National Exhibition of Concrete Art." *Revista do Globo*, January 12, 1957.

Now, the reason why Haroldo de Campos's manifesto is particularly famous is because it sparked a decisive episode in the Rio-São Paulo schism that followed the "National Exhibition." Campos submitted it to Gullar for publication at the *SDJB*, but the text met the latter's severe opposition—Gullar did publish the manifesto but not without first penning an accompanying point-by-point rebuttal of the São Paulo position. This is the text I introduced a few paragraphs earlier, in which Gullar reverts Cordeiro's notion of the object.[67] The move can be summed up as follows: to Campos's proposal of bringing poetry closer to Pedrosa's reading of concretist painting, Gullar responds by simultaneously questioning both painter and poet via Cordeiro's object, and by formulating a proposal that was not only closer to Pedrosa's description of a phenomenologically oriented concretist poetry, but also to the earlier conception of the artistic object that the senior critic had advanced in his 1949 thesis.[68] With this in mind, it is easier to realize that Gullar's position was neither a simple refusal of Gestalt theory—just like Merleau-Ponty's critique also praises particular aspects of Gestalt—nor a critique of it solely based on its employment by the São Paulo concretists. It was also an updating of the driving force behind Pedrosa's own interest in Gestalt theory: the defense of the autonomy of artistic experience against heteronomous determination.

Accordingly, then, Gullar's ultimate "durable objects," his own non-objects, lie also on the threshold between poetry and visual arts. I refer here to his neoconcrete *Spatial Poems*, like *Noite* (Night) and *Lembra* (Remember/Reminds).[69] *Ara* (an unusual Portuguese word meaning a ceremonial or sacrificial altar or tabletop), the first of the series, is Gullar's most Brancusian poem, in the sense that it eventually incorporates its own "plinth" (i.e., the entire wooden structure, reminiscent of the book pages, which is opened in order to reveal the printed word) into the whole of the form the poem installs, as it is manipulated/read. The usage of a single word (which Gullar would repeat in various *Spatial Poems* and in the *Buried Poem*) is crucial, as it enacts a temporal structure that is noncoincident with the rhythm of reading a sentence or even a group of equivalent words (in the sense of them sharing the same experiential space). In short, the particular meaning of the word becomes highly condensed, to the point of excess; instead of either inserting itself in the syntagmatic flow of meanings or letting itself be paradigmatically measured against other words arranged on a page, the reading of these words sparks a kind of loose, overspilling temporality that impregnates the visual support of the poems.[70] So, in *Lembra*, one's perception of the visual ensemble of the poem is irrevocably contaminated by the memory of the word that was read—as the title's allusion to memory implies, one cannot help *remembering* that there is a word below the blue cube. Likewise, in *Ara*, the three-letter word graphically translates into the triangular shape of the cover; semantically speaking, after the word is read and the poem is once again "closed," the superimposition of the triangle over the square base becomes evocative of the very shape of an altar. But, most crucially, the connotation of the altar, a space meant for the temporally charged moment of ritual, becomes a token of self-reflexivity.

Something is fundamentally changed with the "reading" of all *Spatial Poems*. The original form the viewer/reader encounters cannot revert back to its original state; that is, one cannot dispel the meaning that now impregnates it, even if the word is again covered. It is telling in this respect that the word *ara* not only means a sacrificial altar

ovo
n o v e l o
novo no velho
o filho em folhos
na jaula dos joelhos
infante em fonte
f e t o   f e i t o
dent ro   d o
centro

nu
d e s   d o
nada até o hum
ano   mero   n u
mero   d o   zero
crua criança incru
stada no cerne da
carne viva en
fim nada

o
p o n t o
onde se esconde
lenda ainda antes
e n t r e v e n t r e s
quando queimando
os   seios   são
peitos   nos
dedos

no
turna   noite
em torno em treva
turva sem contorno
morte negro nó cego
sono do morcego nu
ma sombra que o pren
dia preta letra que
s e   t o r n a
sol

1.8
Augusto de Campos, *Ovonovelo*, 1956.

com   can
som   tem

con   ten   tam
tem   são   bem

tom   sem
bem   som

1.9
Augusto de Campos, *Tensão*, 1956.

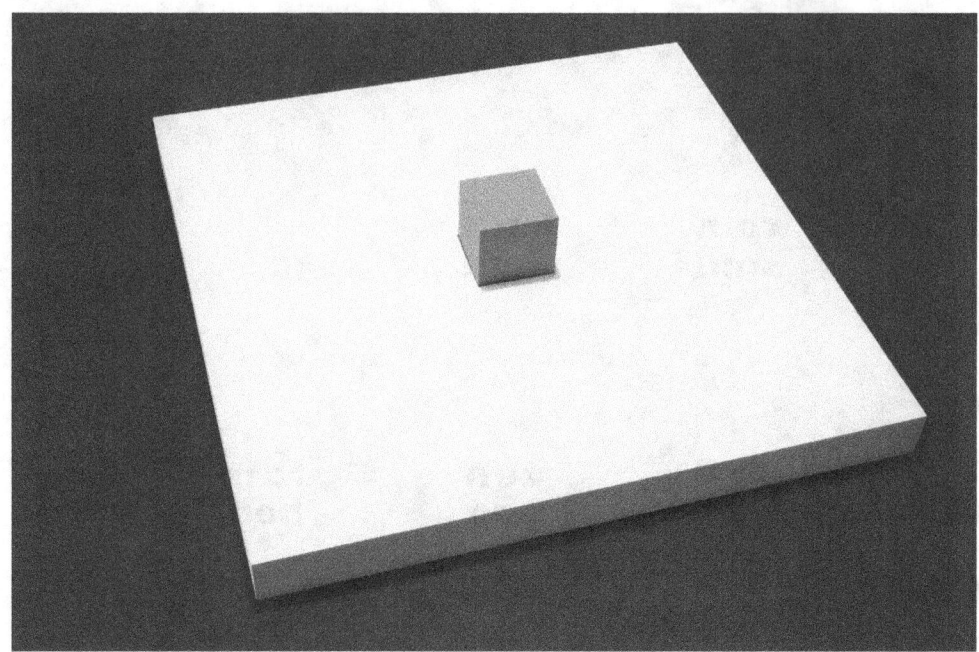

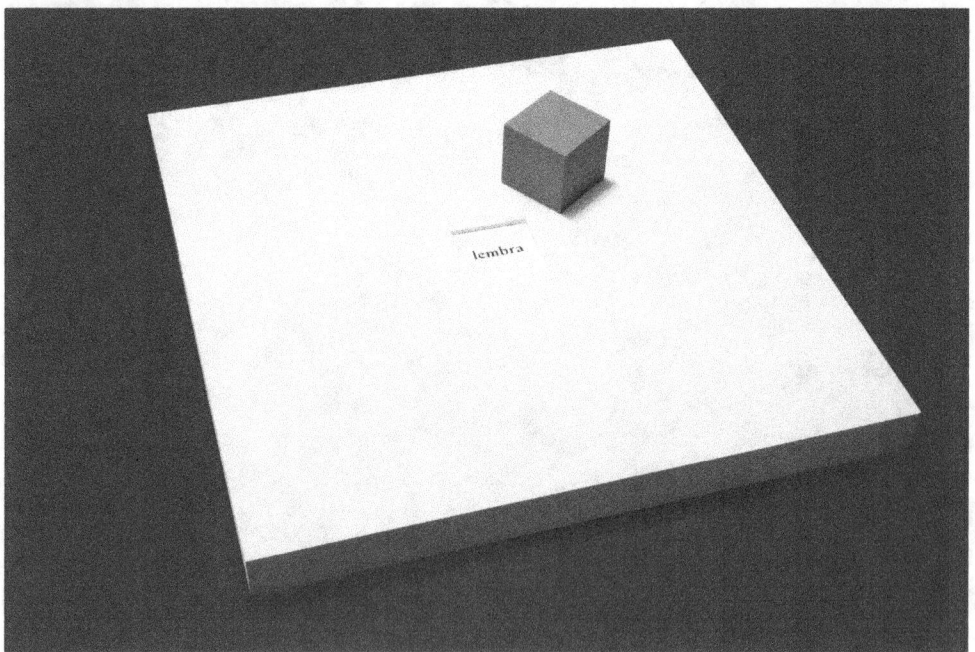

1.10
Ferreira Gullar, *Lembra*, 1959 (reconstruction).
Acrylic on wood and vinyl, 40 × 40 × 5 cm.
Collection of the artist. Photo: Erika Tambke.

1.11
Ferreira Gullar, *Ara*, 1959 (reconstruction).
Acrylic on wood and vinyl, 40 × 40 × 4 cm.
Collection of the artist. Photo: Erika Tambke.

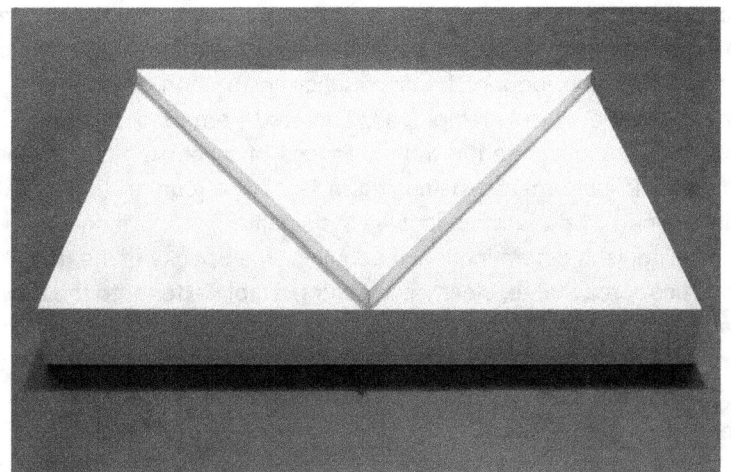

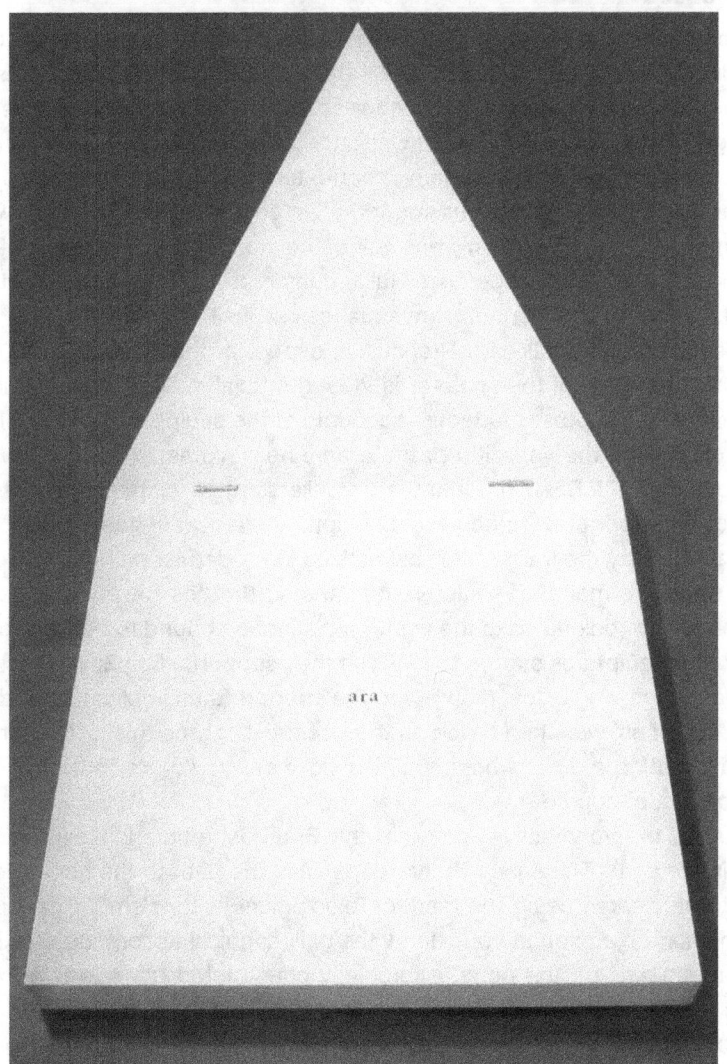

(in its pagan connotation) but also, within a Christian context, the specific table on top of which the communion chalice and wafers lie. A sense of transubstantiation through signification—akin to the logic of transcendence in the non-object—is set in train.[71] By the same token the word is reciprocally liberated from its ordinary role. For Gullar, everyday objects "are exhausted in the references of meaning"; that is, they are fully determined by their instrumental belonging in language (our relationship with a pear would be determined by our access to it via the signifier "pear"); if an ordinary object is stripped of this linguistic determination, it acquires "the opacity of the thing," becoming "impenetrable, unapproachable, clearly and insupportably exterior to the subject."[72] The *Spatial Poems* aim at undoing this duality by enacting a relation between language and plastic form that, instead of using words in order to determine objects, lends them an afterlife, in the subject, as a mnemonic catalyst—it is in this precise sense that poetry gives the reader a durable object.

EXCLUDED OBJECT

My main concern so far has been to reconstruct and historicize the intricate conceptual origins of the non-object by showing how it thrived on Pedrosa's use of Gestalt theory to carve a legitimized autonomous space for abstraction while simultaneously rejecting the tautological closure of form Gestalt was later taken to prescribe. In other words, the non-object strived to keep the question of nondetermination an open one, and one that should bear not only on the demand for figurative content, but also on the very formal constitution of artworks. This is only one half of the story, and it is important to turn now to the historical narrative of modernism Gullar constructed for the non-object, since this narrative is not without conceptual consequences as well.

In this context, my talk of a Brancusian aspect of the *Spatial Poem* is not arbitrary: Gullar's treatment of the sculptor is indeed crucial in this respect. It is also very similar, at first sight, to other modernist accounts of the sculptor. The crux of the poet's reading is clear from the very title of the article he devotes to the matter: "Brancusi and the Problem of the Base in Sculpture."[73] Gullar is mostly interested in stressing the way Brancusi incorporates the base as a sculptural element in itself, which he sees as analogous to the way the frame is problematized in modernist painting. He argues that the earlier, figurative matrix of sculpture guaranteed that the base would be "naturally apprehended as not belonging to the work," a distinction bound to become problematic as nonfigurative sculptures started to look like their supports. For Gullar, this meant that sculptural language would "overflow" onto the support, thus implicating and eventually including it. Brancusi was then hailed as the first artist to face this problem head on, to the point of creating a work where "there is no more *sculpture*, but only *base*"—the *Endless Column*, of course.[74]

That said, the very last sentence of the Brancusi article leaves no doubt as to Gullar's ultimate aim: "There is in Brancusi, as well, the path to the non-object."[75] This assertion, to be clearer, bears the mark of teleological historicism.[76] There is a double matrix to the non-object: on the one hand, the philosophical absorption of existentialism and phenomenology; on the other, a forcefully constructed genealogy about the end of medium specificity. After all, the non-object was meant to deny the separation of painting, sculpture, and even relief.[77] That was carried out, in the pages of the *SDJB*, by means of a step-by-step interpretation of modernist artists and movements "from the neoconcrete viewpoint."[78] Cubism, constructivism, neoplasticism, futurism, Bauhaus, concretism (but *not* expressionism or surrealism) … all of these were there *as well* as Brancusi. Any given series of articles was often followed by sections entitled "Attempt at Comprehension." The neoconcrete interpretation of modernism was consistently confident, but it was also imbued with a certain experimental caution, and even with outright honesty about its tentative historical viewpoint—and yet more often than not these "attempts" ended, like the Brancusi article, by implicitly or explicitly locating the movement or group in question as yet another step in the path to neoconcretism and the non-object. Hence the very title of the series: *Stages of Contemporary Art*.

The purpose of these articles, then, was fully to flesh out the historical account present in both the "Neoconcrete Manifesto" and even more so in the "Theory." Gullar claims that developments in the fields of painting and sculpture are equivalent in that both "[converge] toward a common point" in which "the denominations *painting* and *sculpture* perhaps no longer apply."[79] For the poet, base (in sculpture) and frame (in painting) are equivalent problems that art was in the course of overcoming. Without such categorical mediation, only the non-objecthood of the work would remain as an artistic parameter. We should ask ourselves, however, to what extent are painting and sculpture equivalent in this account? Otherwise put: does the non-object deny both categories equally in order to constitute itself? It may not be so, and I think that it is precisely from this fundamental imbalance that we can start to think the non-object in terms beyond its original historicism.[80]

The different historical inflection of the "Theory" in relation to the preceding "Neo-concrete Manifesto" is nicely summarized by Michael Asbury: "[No] longer directly concerned with establishing parameters of distinction for neoconcretism, Gullar's text centers on the unfolding of the two-dimensional plane within space as a general art historical development."[81] There is more to it: with the non-object already situated within his theoretical horizon, Gullar is able to include even groups and artists he had previously dismissed, positing neoconcretism as a dialectical synthesis. So, whereas the "Manifesto" had hastily glossed over Dada and surrealism, mentioning them only as "irrationalist" reactions to "rationalist extremism," the "Theory" engages in a more specific discussion of the estrangement generated by the Duchampian readymade and by the surrealist object (which was certainly familiar to Pedrosa, close as he had been to the surrealists).[82] Gullar's critique thus becomes more refined, as he argues that the problem is that the readymade's "process of transfiguration of the object is grounded not so much in the formal qualities of the object, but in its connection with the object's quotidian use. Soon that obscurity that is characteristic of *thing* returns to envelop the *work*, bringing it back to the common level. On this *front* the artists are defeated by the object."[83]

Gullar thus recognizes both the attempts of transposing art into direct friction with everyday objects (as in Duchamp and surrealism) and the self-critical stance painting and sculpture adopted toward their own "metaphoric space" (common to most constructive tendencies) as participating in the same telos. Duchamp was quicker to point toward the object, true, but his procedure was too nihilistic; already in the "Manifesto" Gullar questioned the point of understanding Mondrian "as the destroyer of the

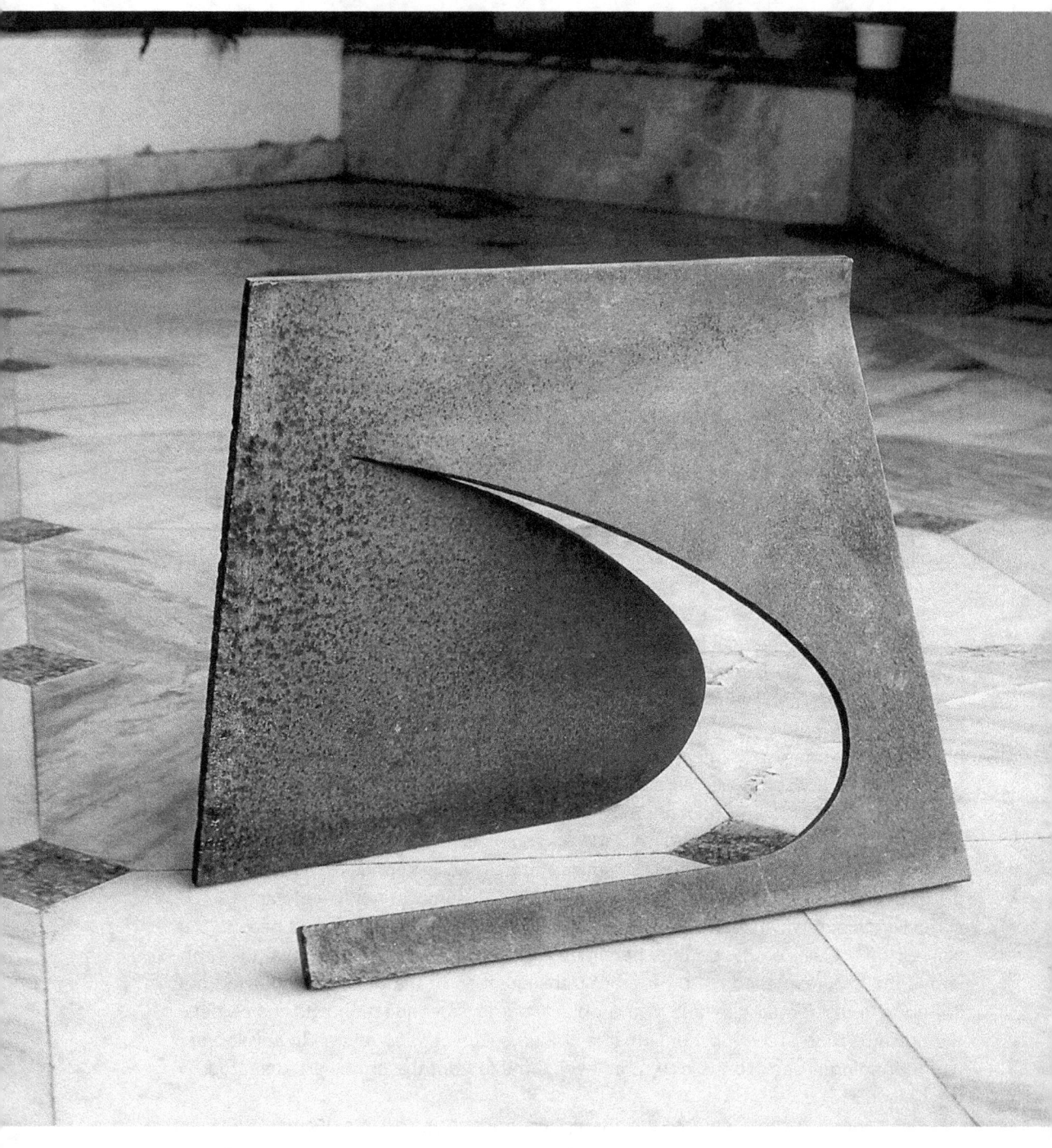

1.12
Amilcar de Castro, *Untitled*, early 1960s. Steel,
54 × 54 × 1.2 cm. Private Collection. Licensed
by inARTS.com. Photo: Daniel Coury.

surface, the plane, the line, without paying attention to the new space constructed by this destruction."[84] The avowed transcendence inaugurated by the non-object (i.e., the redemptive perspective of subject-object relation it offered, consonant with its utopian cultural context) was thus, in this precise sense, a *constructive* requirement that depended, as such, on its unequivocal articulation via *constructive* forms. A contextual requirement, for sure, but also one inherent in the very historicity of the non-object: the obligatory passage via the figure of the *plane* signified its hard-fought position at the end of a dialectical history of modernism, a position that was now able to surpass and incorporate even those seemingly antithetical historical episodes (and thus to assure its superiority and distinction from them).[85]

This pivotal role assumed by the plane—as the metaphysical backbone of constructive art—will ground both the explicit prominence of painting in Gullar's history of modernism and its implicit grip over the interpretation of neoconcretism (it is noteworthy in this respect that the title of the *Stages of Contemporary Art* series would eventually change into *Stages of Contemporary Painting*).[86] The case of Amilcar de Castro is exemplary here, as the misleading simplicity of his sculptures makes them privileged screens for interpretive projections. What may have been initially a critical description of his work became, over the years, a hackneyed formula, an obstacle to further critical reflection. I refer to the idea that his trademark sculptures originate with a cut-and-fold operation that opens up the two-dimensional plane to three-dimensionality (to which I shall refer, for brevity's sake, as the *2D-3D account*).[87] There are two points to consider here. First, while the emphasis on the cut-and-fold process is undoubtedly accurate (as a drastically brief inventory of sculptural actions), it is also, as critic Rodrigo Naves was one of the few to point out, too schematic, in that it clearly fails to account for the experiential complexity of these works.[88] After all, they convey a temporal sense of *imminence*—as if they had just been cracked open or could be folded slightly further—rather than communicate a step-by-step process. Second, and most important, there is the incredible assumption that these sculptures originate in a movement that is strictly analogous to that of the neoconcretist history of modernist painting: the passage from the two-dimensional plane to three-dimensional space. It may be unsurprising that Clark's trajectory from her *Cocoons* and *Counter-Reliefs* toward the *Bichos* (and it is worth recalling that this is the avowed site of Gullar's encounter with his primordial non-object) practically invites such a reading, or that Oiticica would cast his own neoconcrete production as the "transition of color from painting into space"—both were originally painters, after all.[89] But shouldn't we stop and ask whether it is proper also to interpret Castro's sculptures with such painterly eyes?

Of course, one might object to my incipient critique at this point by pointing out that Castro himself endorsed this reading.[90] His sculptures, he would explain, are "made from iron slabs … because I want to demonstrate, departing from the surface, the birth of the third dimension."[91] Art historian José Francisco Alves further emphasizes Castro's obsession with the origin of the sculptures in drawing, noting that the sculptor would draw several lines on a white sheet of paper, with a hard pencil, in order to come up with shapes and ways of cutting his steel plaques and slabs.[92] It is here that the potential objection falls short. That Castro—the artist—would easily envisage a smooth passage from the moment of production to that of the finished work is understandable, but this

1.13
Amilcar de Castro, preparatory drawing,
undated. Licensed by inARTS.com. Photo:
Daniel Coury.

does not entail that this passage is so smooth once we start from the viewer's side. This is especially true vis-à-vis the neoconcretist paradigm of experience. Gullar's articles and manifestos often couple phenomenological primacy ("by virtue of being the first appearance of a form, [the non-object] founds its signification in itself")[93] with a remarkable lack of interest in the production side of art making, to the point of overlooking this aspect even in extreme cases such as Russian constructivism.[94] It is not that those preparatory drawings are irrelevant (and I will return to them). But to see them determining the meaning of experience is to ignore that the autonomy of phenomenological experience over making, or perhaps their evident out-of-jointness, is one of neoconcretism's most basic tenets (in keeping with Pedrosa's Gestaltian emphasis on reception). Folding the meaning of experience onto that of production is a concretist gesture, not a neoconcretist one.

This is something Haroldo de Campos ignored when, forty years after the "National Exhibition," he maintained that the difference between the likes of Sacilotto and Castro was merely one of "personal accent," meaning that their common repertoire—cutting, folding, usage of geometric shapes, and so on—essentially brought them together.[95] That said, comparing Castro to Sacilotto is useful in order to clarify a problem raised by my contentions against the 2D-3D account: what about the plane? To put it in a nutshell: even if one accepts that the idea of a two-dimensional origin of Castro's sculptures is flawed, it does not mean that the plane plays absolutely no role in them. It clearly does, but the exact nature of this role is much more complex than it appears at first.

As we have seen, Sacilotto's sculptures present planes that include empty intervals. It is easy to see how those gaps are not meant as openings for our gaze, or frames for the space that lie beyond them. This kind of transparency is not *meaningful* to the sculptural form they take part in. On the contrary, those spaces become equivalent to (i.e., occupy the same plane as) the material segments of the sculpture, thus becoming an equally positive predicate; both become complementary, and it is because of their complementarity and regularity that they are able to form a gestalt, as if both took part in defining a planar geometric form (in this particular sense, they do aim at flatness). Experience thus becomes a closed circle (or square), since the plane is reaffirmed and expanded at every sculptural move.

In contrast, Castro's sculptures are based on the plane as that indispensable structuring element that is nevertheless *unattainable* to experience as such, in the sense that the actual form of the sculpture is at a remove from it.[96] What is more, this is a somewhat incommensurable remove, since its temporality—once again, its sense of imminence—cannot be grasped as a regular sequence of steps. The plane thus remains on the negative side of things, since it is never empirically ascertainable, but it also remains somehow attached to the experience of these sculptures—it continuously lurks there.[97] In other words, by virtue of its insistent reluctance to form itself (or at least to do so in a satisfactory way), both actually *and* virtually, the plane here acts, so to speak, as a *negative* benchmark, an absent "ground" that lends formal consistency to the visible configuration of the work. The sculpture is not measured against the plane (as if it were a ruler of sorts), but against its absence (as if it were a failed structural function). So, far from determining the sculptural form in any positive way, the plane becomes the name of that irresolvable tension that animates the sculpture. We cannot get rid of it, but we cannot achieve it either. Last, but not least, this account by no means ignores the sheer materiality of these works. On the contrary, the plane is initially excluded also as a result of an opaque materiality that denies its abstract autonomy. After all, why should we ascribe to these densely material plaques and slabs of steel—rusting ones, moreover—the automatic and abstract identity of planes?[98]

Thus the peculiar sense of becoming which these works mobilize, consonant with Gullar's assertion that the non-object is "an open immobility [that is open] to an open mobility [that is open] to an open immobility."[99] Faced with Castro's sculptures, this elliptical formulation, so brilliantly enacted, draws attention to the works' elusive foundation as an incessant differentiation from the plane. That the passage is so temporally convoluted is proof of an important point—namely, that Gullar's theoretical repertoire obviously lacked a fully articulated concept of negativity; more often than not, definitions of the non-object convey experiential fullness instead of acknowledging constitutive gaps in perception. By taking the latter into account, however, we can suggest a crucial distinction between *multiplication* in Sacilotto and *repetition* in Castro: in the former, the negative is additive (and thus no longer strictly negative—I am referring here to the intervals that help to multiply the planes)—while in the latter the negative remains as such (since the plane is never in sight). Castro's famous coherence, his insistence on the same sculptural matrix throughout his career (with a few variations), can thus be reinterpreted from this viewpoint. The reason his cut-and-fold sculptures uncannily read as being all the same and yet different from one another is that, being based on sheer negativity, their relation to the plane can never be pinned down. This failure is a structural, constitutive character of the works themselves. Castro's confident repetition of the same procedure over and over again was supported, paradoxically enough, by the certainty of knowing that each and every sculpture he set out to make would stumble upon the same, irreducible incompleteness—what is fundamentally constant in them is not their formal repertoire per se, but the absence they articulate without ever representing.

This phenomenology of the negative may be at odds with Gullar's Merleau-Pontian approach, but it is properly theorized elsewhere: in psychoanalysis. What I have in mind here is Joan Copjec's argument that phenomenological consistency (or "reality testing," for Freud) is not a matter of finding "an object in real perception which corresponds to the one presented, but to *re-find* such an object, to convince oneself that it is still there."[100] My point is that Castro's sculptures do not attempt to correspond to or present the plane (as the multiple facets of Sacilotto's sculptures do). What they try to do is to convince us that the object—the absent plane—is somehow still there. But this effort can never be fully successful (we can only keep trying to refind the object as long as it is never there to be found). As Freud often insists, the "refound" object is never an actual object once experienced by the subject (it is not a memory), but an always-already lost object. Reality testing is thus the paradoxical name of "the permanent *loss* of that reality—or Real: a reality that was never present as such—which is the precondition for determining the objective status of our perceptions."[101] Perceived objects, Copjec continues, are then "fleeting perceptions" that seem to acquire "the weight of objectivity only when they are weighed or anchored by the excluded real object."[102] From this standpoint, it is clear that the negativity Castro's sculptures articulate is ultimately at odds with the non-object: the works acquire their specific consistency as they become negatively anchored by their unattainable planarity.

But what exactly does it mean to say that the plane is lost? It has been already noted that neoconcretism as a whole represents a critical limit of what would be eventually termed the "Brazilian constructive project"; in other words, that it prefigured its implosion.[103] But here we achieve a striking formulation: Castro goes as far as accepting the geometric plane, that pillar of concretist aesthetics, as an object. In this sense, his work constitutes a critical limit of the constructive project not simply because it participated in its undoing, but because it took it beyond its limits of *representability*; it acknowledges and affirms the breakdown of the constructive form, excludes it from perceptual reality, but nevertheless retains it as a negative benchmark.

I can now propose that even Castro's preparatory drawings strengthen rather than undermine my case. Citing Paul Valéry, critic Ricardo Fabbrini imagines Castro's relationship with that mesh of lines traced "without any previous calculation" on paper so as to suggest that the sculptor "'goes forward, backwards, bends himself, blinks, behaves with all his body as an accessory of the eye, becomes one and all viewing, aiming, modulating or focusing organ' in order to, then, with a well-aimed trace, detach from this labyrinth of lines a project of the work."[104] So the project—supposing we can still use this term—would come *after* the work of the eye. As Pedrosa noticed, the sculptor "doesn't depart from an a priori, but from a vague drawing on paper."[105] Castro's interwoven lines and curves become a sort of field through which the eye would be able to search for the sculptural form. But what does Castro find? Again, it is never the flat plane, but a partial view of a future sculpture, a form that he will still *actually* have to find by cutting yet another piece of paper. This is what is the most striking: Castro does not turn the flat sheet into a sculpture, but tries to capture an already-formed sculpture—even if only a partial "view" of it—as it springs forth from his drawn mesh. Or perhaps, and even more precisely, Castro lets his searching gaze be caught by the web of lines he draws on the paper, and the sculptural form is the product of this encounter. This mesh is, in this particular sense, far removed from that quintessentially modernist form of the *grid*. In Rosalind Krauss's famous argument, the grid underscores the illusion "of the originary status of the pictorial surface" by creating a double, a "representational text" that manages to become even *more* originary than the blank canvas itself.[106] The name of this illusion is, of course, the *picture plane*. And we can thus glimpse the full extent of Castro's radical gesture: rather than taking the drawings as evidence in favor of the 2D-3D account, I can now suggest that the plane is absent from them *as well*. Instead of doubling a blank surface that would be receptive for a projective look, the drawings act as screens that capture a gaze fraught with anxiety: they already stage the failed refinding of the lost object.

Castro's sculptures thus make evident that the negative is the blind spot that remained untheorized by Gullar and undertheorized by most later commentators. More specifically, they question the ultimate coupling in the "Theory" of phenomenological openness and historicist closure. For those sculptures, hinged as they are on the plane qua lost object, are not simply expressions of the heterodoxy of the Brazilian constructive project, but also revelations of its historical crux; in fact, what makes the idea of the lost object more compelling in this case than, say, a late Merleau-Pontian emphasis on the "generating axis," is the fact that the former reaches beyond the limits of the phenomenological encounter and operates critically also vis-à-vis this crux.[107] Let me put it another way: what if we substitute the "real satisfaction" the lost object is supposed to offer (in Freud's theory) for, so to speak, a "historical satisfaction"? Doesn't utopianism, especially in the quasi-positivist tone it had in 1950s Brazil, legitimize this operation? With hindsight, we may perhaps suggest that Castro's sculptures, from neoconcretism onward, articulate the loss of a neat identification between the language of geometric abstraction and a palpable sense of historical fulfillment. We might thus be led to think of his oeuvre as a melancholic and repetitive reenactment of a lost utopia, but I don't think that is all there is to it. When it is said that neoconcretism introduced negativity at the very core of the Brazilian constructive projective—as Brito does say—it does not follow that it simply led to its eventual demise. It also means that this negativity was itself *objective*, and that, as such, it was prone to being reclaimed and redeployed—precisely as the non-object would be in the late 1960s. It is true that constructive *identity* was quickly losing its ability to provide a legitimate historical ground for art practice, but it may be that the same negativity that disrupted a certain notion of the constructive may have simultaneously opened up the possibility for another, different one to emerge.

Although Gullar's teleological historicism has been undoubtedly crucial for the consolidation of the "Theory" (and for its very inception), my point here is that the non-object itself has been limited *by*, but is not essentially limited *to*, the historical-theoretical terrain this historicism defines. It follows that to think the relay between the non-object and contemporary art is different from thinking contemporary art within the historical coordinates of neoconcretism. Gullar's own critical trajectory—his rejection first of the avant-garde and later of contemporary art as a whole—is not contradictory. It may be evidence that the poet himself could not break free, in the long run, from the teleological trap he inadvertently had set up. In this context, what Castro's sculptures offer, in their resistance to the notion of an "original" plane, is precisely a critique of these limitations, one that may help in rescuing the non-object from sharing that same historicist cul de sac (significantly, Castro also resists yet another major neoconcretist narrative of passage, from temporality to participation). One need not look far to find alternative models for constructing another tradition: Gullar's adversaries Haroldo de Campos, Augusto de Campos, and Décio Pignatari had one; so did Hélio Oiticica, starting from the very moment neoconcretism broke down (it is not by chance that he would eventually heal the wounds and get closer to the São Paulo poets). The name Oiticica's conception of history took in the 1960s is—either surprisingly or unsurprisingly, it's hard to tell—the *constructive*, to which I next turn.

2

The Constructive

Hélio Oiticica once noted that *Tropicália* gave him "the powerful sense of being devoured," thus rendering it "the most anthropophagist work in Brazilian art."[1] Such a description effectively made a claim for the place of *Tropicália* at the heart of Brazilian avant-gardism. One has just to refer back to the "General Scheme of the New Objectivity," an ambitious text Oiticica published in 1967, accompanying *Tropicália*'s unveiling, to find explicit mention of poet Oswald de Andrade and his 1920s concept of "anthropophagy" (a term meaning "cannibalism"). Oswald had envisaged the anthropophagic operation as a symbolic avant-garde procedure whereby foreign cultural influences were not to be simply opposed, but rather internalized and redeployed by local artists and thinkers.[2] The rediscovery of his ideas marked a period of effervescence and dramatic changes in the Brazilian artistic avant-garde of the 1960s, and the very notion of Brazilian identity was to be strategically linked to the anthropophagic operation in a clear negation of essentialist positions—as Oswald's motto goes, "only anthropophagy unites us."[3] From this perspective, for example, the musical output of the tropicalist movement can be largely (though not exclusively) characterized as an updating of anthropophagy. Oiticica, however, was coming from the 1950s debates over concretism and neoconcretism, and remained interested in concepts that had originated back then, such as the non-object, and also in evaluating his own historical role. Setting things out more programmatically, he thus seized anthropophagy as a procedure that would allow him to *re*define both avant-gardist activity and Brazilian cultural identity, as well as to reflect on how these stances related to each other.

Crucially, then, Oiticica was not simply a "neo-anthropophagist." My suggestion is that anthropophagy was for him actually a means of expanding an operative mode he had been already formulating in his own earlier artistic practice to a broader cultural field. I will try to substantiate this claim by following the shifts and developments that inflected the way he conceived of what he termed "the constructive," which was the object of a lifelong commitment, but never a stable concept. Oiticica's assimilation of anthropophagy would then be one episode—albeit a crucial one—in a succession of shifts that characterize the history of the constructive in his trajectory. Reciprocally, it can also be argued that anthropophagy provided him with a suggestive way of rereading this very trajectory, indebted as it had been to high modernist, abstract painting.

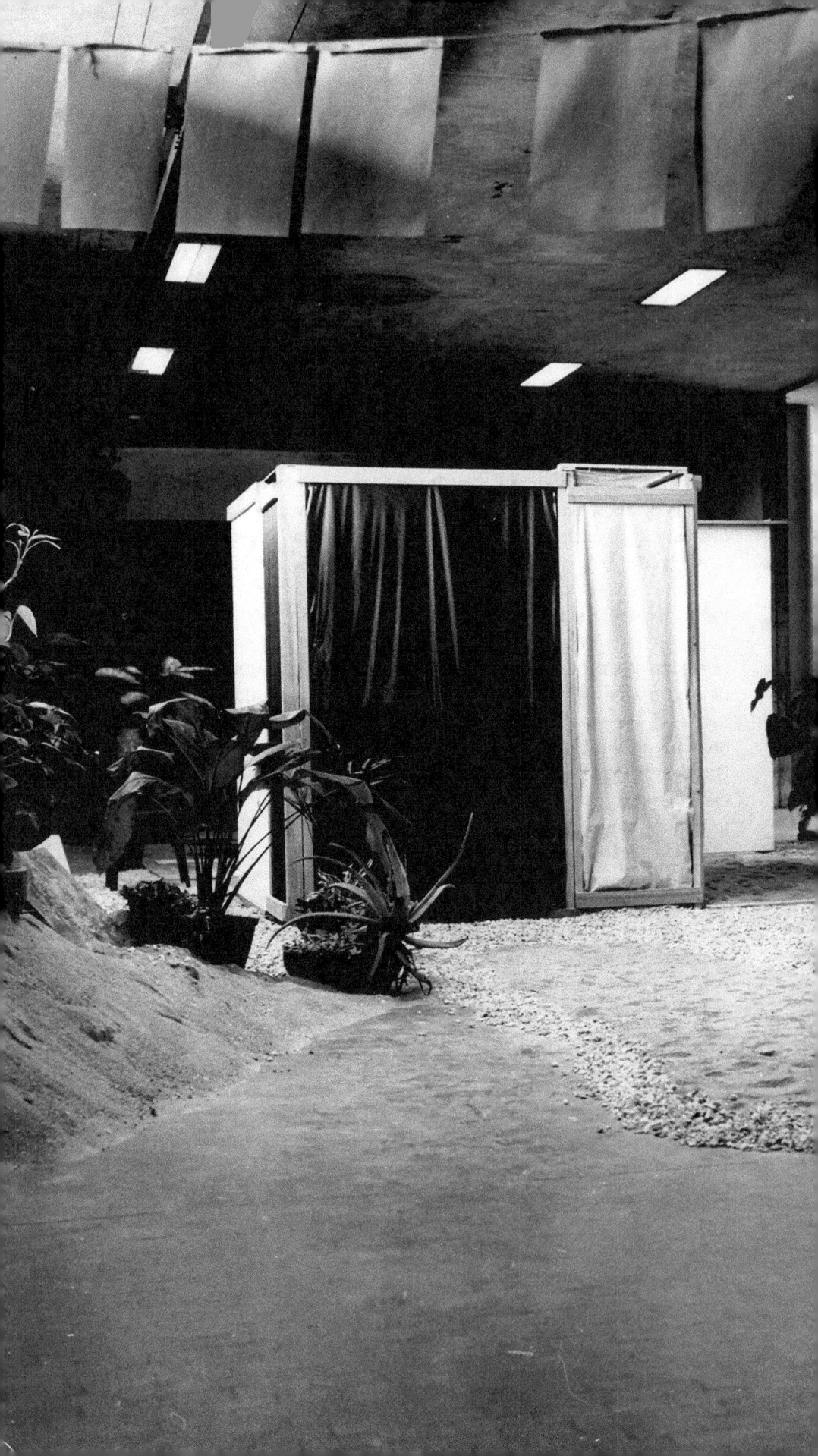

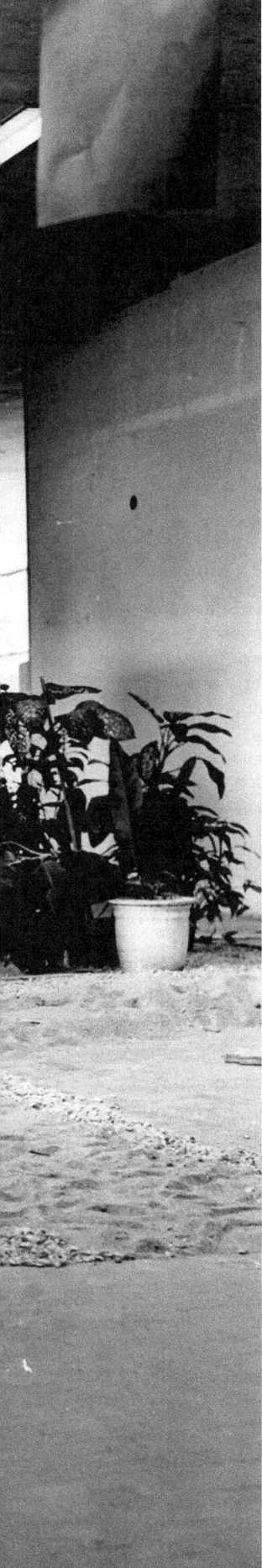

2.1
Hélio Oiticica, *Tropicália, Penetrables PN2 Purity Is a Myth* and *PN3 Imagetical*, 1966–1967. Mixed media installation, variable dimensions. Courtesy Projeto Hélio Oiticica.

As such seemingly opposed terms—"anthropophagy" and "the constructive"—become inextricably entwined, Oiticica ends up positing the constructive as an operation rather than a movement, something quite different from what is usually understood by "constructivism"—or so I will argue.

All of this also suggests that prior to resorting to Oswald's anthropophagy as a means of cultural critique, Oiticica had to cannibalize one of his greatest modernist father figures: Piet Mondrian.[4] This assumption would support Michael Asbury's claim that Oiticica's "radical leap" toward the *Parangolés* and ultimately toward *Tropicália* was theoretically prefigured in his earlier work.[5] Furthermore, I want to think of this coupling—of a reading of European modernism with the imperative of reinventing Brazilian culture under the sign of the constructive—as crucial to a larger consideration of the matrix of avant-gardism in that country, with consequences that may well exceed the scope of Brazilian art and prove itself foundational of a reradicalized historical perspective on modernism as a whole.[6]

DESTRUCTIVE CONSTRUCTION

In 1959, Oiticica transcribed what he called some "prophetic words" by Mondrian:

> What is certain, is that there is no escape for the non-figurative artist; he must stay within his field and march towards the consequence of his art. This consequence brings us, in a future perhaps remote, towards the end of art as a thing separate of our surrounding environment, which is the actual plastic reality. But this end is at the same time a new beginning. Art will not only continue but will realize itself more and more. By the unification of architecture, sculpture and painting a new plastic reality will be created. Painting and sculpture will not manifest themselves as separate objects, nor as "mural art" or "applied art," but being purely constructive, will aid the creation of a surrounding not merely utilitarian or rational, but also pure and complete in its beauty.[7]

That was a "prophecy" Oiticica took seriously, though not uncritically. Five years later, for instance, he made a point of reproaching Mondrian's habit of formulating principles, warning that these risked being wrongly read as "dogmatic and absurd," thus precluding "the development of the extremely rich possibilities opened by his conceptions of painting (and art in general)."[8] In the same breath, he praised Mondrian's ability to subvert his own concepts according to "the aesthetic judgment that presided over his creations"—in other words, Oiticica was definitely not interested in taking the Dutch master's interpretation of his own work at face value, preferring to engage instead in a visual dialogue.

A good starting point for retracing this dialogue is Mondrian's introduction of double lines in the 1930s. As Yve-Alain Bois has argued, "What we find [in this period] is an inflexible demolition, one by one, of all the pictorial presuppositions of neo-plasticism."[9] It is not by chance that the text Oiticica cites was written precisely in this destructive period. My point is that he was more focused on Mondrian's creative impulse than on his finished work—and, more importantly, on the way this impulse could actually run counter to his finished work. Taking Mondrian's trajectory as a potential—or rather necessary—site of dialogue instead of a fixed, oppressive formal paradigm, Oiticica can be said to have embraced the former's steadfast commitment with "finding things out."[10] We can spot here, in embryonic form, a line of thought that would not only inform the concept of "the constructive," but also run through terms such as "invention" or "the experimental," which Oiticica would only later add to his vocabulary.

A brief look at some of his early paintings can help us to visualize the material concreteness of this engagement. Take the *Sêco 27* (1957), for example. The yellow lozenge becomes a distinctive color-saturated puncture that provokes a tilting effect, destabilizing a presupposed balance: the picture's suggestion of symmetry becomes stillborn as this pulsating movement is perceived as always-already operative in tearing it apart.[11] But doesn't that obviously run counter to Mondrian's use of color to bring an asymmetrical composition into balance? Indeed it does, and this is where we should remember that Oiticica's take on Mondrian is procedural rather than formal. As a matter of fact, the Dutch painter himself had countered his early emphasis on "repose" with a renewed notion of "dynamic equilibrium."[12] What Oiticica thus retraces in Mondrian is not a particular "solution," but rather his ongoing restlessness toward whatever kind of stability painting might have seemed to achieve at any given stage, as in his later use of color as a means of destroying his own lines.

It is unsurprising then that Oiticica's subsequent *Metaesquemas* deploy color in order both to assemble and undo one and the same structure, without ever fully succeeding in any direction. As Briony Fer elegantly describes it, there is in them "an uneasy oscillation in play between the chromatic and the schematic as two drives working themselves out but also intertwining and at moments fusing one with the other in a way that absolutely collapses all the distinctions between color and form."[13] This is a subtle but key change. Previously restricted to a discrete point of destabilization, color now takes part in a sense of "oscillation" and its role grows in ambivalence. First introduced in *Sêco 27* as a local, destructive slit, it is now made literally, as Mondrian once said of neoplasticism "as destructive as it is constructive."[14]

Apropos of Mondrian's dictum "if we cannot free ourselves, we can free our *vision*," Bois further remarks that "to liberate our vision is also to accept that we no longer master it."[15] In 1972, Oiticica wrote a list of aphorisms on his *Metaesquemas*. One of those is read as "infinitesimated mondrianstructure," while another one goes by, simply, "re-insistence."[16] The latter does indeed conjure the sense of an unmastered vision, and it is telling that Fer designates the chromatic and the schematic as *drives*—doesn't the drive correspond to a "headless subjectification," as Jacques Lacan puts it, that is defined precisely by its constant pressure, by its *insistence*?[17] And doesn't this "subjectification without subject" run counter to the sense of a self-sufficient—that is, mastered—subjectivity?[18] From a Lacanian viewpoint, the theory of the drives is the basis for a "negative ontology" that plays against the "*I qua synthetic unity.*"[19] With that in mind, my suggestion is that the a priori time-space coordinates that Oiticica seeks to dismantle by grounding the temporality of painting on a drivelike deployment of color correspond to an incisive critique of the experience of painting as a "subject-object duality."[20]

Such duality can be nicely described as *egomorphic*—to use another term by Lacan[21]—in that it sustains a certain kind of viewing subject that could thus be more properly termed a "viewing I." This is a viewing subject who fantasizes the act of painting as preceded by a given set of time-space relations that make it available to viewing while keeping the viewer untouched by the object it apprehends.[22] By attacking these coordinates, then, the *Metaesquemas* temporally imply the viewing I in what it sees, giving rise to a proper—unmastered—"viewing subject" (inasmuch as this implication is

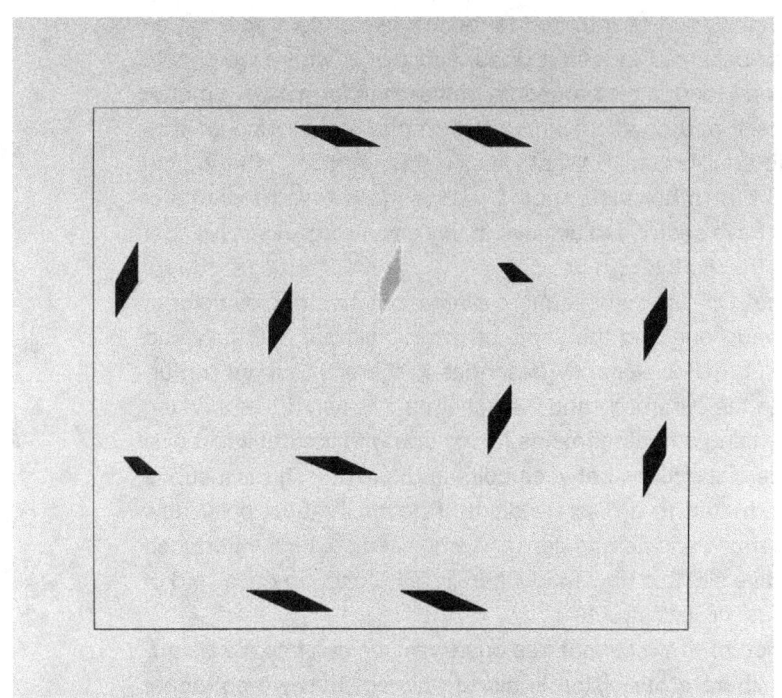

2.2
Hélio Oiticica, *Sêco 27*, 1957.
Gouache on cardboard,
39 × 43 cm. César and Claudio
Oiticica Collection, Rio de
Janeiro. Courtesy Projeto
Hélio Oiticica.

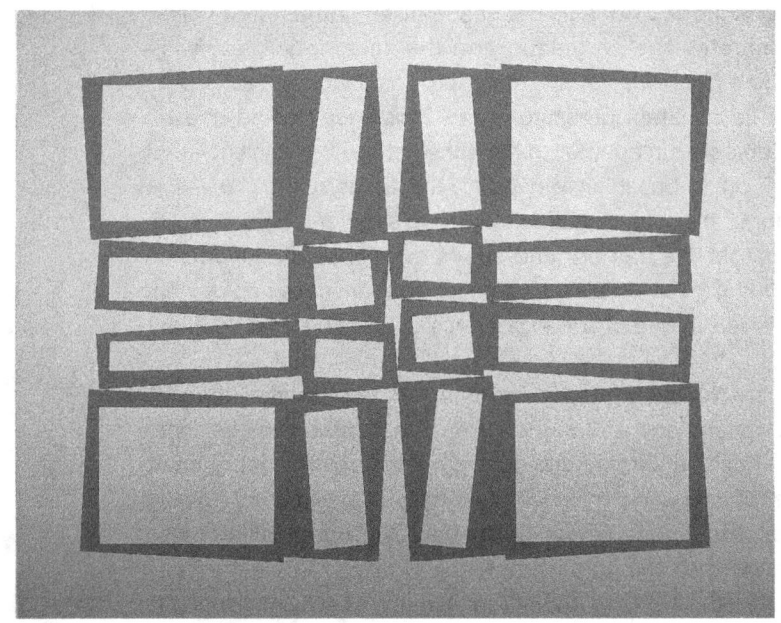

2.3
Hélio Oiticica, *Metaesquema*,
1958. Gouache on cardboard,
39 × 43 cm. César and Claudio
Oiticica Collection. Courtesy
Projeto Hélio Oiticica.

already a *bodily* one, the viewing I ceases to be a "viewing eye"). If we follow Oiticica from *Sêco 27* to the *Metaesquemas* (and on to the *Inventions*, as we will see), it becomes clear that he is searching for this ongoing, hard-to-fix (but also hard to disavow) quality of experience. In this sense, "free vision" was not something that could be translated to any particular painting, not even to some mythic painting belonging to a projected future, a kind of endgame work that would have eventually realized Mondrian's prophetic telos had he just lived "long enough" to paint it—to cite a teleological speculation by Ferreira Gullar.[23] What Oiticica found truly revolutionary about Mondrian was the fact that his "free vision" involved a temporality that exceeded individual paintings, thus dismantling egomorphic attachments to artworks in particular. No wonder Oiticica was one of the earlier enthusiasts of Mário Pedrosa's motto of art as "the experimental exercise of freedom."

It is telling here that Oiticica retrospectively reads his works as "METAESQUEMAS of the non-gratuity of space: space-husk exercise book of non-waste space."[24] Not a rulebook, but an exercise book: principles arise from experience (being therefore *experimental*), and not the other way round. For Oiticica, space could be meaningful only insofar as one was *driven into* experiencing it (it is in this sense that the space of representation is wasted). And he was not alone: Lygia Clark wanted her *Modulated Spaces* (1958–1959) and *Unities* (1958) to ensnare and frustrate egomorphic expectations, thus opening the way to a similar kind of experience. For Clark, the square was the perfect expression of the plane, which she denounced as a mirror of "a rational and false concept of [man's] reality." However, and precisely on account of this metaphoric reflexivity, the square could be subverted by the constructive artist and made into a means of transforming "a total vision of the world."[25] This is exactly what she tried to do by painting deep white lines, like grooves, on the border of the *Unities*. These "light lines," as she called them, gradually unsettle the visual experience of those squares by introducing an "oblique tension" that perceptually tilts them.[26] For Clark, such precise acts of constructive destruction were a sine qua non condition for an experience of "free vision" (and we should recall that Bois's canonical reading of Mondrian is admittedly indebted to Clark's).[27] Likewise, in their dialogue with Mondrian, both Clark and Oiticica pursued nothing short of a destructive reconstruction of the subject of painting. The difference, of course, is that color, and not line, was Oiticica's designated bulldozer as he carried this project on.

As a matter of fact, it was in Oiticica's *Inventions*—also a series of square paintings—that color eventually closed its destructive cycle. What is crucial here is the unusual absence of a "structural" quality. Readable in the presentation of discrete planes, this feature can be found not only in the artist's earlier gouaches, but also in his *Spatial Reliefs*, which enlist the spectator as a body moving around their clustered facets. What persists in them is an underlying principle of *articulation*. The *Inventions* are another matter altogether. Their superimposing layers of different colors open up to duration without relying on a sequential progression: there is no distinction of planes that may tabulate time. What is more, their condition as *quasi-monochromes*—in the sense of them being defined by an initial expectation of them being monochromes—can be related to Mondrian.[28] As Bois has argued, Mondrian's practice was antithetical to the monochrome in that the latter would amount to a refusal of painting instead of a critical

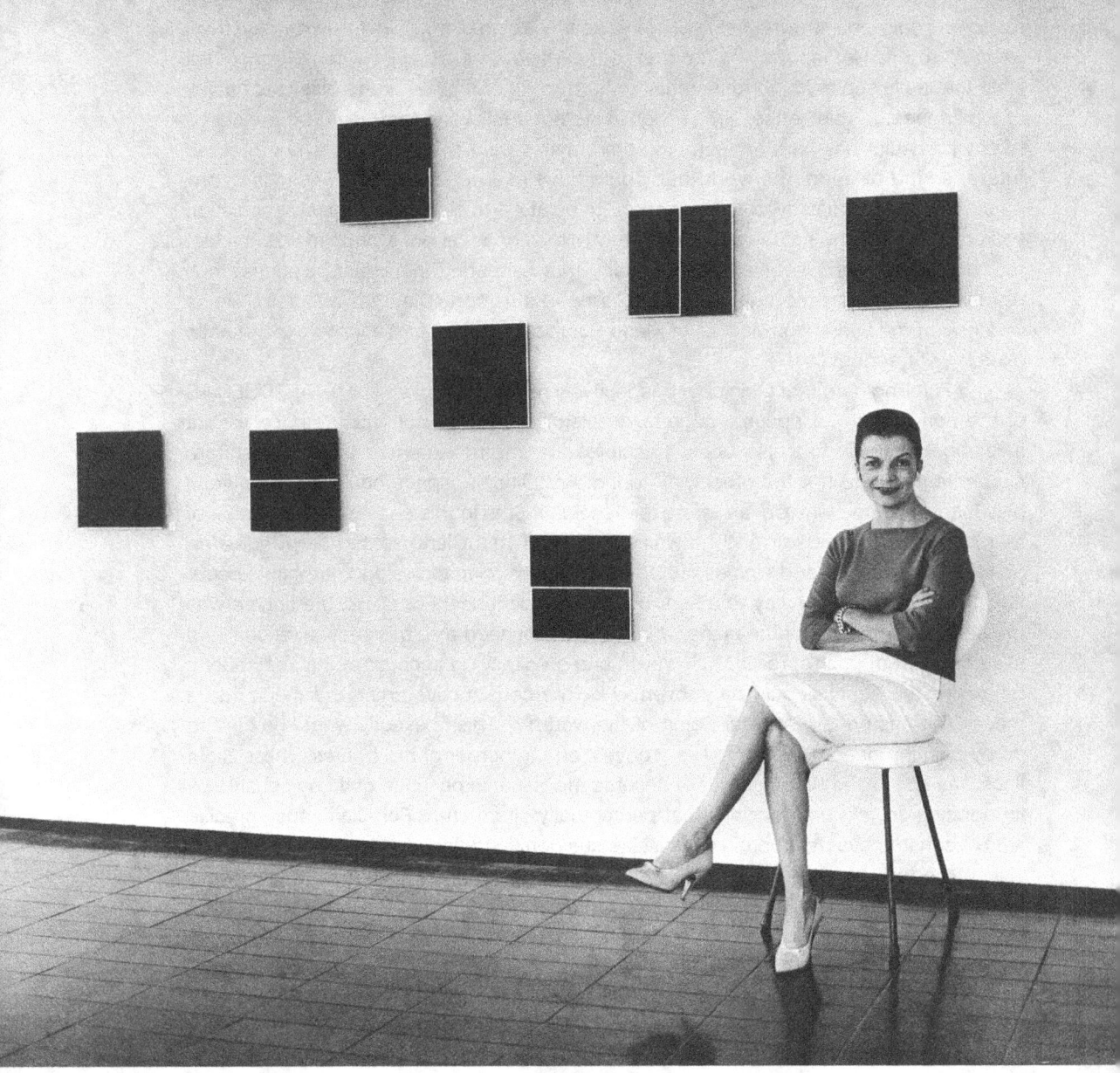

2.4
Lygia Clark in front of her *Unities* at
the "Second Neoconcrete Exhibition."
Photographer unknown. Courtesy
of The World of Lygia Clark Cultural
Association.

dismantling of it.[29] The *Inventions* supersede this polarity by making duration the agent that brings the monochrome into the scope of, so to speak, "valid" painterly problems— it makes them *non-monochromes*, as light reflects on the free brushwork and glimpses of underlying colors insinuate themselves to the viewer.

Mondrian also suspected color blending to be impure, and thus advocated its deployment in discrete units. The problem here was that he could only conceive of these atoms as synchronically coexistent. This is also resolved in the *Inventions* by virtue of their durational existence. Oiticica speaks of "superimposition" and "verticality of color," so the point here is that colors are not conceived as being previously mixed. In short, these paintings demand to be perceived neither as monochromes nor as mixed colors, but as something that gravitates in between the two without ever becoming either of them—a clear radicalization of the "reinsistent" movement that characterized the *Metaesquemas*. Needless to say, this gravitational movement is carried out by color alone.

This arc of development that runs from the *Sêcos* to the *Inventions* is thus driven by Oiticica's growing realization that color had to be wrested away from merely instru-mental functions—such as conveying depth, flatness, movement, and so on. It was no longer to be subordinated and "used"—alongside lines and shapes, for instance—in order to delineate or represent the space of experience (as it still was in *Sêco 27*, albeit partially). It was now this space—or rather this duration—that was to be brought about by color. We can thus glimpse what Oiticica meant by his notion of "color-time," by means of which, he says, "structure rotates, then, in space, becoming itself also temporal: 'structure time.'"[30] Thus were Mondrian's "prophetic words" enacted through color.

2.5
Hélio Oiticica, *Invention*, 1959. Oil on wood, 30 × 30 cm. Photo: César Oiticica Filho. Courtesy Projeto Hélio Oiticica.

OPERATIVE CONSTRUCTION

This destructive take on construction would lead Oiticica into a discursive position that parted from the evolutionist rhetoric that characterized the 1950s debates over concrete art. This occurs at a moment when an all-encompassing nationalist project of modernization, which included artistic practice, was failing in ways that would eventually inform Oiticica's own conception of the avant-garde, and to which I will return. For now, let me suggest that the constructive was "materially" born, for Oiticica, in his earlier formal experiments, but ended up acquiring a life of its own as a signifier. That allowed Oiticica to reorient the parameters of his practice in relation to new conditions of operation.

A long essay from 1962, suggestively titled "The Transition of Color from the Painting into Space and the Meaning of Constructivity" will help clarify how Oiticica's adoption of Mondrian's destructive procedure proves to be fundamental for his own particular conception of construction. He picks the *Inventions* as the fundamental starting point for a discussion that turns out to be mostly apropos of his *Nuclei* and *Penetrables*. This is a curious choice: aren't the *Bilaterals* or *Spatial Reliefs* more obvious precedents? I take this to indicate that he conceives of his newfound constructive paradigm as the aftermath of his Mondrianesque painterly investigation. In other words, the *Inventions* make it possible for Oiticica to conceive new works where the easel can no longer be "an a priori field in which to develop the 'act of painting,' but that the very structure of this act take place in space and time."[31] Again, it is crucial here to keep track of how this subtle temporal conflation is indebted to that earlier dialogue. The idea that whatever painting achieves must be temporally coincident with the realization of its conditions of possibility (i.e., the "structure of the act" that "takes place in space and time") refers back to his understanding of Mondrian as process-oriented rather than object-oriented. I mean "process-oriented" here as taking into account previously produced art objects not as enclosed or discrete entities, but as part of an ongoing process, so that the truth of their meaning depends on that relation.

It is crucial to stress here that the very notion of the constructive undergoes an analogous transformation. In short, its ceases to be the product (like a pictorial language) or given name of a clearly defined historical space or narrative (such as, say, a *style*) and achieves a kind of transformative conceptual autonomy in relation to the very past it designates. It is as such that it becomes a key motif in Oiticica's discourse: now redefined as a "sense," constructivity could be deployed in different directions and contexts, and relate to various, seemingly unrelated sets of practices (with ethical and political consequences that I will yet explore).

Let me clarify this with reference to the text I introduced. After discussing the *Inventions*, Oiticica proceeds to define his own constructive take at the time:

> To me, then, constructive artists are those who establish new structural relations in painting (color) and in sculpture, and open up new perceptions of time and space. They are the *constructors*, builders of structure, of color, of space and of time, those who add new perspectives and modify the ways we see and feel; those, therefore, who open up new directions in contemporary sensibility, those who aspire to the spiritual hierarchy of construction in art. Art is not meant to be understood here as a symptom of crisis or of the age, but as the foundational meaning of the age itself.[32]

One shouldn't take this simply as the lingua franca of the time. If Oiticica agreed that his was a "new constructivism,"[33] he stressed that it wasn't simply a continuation of prewar constructivism under a new guise, but a certain return to a permanent, universal quality that he saw as operative in the work of the original constructors and, more important, as particularly pertinent to his own project. He searched for a common denominator between his conditions—as he understood them—and his artistic precedents, but not a formal one. As critic Celso Favaretto puts it, he was worried not to "place experimentation in the register of the 'isms,' but at a level he understood as a 'contemporary tendency': the foundation of new structural relations aimed at the opening of new paths in contemporary sensibility."[34] The "sense of constructivity" pointed to a founding attitude rather than a telos, and, most crucially, one defined vis-à-vis Oiticica's own present.

Subtly enough, then, a reversal is put in operation. First, through his painterly activity, Oiticica is able to situate himself as the continuation and apex of a constructive project—Mondrian's. He then achieves a turning point that allows his procedures to break free from the painterly limits without which they would never have been conceived in the first place. These procedures are subsequently defined as a conceptual locus—the "constructive"—from where they can be strategically redeployed onto previous practice. It is in this sense, and for this use, that Oiticica would redeem the constructive out of and beyond the scope of constructivism and subsequently put it to bear on history in a retroactive movement, creating from his own standpoint the very historical meaning and pertinence of the term. That much becomes evident when, still in the same text, Oiticica starts to recast certain artists he finds crucial under the light of his newfound concept: Pollock, for example, becomes the "constructor of 'hyperaction.'"[35] Other so-called constructors would include Mondrian, of course, and also Kandinsky, Schwitters, Calder, Wols, Brancusi, Picasso, Gris, Gabo, Pevsner, Boccioni, Max Bill, Lygia Clark, Albers, and Fontana, just to name a few.

There are good reasons to think that this operation isn't simply a rhetorical gambit or another display of historicism. It is hard to imagine that Oiticica wouldn't have realized how different his own retrospective synchronism was from Gullar's teleological linearism—especially considering that the former emerged precisely when the possibility of a positive, integrated avant-garde fell apart in the midst of political turmoil and aesthetic radicalizations. Let us then turn to back to something that I have only briefly noted and pay attention to the *ethico-political* aspect of Oiticica's notion of construction.

ETHICAL CONSTRUCTION

A caveat is due here: Oiticica's "sense of constructivity" not only had to be pertinent to his specific context and project, it also had to be *more* pertinent than it ever was before. This is directly tied to his understanding of the "universal." As art historian Sônia Salzstein puts it, Oiticica's use of the term "constructive" comes "to designate the creative will of a culture in the making."[36] Salzstein locates Oiticica's discussion of the constructive in his need to establish some sort of "cultural zero" that would undo what he diagnosed as a relation of dependency toward European culture.[37] By locating the universality in constructivism from his own historical standpoint, the artist would not so much subscribe to constructivism as he would pose the constructive as a "true" meaning of constructivism that could only be revealed under the conditions of the Brazilian avant-garde practice of that period. It was through such a gambit that Oiticica imagined a "refounding" of Brazilian culture.

This gambit can only be understood vis-à-vis the dramatic pressures increasingly felt by local artists and intellectuals in the 1960s. As I discussed in chapter 1, avant-gardism in the 1950s was fueled by the perception of modernization as the new harbinger of national identity. Governmental slogans such as "fifty years in five" heralded an era of industrialization and progress, while the project of Brasília seemed to put a definitive stamp on Brazil as the "country of the future." Such rhetoric was well suited for cultural producers eager to get rid of the constraints put on them by academic-oriented art institutions, as they managed to equate these with an aspect of Brazil that would be better left behind (and Oiticica would indeed refer to Brasília in 1960 as "the city of the future").[38] Pedrosa's famous verdict, written apropos of the new capital, adamantly asserts the conflation of developmentalism, constructive language, and national identity: "Brazil is condemned to the modern."[39] A condemnation, in a sense, *to* and *by* modernity.

The 1960s were another matter altogether, as the enthusiastic promise of modernity gave way to latent political tensions and to economic faltering. Within an increasingly polarized intellectual sphere, where conservative segments of society faced a cultural clash with the student movement and a nationalist left, skepticism of non-objective artistic experiments grew. Surprisingly enough, one of the starkest signs of this shift occurred within Oiticica's inner circle: Ferreira Gullar's defection from neoconcretism and subsequent embrace of the didactic aesthetics of the student movement, with its emulation of popular and folkloric art forms and its underlying Marxist orientation.[40] There are three important points to be noted here. First, that Gullar conceives of his shift as the result of "critique, practical and then theoretical," and a "rejection" of the "European cultural inheritance."[41] This was obviously a major issue for neoconcretism and also for Oiticica, and it was clear that the position of the 1950s avant-gardes in this regard had reached an impasse, the one I have addressed in chapter 1 as the breakdown of constructive *identity*. Let me now suggest that, notwithstanding his drastic shift from a constructive to a national-popular identity, Gullar's political stance is ultimately coherent in that it remained dependent on a securely identified intellectual position from which to operate. Oiticica's reworking of the constructive provides an alternative response to the same impasse, but one that was more self-critical, curiously enough, precisely because it remained faithful to avant-gardism as a means to criticize and overcome the avant-garde's own reliance on identity. From this perspective, the contradictions of the non-object on the one hand and the constructive on the other can be historiographically mobilized to negotiate the passage from the 1950s to the 1960s without turning those different contexts into overdetermining zeitgeists. Counterintuitively, then, Oiticica's critical insistence on the avant-garde represents, at the structural level of subjective engagement, a more radical move than Gullar's.

My second point follows from this one. I have already noted how fundamentally distant Oiticica's and Gullar's conceptions of history became. The poet becomes trapped here in his own evolutionism: in the face of impasse, the only coherent choice available to him was to reject past commitments and start anew.[42] Oiticica, in contrast, envisaged the choice of affirming his own stance and thinking of the past not as a succession of givens, but as making possible a radical openness in the present, just as Mondrian's paintings were to be understood as part of a process rather than individually meaningful. By shedding its reliance on identity, the constructive opened itself to a renewed historical charge—indeed, its later conflation with anthropophagy would be intimately related to this same development.

Third, and finally: Gullar's defection did strike Oiticica as a shock.[43] But it was also a formative shock, since the artist was now faced with the opportunity—and perhaps the need—of publicly establishing his own voice (as his 1962 article attests).[44] On the one hand, he now had to defend his understanding of the avant-garde against accusations of alienation or political ineffectiveness from left-wing positions such as the one Gullar had now embraced. On the other hand, Oiticica had to negotiate his own position in relation to a sustained interest in and respect for Gullar's ideas, both old and new. This meant not only continuing to reflect on the non-object, for example, but also positioning artistic practice in the terms of its social insertion.[45] Concerns such as these were played out in a number of exhibitions and manifestos throughout the 1960s. The most polished version of both came in 1967, with the "New Brazilian Objectivity," which takes me back to my starting point.[46] Again, this was the show where Oiticica—one of the organizers and its main theoretician—first exhibited *Tropicália* and reclaimed anthropophagy.[47] The show also displayed works by a number of mainly young artists whose ensemble, in Oiticica's judgment, demonstrated the idea of a "new objectivity" as a "typical state of current Brazilian art," which he itemized as follows:

> 1—general constructive will; 2—move towards the object, as easel painting is negated and superseded; 3—the participation of the spectator (bodily, tactile, semantic, etc.); 4—an engagement and a position on political, social and ethical problems; 5—tendency towards collective propositions and consequently the abolition, in the art of today, of "isms," so characteristic of the first half of the century (a tendency which can be encompassed by Mário Pedrosa's concept of "Post-Modern Art"); 6—a revival of, and new formulations, in the concept of anti-art.[48]

Oiticica emphasizes the first item, saying that if "new objectivity" is to be seen as a "state" to be aimed for by the Brazilian avant-gardes, then the "general constructive will" is no less than its "principal item, its spiritual mover."[49] Crucially, it was under this rubric that he presented his updated concept of "anthropophagy," which he took as the first sign of such a constructive will in the history of Brazilian culture.[50] Oiticica recasts Oswald de Andrade and the avant-garde group he belonged to in a manner resembling that of Pollock and others in the 1962 essay: as a group distinct for their "striking constructive will." Andrade's 1920s avant-garde was marked by a nationalist approach to the laying down of a "cultural zero," to use Salzstein's term once again—but as a remarkably non-essentialist, negatively defined one, as if the cannibalistic take on foreign cultures were the only possible definition of a properly Brazilian position. "Only anthropophagy unites us," Andrade starts his 1928 manifesto. "Socially. Economically. Philosophically."[51] In another passage, Andrade proposes to critically advance "from the equation—*I* as a part of the *Cosmos*—to the axiom—the *Cosmos* as a part of the *I*. Subsistence. Knowledge. Anthropophagy."[52]

As philosopher Benedito Nunes compellingly argues, Andrade operates a logic of cultural *diagnosis* and *therapy*; within the scope of his intellectual references the two correspond respectively to Freud and Nietzsche.[53] The rise of the sociocultural superego in *Totem and Taboo* would thus be met with a relentlessly Nietzschean demo-lition of morals. But this is not simply to affirm a law/transgression polarity. The terms and references of cultural diagnosis in Andrade's manifesto are actually put into friction, generating jolts of signification (as in the famous aphorism "Tupy or not Tupy, that is the question").[54] As Nunes puts it, anthropophagy becomes in this context "a guide-word like *dada*, which leads thought in the hunt for ideas."[55] Likewise, the *construction* of Oiticica's radical present is nothing but the continuous and creative short-circuiting of historical references and social norms.

This is to stress, in the light of what I have been discussing, that the construc-tive as it was theorized in 1962 already contained the seeds of the anthropophagical reclaiming—it is as if, from Oiticica's perspective, anthropophagy was always-already embedded in the constructive. For it was precisely the possibility of juxtaposing the dialectical synthesis of Oiticica's earlier activity with this newfound concept that allowed the constructive to become for him the ethical blueprint of the Brazilian avant-garde. It is then necessary to pay sustained attention to *Tropicália* in this respect. Not because it is to be taken as the definitive "high point" in Oiticica's career, just as he is not to be taken as a sort of founding father of contemporary Brazilian art, but rather because in his production, and more specifically in this work, the encounter between different avant-garde conceptions, and even the very attempt of thinking the coherence of an avant-garde in Brazil at that time, became clearest.[56]

CONSTRUCTIVE MAPPING

Tropicália includes, both inside and outside its two "penetrables," a vast array of materi-als, such as gravel, sand, tropical plants, live parrots, poems, a TV set, scented sachets, a curtain of plastic strips draped from the ceiling, and a gray carpet.[57] From the outside, the penetrables look like improvised shacks erected amid a mix between a sandy, tropi-cal garden and a vacant lot. The first penetrable is a small, colored shack, where the visitor encounters a written statement, which happens to be the penetrable's title: *Purity Is a Myth* (*A pureza é um mito*). The second one, called *Imagetical* (*Imagética*), is a labyrinth of heterogeneously decorated wooden panels that grows darker as one enters it and ends up in a small area with a bench and a turned-on TV set broadcasting a local channel.

Carlos Zilio, who exhibited his work alongside Oiticica in "New Brazilian Objec-tivity," sums it up in a lapidary formula: "The calculation implicit in that work is to provoke the implosion of the obvious. That is, a rupture with attempts of updating the realism of national-popular ideology."[58] This is actually a definition of the structural effectiveness of *Tropicália* in relation to a series of political and cultural concerns current at the time, including the work's contribution to the discussion of Brazilian identity and the presup-posed dualities that fueled it.[59] Such a structural effectiveness can be better grasped if we begin by following the experiential model proposed by *Tropicália* in relation to Oiticica's earlier production. I have already proposed that the *Bilateral* and *Spatial Reliefs*, on the one hand, and *Inventions*, on the other, define two distinct, even opposed, possibilities of exploring actual duration. The tension set by these two different models did not escape Oiticica, and much of what he did in the period preceding *Tropicália* can be seen as the dialectical exploration of these poles, in search of a way out that could problematize the viewer's position even further.

Take the *NC1 Small Nucleus*, for instance, where a mirror is placed just below the work, which hangs in the fashion of a *Spatial Relief*. This mirror has been discussed in terms of enhancing the light-related contrasts of the work, by expanding the field of vision to reveal the innermost concavities of the construct, and even of including the viewer.[60] I tend to think, however, that the mirror stands less for an act of completion than a statement of incompleteness, for it perforates a syntactical sequentiality of experience that could otherwise have resembled that of the *Spatial Reliefs*. If these relied on the contiguity of their facets to produce a sense of articulation—like, say, early cubist paintings—the *Small Nucleus* interrupts this potential sense of sequentiality by luring the spectator into a further temporal exploration at the same time as it draws attention to the incompleteness of this same mode of exploration. The more views it provides, the more dramatic the sense of failure in summarizing the whole thing. This interruption would be further developed in the *Grand Nucleus*, where the planes are not bound into a whole, leaving such an articulation (and the inherent sense of its insufficiency) to the spectator. Space is incorporated, Oiticica says, "as a sign."[61] Like *Tropicália*, this work is also composed of a juxtaposition of different "proto-works," as the resulting labyrinthine feeling attests.

In *Tropicália*, this tension is productively exploited. As the spectator enters the work, a number of different elements come into view, but they lack any clear sense of articulation with one another. They are rather experienced as an *accumulation*. It is as if the spectator has no time to make sense of each element, as if a new one piles up in front of the former before that can be done. The disconnectedness comes then *before* one makes sense of the thematic whole presented by the work, and is further enhanced in the vertiginous dive into the labyrinth of the *Imagetical* penetrable, which keeps narrowing as one advances, prompting an urgent pace that forestalls the possibility of careful assimilation. For sure, the images in *Tropicália* are stereotypical icons of "Brazilianness," but paradoxically presented ones: an accumulation of "Brazilian" images that fail to coalesce into a smooth sense of identity. The viewer, previously enlisted to make sense of the *Grand Nucleus*, is now drawn into making a whole array of supposedly familiar images into nonsense.

But nonsense has a sense of its own. At the end of the labyrinth, as a sudden halt to the accelerating movement of accumulation, awaits the solitary television set. It punctuates an encounter meant to reinstate a constructive sense to the now imploded "obviousness." Oiticica doesn't simply include the TV set as a mere critique of television, mass culture, and so on. On its arrival in Brazil, far from installing the crystallized form of spectacle known as the corporate network, television shared in the impulse of modernization in the 1950s[62] and it wasn't until the early 1960s, with the introduction of the videotape, that shows could be imported.[63] This meant that all television programs were locally produced, employing a workforce that came from other cultural media, notably theater and radio. For those professionals, television offered the potential to expand their own artistic languages and the scope of their practices.[64] To be sure, by the time *Tropicália* was shown, TV *was* becoming corporate, but the fact is that its "heroic"—so to speak—aspect was still fresh in the minds of cultural producers.[65] This may well have informed Oiticica's take on television as an ultimate act of anthropophagy: once conditioned by Brazilian adversity, television could become exemplary (as a procedural

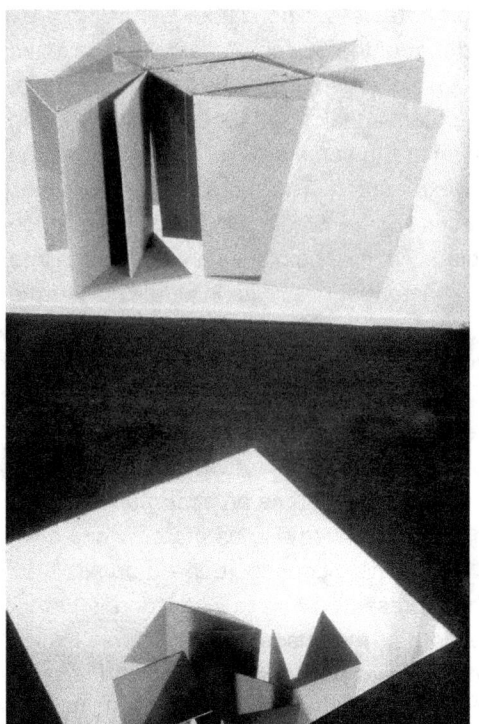

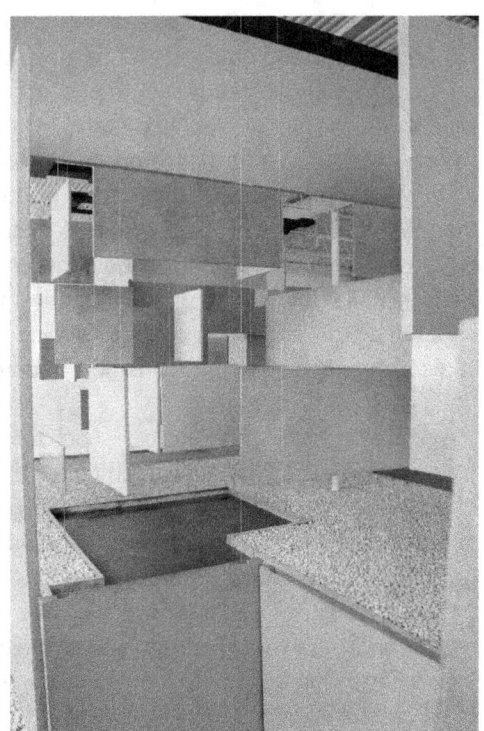

2.6
Hélio Oiticica, *NC1 Small Nucleus No. 01*, 1960.
Synthetic resin on wood fiberboard; mirror,
52 × 37 × 37 cm. César and Claudio Oiticica
Collection, Rio de Janeiro. Photo: Cláudio
Oiticica. Courtesy Projeto Hélio Oiticica.

2.7
Hélio Oiticica, *Grand Nucleus, NC3, NC4 e NC6*,
1960–1966. Oil and resin on wood, fiberboard,
variable dimensions. Photo: César Oiticica Filho.
Courtesy Projeto Hélio Oiticica.

matrix) in that it could "devour" everything, including itself (as a cultural emblem).[66] It follows that turning television onto itself was, in effect, as he summarized in 1970, "to consume consumption."[67]

Tropicália is not simply about the cultural circulation of signs, but refers back to the very apparatus that supports it. The fact that the newspaper drawings of the younger artist Antonio Manuel were exhibited on a table close to Tropicália is telling in this respect. What is more, Manuel would soon start to make his Flans, interventions in clay-based newspaper flongs.[68] These provide a material, tactile, and bodily anchor to the otherwise loosely articulated newspaper sign, pointing to the printing process of the newspaper, within the artist's reach, as a space to be manipulated—a space that precedes the public circulation of news.[69] Such a malleable relationship with the newspaper (i.e., the notion that it is not so much a given terrain as yet another space to be acted upon) is evocative of Amilcar de Castro's famous graphic reform, ten years earlier, of the SDJB, which played a key role in the affirmative ethos of the constructive avant-garde.[70] My point here is that for both Oiticica and Manuel there would be no point in renewing the alliance with mass media, especially in a context of censorship, but this material relationship to the media (in both senses of the word) could still offer a critical perspective.

Oiticica further states that Manuel's drawings were included in Tropicália, lending their violent and kitsch affect to its already charged ensemble.[71] As Manuel puts it, Tropicália acted "like a magnet" that attracted everything around it.[72] The work did indeed aim at a centripetal involvement of its surroundings—and of its public: the artist makes the crucial remark that the TV "is the image which then devours the participant, because it is more active than his sensory creating."[73] Television thus substitutes and radicalizes his previous use of mirrors: instead of standing for what Joan Copjec termed the "screen as mirror"—a locus of imaginary completion (and thus of identity)—the encounter with the TV in Tropicália evokes the "mirror as screen"; that is, it points to the insufficiency of the subject, to the fact that the image it assembles (along with its putative inclusion in it) cannot possibly account for reality as a whole (thus countering its reification in the image).[74] To put it another way, it is not only that the subject is not sutured to the moving image, but also that the moving image itself confirms the breakdown of narcissism. What is crucial (and I shall return to this point) is that these coordinates of narcissism are not simply individual, but rather part of the cultural myth of "Brazilianness." It's also worth remembering that, also in 1967, Oiticica would make his B47 Box Bolide 22, Appropriation, The Plunge of the Body, Poem Box 4 (figure 2.9)—a work whose stark simplicity contrasts not only with its long title, but also with Tropicália, while simultaneously acting as a complement to the latter. It consisted of no more than an industrial water-filled barrel with a stenciled sentence at its bottom: "MERGULHO DO CORPO" (the plunge of the body). In a brilliant (and almost untranslatable) comment, poet Waly Salomão suggests that, as viewers bend forward to see their reflection, they also see the sentence, which then "provokes in Narcissus a detaching shock, a takeoff [um susto decolador e descolador]. A plunge in which the body appears no longer as a fragment of matter, as a bundle of mechanisms, but as animated flesh.... It is in truth a mirror that is fluid, changing, precarious, oblique and dispersive, since one grasps oneself reading a sentence that is superimposed and integrated to one's image, like a scar or a scurf."[75]

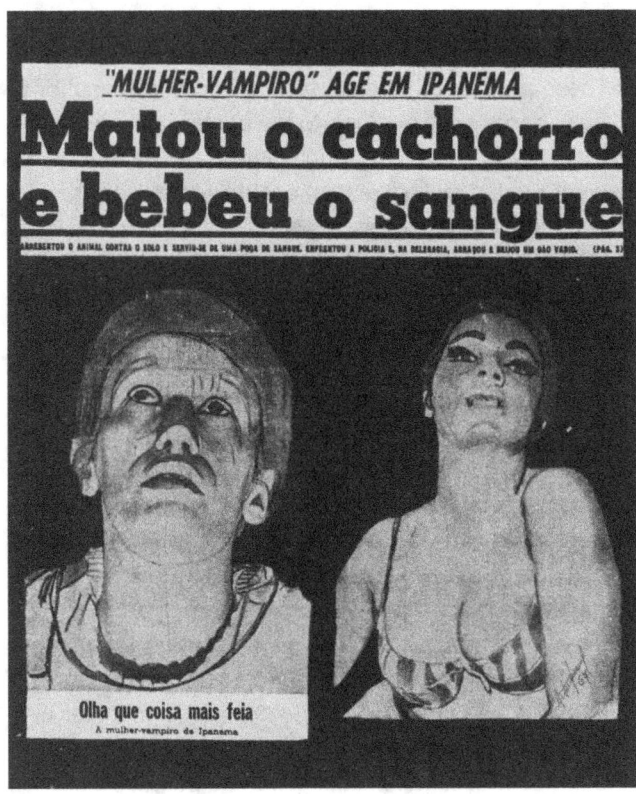

2.8
Antonio Manuel, *Matou o cachorro*, 1967. Crayon on newspaper, 43 × 36 cm. Courtesy of the artist.

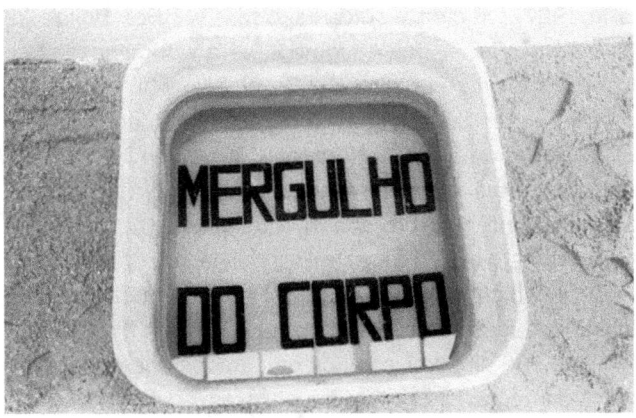

2.9
Hélio Oiticica, *B47 Box Bolide 22, Appropriation, The Plunge of the Body, Poem Box 4*, 1966–1967. Mixed media, 53 × 68 × 63 cm. César and Claudio Oiticica Collection, Rio de Janeiro. Photo: John Goldblatt. Courtesy Projeto Hélio Oiticica.

As in the *Metaesquemas*, Oiticica here seeks to stir an involuntary movement within the viewer.[76] This is precisely the image-driven (and iconoclastic) movement that animates the viewer's trajectory within *Tropicália*.[77] To state it plainly, my argument is that the TV in *Tropicália* is not simply a positive locus of significance; it is rather a reflective center that brings the whole vertiginous trajectory to an uncanny synthesis.

Now, if the contradictions within Brazilian social, economic, and cultural reality held the key to overturning what was already becoming the most powerful machinery for spreading cultural dependency—especially, in the artistic sphere, the "images of international pop and op [arts]"[78] to which Oiticica was so fiercely opposed—then it was easy to believe that this same reality had to be addressed head-on as the starting point for any significant cultural change. In short, it had to be hijacked into becoming the "digestive system" of an updated anthropophagic operation. Statements such as "OF ADVERSITY WE LIVE" are to be understood exactly as an engagement with this process, and so is his 1970 formulation in a virulent manifesto titled "Brazil Diarrhea": "whoever wants to 'construct' (and no-one 'loves Brazil' more than I!) has to see this and dissect the guts of this diarrhea—plunge into the shit."[79]

There is nothing new, of course, in arguing that *Tropicália* employs parrots, sand, and tropical plants in order to *undo* a "typical" portrayal of Brazil. What is important here is to draw attention to the way those images stage an encounter with the specificity of Brazilian culture. What is properly constructive about this encounter is its ethico-political dimension—that is, the imperative of "plunging into the shit." Instead of simply projecting a utopian future, the constructive operates firmly in the present tense, and it does so by internalizing the frictions of its past(s) and by constructing a subject that is drawn into critically sustaining these frictions. More specifically, in *Tropicália*, the encounter with the Brazilian image is staged as a fantasy. That much is evident in what would otherwise be a problematic term in Oiticica's discourse, the *myth*. Caught between the sensorial cacophony I described and the statement that "purity is a myth," which artist and writer Luciano Figueiredo interprets as "an attempt to free art from the perceived oppression imposed on it by centuries of aestheticism and 'good taste,'"[80] one has to face the "Brazilian image" as a radically contingent experience rather than as a well-finished or clearly localizable proposition. In Oiticica's vocabulary, "aestheticism" stands, for example, for the inability to grasp the radical openness of Mondrian's trajectory, which leads to a mistaken fixation on the finished work of art. But one cannot simply substitute "lie" for "myth" and consider that statement an outright denunciation of false reality. Oiticica's use of myth is way too ambivalent for that, and it would seem to me that he calls for a dialectics of myth making. Thus his later assertion that "mythification" should always come accompanied by "demythification." In a sense, then, what Oiticica terms the "objectivation" of a Brazilian image relates to a process of image (and myth) making in which the subject is brought into "experimenting" as the only possible way of critically relating to his or her own ideological closure. In other words, the fantasy cannot be simply denounced from the outside: its critique is indissociable from that earlier—and now updated—attack on the "synthetic unity" that grounds, in one and the same stroke, both the I and its perception of the social reality.

The idea of the myth as an anti-aesthetic stance can be further elucidated if we attend to yet another side of the genesis of *Tropicália*. Since *Tropicália* is also the peak of Oiticica's encounter with Mangueira, a favela in Rio famed for its samba school, it brings together precisely that which the *Parangolés* had inaugurated: the sheer energy of his discovery of dance as creative potentiality and the formalization of his programmatic aspirations. Understanding the exact register of Oiticica's use of the word "myth" in relation to Mangueira is crucial so that one does not fall in the trap of a primitivist reading that would clothe his work in otherness. True, there is a range of contradictions involved in Oiticica's own relationship to Mangueira, and he displayed something of a primitivist take on it himself. Guy Brett recalls how the imagery Oiticica included in his 1969 Whitechapel exhibition catalog—photographs of the favela and of native huts— was criticized by his peers back in Brazil for being perhaps too stereotypical. But Brett also remembers how Oiticica himself "fiercely contested the application of the term 'folkloric' to his projects."[81] So I think it is also possible to understand his radical demand of "universalization" as precisely opposed to such a primitivism; or to understand the latter, at least in Oiticica's discourse, as part of what I just termed a dialectics of myth making.

70

Oiticica first came to Mangueira in 1964, taken by the sculptor Jackson Ribeiro, in order to work in the samba school's workshop. That was the same year his father died, and close friends later recalled that he subsequently changed from an "Apollonian" young, sophisticated artist into a "Dionysian" agitator.[82] My point, however, is not to indulge in psychobiographical interpretation, but to translate that episode into the terms of Oiticica's cultural trajectory. Central to this was the artist's own account of that period as an important moment of "deintellectualization." Far from any rejection of critical thought, this meant an expansion of sensibility that deliberately opposed itself to the refined cultural environment of the Brazilian elites, from which Oiticica came. It also provided him with ways of further exploring the tensions that neoconcretism generated within the constructive project and bringing them to an expanded cultural level. As critic Paulo Venâncio Filho puts it:

> By "deintellectualising himself," he bravely set out to break with fixed places as well as spatial, cultural and social boundaries—without, of course, faking the experience, as experience is either legitimate or non-existent. Put another way, it was a question of finding the vital, true authenticity that only total confrontation with the city (the Rio de Janeiro of the 1950s and 1960s) could offer and validate.[83]

The psychogeographical aspect of this process of "deintellectualization" explains why *Tropicália* has been constantly referred to as a kind of map.[84] This led architecture scholar Paola Berestein Jacques to conclude that "*Tropicália* would then be a lived-through map, a kind of 'sentimental cartography' of lived through places in Rio and, more particularly, in the Morro da Mangueira."[85] What escapes Jacques's interpretation is the element of confrontation identified by Venâncio Filho. For more important than considerations about "sentimental" value is the fact that *Tropicália* defines, as well as maps, deintellectualization as a psycho- and sociogeographical enterprise. In other words, if the constructive was now put in operation as a juxtaposition of affective spaces, then this relates to the way Oiticica negotiates between 1950s and 1960s Rio de Janeiro: it is not actually "he" himself who comes in confrontation with the city, but these two versions—these two *myths*—of the city that are put in friction with one another.

In this sense, it is plausible to suggest that *Tropicália* also proposes a deintellectualization of modernism itself. As an architectural metaphor, the work is often discussed in relation to the favelas. But there is another side to the story, one that requires that we pay attention to an overlooked historical particularity. The "New Brazilian Objectivity" show opened to the public in April 1967, at the Museum of Modern Art in Rio de Janeiro (MAM-Rio), one of the most ambitious and sophisticated landmarks of Brazilian modern architecture. The museum itself had a long history, and Oiticica was one of its firsthand witnesses. It was there that his early artistic education took place in the famous workshops of the older painter Ivan Serpa, the leader of the Rio de Janeiro concretist-leaning Grupo Frente. MAM-Rio was also the setting for a number of important avant-gardist exhibitions both in the 1950s (when most cultural institutions still rejected abstract art) and in the 1960s, including the Grupo Frente exhibition (1955), the "National Exhibition of Concrete Art" (1957), and the "Opinião" shows in 1965 (where Oiticica first showed his *Parangolés*) and 1966. Although the museum did not move to its current location until 1958, it had already occupied another emblematic modernist setting, the Ministry of Education and Health building in Rio. The building had been completed in 1945 by a group of young modernist architects (including Oscar Niemeyer and Lúcio Costa, who would eventually design Brasília, and Affonso Eduardo Reidy, the future architect of the MAM-Rio building), with Le Corbusier acting as a consultant. So *Tropicália* emerged at the heart of Brazilian modernist architecture. Can we thus surmise that it simply opposes modernist grandeur with references to the vernacular?

Not quite: by the time *Tropicália* was unveiled, in April 1967, the main building of MAM-Rio was still receiving its final touches and would only be opened to the public later that year. This means that the whole show took place in the museum's school section. This is not extraordinarily significant per se, as all shows for the past nine years shared that same space. My point lies elsewhere, namely in the fact that *Tropicália*, a proto-architectural environment with its bricks, sand, and pebbles, was opened in a museum that was itself a *construction site*. And it was as a construction site that Oiticica had known it since 1958, and even before. By the time the exhibition wing opened, later in 1967, the museum had been under construction for thirteen years, which involved notorious delays. And its final opening was not so final, since part of the original plan (a theater wing) had been abandoned, leaving behind the project of a building that would integrate different artistic forms and cultural activities. As art historian Maria Cecília França Lourenço puts it, "during the period encompassing the initial plans, the making of the project, the protracted construction, and finally the death of the architect in 1964 ... some of the expectations and intentions [that informed the original project] were forgotten, and others never got off the ground."[86]

Bricks, sand, pebbles—these are tokens of improvisation (in the favelas), but also of incompleteness (of the modernist monument). As exposed materials, they connote simultaneously architecture (in the case of the former) and architectural failure (in the sense that the museum literally failed to *live up* to its expectations, which is by no means to downplay the historical role it actually played). It is telling in this regard that one of the photographs of improvised "constructions" that reportedly inspired the *Parangolé* concept was taken at the parking lot of MAM-Rio in 1965 (figure 2.10).[87] It didn't contain bricks or anything like that, but it is tempting to see in the juxtaposition of this small tree (surrounded by rags, clothes, tins, and bottles) with the building in the background a first visualization of the architectural incongruity *Tropicália* would condense.

By addressing MAM-Rio as a construction site, *Tropicália* itself became a site-specific work. Its site, of course, must be understood at a broader level, for it is located at the contradictory crux of Brazilian modernization. Gullar felt this contradiction as well when, in 1961, as the *SDJB* ceased to circulate, he was invited to direct the Fundação Cultural de Brasília (Brasília Cultural Foundation): "Brasília is the fusion of the new, it is what there is of most advanced and most antiquated in Brazil. With the architecture of Oscar [Niemeyer] and Lúcio [Costa] and the northeastern workforce. And there I am to make both avant-garde art and popular art."[88] The poet then attributes his shift in great part to the experience of witnessing the poor social conditions of those immigrant workers who moved to Brasília in order to build it—that invisible underside of the modernist emblem—which would have prompted a "renewed contact" with his own, northeastern origins. Brasília could indeed provide shocking images: for example, picture the slum *Sacolândia* (Bagland), aptly named for the empty bags of cement left over from the construction work that were then used as building materials for its shacks. It was to this kind of situation, simultaneously pungent and ironic, that the poet may have been exposed.[89] Can't we think of it also as a striking precursor to *Tropicália*, a juxtaposition at least as extreme as the one in the parking lot photograph? For Gullar, such contradictions demanded a radical choice; for Oiticica, they demanded one live through them, and this is what *Tropicália* ultimately stands for.[90]

I think it is possible to go one step further and suggest that *Tropicália* maps a phantasmatic terrain. The point would not be to "read" it—that would lead to a superficial assimilation of its imagery as "typical"—but to traverse it; that is, to live it to the point that it doesn't so much point to any coordinates, but becomes active in the refounding of those coordinates. Let me put it another way. Jorge Luis Borges once imagined an effort to make the perfectly detailed map of an empire. Striving for perfection, the cartographers ended up needing a map so large that its area coincided with that of the empire itself.[91] The point, of course, is the absurdity of not recognizing language—and thus cartography—as loss. *Tropicália* not only operates in full understanding of this condition, it assumes it to the point that its mapping ultimately refers to loss alone. It maps the loss of an image of Brazil, thus aiming at a purely operational, rather than representational, take on mapmaking. And by doing so it *locates* the constitutive gap upon which concepts like anthropophagy and the constructive, staked as they are in signifying operations, can intervene. It is in this precise sense that the disconnectedness of its imagery can be understood in the terms of cartography, opening the way to yet another shift, where cartography will be recognized as a critical procedure vis-à-vis the image *tout court*.

Thus we arrive at a point where Brazilian cultural and social reality, understood as fantasy, is mapped (swallowed) into dissolution. This assertion can be verified by casting its terms onto the terminology of "Brazil Diarrhea." We can then translate Oiticica's proposal as follows: "dilution in the diarrhea" stands for the subject imaginarily frozen in a social reality that reproduces conservative values. This state of affairs is named, from the subject's viewpoint, as *convi-conivência*, a term that assembles ideas of "living together" and "connivance" and thus conveys in a nutshell what it is to be (as in to exist) in ideology. By proposing "transformations in the behavior context" the "experimental" is able to "swallow and dissolve" the *convi-conivência*, a traumatic moment that involves "plunging into the shit." Let me evoke, once again, the final lines of "Brazil Diarrhea": "In Brazil, therefore, the experimental and a permanently critical and universal position are constructive elements. All else is dilution of the diarrhea."[92] The "universal" is once again key here, and it becomes clear that there is no essentialism in it.[93] It is not enough for Oiticica to counter a local myth. It is necessary instead to pull the whole mechanism of mythification into the dialectical process I have described. The constructive is the ethical guarantor of such a *permanent* critique, a metacoordinate of *Tropicália* as cartography, thus the genesis of the constructive attitude as the "opening of new paths in contemporary sensibility."[94]

As art historian Paulo Reis argues, "Oiticica widened the borders of the exhibition, public locus for the *vivência* and understanding of art, to the scale of the city. Urban and social geography were united with the art show, and the New Objectivity, through [the concept of the] object, realized the transit between these spaces."[95] I take this to imply that the artist's ideas on participation must be understood on this same confrontational, psychogeographical level, and not on one of purely ludic individual liberation (it would be incredibly naïve to believe that spectators systematically had moments of mind-opening epiphany while experiencing Oiticica's environments).[96] It follows that we cannot assume the immediacy of experience as a positive, joyful, irreducible, and continually valid kernel of radicality.[97] Take two photographs of the *Bolide* Oiticica made as an homage to his friend Cara de Cavalo, an outlaw who was named an "enemy of society" and shot dead by the police. I want to draw attention to the contrast of Oiticica's stern, confrontational attitude with the more absorbed, joyful one of many of his Mangueira friends while interacting with his works. The latter attitude would be easily readable in conjunction with a dance-driven *Parangolé*, but what to make of it in the face of such a solemn, antagonistic work? I take it to mean that joyfulness relates more to the subject position apropos of which the liberating charge of the work is constructed than to the experience of a self-sufficient moment. With the *Parangolés*, Oiticica also identified as participants those who watched other participants don the capes—even those who were actually outraged by the excessive joy the Mangueira dancers brought into the MAM in 1965, as their entrance was unexpectedly barred.[98] Thus these modes of participation are far from symmetrical: upper-class spectators were unlikely to join the dancing as immediately and wholeheartedly as Mangueira dancers summoned for that purpose and fellow avant-garde artists.[99] They were participants, then, in the sense that they were confronted—confronted by the same subjective position Oiticica saw society attempting violently to repress in Cara de Cavalo, and which returns in the image of his traumatized body and of joyful identification with the defiant statements displayed by so many Parangolés, such as "I embody revolt" (*Incorporo a revolta*) and "I am possessed" (*Estou possuído*).[100]

This antagonistic dimension of the *Parangolés* is an important reminder that Oiticica should not be taken as the predecessor of contemporary practices where participation is fetishized.[101] What is more, it is also a way of challenging a buzzword that risks blocking from our view a fundamental guiding thread in the artist's trajectory—the

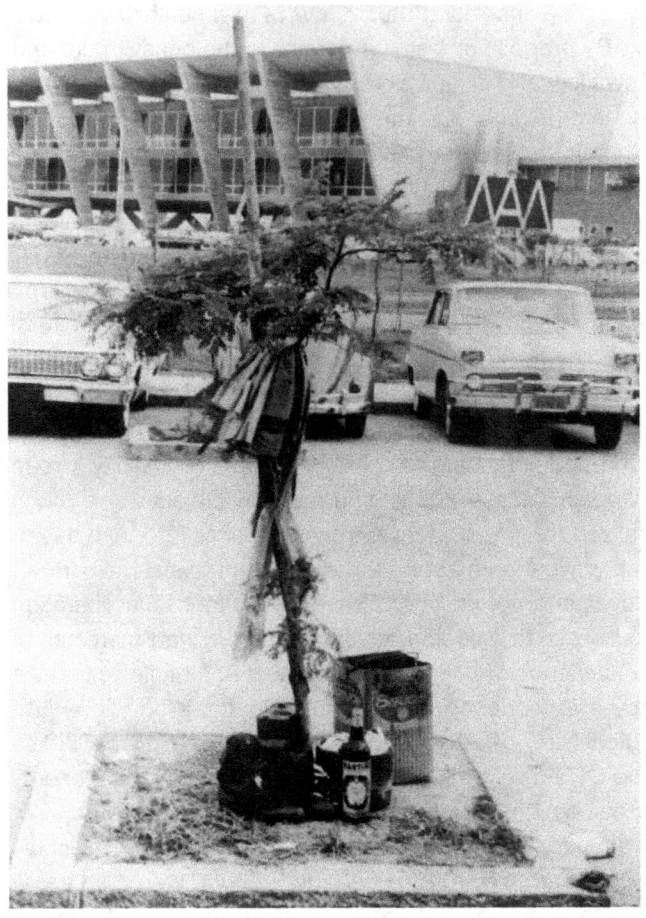

2.10
Photograph taken at the parking lot of the
Museum of Modern Art in Rio de Janeiro and
associated with the genesis of the *Parangolé*
concept. Photo: Desdemone Bardin. Courtesy
Projeto Hélio Oiticica.

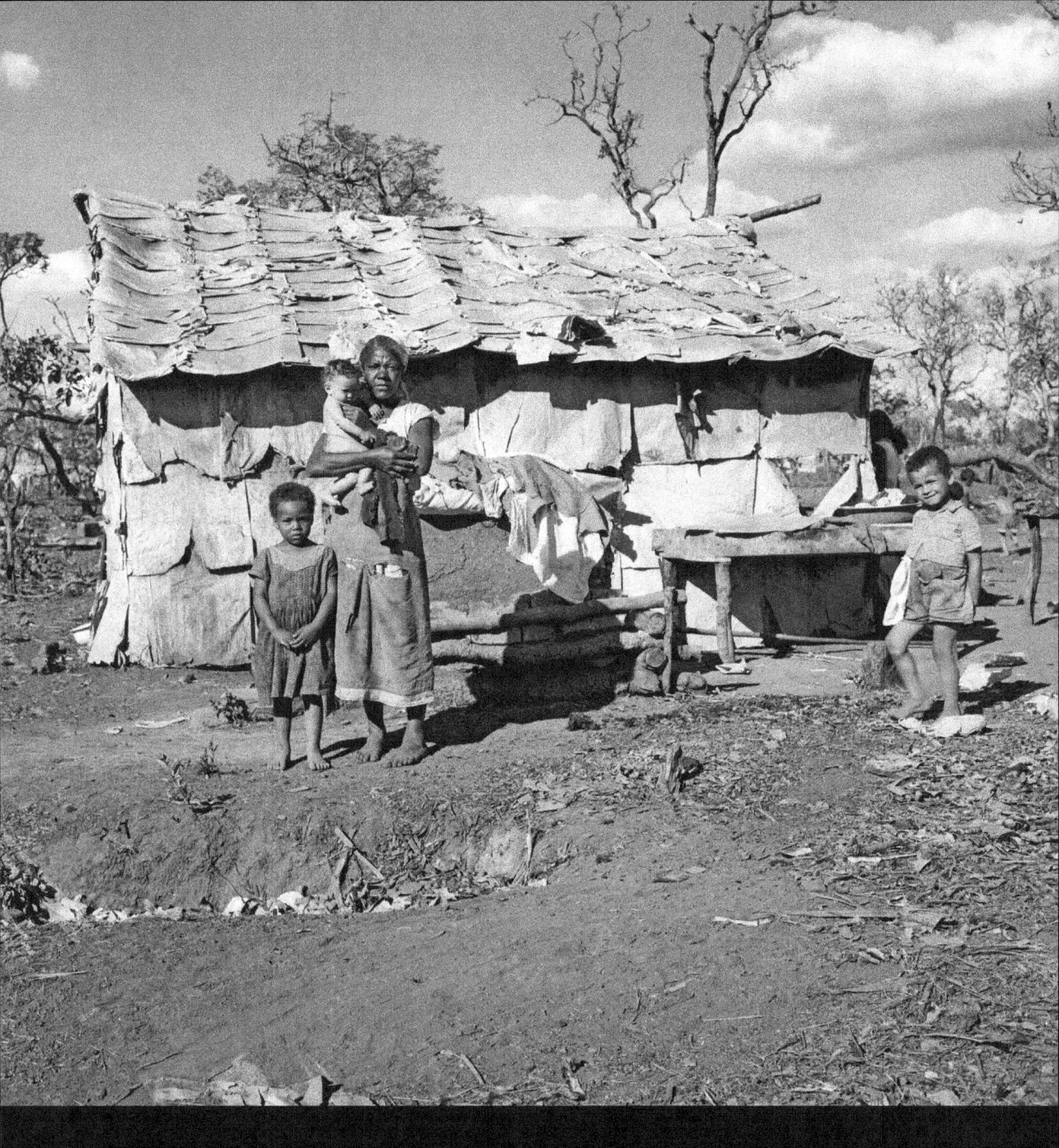

2.11
Marcel Gautherot, *Sacolândia*,
ca. 1959. Marcel Gautherot /
Acervo Instituto Moreira Salles.

constructive—that runs from his questioning the givens of painting through color to the confrontational arena he sets up vis-à-vis the ideological foundations of modernist history, urban experience, and national identity. Needless to say, those are precisely the three dimensions that *Tropicália* critically assembles. To fetishize participation—either as an epiphanic experience or as a privileged interpretive motif—is thus to risk losing sight of the ambitious breadth and scope of Oiticica's artistic and intellectual activity.

I have already remarked that the historical charge of Oiticica's *constructive* is staked on its rejection of identity. This is precisely what neoconcrete theory failed to articulate due to its teleological closure.[102] Conversely, the starting point of the relation between the constructive and history is its denial of historicism, its articulation of history in the terms of a present urgency that exceeds available narratives (much like Clark's reading of Mondrian exceeded available interpretations). In many ways, of course, the constructive refers back to the achievements of neoconcretism. What is crucial is that it does so without resorting to a theoretical armature that would forestall the full development of its newfound historicity. In this sense, Oiticica's emphatic refusal of framing his efforts as a new "ism" must also be taken very seriously, and not simply as a rhetorical cliché. By the same token, to ground it too strongly in participation—or in any isolated aspect of Oiticica's work, for that matter—would amount to a similar turning away from the radical openness of the concept, turning it into, say, a kind of "participationism." Participation in *Tropicália* must be understood rather as short-circuiting the fantasy that uncritically conflated both national-popular and "aestheticist" discourses under the amorphous regime of *convi-convivência*. By subordinating such an operation to the constructive, then, I intend to restore its validity as a historical intervention in the course of modernism and the avant-garde, thus distinguishing it from the postmodernist—in the sense that it mirrors a late-capitalist procedure—field of participation.

Tropicália is then less a map of the constructive than the realization of a constructive way of mapping—like color before, the constructive is now effectively "in charge." This points to a model of historical meaning that draws on Oiticica's anthropophagic redefinition of "construction," or, more precisely, on his constructive reclaiming of anthropophagy; in other words, it builds on his 1962 definition of a "sense of constructivity" and completes it by adding an element: the "adversity" of a Brazilian cultural reality understood as psychic scenario. This results in the formation of a position that makes historical intervention possible. Oiticica effectively reverses Pedrosa's terms and condemns modernity to be Brazilian instead; he takes up a position in a radical present that is constructed in relation to history. In Slavoj Žižek's reading, Walter Benjamin's image of the historical materialist making a "tiger's leap into the past" means that "we do not have to look for the connection between past and present constellations in the diachronous time arrow; this connection reinstates itself in the form of an immediate paradigmatic short-circuit."[103] Isn't that the way Oiticica reclaims his designated constructors? And more importantly: isn't that how he proceeds to reclaim anthropophagy, as a procedure that is constructive exactly in its power to short-circuit the *convi-convivência*?[104] And isn't that, in its turn, the procedure implied by the disconnectedness in *Tropicália*; isn't that the way *Tropicália* can be conceived as a work that reflects on the status of the image, especially if we understand image in the register of fantasy? It is precisely this fantasy that supposedly is enacted by the "centuries of aestheticism and good taste"

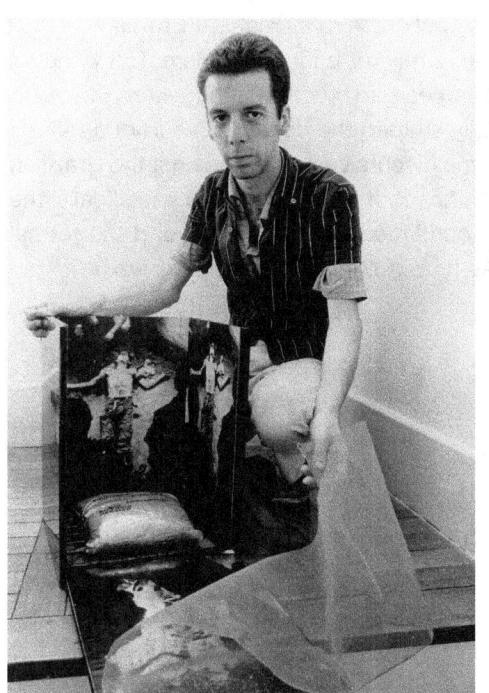

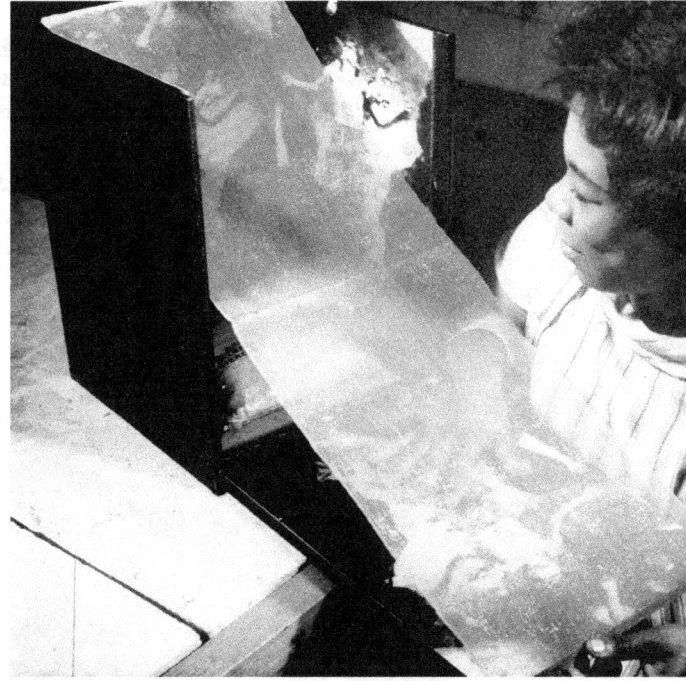

2.12
Hélio Oiticica with *B33 Box Bolide 18, Poem Box 2, Homage to Cara de Cavalo*, 1966. Wood, plastic, photograph, nylon, iron, pigment. Photo: Cláudio Oiticica. Coleção Gilberto Chateaubriand, Museu de Arte Moderna do Rio de Janeiro. Courtesy Projeto Hélio Oiticica.

2.13
Luiza with *B33 Box Bolide 18, Poem Box 2, Homage to Cara de Cavalo*, 1966. Wood, plastic, photograph, nylon, iron, pigment. Photographer unknown. Coleção Gilberto Chateaubriand, Museu de Arte Moderna do Rio de Janeiro. Courtesy Projeto Hélio Oiticica.

Luciano Figueiredo alluded to, and against which *Tropicália* can be said to mobilize myth as an anti-aesthetics; this is what Oiticica's avowed deintellectualization ultimately amounts to.

As concepts go, it may be that anthropophagy is easier to retrieve from our contemporary critical viewpoint than the constructive—indeed, anthropophagy has undoubtedly become an (un)critical cliché that seems applicable to all matters Brazilian.[105] And the constructive, after all, strikes us almost as a relic of past utopianism. But bringing both back *together* seems relevant not as a synthesis so much as a trigger for rethinking histories of recent Brazilian art. Oiticica initially shaped the constructive from a refined process of formal dialectics. But having become discursive and set against the Brazilian "adversity," it becomes fully operational as a concept. It becomes, more specifically, the signifier of Oiticica's radical present, whose continued validity lies beyond the formal immediacy of his works and propositions. As he put it in 1972: "*the experimental* can reclaim never *relive*."[106]

78

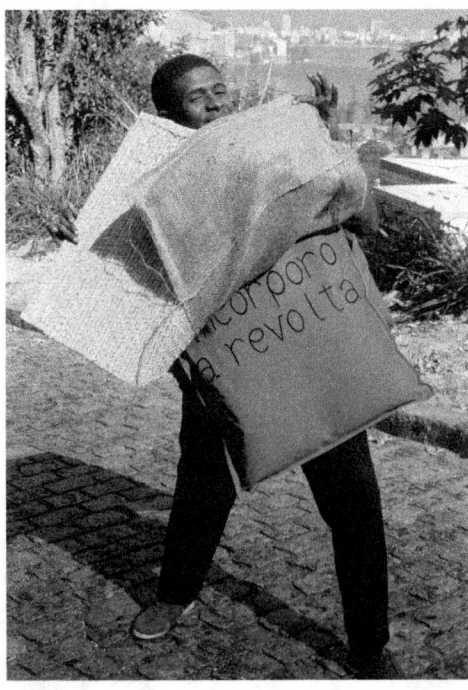

2.14
Nildo da Mangueira with *Parangolé P15 Capa 11, Incorporo a revolta*, 1967. Straw matting, cotton fabric, burlap. Photo: Cláudio Oiticica. Courtesy Projeto Hélio Oiticica.

Taking Positions

A man advances alone along a street, in broad daylight, nervously pressing his back against walls and gates. We don't get to see his face; he wears a gas mask. He may be terrified, paranoiac, in flight; or he may be sneaking, spying, an agent of repression (or subversion, perhaps). In some scenes, a huge, cut-out red heart dangles over his chest, swinging like a pendulum against the backdrop of his black shirt; at another moment, he is lying on a bed, in front of a large "DANGER" sign. A muffled voice, probably the man's own, duly pronounces a series of reflections about painting, political struggle, and art making in general. "The painter is a professional," he explains, "but what I do is not a profession. Someone working in painting or cinema always thinks he'll change something."[1]

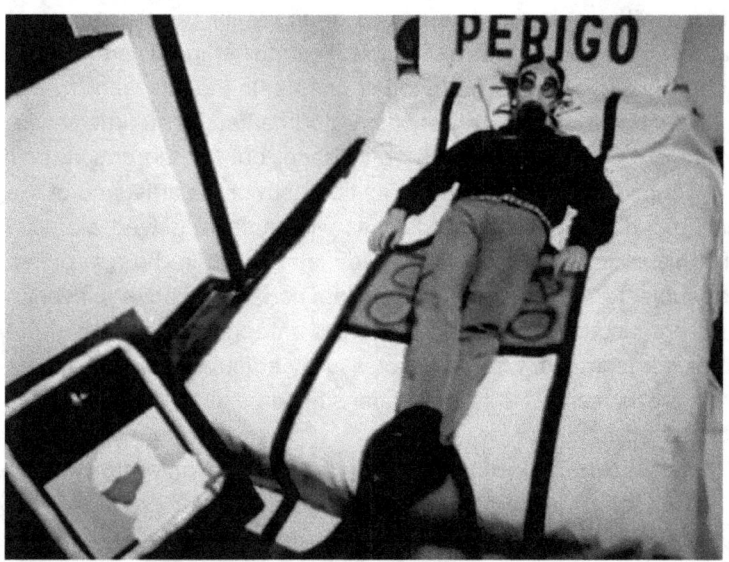

3.1
Still from *Ver ouvir*, 1966. Courtesy Antonio
Dias/Antonio Carlos da Fontoura/Canto
Claro Produções Artísticas.

These scenes come from the middle episode of Antonio Carlos da Fontoura's 1966 short film *Ver ouvir* (See Listen), and it is not until the very last second that the voice positively connects with the character, presenting himself as Antonio Dias at the same time as he produces and displays what he claims to be his identity card. Each episode in Fontoura's film is monographic; others focus on Roberto Magalhães and Rubens Gerchman, also artists associated with this generation. What all of the episodes have in common is that they approach each of the portrayed artists from the viewpoint of the strategies of *self-inscription* they employ. Magalhães is shown at a theme park, recounting events from his childhood and adolescence while his face is either caught in a distorted mirror image or smeared with paint he has applied, in order to resemble the human figures (self-portraits included) so common in his 1960s work. Gerchman's episode starts with his self-presentation: "My name is Rubens Gerchman, I am 1.70 meters high and my ID card number is 1,566,166. I am a painter."[2] It draws on the fact that his work often includes stylized versions of ID cards as signs of urban anonymity and failed individuality. "I open the newspaper," Gerchman's voiceover continues, "and suddenly read about John, who tried hard to be no longer an unknown, or simply an ID card number."[3]

As a series of cinematic portraits, *Ver ouvir* mirrors the fact that artists belonging to this circle shared an intense engagement with portraiture (and especially self-portraiture). All we need is a cursory glance at works like *Identity Card: Self Right Thumb* (1965) and *Self-Portrait* (1968), by Gerchman; *Self-Portrait Speaking* (1965) and *Self-Portrait on the Left Side* (1965), by Magalhães; *My Family* (1966) and *Anna* (1967), by Anna Maria Maiolino; *Self-Portrait with a Carajá Indian* (1968), by Carlos Vergara; and finally *Self-Portrait for the Counterattack* (1966) and *My Portrait* (1967), by Antonio Dias. These works mark a period when their authors were increasingly claiming for themselves—in an alliance with some representatives of an earlier generation, most notably Hélio Oiticica and Lygia Pape—the Brazilian avant-gardist stage. Therefore, my aim in raising this subject is not to establish yet another chapter in the critical history of portraiture, nor to further deconstruct a much-deconstructed genre. Those artists were reclaiming the remainders of this genre not for its own sake, but for the critical possibilities it offered in the context of a crisis of self-definition both of the artist and of the avant-garde qua collective endeavor (a similar crisis, as will be seen, played a crucial role in cinema as well). This is an issue that was already latent both in the non-object and in the constructive, subjects that I have already examined, and whose relevance in the context of the present discussion I will address. The anti-egomorphic drive that informed the constructive, for instance, was a way of visually articulating Oiticica's disjunctive engagement with modern art, and its implications become all the more obvious against the backdrop of self-portraiture.

Yet the imperative of assuming a position faced by the 1960s avant-gardist stage cannot be properly addressed solely via the portraits and self-portraits then produced—so much is evident already in the fourth topic of the "General Scheme of the New Objectivity": "position-taking in relation to political, social and ethical problems."[4] Therefore, in order to analyze this imperative as part of a broader discussion, I will explicitly address how important historical and artistic landmarks (especially the construction of Brasília and the reception of pop art) came to play a decisive although often contradictory role in the

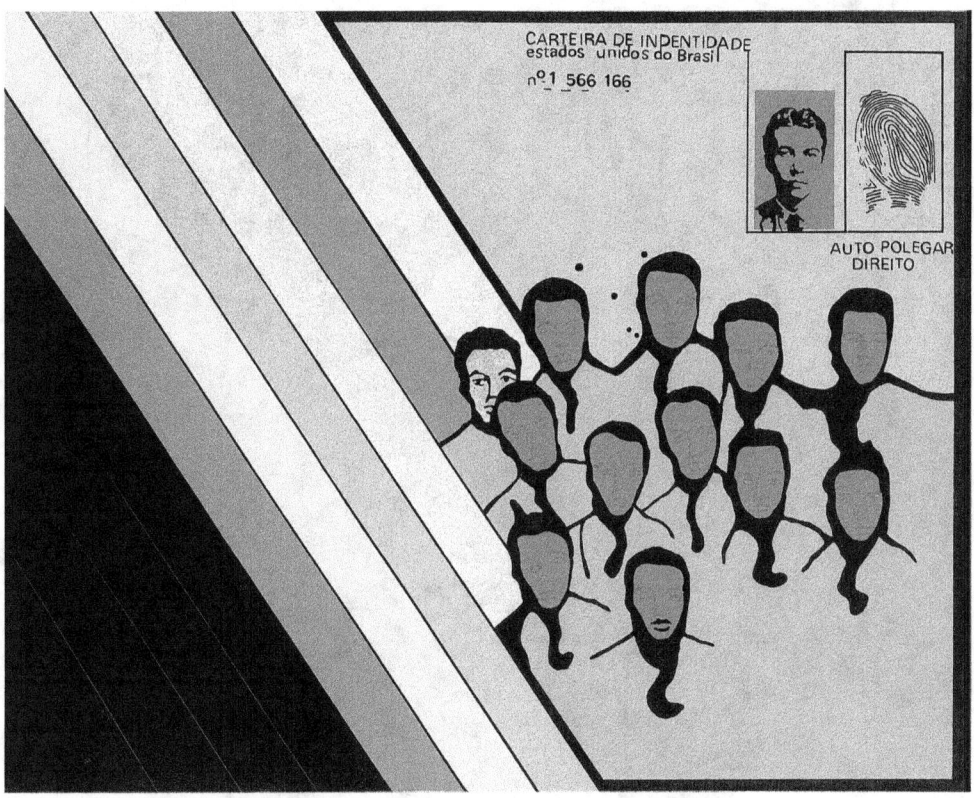

3.2
Rubens Gerchman, *Identity Card (Self-Right Thumb)*, 1965. Acrylic on canvas, 110 × 135 cm. Coleção do Museu de Arte Moderna de São Paulo—Fundo para aquisição de obras MAM-SP—Pirelli. Licensed by inARTS.com. Photo: Romulo Fialdini.

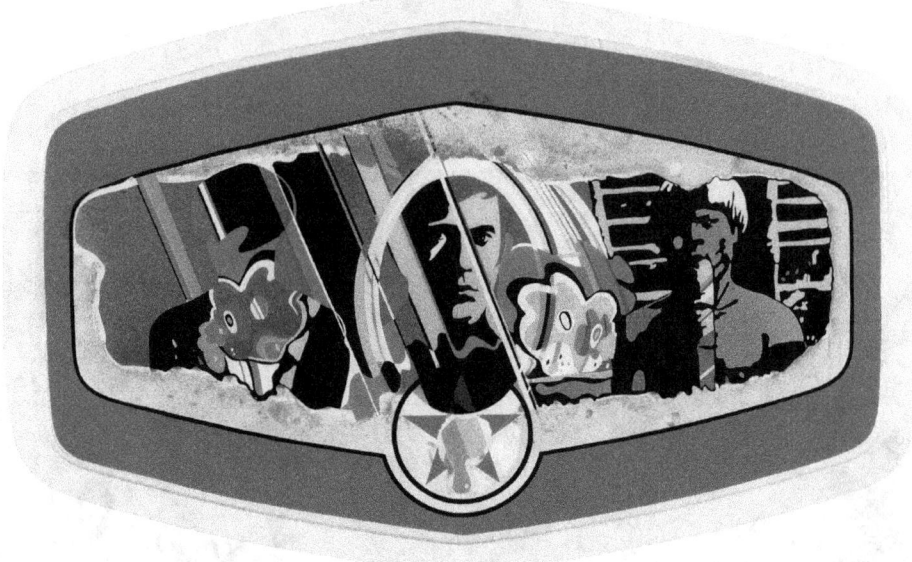

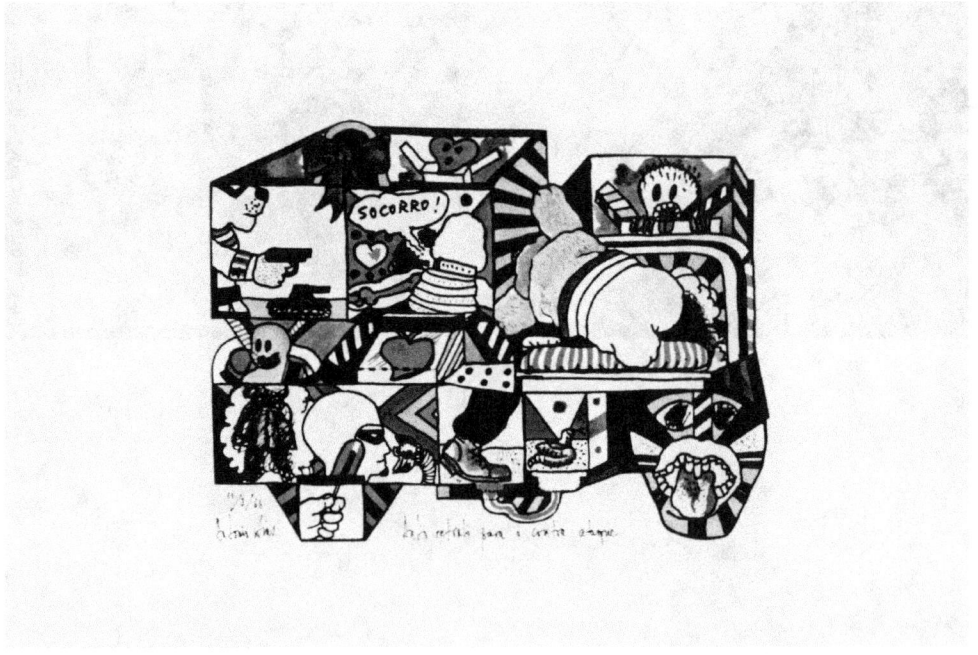

3.3
Carlos Vergara, *Self-Portait
with a Carajá Indian*, 1968.
Paint on molded acrylic, 90 ×
130 cm. Coleção Gilberto
Chateaubriand, Museu de Arte
Moderna do Rio de Janeiro.

3.4
Antonio Dias, *Self-Portrait
for the Counterattack*, 1966.
Ink and watercolor on paper,
41.7 × 47 cm. Geneviève
& Jean Boghici Collection.
Courtesy of the artist.

3.5
Antonio Dias, *My Portrait*,
1967. Acrylic and vinyl on
wood, canvas and wire,
120 × 120 × 45 cm. Private
collection. Courtesy of
the artist.

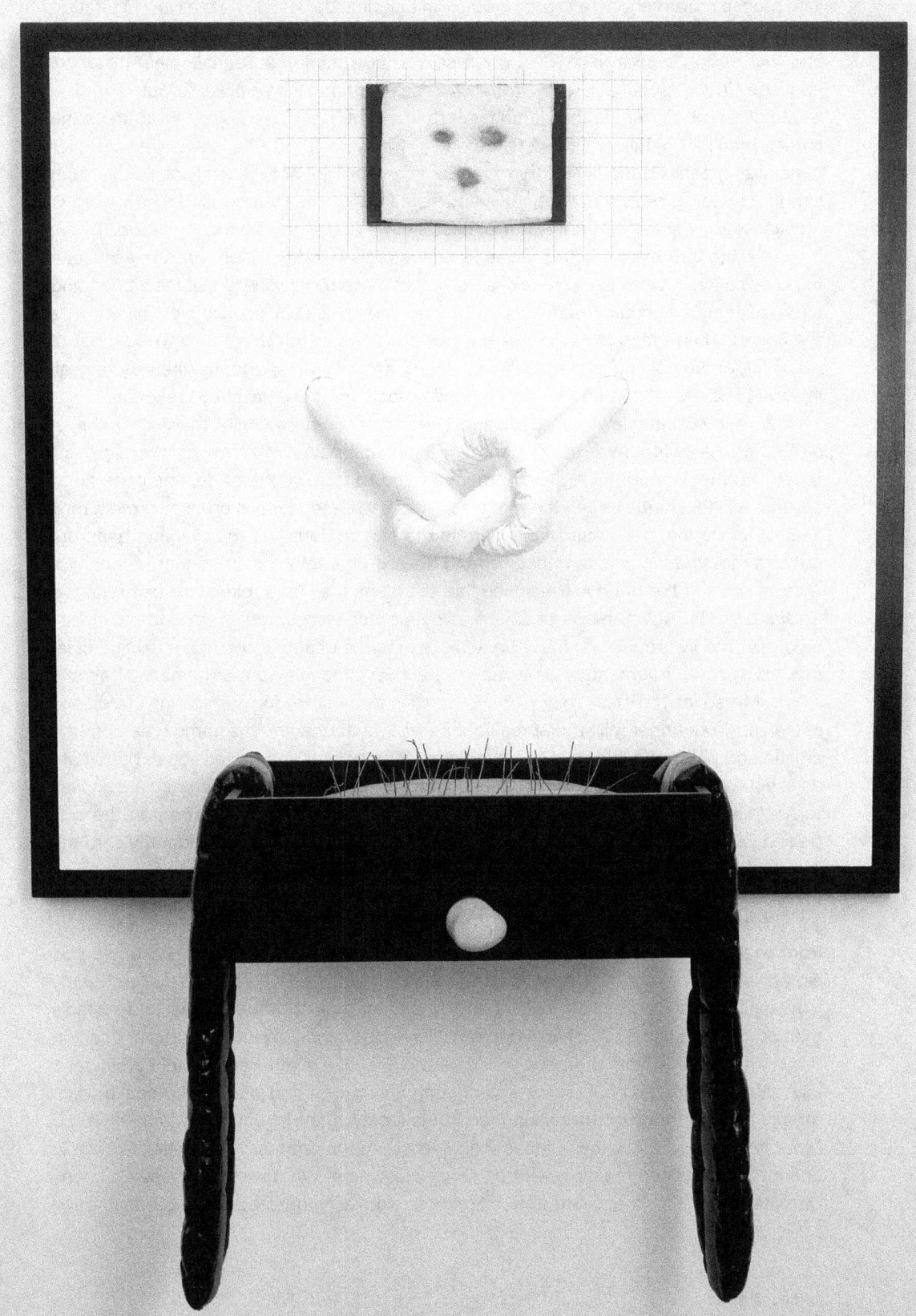

reconfiguration of the 1960s avant-garde. The works I listed are commonly associated with a loose movement or tendency in Brazil in that decade, known as the New Figuration. Such a denomination implies a clear-cut rupture between the art of the "abstract" 1950s and that of the "figurative" 1960s, often said to accompany an equally neat historical passage, in the political arena, from wholesale optimism to social turbulence. The assumption, of course, is that figurative art would be better equipped to address the latter's manifold manifestations.[5] Once again, however, it may be wiser to avoid over-generalizing periodizations and try to render this passage more dialectical. Rather than simply choosing between continuity and rupture, I want to reconsider how certain artistic issues were redefined—but not cast away—during this historical period. To put it bluntly, the turn was not simply one from abstraction to figuration, or from alienation to politicization. It was instead a *self-reflexive turn* in which notions of self-inscription and urban experience became particularly pressing and potentially productive. This may be the key for interpreting the complex relay of positions enacted in those works: that of the artist, of the political agent, of the spectator and, more importantly, the way they all intersect in different media (film, as *Ver ouvir* attests to, is central in this respect).

In a 1966 interview with Dias and Gerchman, Ferreira Gullar makes a point of stressing their recourse to spray guns and industrial paints in place of "the old paint-brush and the paint tube," that is, of more traditional tools of the trade, and goes on to say that this technique forced them to wear masks while working in order to protect their health.[6] While the gas mask Dias wears in the film obviously is not painting gear, but rather a military relic, it is tempting to read his self-characterization as that of a painter with his tools of the trade in the sense that the mask may be a token of a self-reflexive artistic attitude. Again, much of Dias's voiceover (or voice*under*: from under a mask) revolves broadly around what art can achieve in terms of social change, making it clear that his speech, fragmentary as it may be, almost amounts to a statement of artistic ethics. Moreover, the mask may well stand as a metaphor for the suffocating conditions of life and work under military repression. It displays at one and the same time both the artistic and political position of the character ("The painter is a professional, but what I do is not a profession") while simultaneously covering up the viewer's immediate access to his identity, which is momentarily displaced to a photographic portrait on the wall behind Dias (that is, to an explicit representation) or to the antagonistic identity card the artist exhibits in the end, displaying the pictogram of a skull and two bones alongside the word "ANGEL." In Dias's episode, identification is not a given.

The centrality of (self-)portraiture for this generation thus derived, or so I will argue, from an intricate debate over which positions cultural producers should and could possibly assume. We should understand the idea of a position here in its full polysemy. It was not simply a position in relation to national politics, though it is undoubtedly marked by the tense political environment. Nor was it simply an internal artistic position, though it stemmed from the need to locate the Brazilian avant-garde within an increasingly internationalized art world. It was not primarily concerned with institutional politics, though art as a mode of addressing (and thus locating) the spectator was a key issue. More importantly, all of these ideas inflected one upon another, so positions taken in one regard provoked reactions—often fiery—elsewhere. What is more, these concerns persisted even after the virtual dissolution of a relatively organized avant-garde (though not necessarily of an avant-gardist impetus) under military repression, at the end of the decade.

The question of taking a position applies to art understood both as a mode of political intervention as well as a production-reception relation. If I introduce my argument with reference to Fontoura's film, it is because I take this sense of both maladjustment (of one's position) and alienation (of one's voice, i.e., the disruption of the voice's role as a stable mode of address and self-assurance) to play a crucial part in Dias's works, especially between the late 1960s and the early 1970s, when the radical change his work underwent coincided with the fragmentation of the avant-garde group to which he initially belonged.[7] All of these issues, I believe, are inscribed in some important works of this period, in that their subject is constructed by literally *subjecting* spectators to an extremely tense, yet contained, pressure; that is, in the way different positions apropos of the work are set against each other as contradictions and thus implicated in a kind of reflexive dialectic.

VOLUNTARISM

The end of *Ver ouvir* is very telling in this respect. It brings in Gullar's voiceover, as the poet reads a text of his own entitled "Painting Speaks" (*A pintura fala*):

> In the hubbub of voices and noises, slogans, homes, record stores, invisible electrical circuits, the simultaneous city creates and deciphers itself / Clamor is its reality / Everywhere, the city's speech, unanimous and fragmentary, makes itself heard / Within this hubbub, painting—a man who paints—speaks / Childhood mirrors, violence masks, solitude boxes / Goods the city consumes, disguised in soft drinks, news of war, cookware sets / Painting speaks and the same clamor that muffles its voice makes it shout, like slogans, the dream, the love, the solitude / Language is torn[8]

Gullar's narration is clearly meant to wrap up the three episodes, and it does so by stressing urban experience—"the city"—as their common background. The city is rendered strikingly contradictory, at once "unanimous and fragmentary," and the portrayal of speech circulating in the form of commodities—nostalgia in the guise "soft drinks," violence as "news" and solitude as "cookware sets"—turns it into the object of materialist critique. It is important to remember that this is Gullar after his turn to left-wing militancy. His support of these artists hinges on two fundamental aspects: first, their refusal of an "alienating" abstraction (and especially of *informal* abstraction) in favor of an art that is "full of interest for things of the world, for the problems of man and for the society in which [the artists] live."[9] Second, for their ability to draw these concerns out of the urban cacophony and turn them into "communication." The position of the artist is thus transformative, rendering visible the materialist critical position meant to resist the chaotic (and mystifying) commodification of human relations that takes place in the city.[10]

Such emphasis on the city is key for understanding the poet's active role in ongoing discussions of the position artists should take in relation to Brazil's social and political issues. It is worth recalling the central impact Brasília had in Gullar's critical reevaluation and subsequent abandonment of neoconcretism. It is from this perspective that I want to further develop some issues I briefly introduced in the preceding chapters and address the cultural debate surrounding the inauguration of the new capital, paying special attention to its reception within artistic circles. For, their differences notwithstanding, Brasília and *Ver ouvir* share one crucial feature: in both, the city becomes a focal point on which artists and critics project their cultural and political stances.

As we have seen, the 1950s constructive avant-garde was strikingly confident in the knowledge of its own progressive stance. Or, to put it another way, the identity of the *constructive artist* was itself a construct designating a cultural agent whose effort fitted with the perception of an overall thrust of society away from its archaic past and into a bright, modern future. To a great extent, however, this corresponded to a cultural atmosphere that ideologically repressed the brewing of the rather less optimistic conditions that would visibly shape the early 1960s. One example is the growing power of worker's unions, which the populist government of Juscelino Kubitschek managed to keep relatively calm thanks, in great part, to the influence Vice President João Goulart (who would become the last democratically elected president before the 1964 military coup) had upon the unions. Stronger unions were an obvious outcome of industrialization, and some cultural sectors were quite sensitive to it: think, for example, of the staging at the Teatro de Arena, very early in 1958, of *They Don't Wear Black Tie*, an explicitly political play that explored the dilemmas of a working-class family on the verge of a factory strike.[11] It is important to note here how laden with mixed messages the atmosphere in fact was. Kubitschek's relative political stability was certainly the product of a complex set of political compromises that sustained his national-developmentalism. This was a model of industrial development that coupled strong state presence with foreign investment, and whose public facade was the promotion of modernization as the harbinger of a renewed national unity.[12]

Considering its sheer magnitude, it is not surprising that Brasília became a major trump card in Kubitschek's strategy. It furnished the government with a seemingly nonpartisan platform for its "populist appeal to the mass voter," allowing it to refrain from relying too heavily on polemical arrangements that might generate political anxiety.[13] More importantly, Brasília was shot through with historical and ideological components. These included republican aspirations: the promise of the new capital had been inscribed in the first postmonarchic constitution. Even more significant were nationalist dreams of geographic integration, for the capital was meant to unify the vast interior of Brazil with the coastline where most colonial history had taken place and where major cities were located. And then there was the endemic hope engendered by economic development in the guise of industrialization. All of these forces came together in a monumental aesthetic package. From the tip of its massive concrete constructions, Brasília seemed to pull all of these strings together into a promise of *fulfillment*.

Modernist architecture was the most visible emblem of this seemingly unstoppable élan. It had already passed from an experimental stage, where different young architects toyed with aesthetic possibilities, and with striking an effective compromise between a revaluation of the vernacular tradition and a search for the new, into a solid enterprise well integrated with the state's demand for a unifying national language.[14] As architectural historian Adrián Gorelik puts it, "between the 1930s and the 1950s the architectural avant-garde would be able to produce the symbols of this State constructivist voluntarism, and the State would be able the tap into it as the modernizing lever of its ambition for a national culture, society and economy."[15]

It had also became indelibly associated with Kubitschek's own political rise, all the way back to his time as mayor of Belo Horizonte, when he first commissioned the Pampulha complex, a series of architectural projects by Oscar Niemeyer. Gorelik speaks of a veritable "Niemeyer-Kubitschek publicity factory," noting also the "communicational efficacy" of the architect's striking designs, which lent themselves to widespread replication. Niemeyer would thus be more of an "icon giver" than a "form giver."[16]

That Niemeyer's architecture could perform this function was a consequence of its monumental (and somewhat baroque) take on Le Corbusier's "expressive-brutalist movement."[17] Gorelik, however, refrains from dismissing such monumentality as an anachronistic mannerism (i.e., a symptom of late-modernist overcompensation) or a mere dilution of orthodox functionalism: "It is in this profound sense that the architectures of Brasília are monumental: because, just like real monuments, they bring into the present, materially speaking, the event and the will that produced them as finished representations of a modernity that managed to be ethical, political and cultural."[18] Refusing the charge that Brasília was historically out of step, Gorelik argues that it is, on the contrary, profoundly (and multidimensionally) historical. This perhaps reinforced the feeling, shared by a number of critics and artists at that time, that history itself could be disconnected from its apparently unshakeable Eurocentric path and transplanted onto the Brazilian present.

Mário Pedrosa, for one, was aware of the contradictions surrounding the building of the new capital. He was highly skeptical of the government's motivations, but nevertheless believed that the historical magnitude of the project would rise above its political uses, going as far as naming Kubitschek's determination to finish the new capital his only "non-mediocre trait."[19] Pedrosa was won over by the victory of architect Lúcio Costa in the contest for Brasília's urban plan—or Pilot Plan (Plano-Piloto), as it is more commonly known. The critic praised Costa's simple and elegant drawings over a number of scrupulously detailed projects as the triumph of the "thinker over the technician" and of a conception of the "whole" over one that "loses itself" in "details."[20] This, Pedrosa claimed, was the first attempt at a "collective work" that would forcefully group together and justify the constructive endeavors that had been gaining momentum throughout the 1950s: "the new city—the synthesis of arts."[21] The latter became the title of the 1959 congress of the International Association of Art Critics (AICA) that was partially held in the unfinished capital, giving Pedrosa the unique opportunity to present his argument in situ to a worldwide intellectual audience.

That said, the critic remained exceedingly ambivalent about Niemeyer's buildings, sometimes reproaching him for his lack of attention to function, but often endorsing him as well. That Brazilian modernist architects were not aligned with the tenets of orthodox functionalism was no secret. Max Bill had most eloquently denounced it in his controversial 1953 visit to Brazil. Bill, whose ultimate target was Le Corbusier, had insisted on the importance of functionality, criticizing emblematic buildings like that of the Ministry of Education and Health and issuing a harsh judgment: "Brazilian modernist architecture suffers from a taste for the useless, for the simply decorative."[22]

This is where a remarkable contradiction comes to light. For Brazilian concrete artists and poets, as faithful to functionalism as they were, chose to ignore Bill's warnings and support Niemeyer's and Costa's projects, to the point of titling a crucial 1958 manifesto "Pilot Plan for Concrete Poetry." What makes this particularly striking is the fact that there were other contenders in the Pilot Plan selection who were much more aligned with functionalist principles than Costa.[23] "In truth," Gorelik ponders, "the position of the concrete artists proves to be very characteristic, since 'Brazilian modern architecture,' as an embodiment of the Nation-State, was marked by—and had depended upon—a call for unanimity."[24] This adds a twist to the well-rehearsed argument that the Brazilian constructive avant-gardes developed within the climate of a virtually unanimous modernizing front. More precisely, my point is that this "front" was not simply an organic development, nor did it guarantee a neat correspondence between ideological affinity and aesthetic coherence. It was marked instead by a fair degree of voluntarism—that is, by an impulse toward projecting a coherent intellectual front, despite the artistic incoherence that this projection potentially overlooked.

But this was bound to result in a relatively fragile compromise. In fact, such perceived affinities lasted only as long as different sets of artistic products remained relatively ensconced in their own respective circuits, without entering in open confrontation with one another. This, of course, is what happened at the "National Exhibition of Concrete Art," which took place in the early stages of building the new capital. The show was expected to put a definitive stamp on the very idea that there was a national front of constructive artists, but what it actually staged was a severe case of mutual misrecognition. The groups failed to recognize their respective credos in the others' production, to the point—in some cases—of finding the latter utterly incompatible with what they thought they themselves were doing. The artists who would eventually form the neoconcrete group had no interest in identifying themselves with a predetermined set of plastic principles (such as the idea of "mathematical composition" advanced by poet Haroldo de Campos).[25] Feeling no need of prescriptive rules in order to assert that what they were doing was in fact concrete art, they found these rules an absurd and unnecessary constraint (as in Gullar's counterintuitive insistence on *intuition* as a concretist value). But this is not to say that neoconcretism was a kind of "soft" concretism. On the contrary, and this is what I want to stress, the fact that neoconcretists felt entitled to pursue their unorthodox approach can be partially explained by the profound certainty they had about their status as practitioners of concrete art, and Gullar's disagreement with the São Paulo group only encouraged him to fully articulate his theoretical stance.

In short, the artistic avant-garde paradoxically participated in the enthusiasm surrounding constructive practices while simultaneously experiencing a sort of identity crisis that threatened to undermine those same practices. The paradox can be explained by distinguishing two different moments in the course of this crisis. The first, which I have just described, took place in the aftermath of the "National Exhibition," when each group questioned the results and procedures of the other. It can be characterized as a dispute over the *essence* of the concrete artwork. But since this dispute did not yet read as contradiction, the progressive role the concrete artist was assumed to play remained unquestioned. With hindsight, however, it is easy to see that neoconcretism was not simply a divergent position on concrete art, but the work of this fundamental contradiction that it provisionally ignored. Therefore I suggest that neoconcretist theory cannot be fully taken to coincide with its production, since the ideological space that theory had at its disposal required it to voluntarily share in the overall climate of enthusiasm (and thus to disavow contradictions).[26] Neoconcretism is a spectacular symptom of voluntarism precisely in that its members remained confident of their identities as progressive makers of concrete art, in spite of their equally confident belief that concrete art itself should be open to the point of lacking a clear-cut identity. In other words, neoconcretism itself stemmed from the very work of contradiction (as I have argued in relation to Amilcar de Castro), but this would only become clear to Gullar as the voluntarism that surrounded the Brazilian modernist project at large began to wane. And this is precisely the second moment of the aforementioned identity crisis: the loss of faith on the progressive role of the constructive artist.

As a project—that is, as a somewhat idealized mesh of the projections and discourses that formed a "call for unanimity"—Brasília was highly successful. However, just as the ideal of a constructive front was unable to survive the juxtaposition of actual works, the city itself, once *visible*, exceeded the emblem it was expected to be. It was still (and more than ever) an emblem, but one interwoven with contradictions. This becomes evident in photographs taken by Marcel Gautherot in the period surrounding the construction and inauguration of the new capital. His well-publicized images of Niemeyer's buildings contrast with the pictures he took in the shantytowns that grew around Brasília, housing the construction workers and their families. While the former were readily used to illustrate numerous magazine spreads, publishers remained uninterested, for example, in his pictures of *Sacolândia* (see figure 2.11). As critic Lorenzo Mammì notes, the latter remained faithful to Gautherot's usual anthropological style, in contrast with the formal language of emptiness and visual amplitude he developed in order to portray the monumental architecture of the Pilot Plan. On the one hand, the critic argues, this would signal the impossibility of a common language for both situations.[27] On the other, it leads to yet another fracture, not between two contrasting kinds of photography by the same photographer, but between two contradictory modes of representation that clash within one and the same image. In one particular shot, taken from under the shadows of one of the buildings that were being built at the Ministries Esplanade, similar structures luminously rise from a misty bank, across a road that is itself under construction. For Mammì, the play of shadows is reminiscent of a very diverse kind of image, namely Gautherot's photographs of the Amazon rainforest, a scenario completely devoid of horizon and historically hostile to clear, objective representations.[28] So, in the Esplanade image, the workers who divide the scene not only animate the epic event (the construction itself) but also serve, in the image, as a kind of "dam" that prevents, in the critic's terms, the "anthropological Brazil" from mixing with the "ideal Brazil."[29]

What is important in Mammì's interpretation is that it situates the social segregation of the workers beyond the strictly sociological level of urban or economic inequality. Otherwise put, inequality is aesthetically encoded in the photographs in such a manner that it is forcefully referred back to the profound, irreconcilable historical contradictions at the core of Brazilian identity. The workers were all immigrants from other parts of the country (they became known as *candangos*, which eventually turned into a nickname for the Brasília-born). Thus the very impossibility of national integration was dramatically enacted in the relay among photography, architecture, and urbanism, and in how these introduced a historical weight that far surpassed the sociological dimension of Brasília's actual construction.

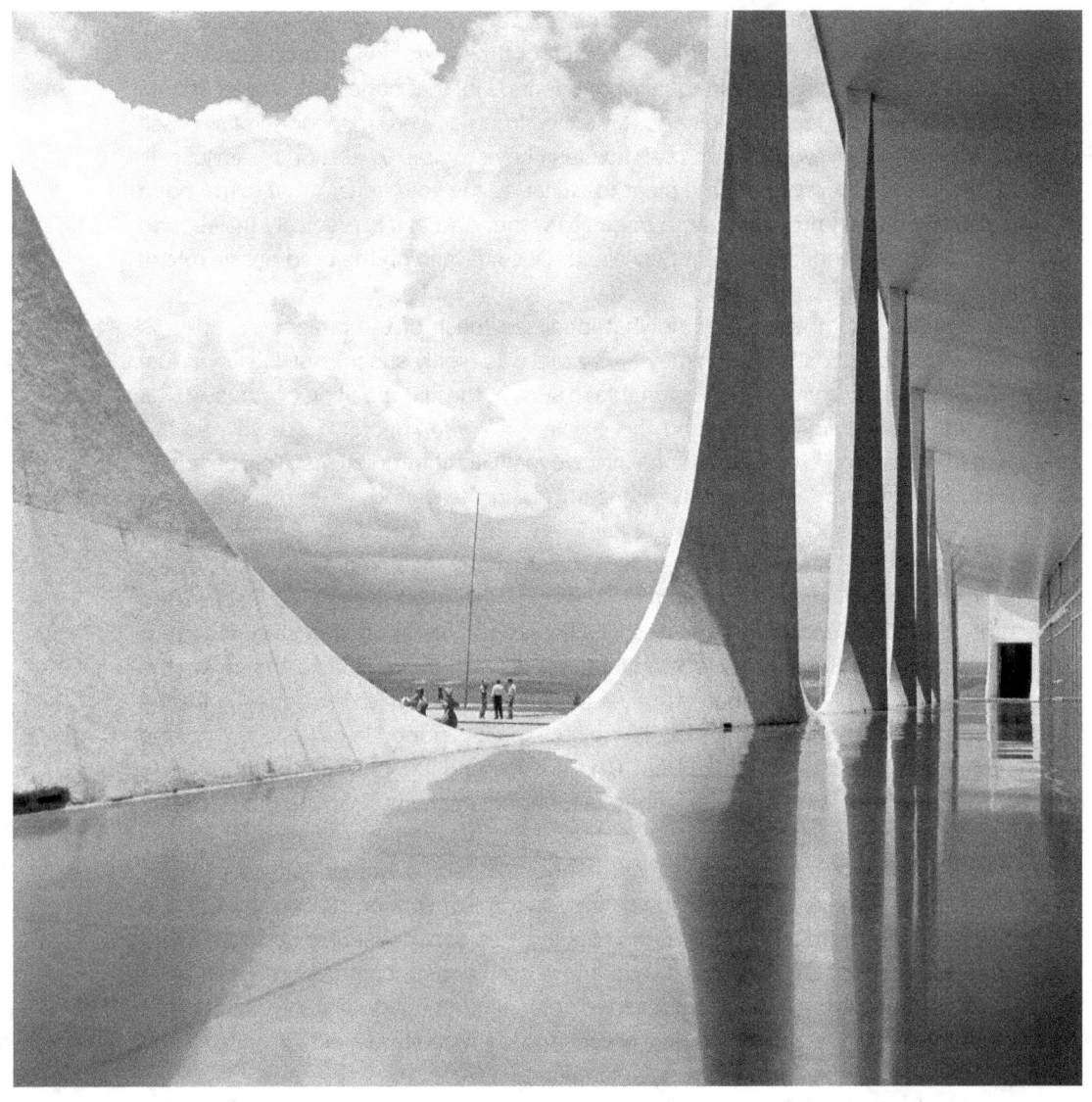

3.6
Marcel Gautherot, *Detail of the Inverted Arches Structure of the Alvorda Palace*, ca. 1962. Marcel Gautherot / Acervo Instituto Moreira Salles.

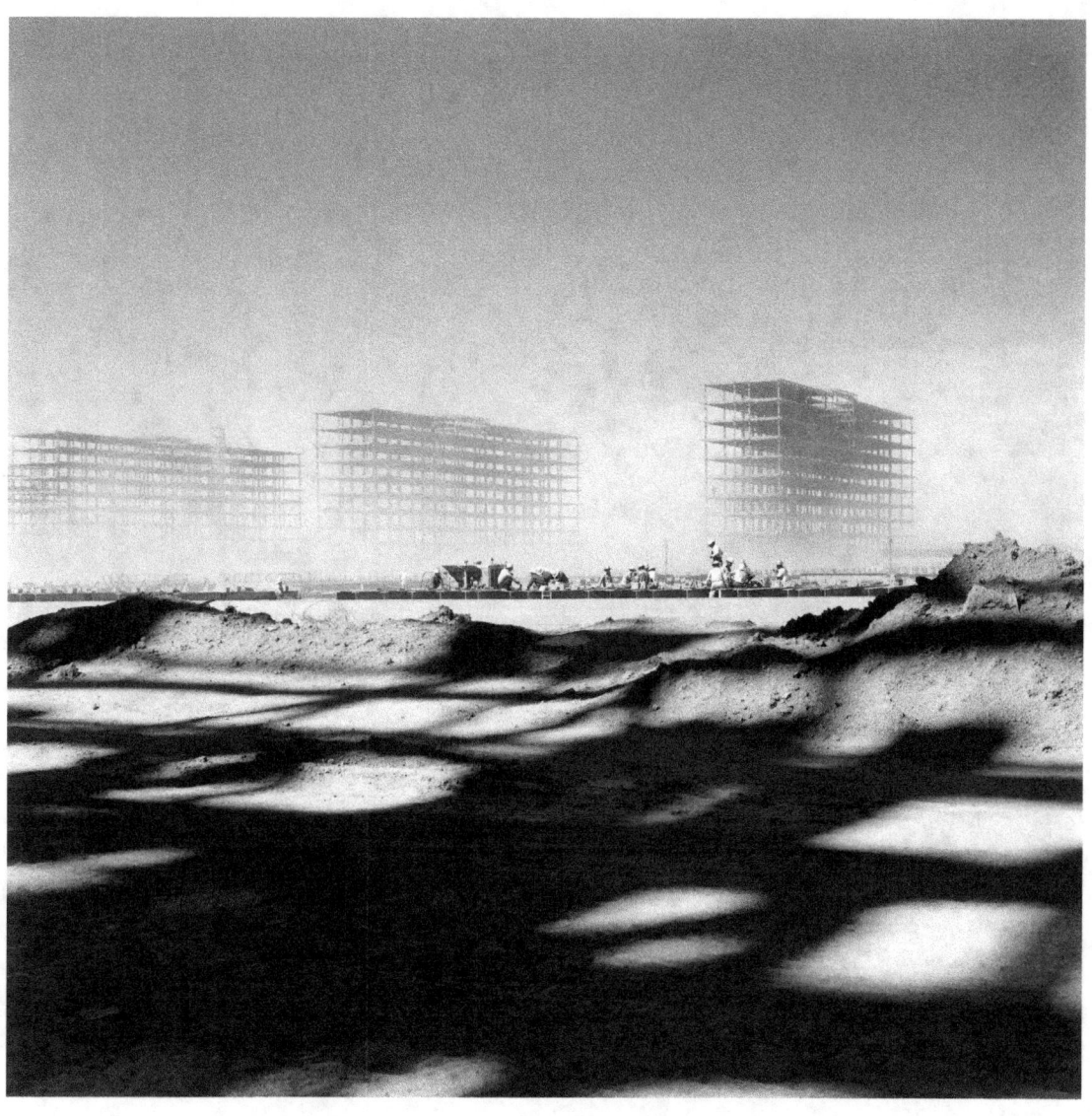

3.7
Marcel Gautherot, *Ministries under
Construction*, ca. 1958. Marcel Gautherot /
Acervo Instituto Moreira Salles.

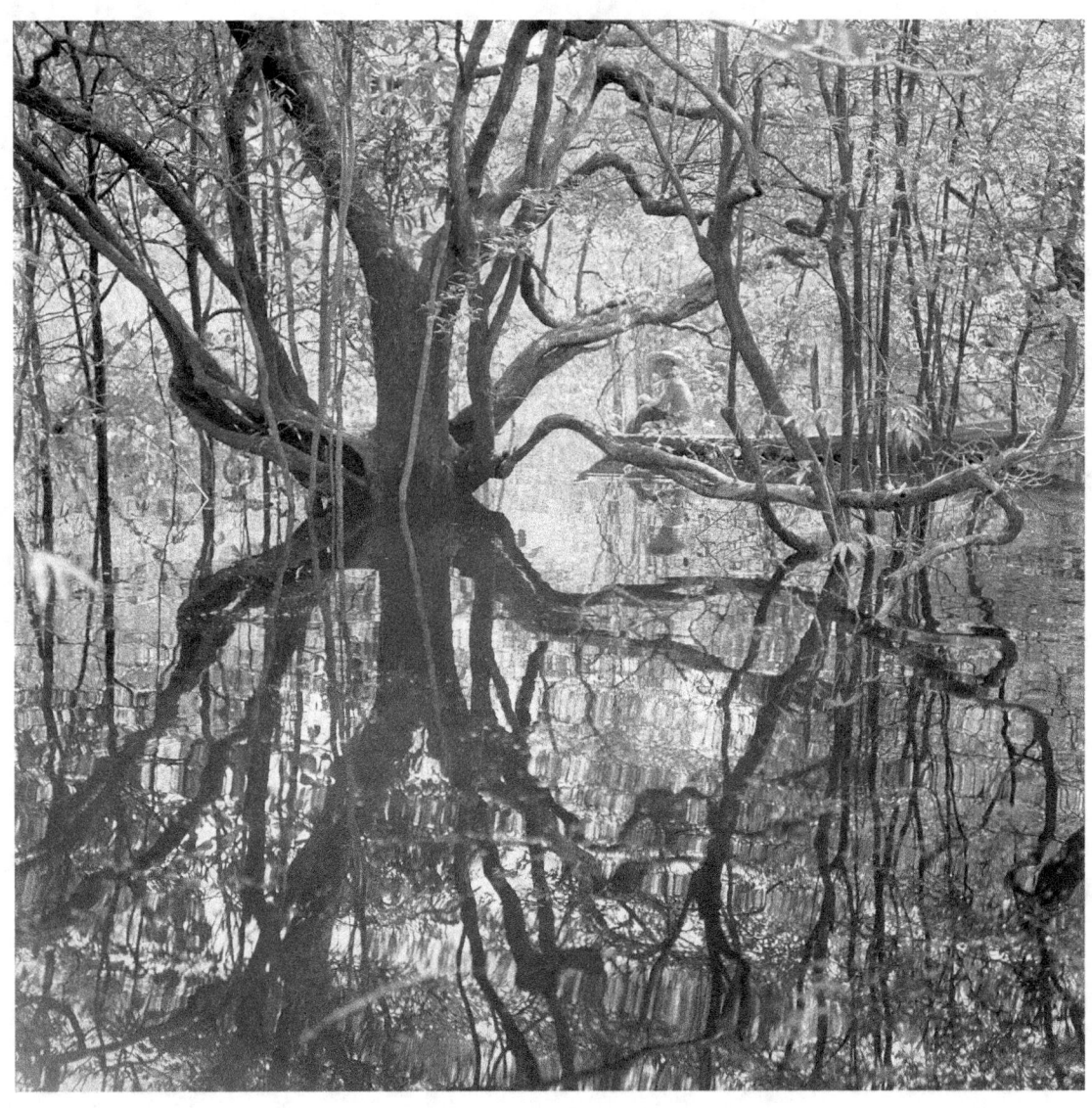

3.8
Marcel Gautherot, *Igapós*, ca. 1955. Marcel
Gautherot / Acervo Instituto Moreira Salles.

This is why the contradictory side of Brasília literally converges with Gullar's rejection of neoconcretism. As we have seen, the poet was struck by the situation of the *candangos*, which brought him into "renewed contact"—as he put it—with his own northeastern origins.[30] This obviously was neither a description of national integration nor of individual reconciliation with one's past, but rather of the geography of class division in Brazil, suddenly mapped onto the (peculiar) history of an individual. Gullar was struck not simply by poverty (which was by no means exclusive to Brasília), but also by the indelible inscription of the contradiction at the heart of the Brazilian modernist project—again, how striking is the use of empty concrete bags in the *Sacolândia* shacks? If one is to consider the poet's turn from a historical perspective, then a careful distinction must be made: it is not simply a question of sudden awareness, as if he awakened to a social reality he previously ignored and that rendered the whole modernist project obsolete. It is rather that the project itself was shown to be constituted by an irreducible contradiction—this is the moment when neoconcretism finally became apparent for what it truly was. The revelation may have been sociopolitical, but it was also aesthetic, in the sense that it jeopardized both the kind of constructive art Gullar endorsed and the very identity construct he embodied. *Sacolândia* is thus the missing link between this second moment in the "identity crisis" of the Brazilian constructive avant-garde and a third and definitive one: the self-imploding synthesis *Tropicália* operates as it levels the disparate elements that floated around the Brazilian ideological scene into an accumulation of images.[31]

COLLECTIVITY

Gullar would stage a return—of sorts—to Brasília in 1967. He provided voiceover narration for director Joaquim Pedro de Andrade's aptly titled short film *Brasília: Contradictions of a New City*. The film starts with the camera coolly traveling all over the Pilot Plan, accompanied by an instrumental track by Erik Satie, while the poet's expressionless voice uniformly describes broader aspects of the urban layout and the more intimate lifestyle projected for the residential superblocks. The latter, viewers are told, are "the domain of comfortable family life."[32] The irony at this point is still very subtle, as if we were being presented a somewhat awkward cinematic prospectus of the city.

But soon the project's letdowns, marked by its "incompleteness" more than five years after the inauguration, are revealed. These are followed by mocking passages, such as the deadpan reminder of the bureaucratic anticlimax of utopia—"for the top ranked [public officials], despite the comfort of their homes, Brasília remains a distant and inconvenient workplace."[33] As the account reaches a critical crescendo, Gullar's narration gives way to various testimonies. These range from University of Brasília students voicing their unhappiness about the scrapping of its innovative academic program by the military government, to working-class families chronicling their isolation in distant areas and shantytowns. The last half of the film centers on the failed promise of social integration and on the exclusion of the *candangos*, which the narrator connects to "the basic conflict of Brazilian art beyond the reach of most people." The narration finishes by claiming that these are problems common to all Brazilian cities, but which "become unbearably exposed" in the capital, and ends up urging: "We need to change this reality so we can see in the face of the people how beautiful a city can be."[34]

These last passages are reminiscent of the social theory of art Gullar developed in his book *Culture in Question* (*Cultura posta em questão*, written in 1963 and published in 1965).[35] Pedrosa had taken Brasília as the "synthesis of arts," a "collective art work" that held the potential to "reintegrate in the conscience the dignity of a social mission."[36] For Gullar, however, Brasília proved to be no synthesis: the fact that Brazilian modernist architecture had been conceived *as art* was evidence, he claimed, of its failure to achieve a collective dimension. In his view, the formal expressiveness of Brazilian architecture was understandable as a reaction to a strictly "theoretical" European functionalism, which had veiled social relations, but it also showed that even a practice so intrinsically embedded in socioeconomic conditions as architecture had become trapped, in Brazil, within an individualist logic.[37] Gullar went on to condemn, in similar terms, neoconcretism's failure to transcend artistic individuality and formulate a collective paradigm for art. Brasília merely confirmed neoconcretism's impasse and "unbearably exposed" it—that is, it elevated it to the status of a broader sociocultural symptom. No wonder then that the poet had proposed destroying neoconcretism by either "scattering his poems throughout the city's gardens" or by blowing them up right after the inauguration of a final exhibition.[38] It is possible to read those dramatic gestures—having artworks destroyed or dissolved within the city—as a pair, whereby one would stand as a metaphor for the impasses of failed individuality and the other for a desperate commitment to collectivity.

There is some truth in Gullar's indictment. If the emergence of new museums and of the São Paulo Biennial played a part in reshaping the agenda of Brazilian art, the institutional consistency thus generated remained too precarious and patchy, failing to overcome, as critic Sônia Salzstein has noted, "a loose notion of the antagonisms between public and private spheres."[39] The Museum of Modern Art in Rio de Janeiro is an illustrative case in point. It has been perhaps more significant for the artists of the Frente and neoconcrete groups as a meeting point where they could develop interpersonal relations (in its canteen, classes, and events), than as the headquarters for the development of a public institutional platform that would circulate and consolidate their program, which remained relatively incipient.[40] More than anything else, then, the museum was a kind of laboratory or "second home," a role it would maintain throughout the 1960s. Even Gullar's extraordinarily innovative experience in the *SDJB* was also short-lived and dependent on relatively spontaneous and unstable personal associations.[41] What the poet thus resented and identified as the "basic contradiction of individualist art" was the failure of the latter to coalesce into a collective experience that would provide convincing social grounds for the formulation of an aesthetic project—a failure echoed and confirmed with a vengeance by modernist architecture.[42]

What the Popular Center of Culture (CPC), a cultural branch of the student movement, offered Gullar as he returned from Brasília was precisely a blueprint for the kind of collective experience he hoped for. Sociologist Carlos Estevam Martins, Gullar's predecessor in the CPC's presidency, would retrospectively justify the CPC's option for a "popular revolutionary art" by pointing to the political atmosphere that followed the unexpected resignation of Kubitschek's successor Jânio Quadros. The rise of the more left-leaning João Goulart, formerly Kubitschek's and Quadros's vice president, was met with resistance and political turmoil to the point that attempts—legal or not—were made to prevent him from taking power. According to Martins, the CPC was born in the wake of a constitutionalist mobilization that ensured Goulart's inauguration, and which was followed by "the perfect sensation that the popular classes had won."[43] In this context, the CPC began to regard art as the catalyst that would accelerate what it perceived as an already ongoing "rise of the masses."[44] Goulart's political gambit relied on perceptions of this kind, as he ambivalently allowed leftist hopes to grow while simultaneously positioning himself as the one politician who would be able to keep tensions in check. However, without the benefit of Kubitschek's economic and symbolic momentum, and in the more radicalized atmosphere that followed the 1959 Cuban revolution, Goulart's strategy went awry and he was eventually overwhelmed by the political tensions that led to the 1964 military coup.[45]

What I want to suggest is that Gullar's "conversion" from constructive to "engaged" was not as extreme as it may seem.[46] With hindsight it is possible to see that, structurally speaking, it was actually a *continuation*. Of what, one might ask, since his political and aesthetic coordinates seemed to undergo such a profound change. The answer is: of one's mode of participation in a *fantasy*. The idea that his shock in 1961 led to a sort of political "awakening," which led him in turn to reject avant-gardist "alienation," is telling in this respect, since the very term warrants a comparison with something that at first sight seems very like a fantasy: the dream. But, as Slavoj Žižek argues, such an intuitive link between alienation and dream would be crucially misguided:

> the only point at which we approach this hard kernel of the Real is indeed the dream. When we awaken into reality after a dream, we usually say to ourselves "it was just a dream," thereby blinding ourselves to the fact that in our everyday, wakening reality we are *nothing but a consciousness of this dream*. It was only in the dream that we approached the fantasy-framework which determines our activity, our mode of acting in reality itself.[47]

I have already noted the deeply teleological component of Gullar's "Theory of the Non-object" and how neoconcretism insisted on the progressive identity of the constructive artist. The point is that these are two sides of one and the same coin: the neoconcrete artist was conceived as intrinsically progressive *because* neoconcretism was supposed to be the historical destination of modern art. In the same way, the activity of the popular-revolutionary artist was sustained by the perception that a popular revolution was inexorably approaching. In both cases, a teleological fantasy is enacted to reinforce political convictions. Gullar's distinctive role in both moments involved the exchange of one set of fantasy coordinates for another without necessarily challenging the structure of fantasy itself.[48] In other words, he rightly noticed that neoconcretism was founded on a contradiction, but ultimately averted his eyes from this contradiction instead of assuming it, as if it were "just a dream." The reality he awakened to was equally a fantasy, albeit one that, in the early 1960s, proved more efficient in keeping that "hard kernel of the Real" — in other words, the crux of contradiction — at bay. Once again, Oiticica's later formulation in "Brazil Diarrhea" about the need to plunge "into the shit" is nothing but a recognition of an alternative path, namely that of delving deeper into the contradictions inherent in one's position.[49]

In short, the collective basis of both the constructive and the national-popular aspects of the fantasy were similarly inconsistent. In the CPC's case, this was due not only to overwhelming external circumstances (the military coup), but also to internal divisions that already were beginning to show. Gullar himself became increasingly skeptical of what he perceived as Martins's excessively narrow "sectarianism." *Culture in Question* was conceived both as a critique of that and of its author's earlier avant-gardism.[50] Martins was not unaware that his aesthetic theory was at odds with the artistic aspirations of many CPC militants, but he nevertheless believed that this was a theoretical problem to be solved *in advance* of actual art making. To embrace a "consequent revolutionary attitude" and abandon formal experimentation was not to conform to a doctrine, but consciously to limit artistic language in order to communicate effectively with "the people" ("It is not from the CPC that [the limits of creative activity] come, but from the artist himself").[51] In other words, artists should not engage in formal investigation or in self-reflexive questions about their role because their very commitment to revolutionary art implied that those issues were already sorted out. Both Gullar and Martins took the collective ground of revolutionary art for granted, but the poet was nevertheless more dialectical in trying to pry this conclusion from a diagnosis of modernist art and architecture. His description of intellectual engagement sounds, in this regard, like a self-assessment: "Such a decision by the intellectual is a direct consequence of the falling apart of that ideal figure of the man of culture, as if he hovered above concrete problems, dealing with absolute values and fulfilling a role that was always beneficial to society."[52] In other words, while Martins took avant-gardism as a futile exercise of bourgeois decadence to be *dismissed*, Gullar regarded it as a serious episode in the history of Brazilian culture that should be critically taken into account in order to be *overcome*.

A particularly polemical affair ensued over *Five Times Favela* (1962), perhaps the CPC's most ambitious production and the only film ever finished in its short existence.[53] As the name implies, it consists of five episodes that revolve around the favelas and the precarious existence of their dwellers. So, for example, one of the stories (Leon Hirzsman's *São Diogo Quarry*) was a tale of collective resistance, in contrast to another, in which individual revolt ultimately proves pointless in face of widespread conformism (Miguel Borges's *Zé da cachorra*). The level of professionalism and formal awareness of the episodes varied immensely, with Joaquim Pedro de Andrade's (*Cat Skin*, which earned international prizes on its own) and Hirszman's (explicitly drawing from Sergei Eisenstein's use of montage) clearly standing out. These discrepancies attracted mixed feedback from the CPC's own ranks. Martins, who was involved in the film's production, criticized the excessive attention paid to formal experimentation and is said to have dismissed Andrade's episode as "the spiritual journey of a cat."[54] Moreover, *Five Times Favela* reportedly failed to engage working-class audiences.[55] Effectively, the film's lack of coherence indicated that the CPC's carefully detailed rationale for a "popular revolutionary art" failed to translate consistently into a cultural product, especially one of the magnitude of a long feature film, thus betraying the collective fantasy that grounded it.

Some of the *Five Times Favela* directors ended up leaving the CPC in the midst of bitter polemical exchanges with Martins. Gullar, for his part, sought to loosen the CPC's orthodoxy during his own term as president, but his efforts were cut short by the military coup. In the years following the coup, *cinema novo* directors gradually engaged in a self-reflexive exercise, seeking to discuss the failure of the intellectual left and the misconceptions they had embraced—Glauber Rocha's *Entranced Land* (1967), with its exhilarating portrayal of populism, failed hopes, political compromise, and misguided identification with "the people," remains the sharpest case in point.[56] It may be too far a stretch to include Andrade's *Brasília* in the list, but there is no missing the significance of having the former neoconcretist leader ambiguously describing the concrete-clad stage of his self-misrecognition. Actually, this particular issue—self-misrecognition—is the critical common denominator between some of the most emblematic exemplars of self-portraiture and self-inscription that Brazilian artists realized in the mid- to late 1960s. From this perspective, self-portraiture may be seen as a means of formulating a countersubject to the voluntarism that marked both the modernist and the national-popular attempts to articulate a collective artistic or political front, or both.

NOWHERE ELSE

In this respect, Dias's *My Portrait* is a striking case in point. Subjective displacement is at play in two of the work's most arresting features: its quasi-facelessness and its pronominal transaction with the viewer. Am I looking at an imprint of a face or at a mask? And if it is a mask, is it simply in front of me, or is it implying (it being *my* portrait, after all) that I am the one expected to don it? Does this body confront me or does it mockingly act as a stand-in for me—or perhaps both?

Dias relies on the fact, as Émile Benveniste has famously put it, that "language is so organized that it permits each speaker to *appropriate to himself* an entire language by designating himself as *I*."[57] What is more, he is employing the pronominal form in explicit opposition to the nonpronominal "self-portrait." By doing so, the nature of the pronominal form becomes instantly perceivable in the failure of the title *My Portrait* to pass off smoothly as a self-portrait. The latter, of course, is the artistic genre par excellence in which the distance between the subject of enunciation and the subject of the enunciated would seem to be eclipsed. Dias's linguistic operation in *My Portrait* inverts such a categorical effect by turning the work, so to speak, into a "wedge" that holds the two stances of utterance apart, and thus productively in tension. This tension, circumscribed within a single artwork, creates an effect similar to that of holding two magnets of opposite polarities a short distance apart without touching each other. It is the moment when we perceive the force that binds them together in action precisely because the actual bond is prevented from occurring.[58] The reflexivity of the "self"—the sense that the portrait is simultaneously and inextricably a product and a representation of the artist's selfhood—is kept in suspension.

Such vacuity is even more pronounced in *Sun Photo as Self-Portrait* (1968), a work in which Dias already adopts a more arid, conceptual vocabulary. As a portrait, it must be admitted, the work is something of a letdown. The only thing its black surface can be said to represent is the purely mechanical consequence of the process described in the title—photographic overexposure to direct sunlight. In this scenario, the word "self" is left unaccounted for; its ostensive but absurd presence ultimately makes it awkward (one might accept a more ironic reading, whereby a photograph of the sun would be presented as a self-portrait, as a symptom of utter egocentrism). However, despite its assumed representational failure, a "sun photo" would still remain functional as a photograph in its barest form, that is, as an index. Dias would indeed take this suggestion to an extreme in *The Art of Transference* (1972), a work he explains with recourse to a childhood memory:

My father went home and darkened a piece of glass with oil fumes. No one had explained to me that it was an eclipse. My father looked at the sun through the glass. Everything went dark and afterwards everything went back to normal. I thought my father was performing magic. Almost 25 years later I repeated the operation of smoking a larger piece of glass with burnt oil. The heat was high and I sweat a lot. I knew that with the passage of time the grease from the body could print in the glass. When it was completely covered with soot I put it on a flat surface and I hit it with my face. After I cleaned the excess of soot there was my portrait as if it were a negative.[59]

Read together, *Sun Photo as Self-Portrait* and *The Art of Transference* describe the photographic self-portrait caught in a Bataillean fall of Icarus. Once the self-portrait gets too close to its supposed truth, "it is no longer production that appears in light, but refuse or combustion" (a failure that resonates with the tragic outcome of the intellectual hero in *Entranced Land*).[60] The closest thing to the blackness of the earlier work is not the precision of its graphics, but the utter lack of self-reflexivity of grease and soot in *The Art of Transference*, where a (negative) self-portrait is paradoxically imprinted on a base material that obscures transparency (of both glass and self).

Now, there is a proper conceptual denominator for these various efforts of short-circuiting the coalescence of the self: *anti-egomorphism*.[61] What is striking about *My Portrait* and other related works is that this remainder of earlier avant-gardist formulations is now smuggled into the heart of a genre that, at first sight, is utterly antithetical to it. And yet there is a telling precedent for such an operation: Hélio Oiticica's *B33 Box Bolide 18—Poem Box 2 "Homage to Cara de Cavalo."*[62] The work displays a photograph Oiticica bought from newspaper archives showing the body of Cara de Cavalo, a famous outlaw who was shot dead by the police and whom Oiticica had befriended in his forays into the Rio de Janeiro favelas. It is true that *Box Bolide 18* is not simply a portrait, and even less a self-portrait. But let us recall the reason why I first mentioned this work and look again at two of the best-known photographs ever taken of it (see figures 2.12 and 2.13): the strangeness of Oiticica's confrontational attitude in exposing *Box Bolide 18* fully open to the camera, as opposed to the usual attitude, visible in the photo of his friend Luisa with the same *Bolide* (and consistent with existing images of Oiticica himself manipulating earlier *Bolides*), of joyful absorption in the experience of manipulating the work. The inscription in *Box Bolide 18* confirms that the martyred Cara de Cavalo is *exhibited*: "HERE HE IS AND WILL REMAIN! CONTEMPLATE HIS HEROIC SILENCE."[63] It is as if Oiticica is kneeling beside the work in defiant reverence (defying the viewer and reverencing the work, that is), about to exclaim: "Lo!" He effectively flashes the whole thing open to the viewer. Or rather to a *public*, for the fact that this is a newspaper photograph is by no means irrelevant: the work is clearly opposed to the public consumption of that image as an uncritical celebration of the outlaw's demise (it is opposed, in short, to another kind of exhibition of his body: that of a prize).[64] Whatever the offensive or subversive content of *Box Bolide 18*, it is to be thrown in the public's face in an *outward* movement totally at odds with most *Bolides*.

I have also discussed how the contrast between Oiticica's and Luisa's attitudes reflects the contrast at the heart of the *Parangolés* between participants who don the capes and dance and those who only watch.[65] Again, bourgeois patrons of the Museum of Modern Art would never wear the capes as easily or eagerly as samba dancers summoned for that purpose or other artists.[66] This is actually a sign of a social division:

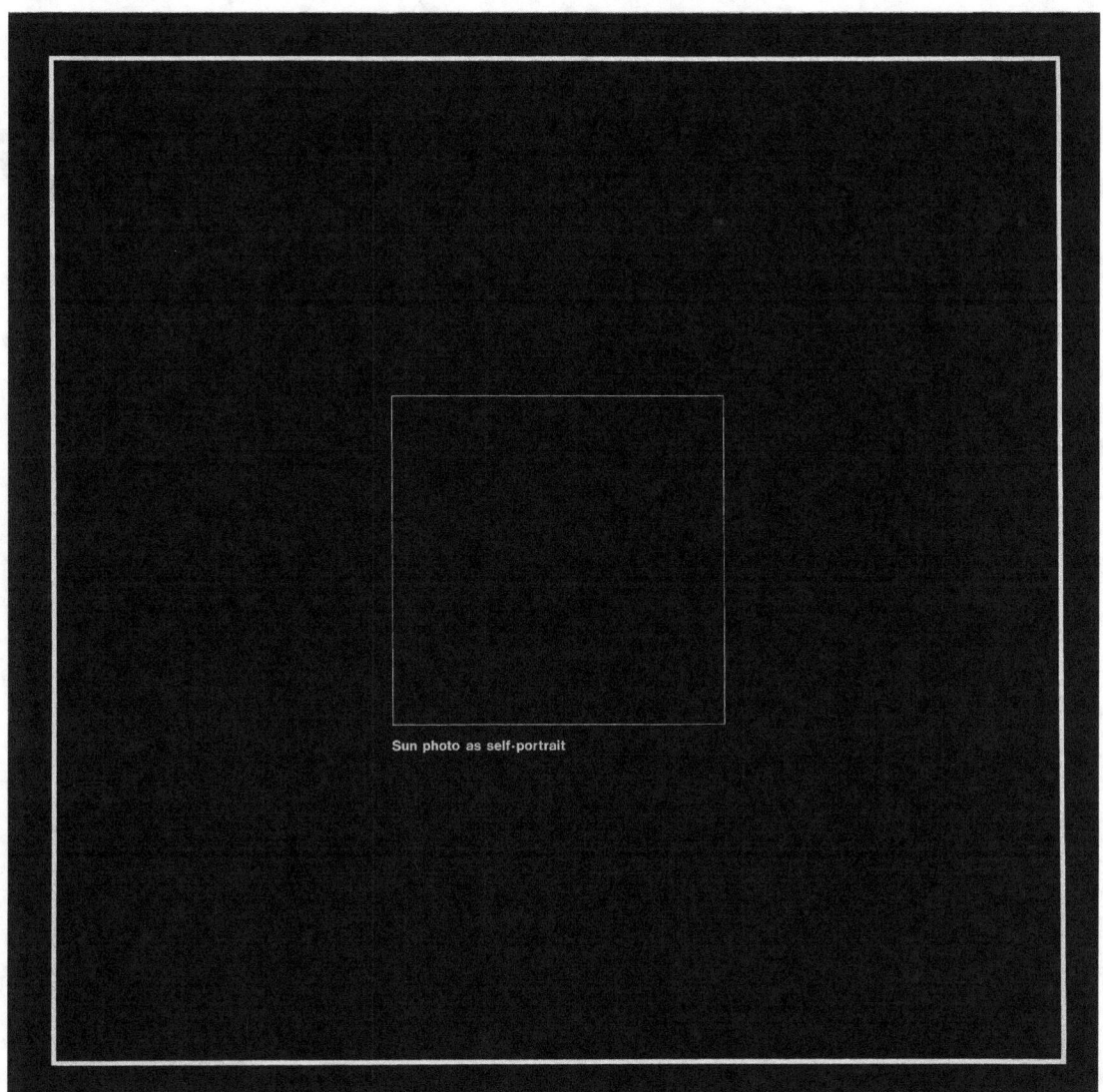

Sun photo as self-portrait

3.9
Antonio Dias, *Sun Photo as Self-Portrait*,
1968. Acrylic on canvas, 150 × 150 cm. Private
collection. Courtesy of the artist.

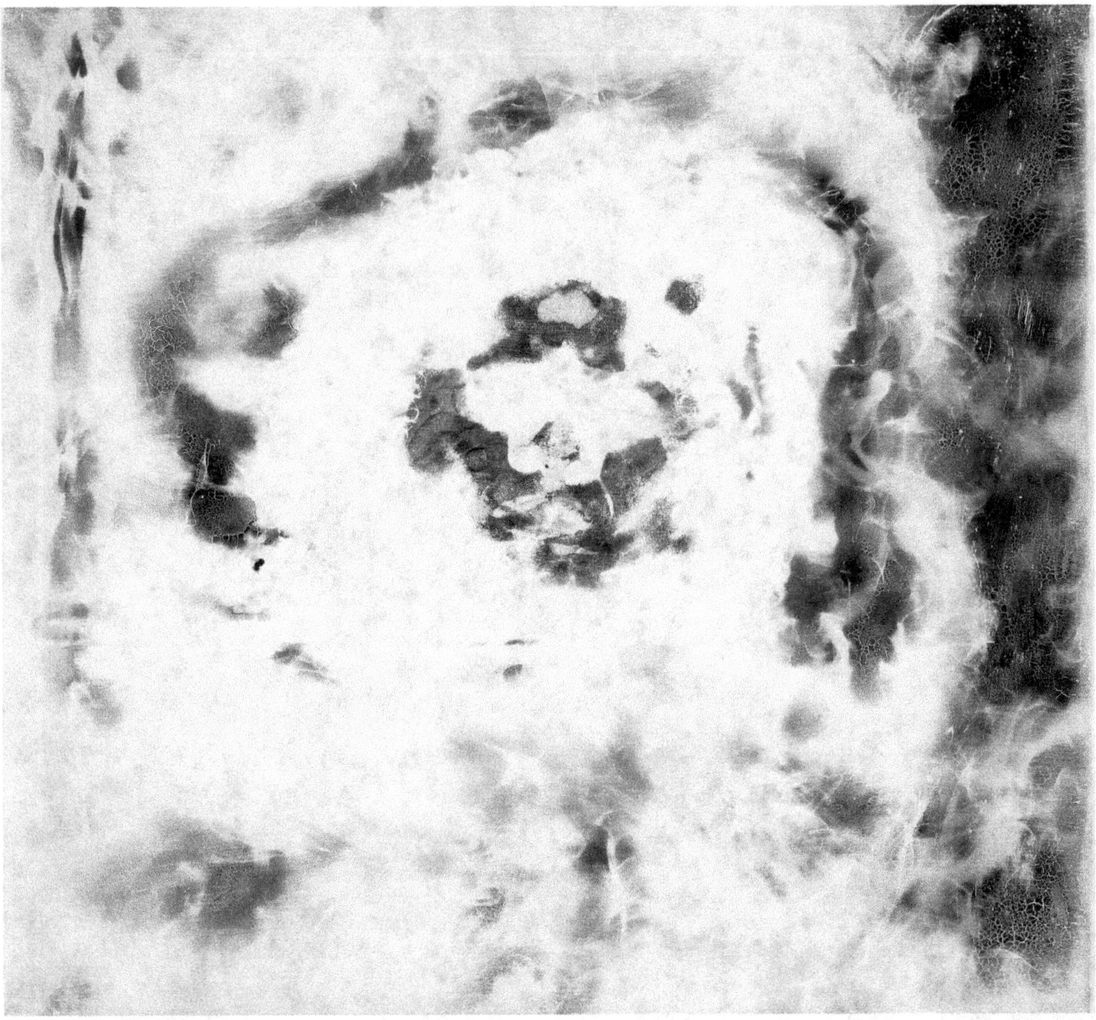

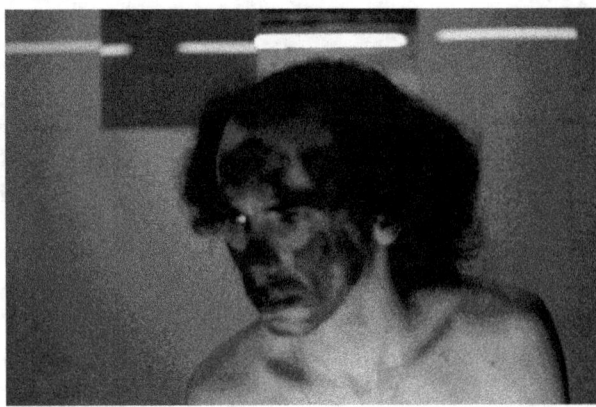

3.10
Antonio Dias, *The Art of Transference*, 1972. Soot on glass, 62 × 67 cm. Collection of the artist. Courtesy of the artist.

3.11
Antonio Dias after the making of *The Art of Transference*. Photo: Iole de Freitas. Courtesy of the artist.

the fact that the dancers, mostly black, were unexpectedly barred from entering the museum at the first showing of the *Parangolé* speaks of this more than of artistic conservatism. Although it is true that Oiticica did at times romanticize his relationship with the favela, sometimes forgetting how much of a foreigner he inevitably was, even the most enthusiastic celebrations of cross-social ease betrayed signs of its actual impossibility. Take, for example, this rhyme written in the aftermath of the "Opinião 65" show by one of its organizers, Romanian dealer Jean Boghici, when a puzzled newspaper arts columnist asked him to explain the *Parangolés*:

What is *Parangolé*?
Parangolé is what it is
It is the myth
Hélio Oiticica, our national Flash Gordon
Flies not through sidereal space
Flies instead across social layers[67]

On the one hand, this is a telling sign of the cultural climate surrounding avant-gardist interventions in the mid-1960s, pointing as it does to the anthropophagic assimilation of pop culture (a topic I will soon turn to). On the other, if Oiticica is treated as no less than a comic-strip hero, this is due to the "heroic" (i.e., herculean) task of crossing social boundaries. Writing one week earlier in the same newspaper column where Boghici's rhyme was published, critic Vera Pacheco Jordão noted that most of the public felt "shocked" and "disgusted" at the works showed in "Opinião 65" and tried to explain part of Oiticica's definition of "vivência-total-Parangolé" (Parangolé-lived-through-experience), but not without ironically remarking that it was "a state we hope to someday achieve, either in this incarnation or in the next."[68] This is unusual for Jordão, who was usually supportive of the avant-garde. Her ironic posture may well be an ambivalent nod to a traditional public that, at least according to the newspapers, was feeling somewhat bemused or alienated.

If Oiticica's photograph excluded viewers by antagonistically addressing them, Luisa's photograph further increased this exclusion instead of appeasing it, for she embodied a kind of experiential joy that viewers could witness, but that was ultimately out of (socially accepted) bounds. The same applies to the fact that Nildo, one of the Mangueira dancers, reportedly coauthored one of the *Parangolés* by suggesting the rebellious statement embroidered in it—"I am possessed."[69] The idea of possession indicates a kind of bodily ecstasy that is socially and geographically circumscribed, for example, in the poor *terreiros* (backyards) of Afro-Brazilian religions. This is a further sign that Oiticica's cross-social "flight" was far from easy or unproblematic—least of all for himself, as close friends such as Waly Salomão later recalled.[70] Hints of this conflicting experience began to emerge, and this is precisely what I take his photograph to be: Oiticica's stern, confrontational gaze, at odds with the usual experience of the *Bolides*, means that he could not possibly identify with the favela in a complete manner. But he could nevertheless ground his self-inscription on the antagonism set up by the work, making it act not as a mediator, but as an edge, an embodiment of antagonism per se, a point of confrontation between two conflicting realities. In other words, if he couldn't "belong" to the favela, he could at least choose to belong to nowhere else than the confrontational ground opened up by his own work.

My Portrait echoes, at least in part, the manipulatory experience of *Bolides* (the penile protrusion in Dias's work actually has a built-in coil, as the artist expected viewers to touch it or pull it). But, more importantly, it brings the antagonist friction of *Box Bolide 18* to bear on the viewer's phenomenological, semiotic, and political self-awareness. Indeed, the work is very focused in this respect. Most of Dias's earlier works resembled comic strips or storyboards, thus suggesting proto-narratives or offering plenty of disparate elements for the viewer to free-associate. But *My Portrait*'s bodily ensemble introduces a considerable semiotic constraint. This looks like a more controlled experiment, but one that paradoxically undermines the stability of the viewer's position. Take the "arms" of the figure, for example: art critic Paulo Herkenhoff has described these as knots that "indicate the ability to say no; they install political resistance."[71] What the critic alludes to is the expression in Portuguese "being with one's arms crossed." This can connote either an attitude of passivity ("being with one's arms crossed" while something is happening means the refusal to take action, that is, a potential alienation) or of active resistance (newspaper language typically states that workers "crossed their arms," that is, initiated a strike). Both meanings, though opposed, derive from the same point—of doing nothing. Yet under an authoritarian government committed to the protection of business interests, to have workers "doing nothing" is potentially disruptive and outright confrontational.[72]

In different ways, then, such works engage in a disturbing mode of self-reflection, which was also a way to reflect on the dilemmas involved in the perceived urgency of articulating aesthetic and political stances at the time. In keeping with the work of *cinema novo* filmmakers and tropicalist musicians, the visual-arts avant-garde elaborated on the realization that there were no sure coordinates grounding one's aesthetic position or attaching it unequivocally to a progressive political project. In short, politically informed artistic practices no longer were to be associated with particular projections (or fantasies) of collectivity. Oiticica would still call for a collective "position-taking in relation to political, social and ethical problems," but not without making the proviso that this should start from the effort of extracting "from individual creative efforts the principal items of these same efforts, in an attempt to group them culturally," and not the other way around.[73] While this "attempt" was obviously at odds with the strategies advocated by the student left, this was by no means the only critical counterpoint to the 1960s avant-garde.

POP

In many of his best-known works, Rubens Gerchman represents various settings of urban life, such as buses and apartment blocks, as boxes filled with the anonymous, serialized silhouettes of dwellers and commuters. These works may well propose a critical viewpoint on a commodified everyday life, but do they readily suggest alternative collective experiences? On the contrary, it might seem that Gerchman's work often compensates for oppressive anonymity with an iconographic immersion in a domestic universe of suburban kitsch. As the artist puts it, in his interview with Gullar and Dias: "There are too many people making boxes nowadays.... I will make a 'dying box' and close the series. I thought of making a whole city with all its 'boxes'.... I now want to paint the city from the inside, what happens in the homes. I'm very interested by the suburban homes, by their curtains, their embroidered towels and their 'bad taste' jars. I want to paint that."[74] In the interview's introduction, Gullar remarks that their painting is consciously adapted to "an age of mass communication."[75] This brings us to the other side of the "communication" coin, namely pop art and its uneasy reception in Brazil.

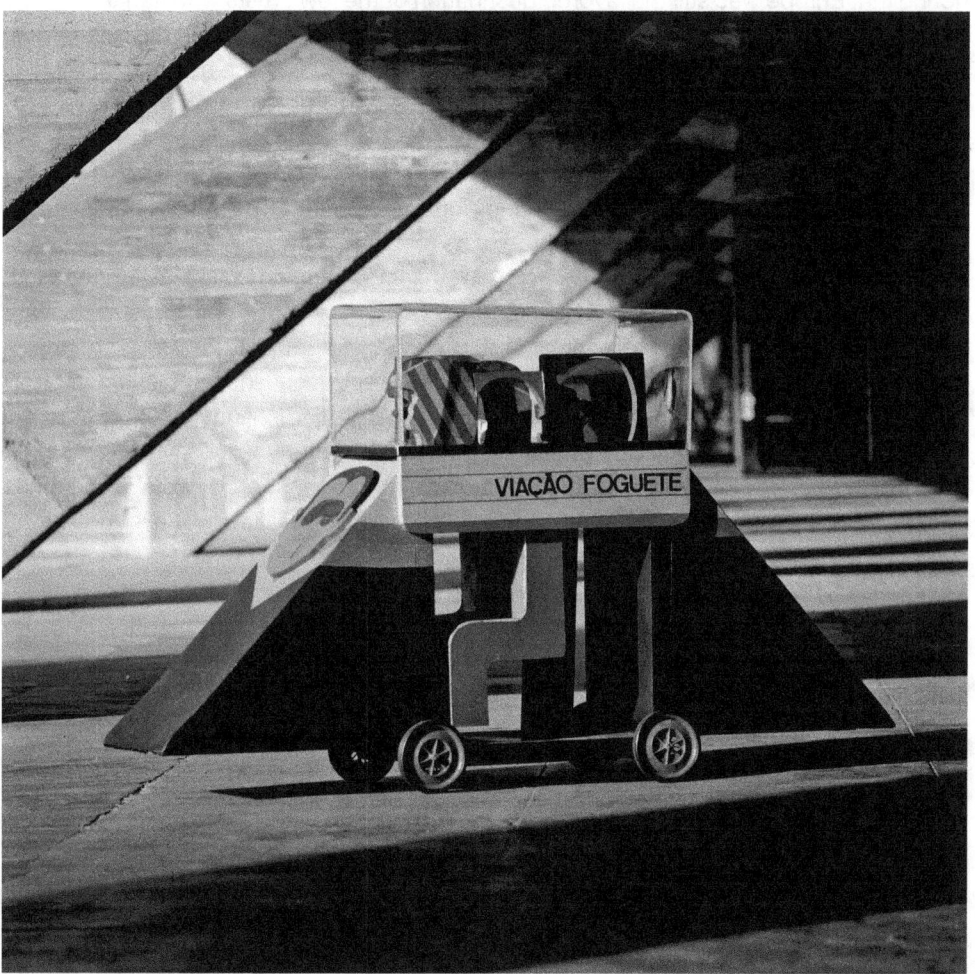

3.12
Rubens Gerchman, *Viação Foguete*, 1965.
Acrylic box and industrial paint on wood,
119 × 208 × 43 cm. Coleção Gilberto
Chateaubriand, Museu de Arte Moderna
do Rio de Janeiro. Licensed by inARTS.com.
Photo: Pedro Oswaldo Cruz.

In an atmosphere charged with political radicalizations, pop was largely frowned upon. It was usually regarded as too acquiescent to consumerist society, if not an outright case of imperialist propaganda. Many critics, Gullar included, were keen to point out how irreducible Dias's and Gerchman's work was to pop (and Nouveau Réalisme), despite whatever similarities one might eventually spot. "They acknowledge a hamburger," Dias himself complained at the time, "And so what?"[76] This verdict that pop was merely disseminating a consumerist iconography was further crystallized due to the lack of direct, physical access to relevant works. Before the 1967 São Paulo Biennial, which brought a massive and representative display of pop art to Brazil for the first time, its circulation in the country was restricted to magazine reproductions.[77] It is also worth noting that Europe was still the favored destination of the few artists who had the means to travel abroad or won travel prizes. It is not surprising then that one of the conceptual pillars of the "New Brazilian Objectivity" exhibition (which took place before the Biennial) was precisely its opposition to pop or, more precisely, to pop *imagery*. From Dias to Oiticica, and from Gullar to Pedrosa, most critics and artists somehow linked to the 1960s avant-garde were skeptical of pop's seemingly compliant iconography.

Their verdicts generally overlooked important aspects of pop, like its reversal of the abstract expressionist ethos. By virtue of its rejection of the public myth of the artist qua privileged individual (and North American) subject—Jackson Pollock being the most emblematic case in point—pop art inverted the equation to show that it was the private arena of the artist and of art making that had entered the public domain. The idea of the artist as a repository of subjectivity had become suddenly anachronistic. One may think of the high-profile desacralization of the artist's atelier in Andy Warhol's Factory, for example, and also of Roy Lichtenstein's reversal of painterly virtuosity into an emulation of graphic patterns. This operation was doomed to be lost on viewers of the small, black-and-white magazine reproductions that circulated in Brazil, who would notice the Ben-Day dots, but not their painterly facture (ironically enough, small reproductions of Lichtenstein's paintings end up looking exactly like the comic strips that motivate them, all but effacing the formal operations involved in his sophisticated transposition from the graphic to the painterly). As Benjamin Buchloh has argued, these artists were able to "articulate the absence of subjectivity," replacing the traditional notion of portraiture as a privileged means of private access to the subject by "the public substitutes of subjectivity, the mere myths of the subject in the spectacular and substitutional appearance of the 'star' and by a 'pathetic residue of subjectivity living on in the comic book, the cheap romance novel, and the advertising image.'"[78]

But pop's blurring of public and private also allowed it to be confidently grounded in *mass subjectivity*, thus opening the path for critical insights into the latter's ideological core—so much so that Hal Foster, for example, was notoriously able to propose broadening Roland Barthes's *punctum* to the level of a mass subject in his characterization of Warhol's images as a case of traumatic realism (a critical reading that would have been impossible without the close attention Foster pays to Warhol's technical subtleties).[79]

In Brazil, however, the 1960s avant-garde dealt less with an internal crack in all-encompassing mass subjectivity than with its outright implausibility as a collective paradigm. Once again, Salzstein's characterization of a dysfunctional public sphere is telling: despite their recourse to appropriated images and mass-production techniques, Brazilian artworks in the 1960s cannot be said unequivocally to inhabit a public dimension of image circulation. What is more, there was a profound shock in the fact that artists did not shy away from juxtaposing state-of-the-art procedures with anachronistic aspects of the context that surrounded them, as if every token of mass consumption asked for an archaic counterpoint coming either from rural traditions or from usually disavowed scenarios of urban poverty. This shock has a proper name in Brazilian cultural history: *tropicalism*.[80] No wonder then that the role of the TV set in Oiticica's *Tropicália* illustrates what I have just explained with a vengeance: the TV "devours" the spectator due to its "more active" creation of images.[81] Oiticica dismisses any potential identification with the world of mass imagery as absurd, as something that ought to be superseded (or devoured). Likewise, Gerchman's interest in suburban kitsch testifies not to a ubiquitous and faceless penetration of commodity culture supposed to transcend the polarity between kitsch and high culture (not a case, then, of Warhol's famous remark that a bottle of Coke tastes the same regardless of one's class), but to an offensive charge of "bad taste."[82] As a matter of fact, one of the tropicalist songs by Caetano Veloso and Gilberto Gil was named after Gerchman's *Lindonéia—The Gioconda of the Suburbs* (1966), a painting that epitomizes the motifs he told Gullar he wanted to paint. Critic Paulo Sergio Duarte's description of the work is highly suggestive:

> She is in the news—a crime of passion … AN IMPOSSIBLE LOVE / THE BEAUTIFUL 18-YEAR OLD LINDONÉIA DIED INSTANTLY. The supposed headline surrounds the frame that surrounds the portrait. Between the public universe of newspaper text and the intimacy of the face, one finds the domestic world of the decorated frame … the frame simultaneously adds relief, materially contrasting with the flat, planar and non-perspectival surface.[83]

For the critic, the kitsch frame "domesticates and privatizes *Lindonéia*": without it, she would remain "a piece of a newspaper that would [in its turn] be a piece of the city."[84] No juxtaposition could create a greater disparity: her suburban anonymity (which her mug shot pose and lack of surname further reinforce) is contrasted with the work's title invoking the single most famous portrait in art history, and whose single name—unlike *Lindonéia*'s—requires no further explanation. The decorated glass of the frame—a kitsch obstacle to reflection—acts as a stark reminder that there is no possibility of identification here for the bourgeois viewer. In other words, art could do little to explore the fissures of a Symbolic consistency that wasn't already there (in mass circulation) in the first place. What it did instead was to transpose to this incipient sphere of circulation a series of contradictions that were usually cordoned off as private and suburban. Anonymity was thus a means of embodying not the "absence of subjectivity," as in Buchloh's reading of pop, but the subject's conflictive grounding in sheer displacement.

As we have seen, this conflictive dimension is what is fundamentally at stake both in *My Portrait* and in *Box Bolide 18*. Oiticica deemed the "move toward the object" that he detected in Dias—together with his *Bolides*, which he categorized as "transobjects"— as central to the political project he was trying to formulate for the avant-garde.[85] In this sense, the *Box Bolide 18* is clearly indebted to one of Dias's most famous works, *Notes on an Unforeseen Death* (1965). With its scenes of physical violence and iconic catastrophes—such as a mushroom cloud—its comics-like partition of the surface, and its sagging appendage, this is a work that synthesizes Dias's aesthetics between 1964

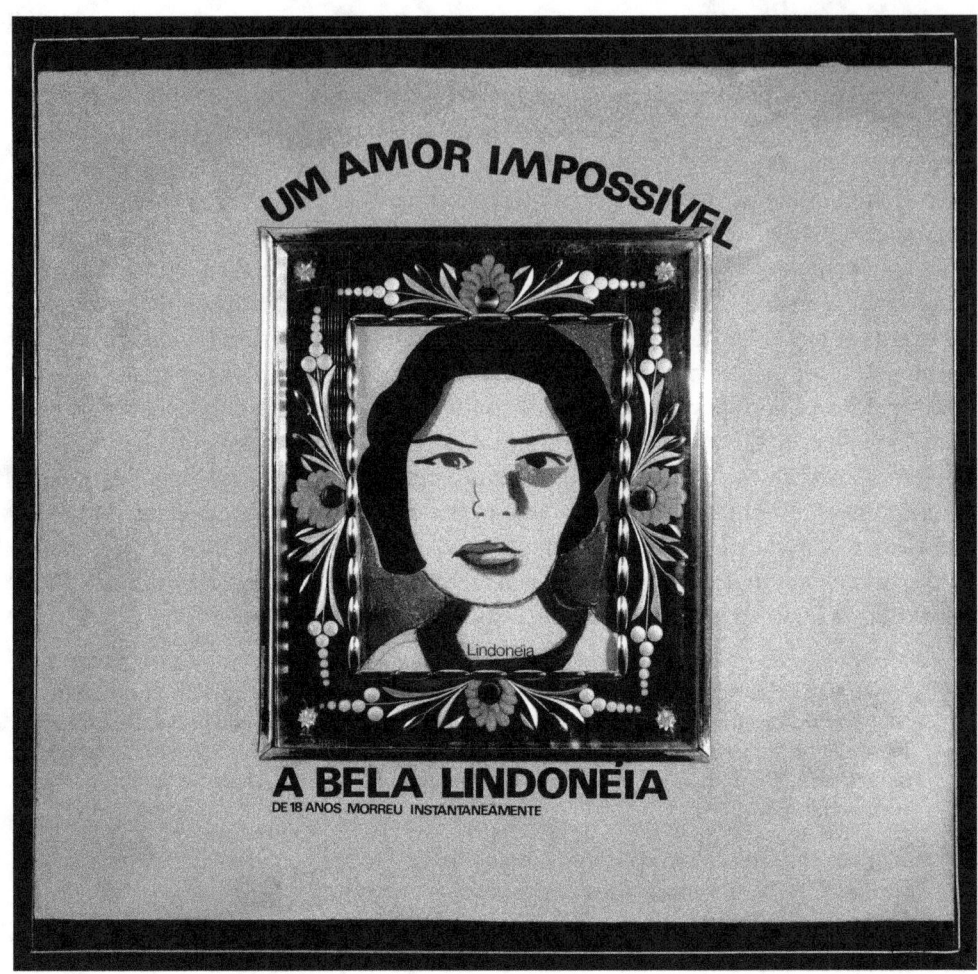

3.13
Rubens Gerchman, *Lindonéia—The Gioconda of the Suburbs*, 1966. Serigraphy and collage on decorated glass and metal, 60 × 60 cm. Coleção Gilberto Chateaubriand, Museu de Arte Moderna do Rio de Janeiro. Licensed by inARTS.com. Photo: Pedro Oswaldo Cruz.

and 1967, that is, in the period when he emerged as one of the main artists active in Rio de Janeiro. In one journal entry, Oiticica writes of a sudden insight—a "revelation" even—he had about the latter while climbing the hill of a suburban favela. On the one hand, he adamantly rejects the view shared by some critics at the time that Dias's work represented "psychological problems on the individual level," stressing that it should be read instead as "a profound lived-experience on the ethical plane, [as] it is connected to a social event that marked our time, the Hiroshima massacre."[86] This emphasis on the imperative of facing current social issues is also a reminder of how attentive Oiticica was to Gullar's ideas even after the poet had parted company with avant-gardist practice.[87] On the other hand, and most importantly, this experience would reveal how "the condemnation of the frame (as a surface of representation or an experimental repository) is revealed as an expression, as an attempt to create an anti-frame."[88] Oiticica says that this suggestion would be meaningless without that earlier consideration on the lived experience, and vice versa. This is crucial: the *vivência*, or lived experience, did not point to a supposed repository of "life" lying beyond artistic considerations—it was not simply external to the dimension of art. On the contrary, it is clear that the strident displacement at play in Dias's works, in *Lindonéia*, in *Box Bolide 18,* and in the *Parangolés*—in relation both to pictorial representation and social demarcations—was at the core of this conception of lived experience.[89]

In other words, the (anti-)formal effectiveness of the works was central to the lived experience they sought to embody. *Notes on an Unforeseen Death*, for instance, alludes to readymade or mass images, like comics, but challenges a stable consumption of those images by rendering a work's affective presence overly intrusive; it is difficult to examine the detailed graphic elements properly without getting too close to the work's abject dangling construct. This is exactly what the *Box Bolide 18* sets out to do as well, against the backdrop of the newspaper picture of Cara de Cavalo. The formal dialogue between the two works is striking indeed: both allude to traumatized bodies, which are brought to the viewers' closeness by the works' overt tactility. The same applies to *My Portrait*, which shares with *Box Bolide 18* the connotation of martyrdom: can we fail to perceive how Cara de Cavalo is exhibited as if crucified? Less obvious, but no less remarkable, is the face in *My Portrait*, a cloth bearing three red stains that stand in for the eyes and mouth. Besides the sexually violent evocation of bloody orifices, there is a potential allusion to the Shroud of Turin, said to bear the imprint of the face and body of the martyred Christ.[90]

When the time came for a face-to-face confrontation with pop works, the critical fate of the latter was already decided, or rather overdetermined by this emphasis on lived experience. One of Pedrosa's most telling responses to the massive North American representation in the 1967 Biennial was an article entitled "From American Pop to Inlander Dias" ("Do Pop Americano ao sertanejo Dias").[91] In the article, the critic flaunts his awareness of pop art by roll-calling Tom Wesselman, Roy Lichtenstein, Claes Oldenburg, Andy Warhol, George Segal, James Rosenquist, and Robert Indiana. All of them were part of the North American contingent in the exhibition; so were Robert Rauschenberg, Ed Ruscha, and Jasper Johns. Johns's *Three Flags* won one of the painting prizes—quite an irony, considering that protesters had graffitied the walls of the pop art room with the inscriptions "Viva Guevara! Fora USA!"[92] The article is mostly

3.14
Antonio Dias, *Notes on an Unforeseen Death*,
1965. Oil, acrylic, vinyl, and Plexiglas on
cushioned canvas and wood, 195 × 176 × 63 cm.
Private collection. Courtesy of the artist.

110

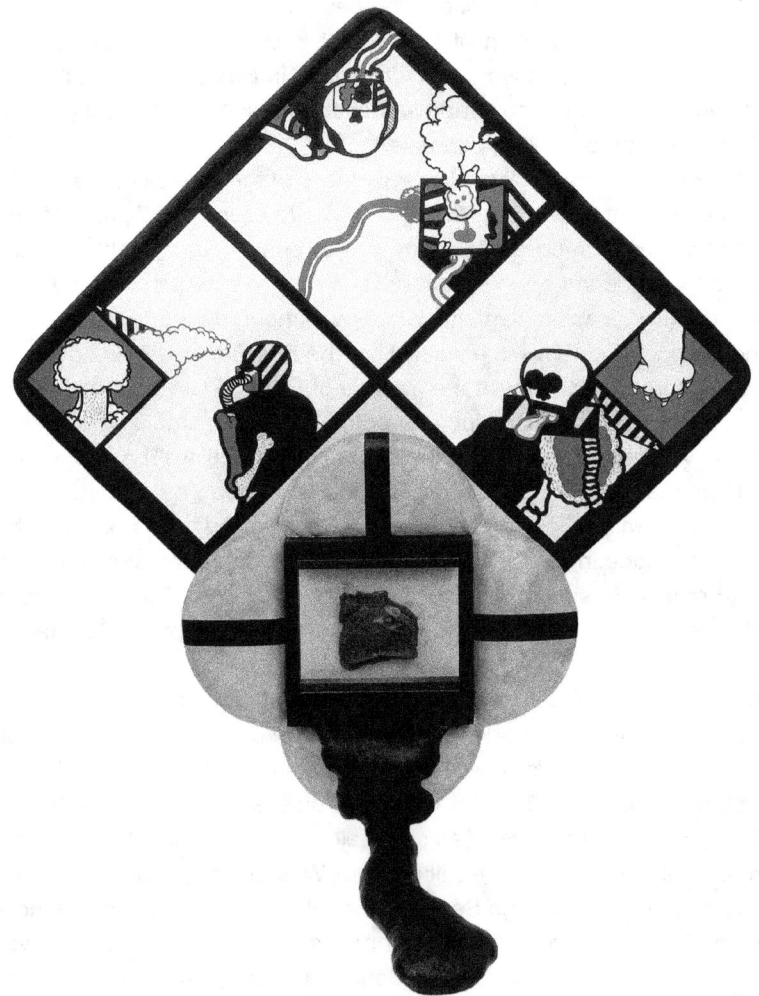

devoted to setting Dias (and Gerchman, by extension) apart from those artists, explaining that he "doesn't provide us with a journalistic comment, as in American pop, but with a raw slice of life."[93] A nude by Wesselman, on the contrary, is described as "a happy body displayed in a market, as if its white teeth took part in a brand new toothpaste ad."[94] Even a "window-shop of sparklingly appetizing cakes" is deemed as appetizing "as ads of beautiful salads or delicacies … in *Life* or in the *Saturday Evening Post*."[95] When it comes to Dias, however, Pedrosa's florid prose embraces a mood of synesthetic intoxication: "In his painting, the three-dimensional volume is not fictitious, a result of perspective tricks; it is real, [and] through the edges of its relief flow all sorts of … organic secretions—blood, excrements, sperm, orgasms, pus, hormones, all with their colours and smells.… With his images, Dias aims not to propose a solution of sorts, but to constantly stir in himself, in ourselves, and in others, the perplexity of the world and the conflicts of life."[96]

Considering that the article renders the pop image so antithetical to the "rawness" of lived experience, it may seem surprising that, after such a lively (and grossly exaggerated) description, Pedrosa still manages to speak of Dias as a producer of images. Or perhaps not—after all, those may be images in the sense that Cara de Cavalo's bullet-riddled corpse becomes an image in *Box Bolide 18*, but one that is to be *thrown* like a bomb at the viewer's face (no wonder Oiticica would later become an admirer of Artaud) rather than passively consumed.[97] Gerchman's "bad taste" fulfills perhaps the same function, and Pedrosa's "tasteless" description of Dias's work confirms this ethos: sex, violence, and bodily instincts literally *exceed* the domestication the image is expected to impose. The power of *Lindonéia* also resides in the fact that it is made *palpable*. The three-dimensional, engraved mirror frame literally negates her smooth entombment in the circulation of flat images; its kitschy, domestic affect suggests a kind of closeness to the viewer that is as physical as the synesthetic rendering of Dias's works. In working against the primacy of a coherent image, all of this—social segregation in reverse, domestic suburban kitsch, individual phenomenological intoxication—also works against stable collective formations, regardless of whether they are based on militant politics (as in the CPC) or in widespread consumer culture (as in pop).[98]

Pedrosa's argument is not completely at odds with Oiticica's depiction of *Notes on an Unforeseen Death* as an "anti-picture." The latter was, after all, an attempt to develop Gullar's urge for an art concerned with "concrete life." And yet this is a point where Oiticica and Gullar parted ways, despite the fact that both approved of Dias's and Gerchman's work. The poet reverted to an aesthetically conservative position, viewing most contemporary art—from informal abstraction to Noveau Réalisme and pop—as a surge of individualist excess following the collapse of the constructive avant-garde. Gullar defended a paradigm of communication that was ultimately staked in traditional representation.[99] For painting's ability "to speak" depended on its capacity for lending sense to the city's muffling "clamor," of providing a coherent representation of otherwise fragmented everyday experience (thus countering individualism, one might expect). What informal abstraction, Nouveau Réalisme, and pop were supposed to have in common, then, was the fact that they attacked this power of mediation by either rendering painting meaningless or failing to provide standards of mediation that would replace those that painting formerly offered. Thus Gullar's scathing attack on what seems to

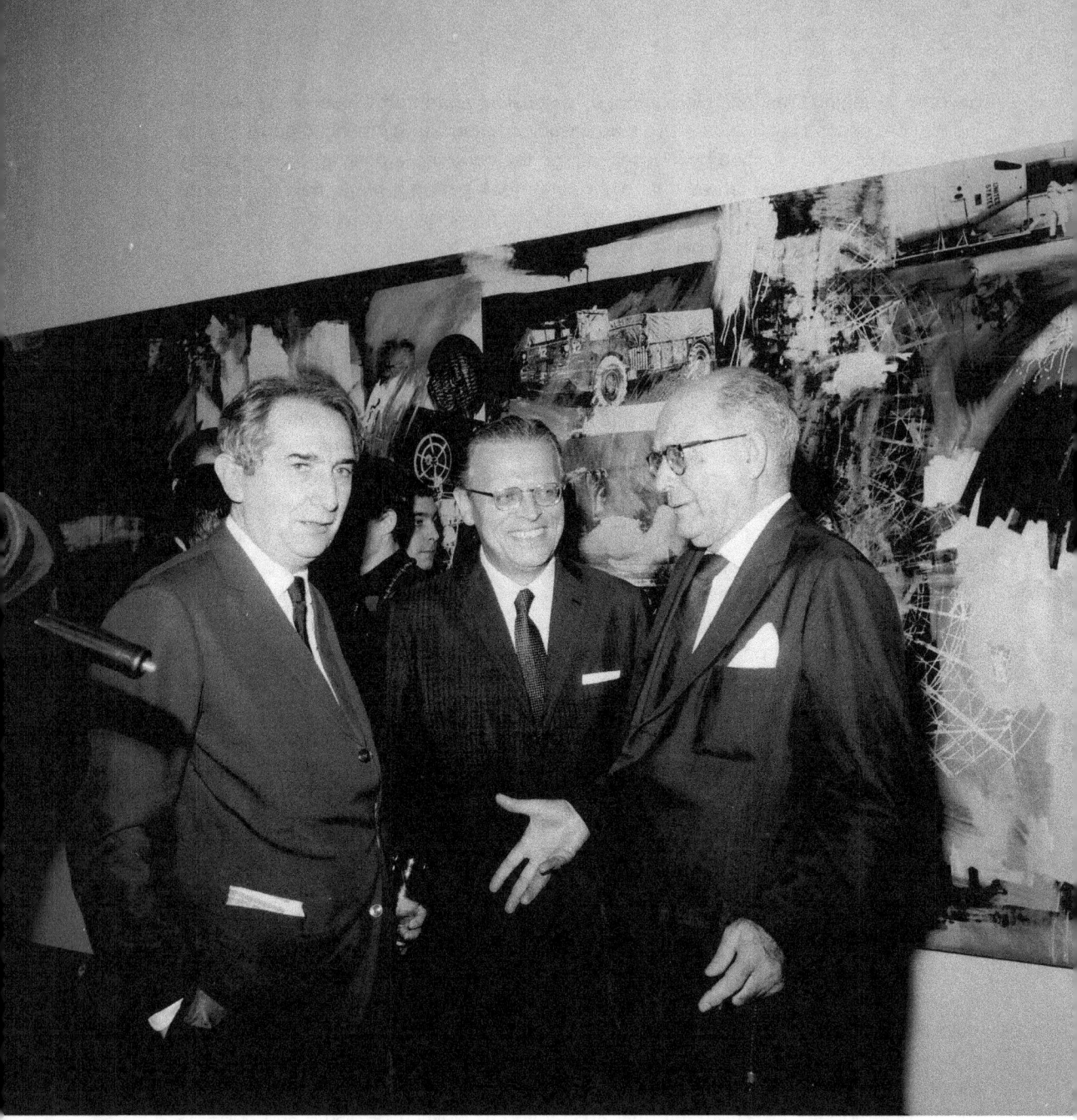

3.15
Mário Pedrosa (left) at the US exhibition during
the 9th São Paulo Biennial, 1967. Photographer
unknown. Arquivo Histórico Wanda Svevo,
Fundação Bienal de São Paulo.

be, from the description he provides, César's *Compressions*: "There is also the case of the sculptor who puts cars under a car crusher and crushes them: a sculpture! How is one supposed to judge them? Should we state that the car crusher is brilliant? That it crushed with the necessary strength, or that it should have crushed it more strongly?"[100]

Ideologically speaking, Gullar's conservative aesthetic stance comes perilously close to the one-dimensional indictment of pop as imagery. In both cases, the centrality of a coherent image was taken to underscore collective formations. And, despite being far more sophisticated, it failed fundamentally to distance itself from the earlier CPC stance. After all, the CPC conception of "the masses" proved to be an idealization, a substitute that provided political legitimacy for the CPC's own projection as the public of their spectacles. Gullar may have perceived that the projection of "the masses" was problematic, but what nevertheless remained in his notion of communication was the imperative that art should be fundamentally grounded in a synthetic representation. This either/or antithesis between communication and meaningless fragmentation was the backbone of his aesthetic theory at that point.

The avant-gardist stance may have had less tangible or immediately ambitious political targets, but these were targets derived from the very limitations and specificities of art's possibilities of address. In other words, by neither projecting a unified public on its interventions nor a unifying image, and by realizing the contradictions inherent in its circulation, the avant-garde addressed the scission in spectatorship without making it seem to coalesce in a projected community. In any case, the project of instilling art with a collectivist ethos would face a definitive crisis with the toughening of military repression late in 1968.[101] As organized initiatives became scarce and almost impossible, many artists and intellectuals faced imprisonment or exile (either compulsory or voluntary).

The case of Carlos Zilio, one of the youngest artists to show alongside Dias's generation, is worthy of notice. Somewhat like Gullar, Zilio tried to reconcile avant-gardism and political activism, but he went in the opposite direction. This was an artist connected to the New Objectivity group who joined the student movement and ultimately embraced armed resistance to the military government. He retrospectively remarked that armed resistance acquired an "aesthetic" quality, like a "happening," and that it also brought to mind "the problem of our frailty when faced by death."[102] The crucial difference between Zilio's situation and Gullar's is that the former no longer had any available fantasies of collectivity at his disposal—no more "masses," for instance. What is more, the artist associated this "aesthetic viewpoint" with an ever more precarious notion of selfhood. Besides the idea of bodily frailty, Zilio also pointed out how political activism required serious "changes in life."[103] A tightly planned routine with constant displacement and changes of identity was, after all, the stock and trade of clandestine opposition movements. Viewed in this light, Zilio's investment in self-portraiture becomes all the more significant.

Take for instance two photographs, *Unknown Identity* (1973) and *For a Young Man of Brilliant Prospects* (1974). Artist and critic Milton Machado has argued that both are actually complementary self-portraits of Zilio, noting the similar position of his feet in both images.[104] Zilio was eventually shot and arrested, spending two and a half years in prison and released only in 1972, at a moment when state repression was more intense than ever, but also when Brazil was experiencing an economic boom that gave rise to a generation of yuppies oblivious of political struggle. In such a paradoxical context, *Unknown Identity* and *For a Young Man of Brilliant Prospects* represent the inadequacy of the artist's position, which Zilio strives to keep vacant, stressing an incongruity that is to be found, quite tellingly, in the expression "stepping into someone else's shoes." This sharply contrasts with his self-portrayal as a revolutionary hero in drawings he made in prison, exposing his wound and ordeals, such as *Self-Portrait Aged 26* (1970) and *Pieces of Mine* (1971). In the drawings, Zilio's broken body is a token not only of moral triumph over his captors (note in particular the red heart in the figure's chest in *Self-Portrait Aged 26*) but of anthropophagic triumph over the conception of pop art as an imperialist stance.[105] The transition from his prison portraits to his so-to-speak "yuppie" series is, above all, a demonstration of portraiture as the privileged point of articulation and criticism of the collective failure of a generation. It is as Zilio himself describes his shocking encounter with such an alienated feeling of economic optimism: "I left prison very scared with a feeling of defeat. It was the opposite sentiment I had when I was arrested. I came there dead but triumphant. I was released alive but defeated."[106]

114

3.16
Carlos Zilio, *Unknown Identity*, 1973.
Photograph, 18 × 24 cm. Courtesy of the artist.

3.17
Carlos Zilio, *For a Young Man of Brilliant Prospects*, 1974. Multiple, photographic series, 18 × 24 cm. Courtesy of the artist.

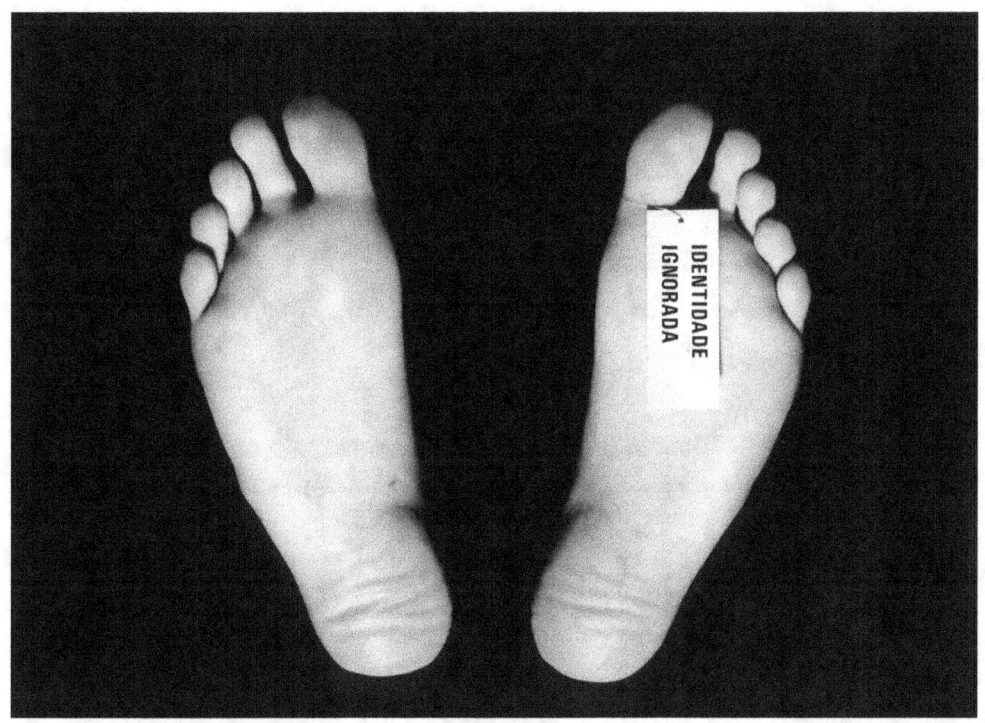

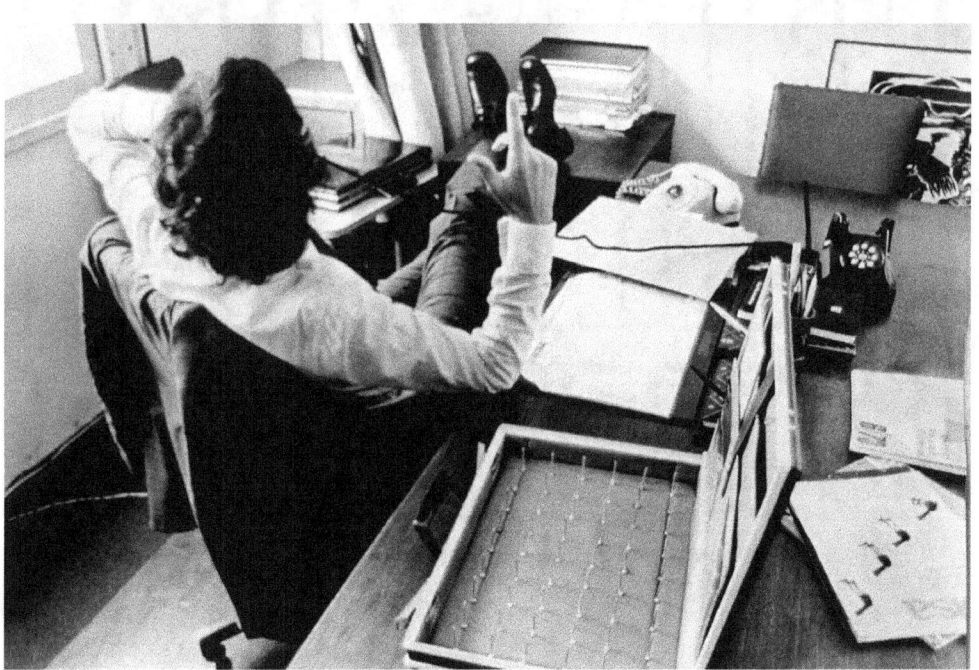

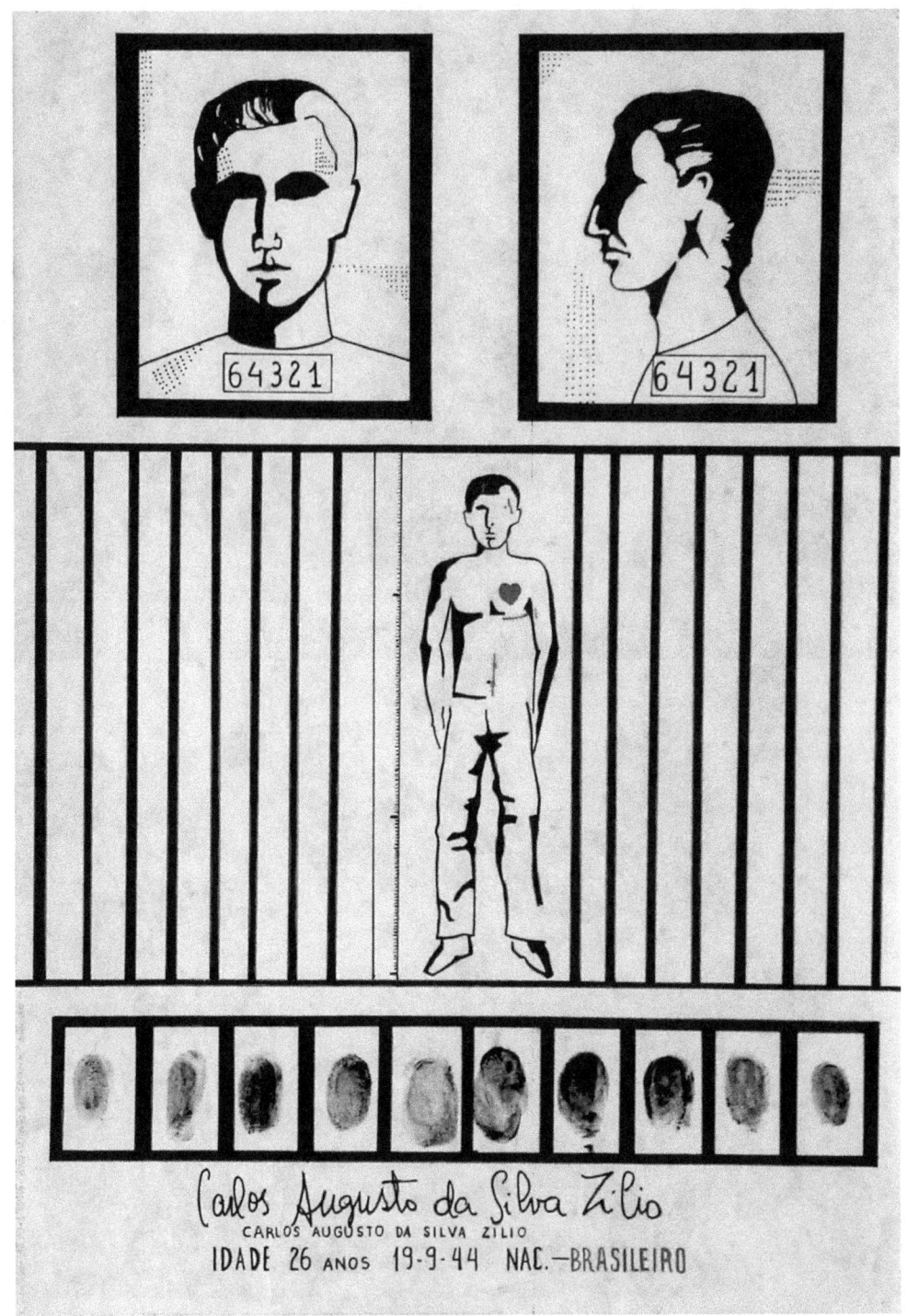

3.18
Carlos Zilio, *Self-Portait Aged 26*, 1970.
Hydrographic pen on paper, 47.3 × 32.5 cm.
Courtesy of the artist.

3.19
Carlos Zilio, *Pieces of Mine*, 1971. Gouache on
paper. 50 × 32.5 cm. Courtesy of the artist.

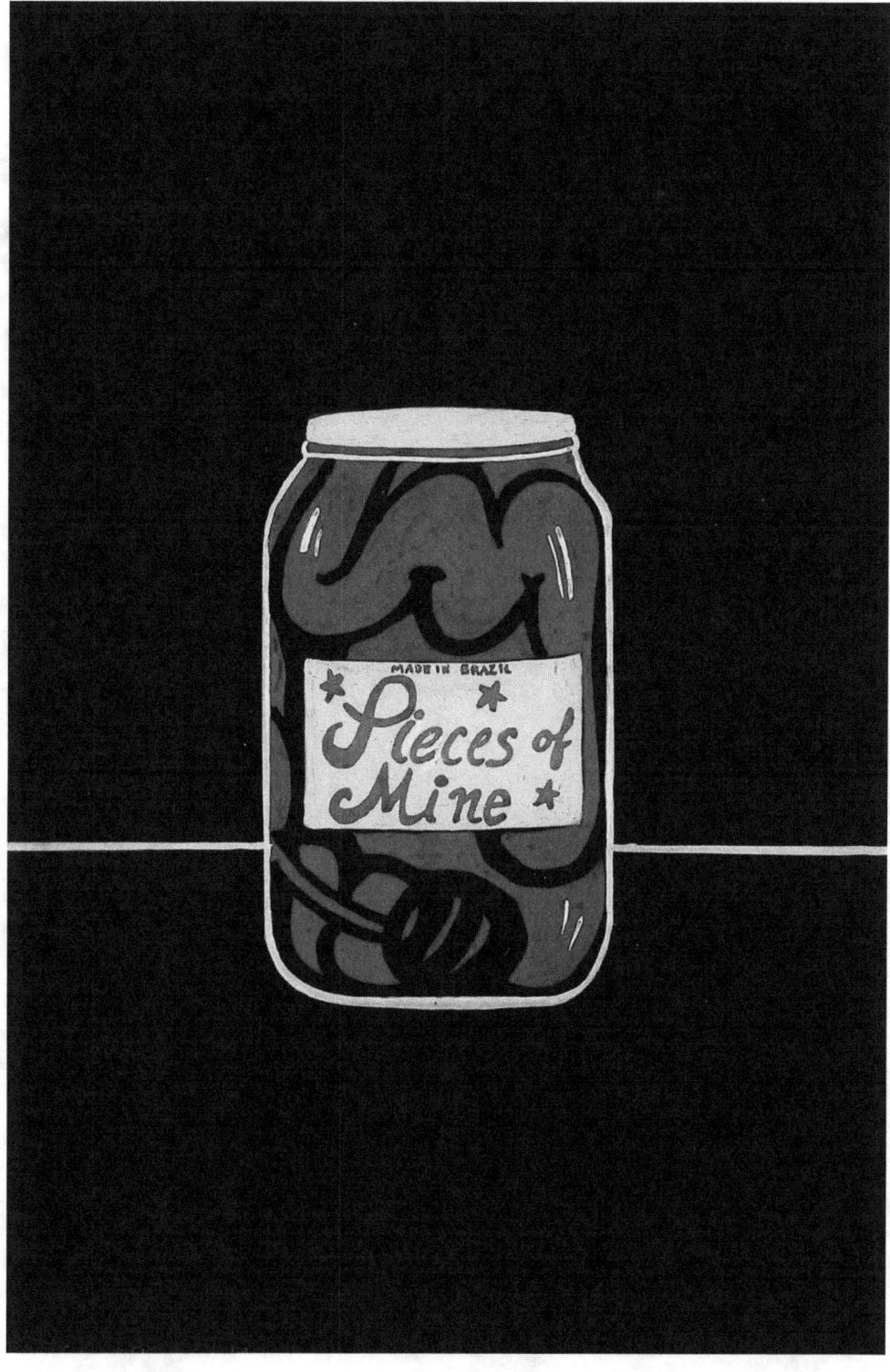

4

Enigmages

"With *Tiradentes*," Cildo Meireles explains, "I was interested in metaphor and in the dislocation of the theme. I wanted to use the subject, life and death, as the raw material of the work. The dislocation is what matters in the history of the art object."[1] Meireles refers to his 1970 work titled *Tiradentes: Totem-Monument to the Political Prisoner*, in which live chickens were tied to stake, soaked in gasoline, and burned alive. Performed in the city of Belo Horizonte, this extreme act was a direct response to an event taking place in the nearby historical town of Ouro Preto. The military government had temporarily transferred the capital of the country from Brasília to Ouro Preto in order to commemorate the death of Tiradentes (Joaquim José da Silva Xavier, who was imprisoned, executed, and quartered in 1792 after leading a revolt against the Portuguese colonial rule, is commonly known by this name). Or, rather, the military's intent was to appropriate the event for the sake of its own nationalist self-legitimizing rhetoric, made all the more cynical by the fact that one of the main detention centers for political prisoners at that time was called ... Tiradentes Prison. For Meireles, then, the work was first and foremost a way of subverting that commemorative relocation of the capital from Brasília, itself the product of a major human and material displacement, with a displacement of another kind—one that exceeded pure symbolism and crossed the threshold of trauma. "Of course I would never repeat a work like *Tiradentes*," Meireles adds, "I can still hear the poor hens in my emotional memory. But in 1970 I felt that it had to be done."[2]

Critic Paulo Herkenhoff has argued that this work generates "an image of liberty by linking the complex figure of Tiradentes into present-day politics."[3] There was indeed a fundamental distance inscribed in *Tiradentes*, as if its shock was meant to possess a muffled rather than vivid quality—the work took place in a courtyard, and the public witnessed it from inside the exhibition space, separated from it by a glass wall.[4] This is perhaps what an "image of liberty" could be expected to retain and circulate. As a matter of fact, Frederico Morais, who curated the "From Body to Earth" exhibition, where *Tiradentes* was performed, recalls that the work did provoke scandalized reactions in members of the local Chamber of Representatives.[5] This is also a sign of Meireles's awareness of conceptualist strategies of circulation, and of the way information can be made to supersede the actual work.

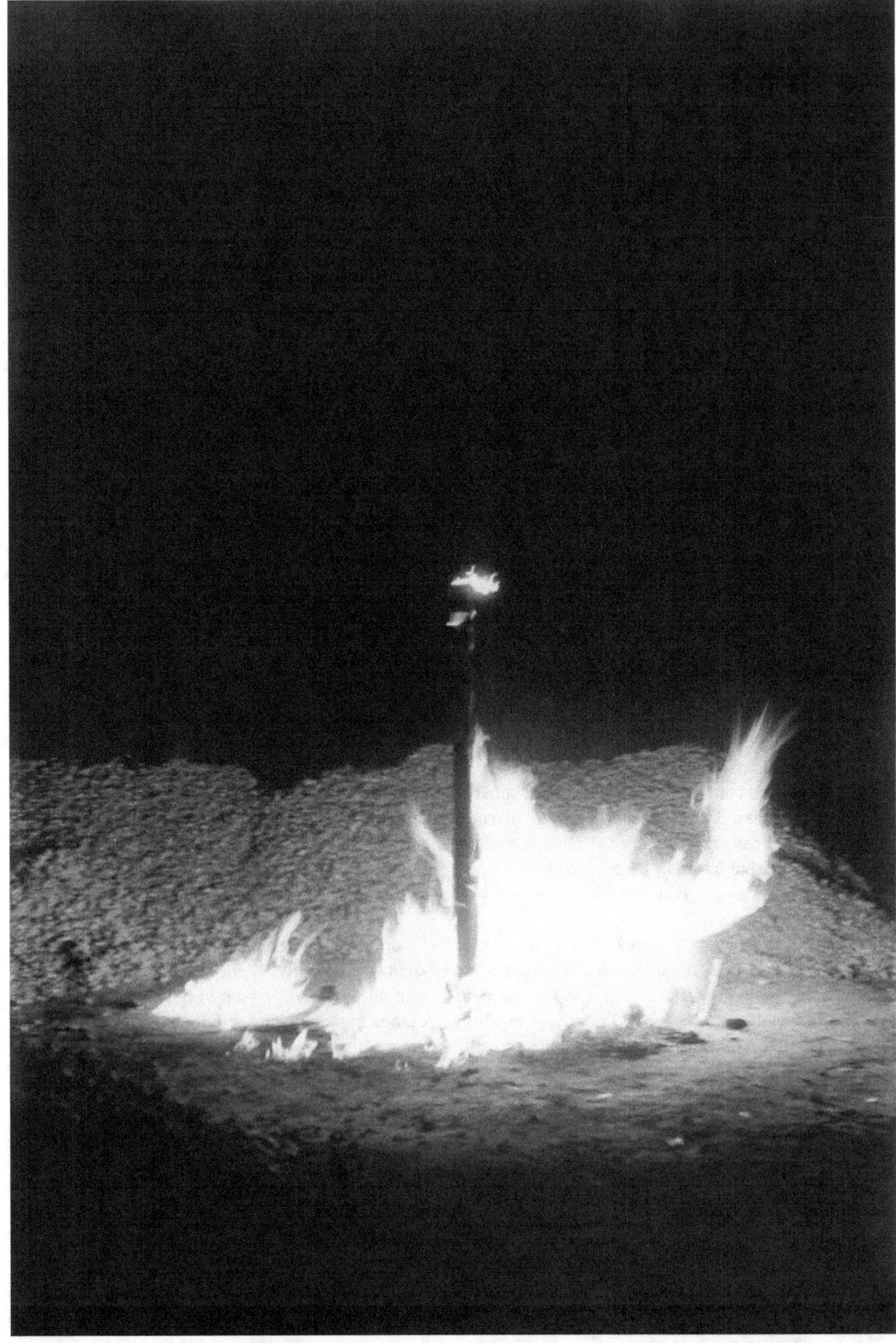

4.1
Cildo Meireles, *Tiradentes: Totem-Monument to the Political Prisoner*, 1970. Wooden stake, white cloth, clinical thermometer, ten live chickens, gasoline, fire (photographic documentation of performance). Photo: Luiz Alphonsus. Courtesy of the artist.

4.2
Cildo Meireles, *Tiradentes: Totem-Monument to the Political Prisoner*, 1970. Wooden stake, white cloth, clinical thermometer, ten live chickens, gasoline, fire (photographic documentation of performance). Photo: Luiz Alphonsus. Courtesy of the artist.

Enigmages

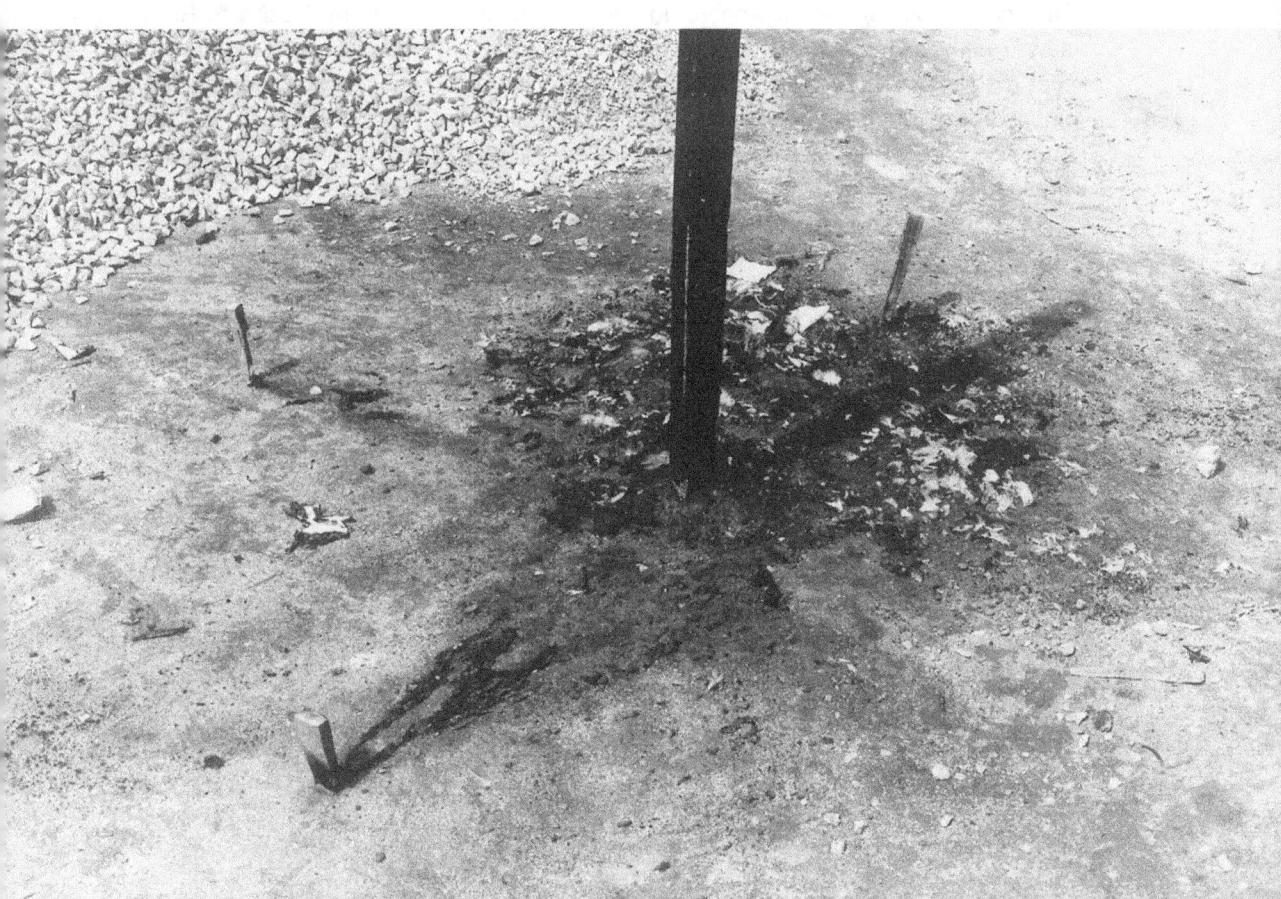

But the real effectiveness of the images in enacting this circulation is complex, to say the least. All we get to see in the photographic registers of *Tiradentes* are rather generic black-and-white images of a bonfire and a few scattered remainders such as feathers—an imagery far too scarce to do justice to what actually took place in that courtyard. And yet I want to suggest that the sheer traumatic power of *Tiradentes* is paradoxically upheld by the very failure of the photographs to convey it, by the gap that separates what they represent and what is conveyed as the work is described. This is consistent with Meireles's interest in *orality*, which he deems "the ideal support for the work of art: it dispenses with the object and can be easily transmitted and expanded in the social sphere. It should be possible to 'recount' a work without it losing much substance."[6] *Tiradentes* adds a twist to this logic, as its affective charge is even *more* vividly captured and transmitted in descriptions than in photographs. In the face of a description of the work, what is shocking about the photographs is precisely their failure to communicate trauma no matter how much one looks for it in them. Note, for example, the paradoxical temporality that stems from the simple fact that captions of the work list *live* chickens as one of its materials. The impossible nowness of them burning in the fire is brought to life, thus revealing the proper traumatic dimension of the photographs— these are live chickens only in the sense that they are both about to die and already dead.[7] Trauma can be appended to the image and even function as its internal limit, but it is nevertheless in excess of its represented content.

This brings me to my initial suggestion: that the work of Meireles and Antonio Dias in the late 1960s and early 1970s takes part in a reconfiguration of representational strategies that increasingly questioned the primacy and sufficiency of the image, and critically compensated for it by mobilizing alternative representational procedures and symbolic repertoires that attest to the need to address an increasingly internationalized (and commodified) cultural sphere. In 1967, Meireles moved from Brasília to Rio and saw *Tropicália* firsthand at MAM. As he recalls it: "that was exactly what I didn't want at that moment."[8] This may sound unexpected for an artist whose installations share an unmistakable phenomenological orientation with those of Hélio Oiticica, and still more so if one considers that, in the same interview, Meireles stresses that he "strategically" presented both Oiticica and Lygia Clark as artists he felt influenced by.[9] *Tropicália* was indeed a formidable attack on representation in the guise of a "Brazilian image," but could its critical edge transcend the imploded visual cacophony it offered? The work's corrosive visual syntax worked against the unifying sense of an imaginary ideological background (the quintessential Brazilian image), but its fragmentary imagery proved to be vulnerable to recuperation, as Oiticica himself quickly recognized. He complained that (the term) "Tropicália" was becoming fashionable but nevertheless maintained that "there are elements here that this bourgeois voracity will never be able to consume: the direct life-experience [*vivência*] element, which goes beyond the problem of the image."[10]

To go beyond the problem of the image, then: as a reaction (in part) to the "imagery" of pop art, *Tropicália* was an attempt to fight fire with fire. The pop primacy of the image would not simply be imitated or locally adapted, but redeployed in order to create, as Oiticica put it, a distinctive way of linking "imagetical relations and social-political impli-cations."[11] Conversely, to recuperate or "consume" *Tropicália* was precisely to deprive its "imagetical relations" of such implications. This would reduce it to a kind of uncritical, pop-like image—at least according to the view, then held by artists and critics in Rio, of pop as utterly complicit with consumer society. As a matter of fact, Oiticica extended his self-criticism of *Tropicália* to the "New Brazilian Objectivity" show as a whole, which he came to see as "entirely immersed in this 'Pop' language, hybrid for us, in spite of the talent and strength of the artists involved."[12]

Dias's work occupies a central position in this debate. If Oiticica's writing at that moment was deeply marked by a concern with the critical insufficiency of the image, Dias's trajectory was its visual counterpart. The flattening of *Tropicália* into an easily consumable image, for example, was analogous to (and contemporary with) the lauda-tory branding of Dias's visceral response to pop and Nouveau Réalisme, in works such as *Notes on an Unforeseen Death*, as a so-called "Antonio Dias style."[13] Crucially, Dias quickly made a point of detaching himself from this awkward trademark: his painting underwent an extreme shift after his move to Milan in 1968, as the main features of its purported "style"—a striking profusion of violent graphic signs and bodily fragments, both in the form of painted elements and amalgamated soft constructs—gave way to a sober display of calculated, if hermetic, precision in works like *Anywhere Is My Land* (1968; see figure I.1) and *Sun Photo as a Self-Portrait* (1968; see figure 3.9). Writing in 1969, Oiticica praised this shift and termed Dias's new works "enigmages"—a hybrid of "image" and "enigma." This placed them in the context of the aftermath of "New Brazil-ian Objectivity": "Antonio Dias' experience emerges from a superlative imagetical vision, towards its synthesis—the *enigmage*, by creating monuments: the *open participation*, provoking a synthesis of his iconographical tendencies (the necessity of continuously building images)."[14]

By describing how Dias overcomes the "necessity of continuously building images," Oiticica suggests a reading of the works—often endorsed by Dias himself in the mid-1960s—as obsessive renderings of psychological interiority that give way, importantly, to a *synthesis*. For, if Dias's experience had had its origin in "superlative" imagery, it was now informed by its negation and thus dialectically turned into an enigmage: "The imagetical world is not sufficient, anymore, to express or put through multiple possibili-ties for *the enigma*, which would be something related to the creative experience in its origin—it lies in creative simplicity itself: the aim is to put through a creative impulse."[15]

This is not simply an amalgamation: the image and that which contains and negates it (the enigma) are actually sublated into the very concept of enigmage. The latter thus arises out of the internal contradictions the work eventually created. And, even though it is posed as the condition for creative experience, the enigma is also negativity precisely in that it signals the end of image proliferation—of image for image's sake. It is important that Dias himself had asked Oiticica to write the introductory text containing the observations I have cited as an introduction to the offset project book he was planning to publish, containing small-scale templates, as it were, for his most graphically clean and conceptually oriented works.[16]

Conceptually oriented, but only to a degree. Far from embracing a dematerialized or overintellectualized version of the work of art, Dias's projects retain something of the structure of *objects*, which is to say, within the context of Oiticica's formulation of the *suprasensorial*, that they aim at a "new perceptual behavior."[17] In fact, this seemingly counterintuitive insistence on keeping within the register of the object is precisely what prompted the invitation to Oiticica—Dias demonstrated enthusiasm about the concept of the "probject," which both artists had previously discussed, and asked Oiticica to consider his new work with it in mind.[18] The neologism evidently brings together the words "project" and "object," but has also been discussed by Oiticica as alluding to "proposition" and "probability" as well: "[the probject] refers to 'open' propositions made by artists … the object, or the work, would be the infinite probabilities contained in most diverse propositions of human creation."[19]

The openness of the concept is radicalized in the text on Dias. The word "open" repeatedly appears, always underlined—he writes of "open participation," "open fields," "open enigma" and "open exercise of significative behavior." Oiticica had just developed his concept—or, in his words, "permanent proposition"—of *Creleisure* (Crelazer), which was for him the culmination of a long theoretical path including the new objectivity, *Tropicália*, and the suprasensorial. In this context, *Eden*—the environment he constructed for his 1969 Whitechapel show—would then stand as a sort of inaugural laboratory pointing to the need for establishing "receptacles open to significations."[20] Compared to *Tropicália*—a comparison the Whitechapel public could actually make, since both environments were installed side by side—*Eden* is more visually austere and allows one to roam it at a slower pace. Whereas the former required visitors to devour images as quickly as possible, so as to put them in friction with one another, the latter offered a more restful setting and a less predetermined path to be followed. *Do It Yourself: Freedom Territory* (1968), which opened Dias's project book and quickly gained an installation version, thus prefigured certain concerns Oiticica was developing at that time. With its extremely concise economy, it radicalized the rejection of imagery that concerned both artists and proposed participation in an utterly unrestrained way, like one part of *Eden*, the *Open Area of Myth*, for which Oiticica devised no instructions: "there is no 'proposition' here."[21] As a space meant for a reflexive act of "self-founding,"[22] the *Open Area of Myth* begs proximity with *Do It Yourself: Freedom Territory* in that both seem equally fit for the "open exercise of significative behavior" Oiticica describes in Dias's text.[23] That description, in turn, clearly evokes a famous dictum by critic Mário Pedrosa, which echoed throughout Rio de Janeiro avant-gardist circles in the late 1960s, namely that art was "the experimental exercise of freedom."[24]

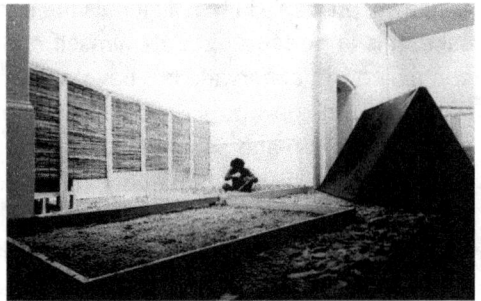

4.3
Hélio Oiticica, *B 54 Area Bolide 1* and *B 55 Area Bolide 2* (partial installation view of *Eden*, Whitechapel Gallery), 1969. Wood, straw, variable dimensions. Photo: Guy Brett. Courtesy Projeto Hélio Oiticica.

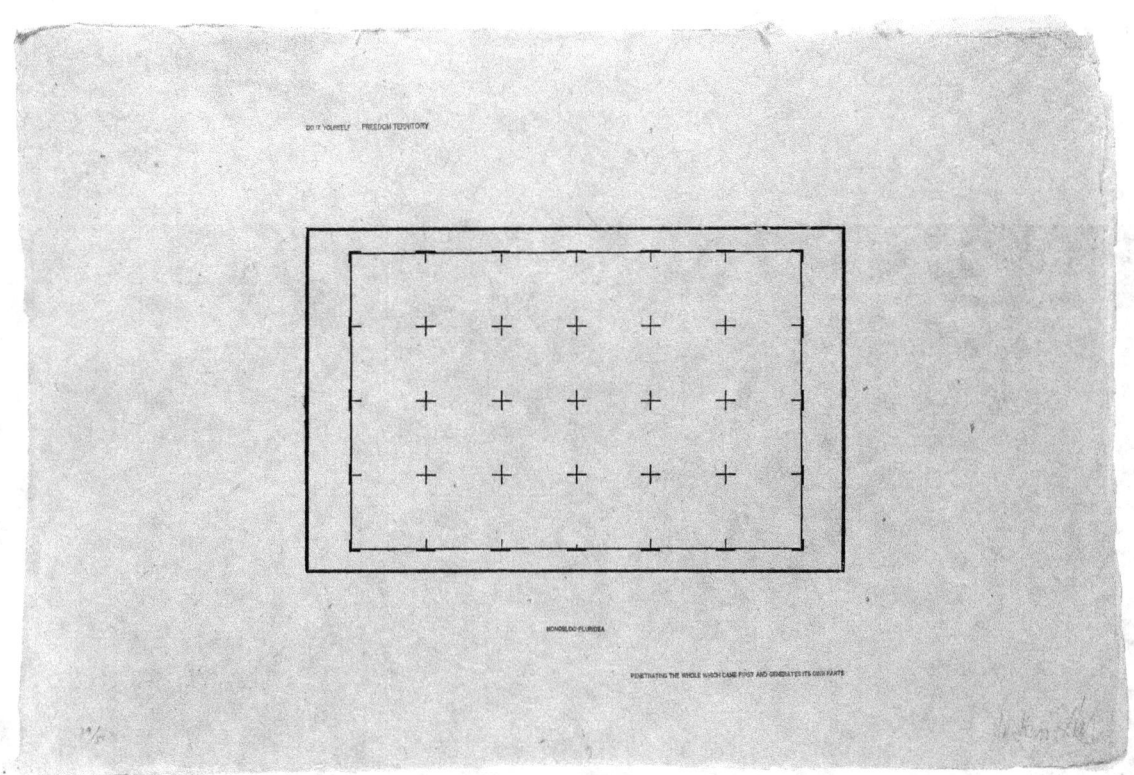

4.4
Antonio Dias, *Trama (Do It Yourself: Freedom Territory)*, 1968–1978. Woodcut print on handmade Nepali paper, approx. 58 × 84 cm. Daros Latinamerica Collection, Zurich.
Photo: Peter Schälchli. Courtesy of the artist.

4.5
Antonio Dias, *Do It Yourself: Freedom Territory*,
1968/2002. Titanium and/or tape, overall
dimensions variable; approx. 400 × 600 cm.
Daros Latinamerica Collection, Zurich. Photo:
Dominique Uldry. Courtesy of the artist.

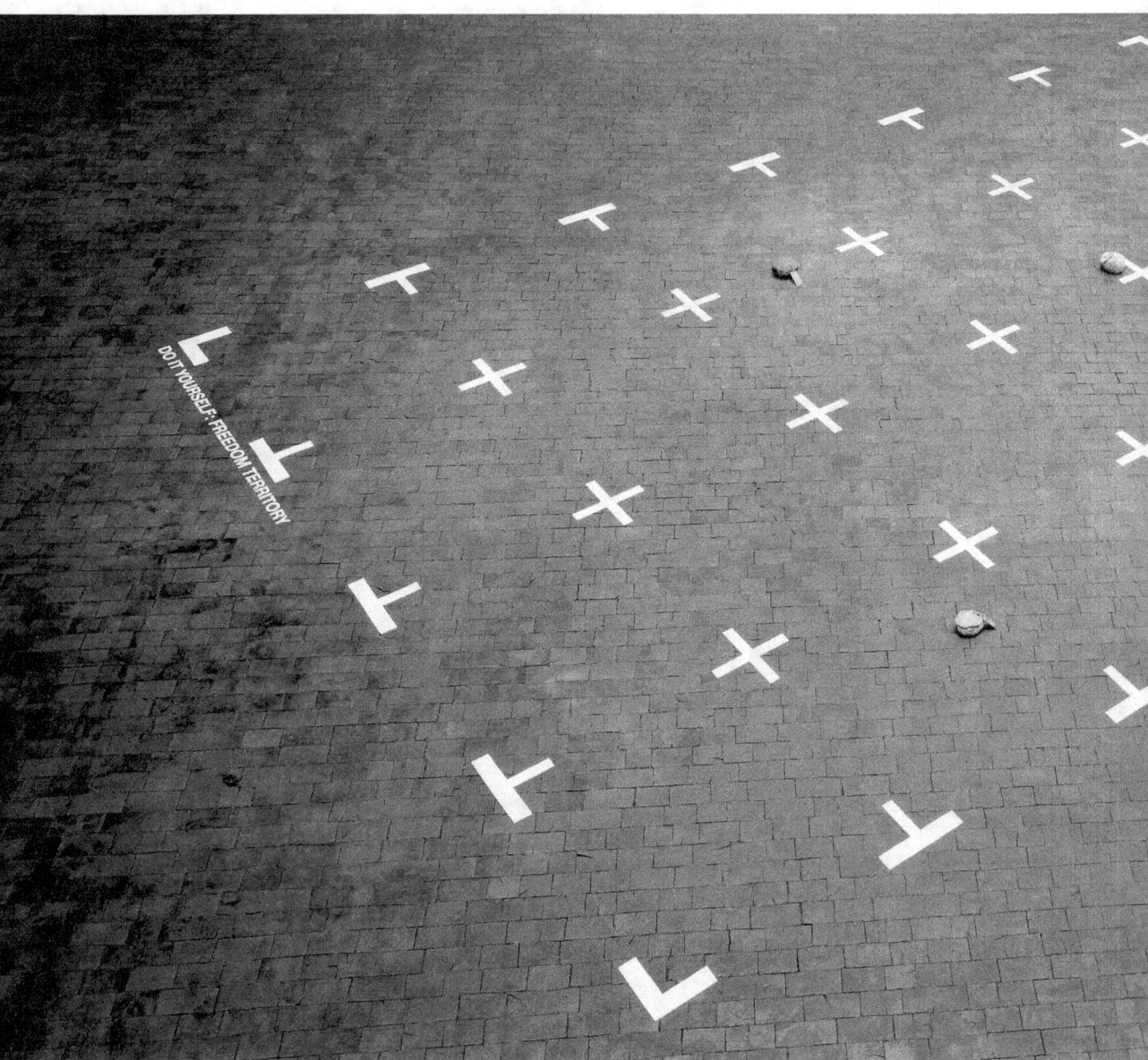

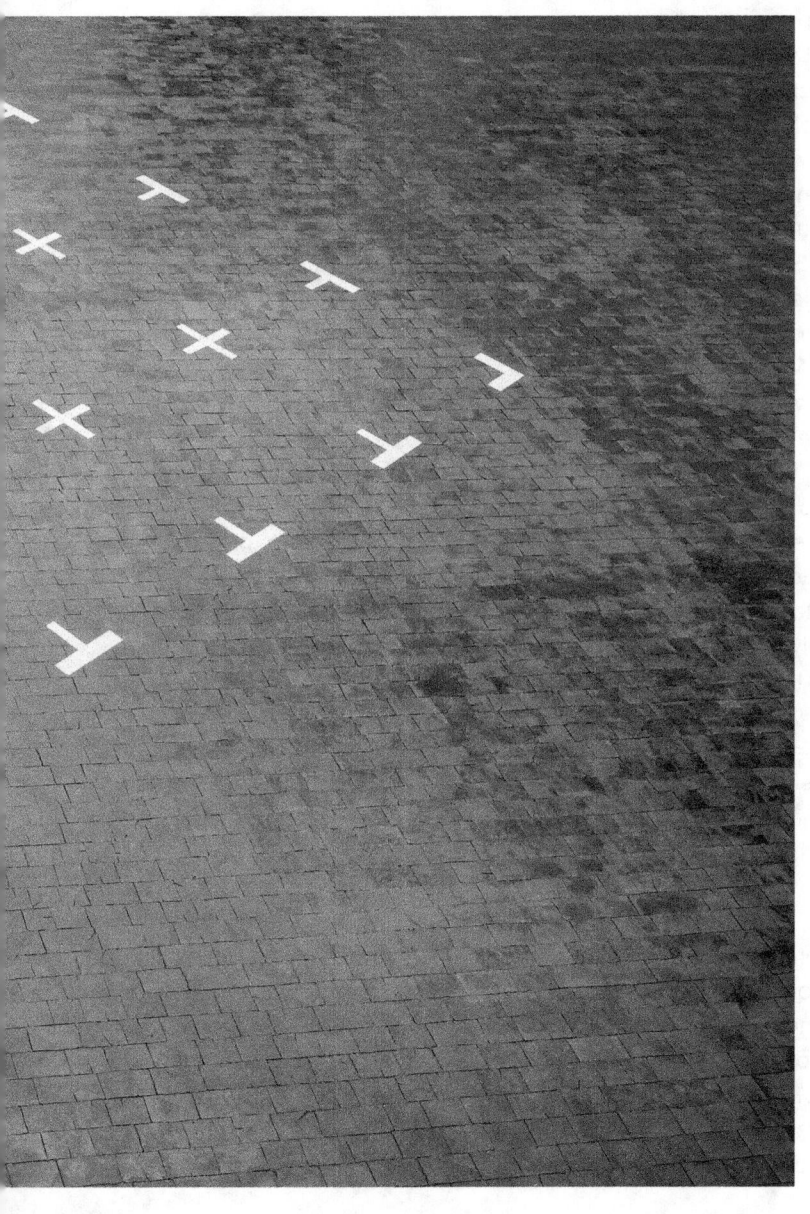

And yet Rio de Janeiro was thousands of miles away. While Dias's radical turn cannot be read simply as a matter of adapting to a newfound international artistic style, it certainly had to do with the new artistic environment he encountered first in Paris and then, more decisively, in Milan, where he finally settled in 1968. "At a certain moment," the artist recounts, "[the Italian critic] Tommaso Trini started to tell me: why make 3 x 4 metre paintings, all black with a little white dot in the middle, written over in white, when it could be a photostat Bristol-board (as Kosuth had used in the past …) … I told him: but for me it is very important that there is the body of canvas, of painting; that inside it a meta-canvas exist, and that it be seen as a figure of inside and outside."[25]

The suggestion that painting remained mainly a *bodily* enterprise would obviously fit Dias's earliest production, but what to make of it in relation to his "black period" in Milan, when his painting was all but reduced to arid, graphic demarcations and neat, written inscriptions? And yet it is precisely the latter to which the statement I have just quoted unmistakably refers. The suggestion attributed to Trini, his description and the passing mention of Joseph Kosuth, leave no doubt about that. The skepticism about the image must be coupled with this double insistence—on painting and on the bodily—if Dias's production in Milan is to be properly addressed.

The artist also recounts that works like these were disdainfully branded "surrealist" by Art & Language, the English conceptual art group alongside which he showed his works.[26] From a certain viewpoint, the accusation is not fully unwarranted. Like Meireles, Dias's assimilation of conceptualism rejects the philosophical rationalism that informed much of its formulations. Meireles puns that his work involves a kind of *humiliminimalism*, that is to say, a concern with scale and regularity that brings in an uncanny dimension within it, rejecting what he views as the absence of "any symbolic or discursive intention-ality" in minimalism (and, to an extent, in conceptual art).[27] What both Dias's insistence in painting and Meireles's insistence on going "through" a symbolic dimension counter is the rationalist dogmatism that informs a certain kind of conceptualism, most clearly that of Joseph Kosuth. Both artists did recognize in the language of conceptualism an opportunity to incorporate certain symbolic codes (such as cartography, as we will see) in ways that are not merely allusive or anecdotal, but this did not entail, to them, that this language would logically lead to a purer state of art.[28]

GODOG …

As a matter of fact, Dias's work after his 1968 turn was often understood and described as a productive friction between visuality and language.[29] For the Brazilian critic Mário Barata, commenting firsthand on the artist's 1969 show in the Milanese gallery Studio Marconi, "the fundamental aesthetic element [of the works] lies in the relationship between mental vectors, and their multiple possibilities, and an ambiguous visual or previsual situation."[30] More vividly, Paulo Sergio Duarte famously suggested in a seminal essay that in order to approach Dias's work "we need a certain strabismus: one eye on what is displayed, the other on the formulated problem."[31] This dual logic in its turn has been imagined similarly by critic Ronaldo Brito apropos of the tilted sink at the end of Meireles's *Red Shift* (1967–1984): "The sink is both a scene and an equation."[32]

As hinted in Dias's answer to Trini, one approach to such tricky paintings is to pay attention to the initial act of differentiation that they perform. Herkenhoff's reading of *The*

Hardest Way (1970) is particularly suggestive in this respect, as it opens up a number of perspectives into a somewhat hermetic work:

> Two monosyllables restore symmetry: GOD DOG. If both were one, this would be a palindrome. There is a double mirror-like quality: both graphic and conceptual. The sounds of the words merge, like a bark or a response. Would DOG be the mirrored image of GOD? Would one be the other's alterity, or its double? What is the place of man? In which cleft would he hide? The space between GOD and DOG in the painting has an undetermined width similar nevertheless to the dimension of each word in writing. This is the space of man: the intermediate gap between dog and god.[33]

As the critic notes, the drama revolves around the unclear interaction of the words, the unresolved position and identity of one in relation to the other. This stems from their formal similarity and is comparable to an unconscious slippage: it happens at the level of the signifier, one taking over from the other, with no regard whatsoever for the signified content of each sign. This is what Dias refers to as the "leash" that connects them in a "horizontal" manner, stressing that language operates according to its own internal logic, with no regard for meaningful hierarchies (while nevertheless affecting them).[34] "We don't have God up there and the creature down here," Dias says, "I wanted to use language to suggest a horizontal relationship."[35] This is a kind of deviation that is actually part of the normal function of language itself, regardless of whether we ordinarily pay attention to it or not (puns, for example, are essentially moments when we play with this feature of language at the expense of its instrumentality, thus noticing how unruly the signifier can be in relation to the signified content).

However, in order to fully elaborate the consequences of this logic, we must go beyond this initial recognition of potential specularity. Mirroring is not an utterly unwarranted metaphor (it actually plays a part in numerous works by Dias), but to interpret those words strictly as mirror images of one another is to lock them in a superficial circular logic, making it difficult to articulate the precise involvement of the viewing (and reading) subject. Thus Herkenhoff's choice to pinpoint the gap between the two words as "the space of man," problematically implying that a relatively traditional space of representation is somehow preserved in the painting. In other words, if we place the indeterminate proliferation of slippages fully within the logic of mirroring, we risk interpreting signification too hastily as a completed process and confusing metaphor for symbol.

But what if we go the opposite way and stick closely to the signifiers? In this case, "dog" will be read as the reverse *spelling* of "god," but not necessarily its flipped form—a subtle, but important distinction.[36] While there is indeed a suggestion of graphic specularity in the painting—two white graphic masses of equivalent size in diametrically opposed positions—it doesn't quite hold up once those masses are firmly grasped as words; strictly speaking, there is no mirroring involved in palindromic reversal. On a third level, that of the referent, specularity returns: the Portuguese word *cão*—one of the possible translations of "dog"—is a popular nickname for the devil.[37] The problem is that the graphic and the referential (or "conceptual") do not form a neat couplet, immediately confirming one another. In the passage from one to the other there is the rather problematic (i.e., nonspecular) dimension of the signifier; or, more precisely, of the verbal signifier in its becoming. Otherwise put, the specular opposition between the referents

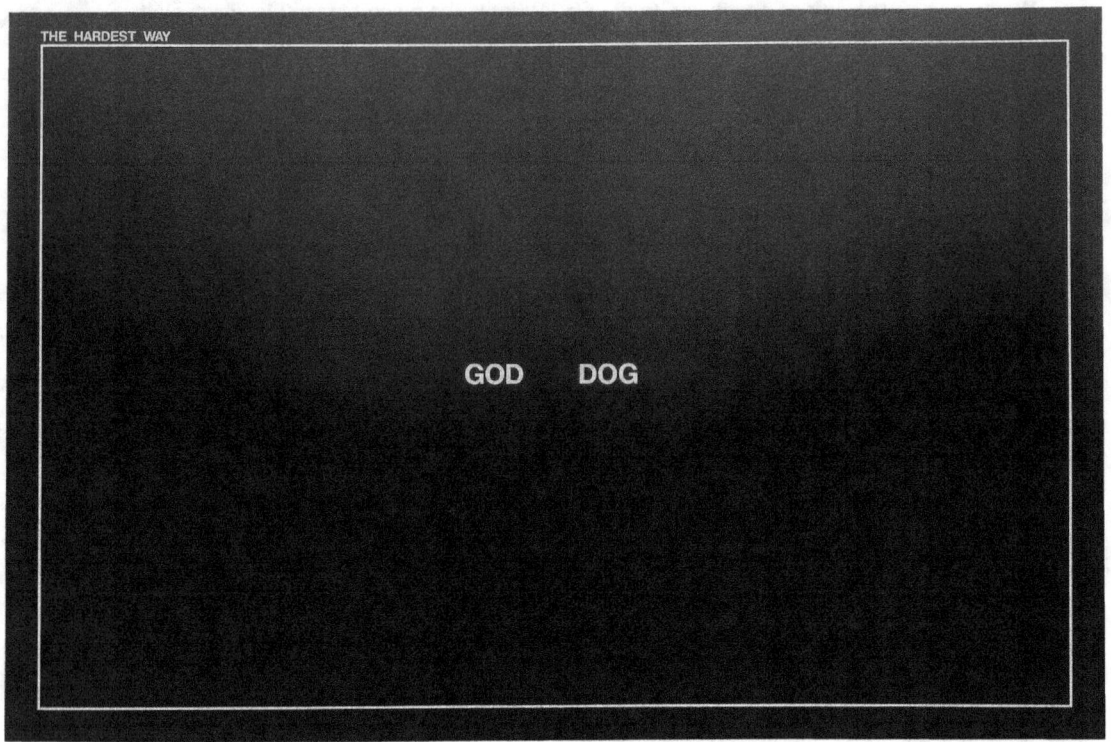

4.6
Antonio Dias, *The Hardest Way*, 1970. Acrylic
on canvas, 200 × 300 cm. Private collection.
Courtesy of the artist.

(i.e., God and the devil) can only take place *after* graphic specularity (i.e., the perception of two similar white masses) is twisted by the emerging signifier (i.e., by the subsequent apprehension of those masses as proper words). If a relationship of homological consistency is subsequently to be maintained, then the signifier's problematic dimension must be covered up, for the latter admits no specularity whatsoever.

The problem with Herkenhoff's reading is that "man" becomes noncorporeal in a way that is supposed to keep a sense of proportionality, so as to fit in the space between GOD and DOG as some sort of missing link that would render the picture complete (or that would at least uphold such completeness as its paradigm). It would thus be the intermediary who guarantees not only the complete image, but also that "god" and "dog" unproblematically mirror each other. This is why this interpretation ultimately relies on preserving a traditional space of representation: at the end of the day, "man" becomes the holder of an ideal proportion that bridges all gaps the painting opens up. In short, the painting is "stabilized" and assumed to be a symmetrical whole. By overlooking the critical dimension of the signifier we also lose, at a single stroke, the sense both of how the erratic slippage between one word and another disrupts rather than stabilizes mirroring and of how this very logic, with its irresolvable temporality, is the actual "trap" that ensnares the viewing subject, the "strabismus" that sets it up, and, crucially enough, the core of its antivisual gambit—of its enigmage. My emphasis on how the work of the signifier must be located somewhere between the graphic and referential aspects of the painting is thus a way of saying that we must take Dias's insistence that these paintings are "non-images" very seriously.[38] This is also to say that the crux of *The Hardest Way* lies precisely in the way it articulates embodiment not as a mirror image, but as something that happens within the dimension of the signifier.

But how? To be sure, this is something that Herkenhoff himself briefly hints at when he writes, "the sounds of the words merge." This is the precise point where specularity fails, for mirror images require a certain level of externality in order to assert similarity.[39] Conversely, these "sounds" are too grounded on the complex material that links them together, and that links also, on the same stroke, body and language: the *voice*. So this is my suggestion: in *The Hardest Way*, the voice qua material dimension of the signifier (either in actual or inner vocalization) lies in the same logical "spot" where spectator and writing meet. As all writing, both words (GOD and DOG) are also graphic marks on a background. In our moment of closing in (we should not forget that paintings are hung on walls, that we approach them from the distance, and that this is a very large painting) we have to apprehend the white, fine, centrally aligned mass on a black background as words to be read. We do not approach them as readers will approach the words I write in the next sentence, that is, as if they were already part of a smooth and operative flow of linked, dynamic words inconspicuously sliding into one another. It is, no matter how briefly, an encounter with language, an *instantiation* of it. This is part of any act of reading, but not perhaps in such an evident way. What ultimately guarantees that *The Hardest Way* is a painting, and irreducibly so, rather than a book, or a poster, is its astonishing capacity to sustain, against all odds, the opaqueness of language. The function of language is denaturalized since it has to be, so to speak, triggered. Thus we get to the main point: because of the way the words are displayed and because of the relationship of progressive closeness between spectator and painting, the words in the painting *elicit vocalization* as the mark of our recognition of them as linguistic signs. It is by virtue of being vocalized—even if not aloud, even if by an internal voice for a split second only—that these words are *distinguished*, as such, from the white marks that materially constitute them.

As I have already pointed out, this distinction comes somehow *before* a third, signifying distinction between GOD and DOG as signs (between what these words actually signify) is fully enacted. It is in this sense that Dias's account of a "horizontal relationship" between GOD and DOG becomes radical: these two words are always-already slipping into one another as they emerge. The fact that we are led into "swapping" materials—that is, into wresting the words away from their graphic support and turning them into phonemes in order to actually constitute them *as* words—is decisive. This action casts a fleeting but dramatic focus on what philosopher Mladen Dolar has termed "the tricky transubstantiation of voices into linguistic signs."[40] That spoken language materially requires the same voice it strives to efface in order to get its message across is a fact of everyday communication.[41] But here we have a case of the intrusion of vocalization persisting *after* its main role of "starting up" language is finished. Vocalization goes awry: instead of, or in addition to, making both words plainly distinct, it keeps stressing their material (phonic) affinity. Again, the proximity of the words is key—of two similar, tonic monosyllables that elicit comparison and juxtaposition. If the two words were placed, say, in opposite corners of a similarly large painting, the effect would be different: we would have the time to discretely make GOD fully legible and signified before turning to DOG, and the hierarchy Dias wanted to undo would probably insinuate itself into our reading of the painting—representation would smoothly install itself. But this is not the case: as quickly as the eye switches from GOD to DOG and back again, the mind's "voice" (and maybe even the actual one) goes about repeating them, turning the two-way "leash" imagined by Dias into a potentially endless loop: "godogodogodo...."[42] So, we are first enticed to utter the words in order to *really* make sense of them—not that we cannot do that by reading alone, but speaking them provides a reassurance of the sense we are offered. And yet this becomes its very undoing, for the voice keeps threatening to collapse both signifiers together into nonsensical babble. The apparent signifying stability, which would authorize an unproblematic exploration of *meaning* as the ultimate arena in *The Hardest Way*, is interrupted.[43]

As (instrumental) *meaning* is interrupted, the way is opened for the eruption of (unruly) *meanings* out of the senseless sound. So, if in the midst of repetition we suddenly feel a prevalence of "god" over "dog," we may find ourselves endlessly repeating "oh, god!" Conversely, if the second signifier happens to momentarily recover its boundaries, or if our inflection shifts just a little bit, we may stumble upon an (ironically) complimentary "good dog!" These meanings will often dissolve back into the senselessness of "godog ...," even if we attempt to retain them. Conversely, it may well happen that one of these particular meanings will stubbornly persist, hijacking our voice as if we were unable to dispel it. It is this unsettling lack of mastery, rather than the notion of the voice as an instrument of the self, that constitutes what can be tentatively termed a *subject of vocalization*, by which I mean that the subject is not actually the unequivocal point of origin of whatever gets vocalized.

132

The vocalization of "godog" in *The Hardest Way* thus differs from an idealized projection of oneself into the empty gap. This is the kind of gap that the subject often attempts to fill either with an imaginary projection (the mirror image) or with a symbolic construct (like, say, the fantasy of a fully mastered and nonintrusive voice that grounds a neat scenario of intersubjective communication).[44] To conflate palindrome and mirror image would be the effect of fantasy insofar as fantasy "functions as a provisional understanding of something which eludes understanding"—in this case, the proper nature of vocalization.[45] Uncannily enough, to fully read "godog"—taking into account the two words' vocal dimension—is to register rather than overlook the elision between them, and thus their irreducible gap. It is this short-circuit in signification that actually places us in front of the painting; our failure to bridge the gap means that the painting *returns* our address. Vocalization calls the spectator forth not in order to *complete* the scene, but to understand him or herself as *incomplete* in relation to the scene. What thus "fills" the gap is not "man," but the voice "in its object-like quality."[46]

This is a rather peculiar—and powerful—version of the "probject" (which, as the catalyst of a "new perceptual behavior," was meant precisely to throw spectators off balance; that is, to frustrate their assumptions and prejudices about what the experience of art entailed). To put it briefly, the gap between GOD and DOG is ultimately a stand-in for another gap: the one between the spectator and the picture, between the work and the subject it posits. This is the gap that fails to be bridged by vocalization. Vocalization is so important, because it reorients the gap in the painting in a way that makes the supposition of a subject related to it (but not integrated in its image) necessary. "If voice implies reflexivity," Dolar argues, "insofar as its resonance returns from the Other, then it is a reflexivity without a self—not a bad name for the subject."[47]

PARODIC WISDOM

The role of vocalization in *The Hardest Way* is indeed a most remarkable example of how radically the gap between language and visuality could be tensioned in Dias's practice, but it was by no means the sole antivisual maneuver he deployed at that moment. If we take a closer look at the production of his "black period," it becomes apparent that this tension often involved the cognitive structures and symbolic codes that are ideologically interwoven in everyday reality and that, as we will see, were also undergoing a crucial historical shift in the turn of that decade. Significantly, critic Sônia Salzstein has recently drawn attention to "the impassive manner by which the artist stretched form to the limit of annihilation as a token of art's cognitive dimension, whether in the output of the mid-1960s or in the works that came later, in which the constant recourse to patterns and reticules surely says something about the difficulty of restoring the intelligence of synthesis that rationalism attributed to form."[48]

Patterns, reticules ... the list can easily be expanded. The basic pictorial operation of *Anywhere Is My Land*, for example, is a superimposition of two quintessential modernist devices, the all-over and the grid. Its spray-painted and dripped areas cannot fail to allude to the likes of Jackson Pollock and Jules Olitski, whose work was so often taken either as a declaration of flatness or an existential confrontation with the large expanse of the canvas—or both. Indeed, *The Desert—Let It Absorb* (1970), one of many works in which Dias employed the figure of the desert, is chromatically similar

4.7
Antonio Dias, *The Desert—Let It Absorb*,
1971. Acrylic on canvas, 130 × 162 cm.
Collection of the artist. Courtesy of the artist.

to certain paintings by Pollock, like *One: Number 31* (1950). But spray-painting was in fact the trademark of Dias's "non-images," making suggestions of expressiveness (and absorption) all but absurd. What is more, the all-overness in his paintings is usually not-all, covering only the "metacanvas" (i.e, the bounded inner space that mimics the shape of the canvas) and thus dispelling any metaphysical association with the absoluteness of the picture plane. By the same token, the grid in *Anywhere Is My Land* becomes curiously displaced, failing to establish a clear relation with its "ground," so that figure-ground distinctions in these conditions can only result from arbitrary projections. The title of the work implies mapping, but it would be a stretch to take its spray pattern as the representation of a particular terrain of any kind. In this context, all quantifications, be they of distance or even of painterly marks, seem equally arbitrary (perhaps the only measurement the grid plausibly undertakes is a pointless count of white dots per square). Instead of demarcating the visible, grid and all-overness actually cancel each other out. If, as Rosalind Krauss puts it, the modernist field of vision is structured as a "cogito of vision" whereby "figure" can only emerge as "non-ground"—that is, as an instantaneous confirmation of the cognitive faculties of the viewing subject in "a limit case of self-imbrication"—then *Anywhere Is My Land* brings this logic to the verge of pointlessness.[49] It becomes a limit case of self-imbrication without a self.

Anywhere Is My Land thus "formalizes an experience of non-identity," and it does so on more than one level.[50] It sets the statement contained in its title against the languages of modernism and conceptualism alike, and also against Dias's own experience of self-exile. This is not to say that the painting simply chronicles a personal situation, but rather that it articulates a sense of subjective displacement that emerged at a moment when notions of geographic, linguistic, and cultural belonging were being profoundly shaken—a perception shared by numerous Brazilian artists and intellectuals who had either to endure political repression and the patriotic pantomimes of the military dictatorship or cope with life in exile. Far from being simply a peripheral narrative, this is actually registered in one of the most significant early documents of conceptual art, MoMA's "Information" catalog, where both Oiticica and Meireles began their written statements by categorically declaring that they were not representing Brazil.[51]

In such a context, it is unsurprising that one's land could be conceived as a radically contingent and unrepresentable situation. This is a point Dias further explores in *The Illustration of Art / One & Three / Stretchers / Model* (1971); what the work illustrates is the absurdity of expecting a meaningful experience of art to be palpably grounded in any particular situation and in the assumed fullness of one's immediate, visual experience. It is not by chance that the two pairs of stretchers in the third set cross over each other at a peripheral position; the spectator is confronted with the insufficiency of self-centered visual experience to deal with the scale of contemporary phenomena. This does not entail that art cannot articulate meaningful experiences, but that such articulation now requires that the expected sufficiency of an individually grounded visual register be questioned from the outset.

Dias's constant recourse to maps is intimately connected with this problem. It revolves around the need to account for the ubiquitous sense of decentralization that, in the late 1960s, seemed to pervade cultural experience at large. This is something that also interested other artists internationally, most notably Robert Smithson. Smithson's

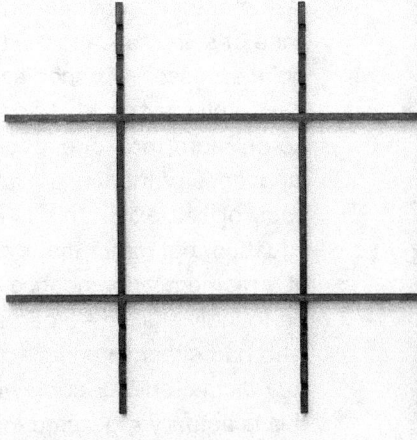

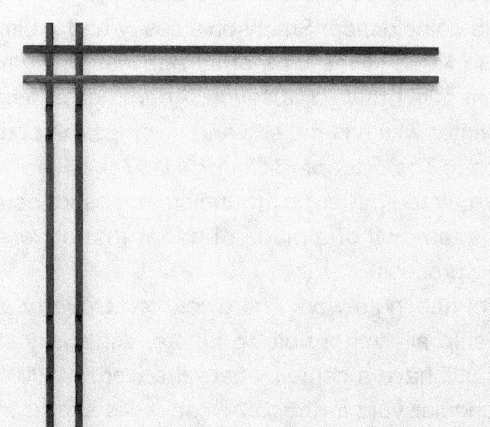

THE ILLUSTRATION OF ART
ONE & THREE / STRETCHERS / MODEL

ALL REDUCTION
OR ENLARGEMENT
IS A MATTER
OF ACCOMODATION

argument in his 1968 essay "A Museum of Language in the Vicinity of Art" takes sprawl-ing suburbs, the work and writing of certain minimalist artists, and even the "vacant and transparent" appearance of actors in Roger Corman's films as symptoms of decenter-ing.[52] The latter is as peculiar as it is telling: "Corman's sense of dissimulation shows us the peripheral shell of appearances in terms of some invisible set of rules, rather than by any 'natural' or 'realistic' inner motivation—his actors reflect the empty center."[53] In other words, Smithson questions the validity of inner motivation and other figures of centrality in providing a useful interpretive key for recent cultural developments. At one point, he turns to Ad Reinhardt's illustration *A Portend of the Artist as a Yhung Mandala* (1956): "From the central vortex, that looks like prophetic parody of 'op art'— I can't think of anything more meaningless than that—to the rectangular margin of parodic wisdom—'Everybuddie understands the Songs of Birds and Picasso,' one is aware of a conflict between center and perimeter."[54]

A "meaningless" center surrounded by a "rectangular margin of parodic wisdom": can there be a better description of Dias's paintings and drawings of the late 1960s and early 1970s? This is no simple coincidence: Smithson's essay had a direct and lasting impact on Dias, who read it in Milan at the time of its publication.[55] Smithson further remarks that "every site glides away toward absence. An immense negative entity of formlessness displaces the center which is the city and swamps the country."[56] This is strikingly suggestive in relation to *The Occupied Country* (1971), where "occupation" is signaled by a formless, spray-painted pattern surrounding an absent center, a negative imprint that resulted from the removal of a piece of paper that covered that part of the canvas during the painting process.

The political overtones of naming a work *The Occupied Country* at the height of the Brazilian military dictatorship are impossible to ignore, especially since an earlier version of that painting does still have a center, where the word "ARMY" can be read. As a matter of fact, the rectangular void in the 1971 canvas is similar in shape to the Brazilian Federal District, famously demarcated at the supposed geographical center of the country and excised from the surrounding state of Goiás.[57] This would lead, of course, to the construction of Brasília, whose utopian aspirations, by 1971, had given way to a bureaucratic and authoritarian state of things. As in *Tiradentes*, geographic displacements, either actual or metaphoric, became an acute way of articulating politi-cal dissent in an increasingly internationalized world.[58] Meireles devotes the entirety of his *Information* essay to a narrative about "a region which does not appear on official maps, a region called the SOUTHERN CROSS."[59] This region, he would continue, was arbitrarily divided into an eastern side that is well known "through post cards, pictures, descriptions and books" and a western side where "people can transform its history into fantastic legends and fables and allegories," thus achieving "a real existence."[60] This is perhaps what *Tiradentes* aimed at: a *détournement* of the geographic displace-ment of the capital into a commentary on the mystification of social reality in Brazil that took the form of a totemic outburst.

Both artists were acutely aware that geography, especially in a country as large and unevenly populated as Brazil, is apprehended mostly in mythic or profoundly abstract, symbolic ways. Cartography thus became a privileged arena for addressing this ideological knotting of language, visuality, and identity, and for artistically questioning it via nonintuitive models of experience. This leads us to the most striking point of contact between Dias and Smithson, which appears only toward the end of "A Museum of Language in the Vicinity of Art" in yet another example of the spatial arrangement the essay's title suggests. Dias recalls his childhood interest in what he called "Lewis Carroll's map of nothing."[61] What he is actually referring to is an illustration of Carroll's nonsensical poem *The Hunting of the Snark*, which Smithson reproduced in his essay. As the pertinent part of the poem goes:

> He had bought a large map representing the sea,
> Without the least vestige of land:
> And the crew were much pleased when they found it to be
> A map they could all understand.
>
> "What's the good of Mercator's North Poles and Equators,
> Tropics, Zones, and Meridian Lines?"
> So the Bellman would cry: and the crew would reply
> "They are merely conventional signs!
>
> "Other maps are such shapes, with their islands and capes!
> But we've got our brave Captain to thank:"
> (So the crew would protest) "that he's bought us the best—
> A perfect and absolute blank!"[62]

Similarly to the inner black square in *Sun Photo as a Self-Portrait*, the *Snark* map displays the failure of vision as a cognitive means. However, the map is not restricted to its blank surface. Like Reinhardt's illustration and many paintings by Dias, it has its own "margins of parodic wisdom." "Mercator's North Poles and Equators, Tropics, Zones, and Meridian Lines" are indeed reduced to "merely conventional signs" that surround visual blankness. As the linguist Jean-Jacques Lecercle has argued, "In *The Hunting of the Snark* we are made to witness the process whereby the figural turns into the semiotic," amounting to "an intuitive grasp of a philosophical problematic that clearly emerged almost a century after [Carroll's] death."[63] This problematic is what informs, in part, appropriations of cartography in art by the likes of Dias, Meireles, and Smithson, as in the latter's complaint:

> When the word "fiction" is used, most of us think of literature, and practically never of fictions in the general sense.... The status of fiction has vanished into the myth of the fact. It is thought that facts have a greater reality than fiction—that "science fiction" through the myth of progress becomes "science fact." Fiction is not believed to be a part of the world. Rationalism confines fiction to literary categories in order to protect its own interests or systems of knowledge.[64]

No work by Dias can be said visually to quote Carroll's map as remarkably as *History/Story* (1971). The title's juxtaposition clearly turns the painting into a display of semiotic difference at its starkest, as the austere inscription of the two similar words highlights their opposition. However, in this case what underlies semiotic difference is nothing but "the myth of the fact" that would make "story" into "science fiction" and history into "science fact."

4.9
Antonio Dias, *The Occupied Country*, 1971.
Acrylic on canvas, 130 × 195.5 cm. Coleção
João Satamini, Museu de Arte Contemporânea
de Niterói. Courtesy of the artist.

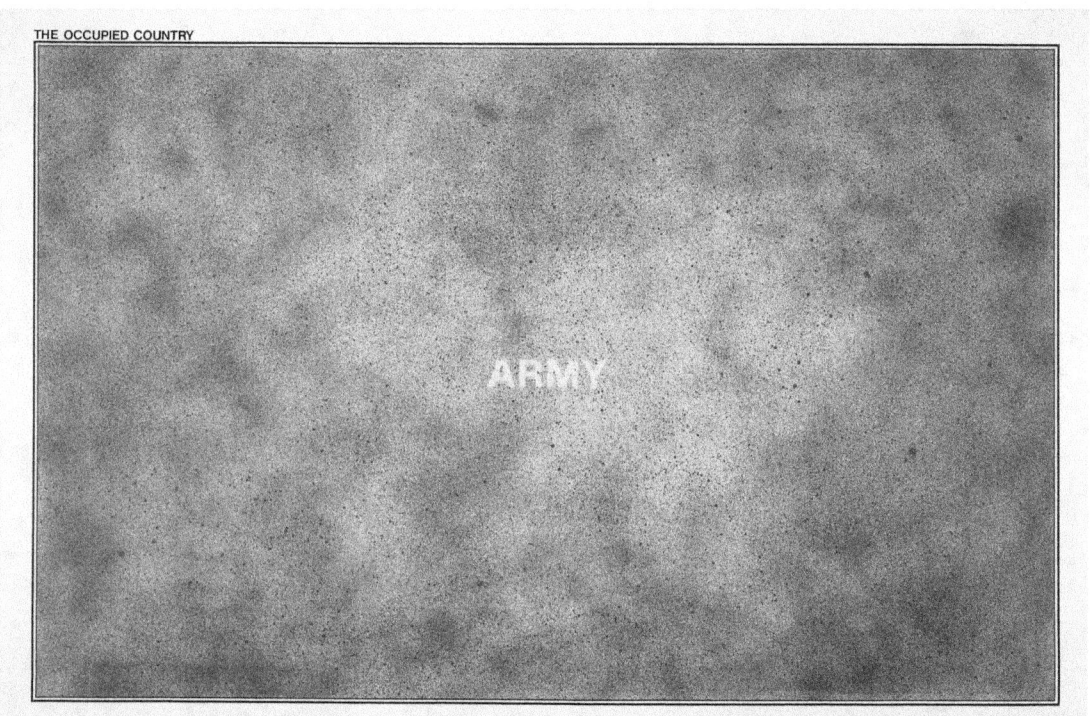

4.10
Antonio Dias, *The Occupied Country*, 1970.
Acrylic on canvas, 130 × 195.5 cm. Daros
Latinamerica Collection, Zurich. Photo: Peter
Schälchli. Courtesy of the artist.

4.11
Henry Holiday, illustration from Lewis Carroll's
The Hunting of the Snark, 1876.

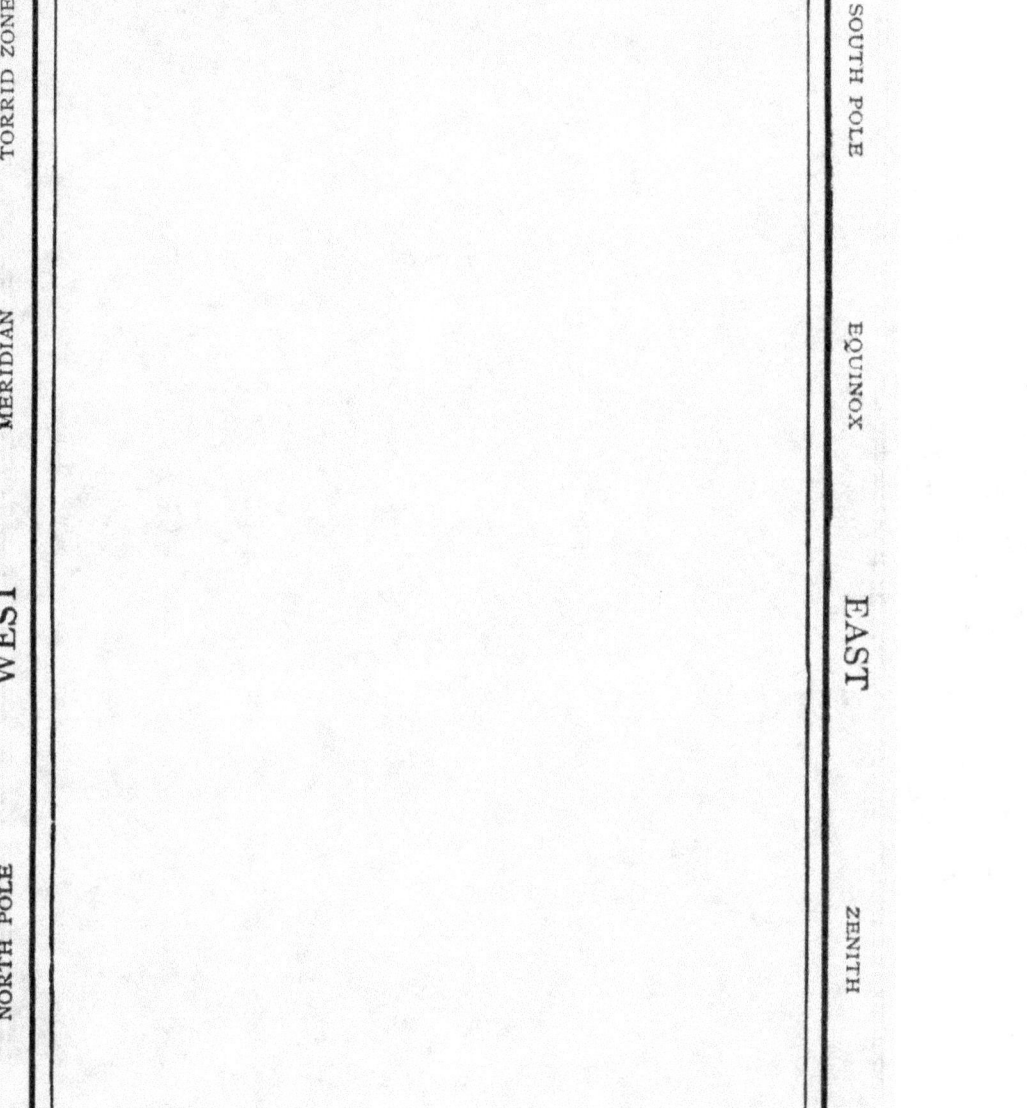

Scale of Miles.

OCEAN-CHART.

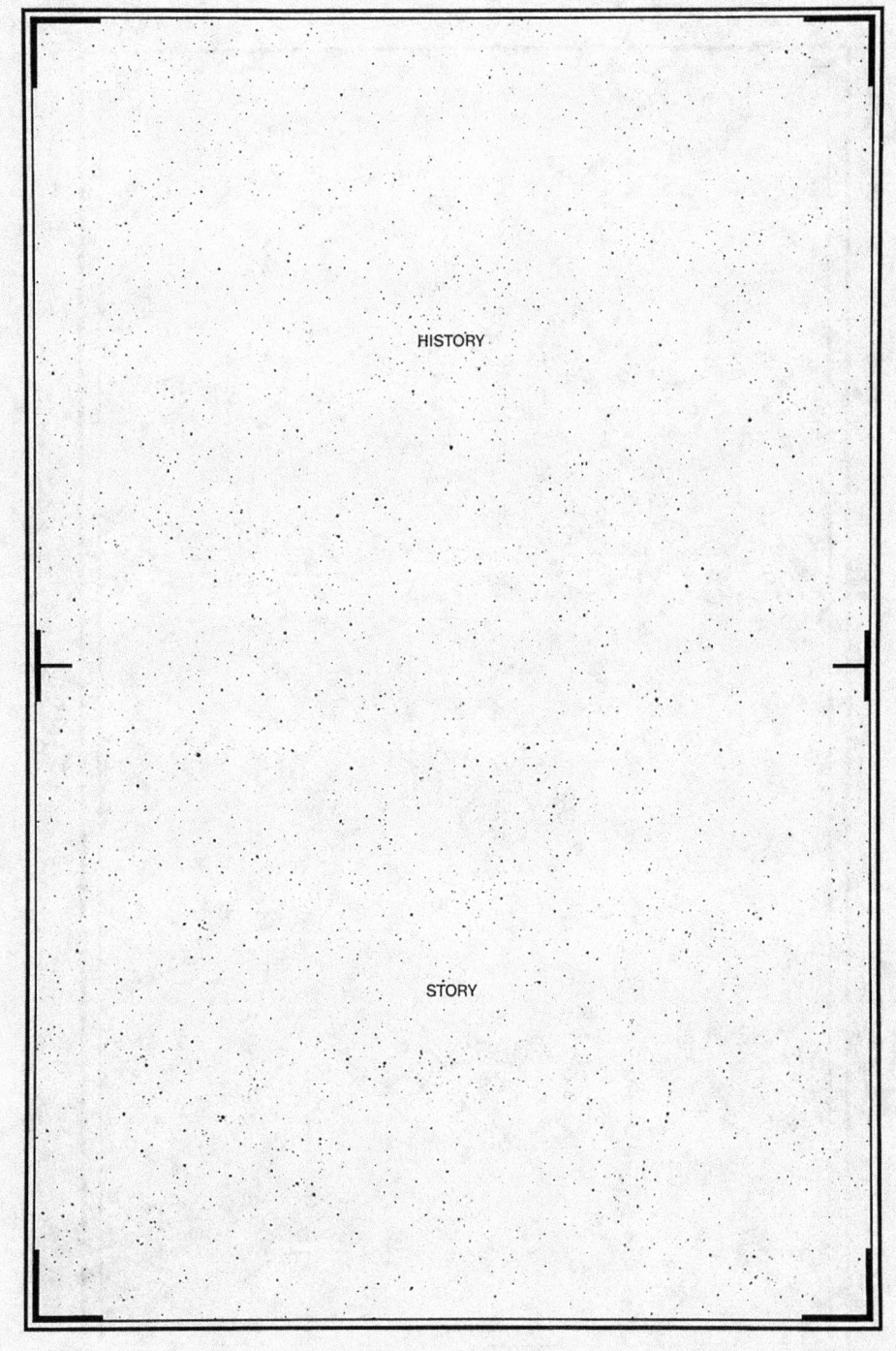

4.12
Antonio Dias, *History / Story*, 1971 Acrylic on
canvas, 195 × 130 cm. Private collection. Photo:
Maura Parodi. Courtesy of the artist.

This is not to propose that fiction is all there is, just as, for Lecercle, the extreme fragmentation of *The Hunting of the Snark* does not authorize "the idea that, in the field of interpretation, anything goes."[65] In *History* (1968), for example, the "myth of the fact" is disrupted not by a direct juxtaposition with fiction, but by taking factuality itself to such an extreme that it loses all self-evidence. Dias collected earth, dust, and debris from the streets of Paris after a demonstration early in 1968 and displayed it in a transparent PVC bag tagged with the word "history." Like the voice in *The Hardest Way*, the inert materiality of the debris is an obstacle in the way of self-evident assumptions about the intrinsic meaningfulness of history and a stumbling block to the coherent sequence of facts that Smithson called "the myth of progress." In Walter Benjamin's well-known allegory, this myth prevents the angel of history from "[awakening] the dead, and [making] whole what has been smashed," so that material history continuously accumulates like a "pile of debris."[66] Benjamin's metaphor is fortuitously reminiscent of *History*, but the point I want to stress is conceptual: once sheer materiality is taken as a dialectical driving force, the duality of fact and fiction is displaced and a new configuration emerges. The assumed inexorableness of the fact gives way to the opaque meaninglessness of the Real, but the former cannot be grounded by the latter, so that reality becomes exposed as what Smithson considered a protection of "interests and systems of knowledge." What is at stake, then, is not an absurd claim of the debris's authenticity, but rather the fact that history, as one of such "systems," has to be subjectively reoriented— that the fictive must be seriously taken into account as the backbone of history (and of everyday experience, for that matter) rather than be ideologically dismissed.

In this sense, Meireles's *To Be Curved with the Eyes* (1970/1975) can also be considered a piece of "parodic wisdom"—one that crucially hints at the efficacy of his work in general. It was meant to be included in every single one of his future exhibitions, to permanently operate as an (anti-)visual epigraph, a warning that vision is no mere cognitive tool but is also, and more importantly, an ideological shaper of everyday reality.[67] What is at stake in this work is the relay between two important Lacanian dimensions, the Imaginary and the Real, as the fabric of lived experience. As Fredric Jameson has noted, this is the same relay that structures the Althusserian critique of ideology.[68] However, Jameson adds that Althusser's Lacanian framework is incomplete, as it fails to consider the play of the Symbolic register. The latter is implied, for example, in the fact that the "two equal and curved iron bars" of *To Be Curved with the Eyes* are placed against millimeter-scale graph paper—in other words, what complicates the relay between intuitive visual experience and the Real is "a proper representational dialectic of the codes and capacities of individual languages or media."[69]

That this paradigmatic shift in representational codes is often addressed in contemporary art with recourse to cartography betrays the fact that cartography has been long equipped to deal with it, as if it were ready to be appropriated, or rather elevated from the status of a specific discipline to that of a major cultural paradigm. This is precisely what Jameson proposes by insisting that the Symbolic register be considered alongside the Imaginary and the Real if an "aesthetic of cognitive mapping" is to emerge from the representational dialectic that this interplay sets in motion.[70] In fact, the historical context of his own mobilization of cartography is not much different from that of Dias, Meireles, and Smithson—it is yet another evidence of the philosophical problematic

146

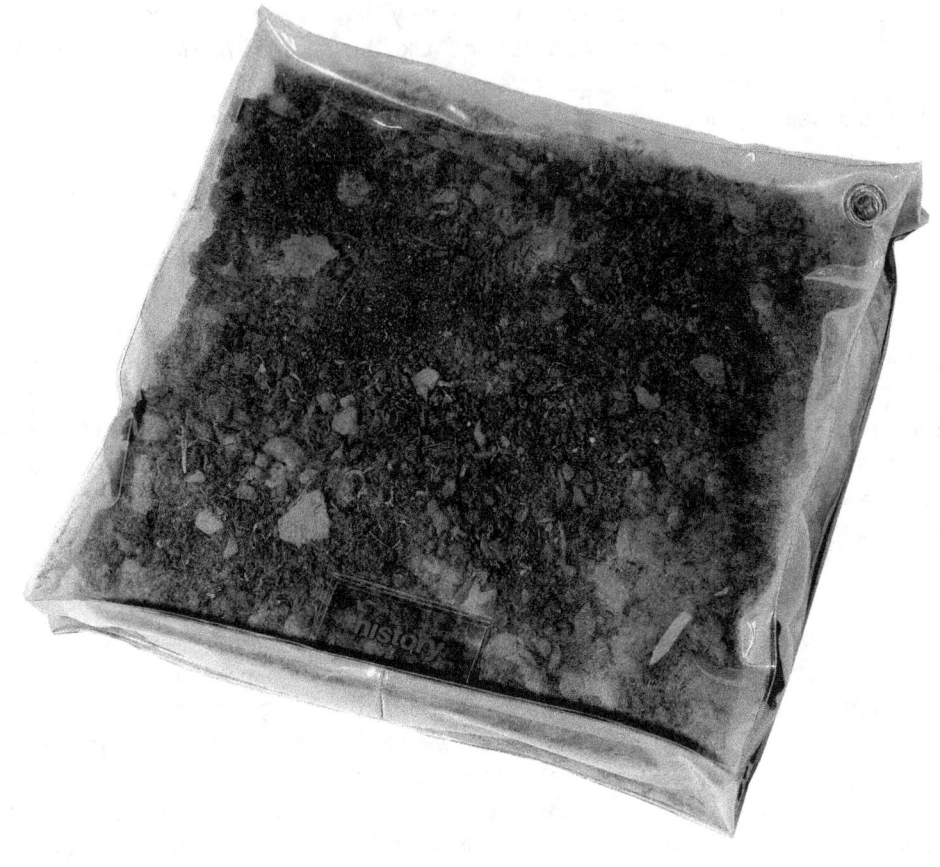

4.13
Antonio Dias, *History*, 1968. PVC, earth, dust,
and debris, 6.5 × 39.7 × 38.5 cm. Daros
Latinamerica Collection, Zurich. Photo: Peter
Schälchli. Courtesy of the artist.

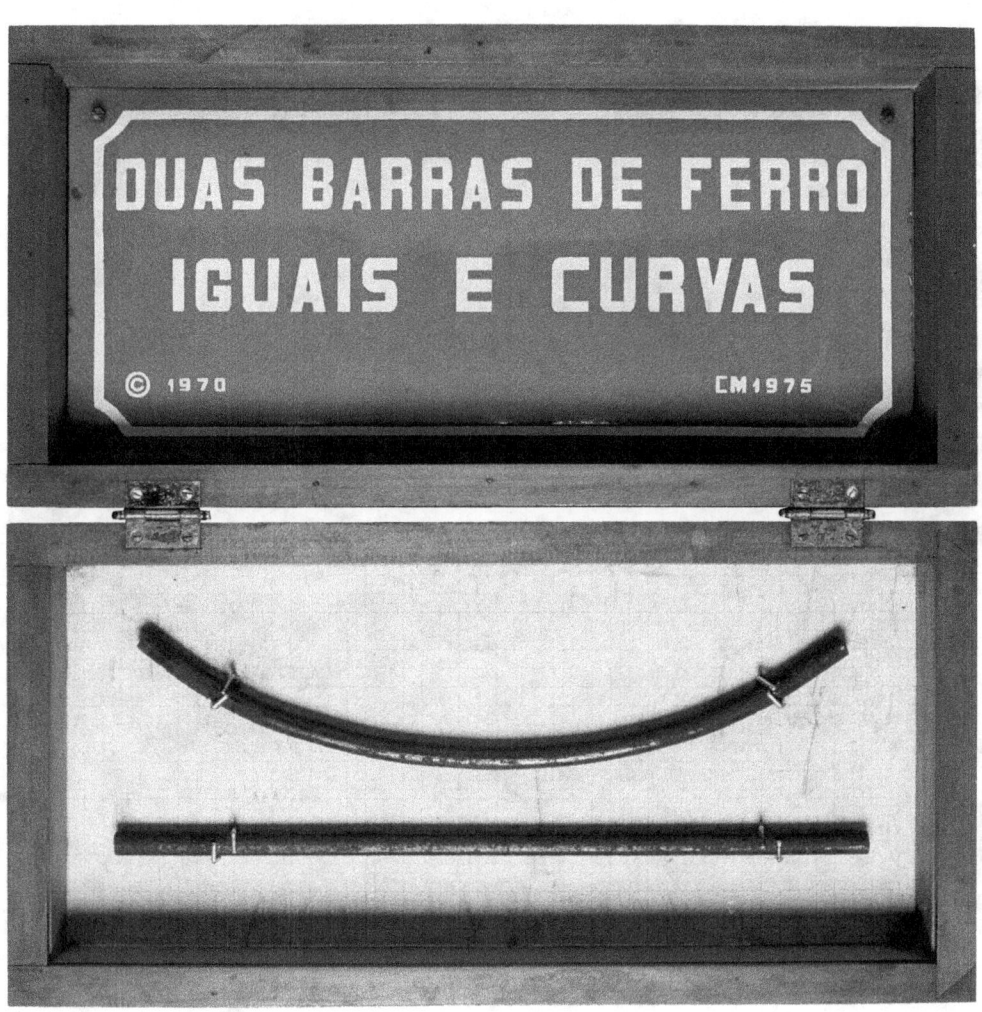

4.14
Cildo Meireles, *To Be Curved with the Eyes*,
1970–1975. Wood, iron, graph paper, bronze
and enamel plate, 25 × 50 × 5 cm. Photo: Wilton
Montenegro. Courtesy of the artist.

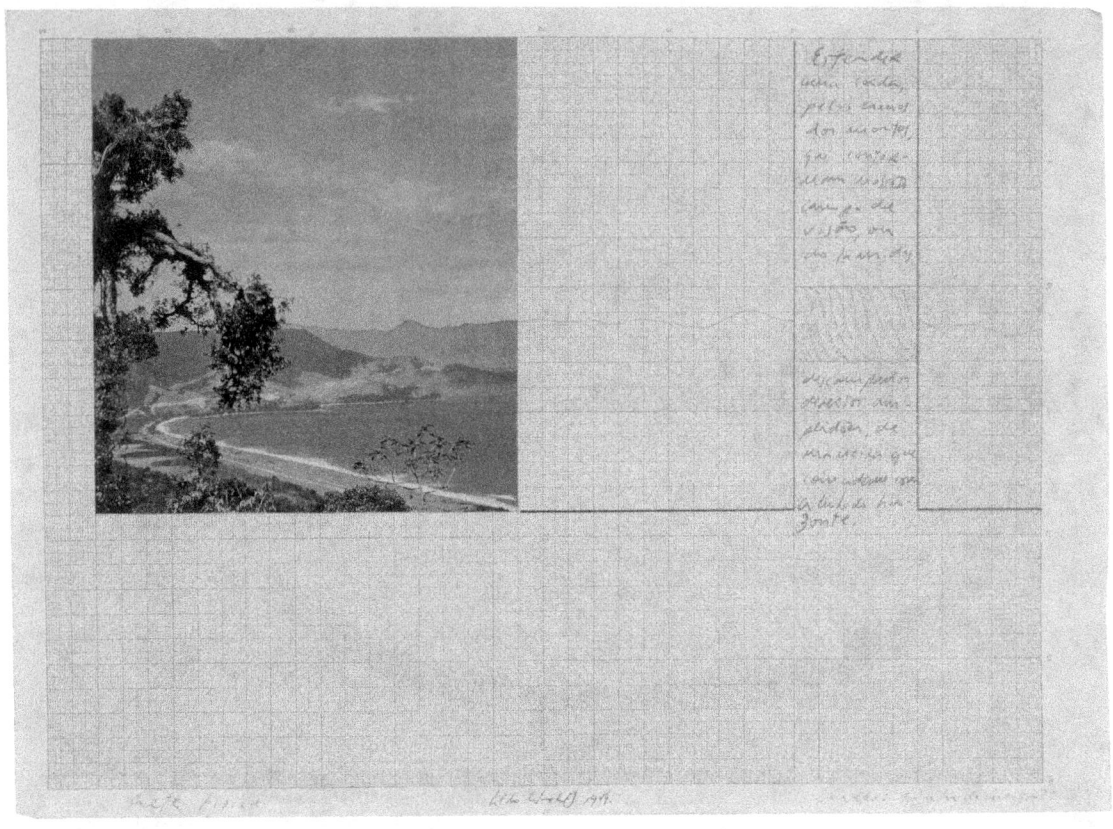

4.15
Cildo Meireles, *Physical Art*, 1969. Ink, graphite,
and collage on millimeter-scale graph paper,
32 × 45 cm. Photo: Vicente de Mello. Courtesy
of the artist.

pinpointed by Lecercle. What is crucial is that cartography in this context means something distinct from precartographic devices, like the itinerary or the sea chart, visual aids in which "coastal features are noted for the use of Mediterranean navigators who rarely venture out into the open sea."[71] The *Snark* map, with its lack of recognizable reference points, would be an example of the latter. Nevertheless, by coupling visual insufficiency with the "parodic" coordinates inscribed in its margins, it points to cartography proper as an entirely different cognitive apparatus. Commenting on the historical emergence of cartography, Jameson further argues:

> the new instruments—compass, sextant, theodolite—correspond not merely to new geographic and navigational problems (the difficult matter of determining longitude, particularly on the curving surface of the planet, as opposed to the simple matter of latitude, which European navigators can still empirically determine by ocular inspection of the African coast); they also introduce a whole new coordinate: the relationship with the totality, particularly as it is mediated by the stars and by new operations like that of triangulation. At this point, cognitive mapping in the broader sense comes to require the coordination of existential data (the empirical position of the subject) with unlived, abstract conceptions of the geographic totality.[72]

Meireles's *Physical Art* series is particularly emblematic in this respect. In one of his unrealized (or rather unrealizable) projects, the artist proposed to "lay a rope along the summit of mountains that contour our field of vision, or at the extremity of deserts, open spaces, expanses, in a way that will match the horizon line."[73] On the one hand, this is a nod to Piero Manzoni, who envisioned a line drawn "around the entire Greenwich Meridian."[74] Indeed, Manzoni's *Socle du monde* is one of Meireles's favorite works and clearly prefigured the latter's frequent recourse to scale shifts and perceptual conundrums that challenge intuitive cognition.[75] On the other hand, Meireles's slips and displacements flirt with conceptualist dryness, but ultimately push its analytical ethos into a kind of cognitive vertigo. The actual futility of that *Physical Art* proposition is obvious, but it nevertheless points to the disjunctive quality of spatial experience Jameson describes. Significantly enough, the project is displayed by means of a deceptively simple collage that brings together different representational registers. Or perhaps, considering its scale shifts, it would be more accurate to say that it pulls them *apart*. Meireles traced a red line on top of the mountains of a landscape photograph, following the horizon line (as seen from the camera's viewpoint). The red line crosses the boundary of the photograph and continues its irregular path on the surface of the millimeter graph paper until it reaches a straight, vertical graphite line. It is then suddenly replaced by a realistic depiction of twisted fibers, in what can be reasonably assumed to be a life-sized rendering of a segment of rope.

The change of scale is abrupt, but it should be not read as a close-up, as if one's viewpoint had simply shifted from telescopic distance to microscopic proximity. In other words, this shift cannot be accounted for by quantifying the viewer's distance to the represented object as a linear value that would consequently structure a homogeneous space, regardless of how far it can be said to extend. On the contrary, what underlies the unbroken and deceptive continuity of the red line is a fundamental incommensurability between different representational registers and their assumed viewing positions. Its initial course over the photograph is motivated by the horizon line, which is not, in turn, an objective trait of the landscape, such as the indexical referent (i.e., the asserted existence a mountain or a forest there). It is rather symbolic and subjective—the symbolic demarcation of a subjectively defined horizon line (in the sense that the latter depends on the camera's viewpoint). As the line breaks onto the millimeter graph paper, however, its motivation is left behind, and so is the particular symbolic function it has performed so far. Even if it is assumed to be the abstract continuation of the horizon line, the fact remains that the empirical reality of the horizon gives way to a kind of projection that has nothing to do with the photograph's viewpoint. In other words, if the horizon line is necessarily defined by the existence of a particular viewpoint, what is the point of representing any particular configuration of it over the unspecific background of the graph paper? In this context, that line would have been no more or less valid qua representation of the horizon had it been as straight as the grid that begins to ground it the moment it leaves the photograph. As such a representation, it is now merely conventional. As a crooked line, however, it is now what Paul Klee described as "[a] walk for a walk's sake"; it trades the pastness of its symbolic attachment to a singular and irrevocable viewpoint for a sense of being a continuously emerging visual incident.[76] An equally incommensurable gap separates red line from red grid, in contrast to the negligible visual difference between them, as the abstract space erected by the grid is temporally at odds with the ongoing present of the line's erratic path.

Last, but not least, the drawn segment of the rope also addresses the here and now, but for different reasons. A subtle reversal is put in play: instead of using scale to abstract the actual dimension of the drawn form, the empirical tendency to perceive this as a life-sized drawing potentially projects a 1:1 ratio over the whole scale of the grid. It follows that the grid ultimately measures the size of the sheet of paper itself, reaffirming its objecthood in the face of an actual viewer. Likewise, by virtue of its iconic and life-sized quality, that segment becomes a reminder of that viewer's presence and of how the scale of one's everyday visual reality ultimately refers back to the scale of the body. "It was perhaps a playful comment on [the idea of] visual arts," Meireles explains, "you needed to use the eye in order to think about it, but at the same time the eye couldn't access it. Visuality had to be worked out through faith."[77] Visuality is thus a double leap, both of faith and of scale—just like distance is properly a "double distance," as Georges Didi-Huberman puts it, an uneasy dialectical friction in which the very object becomes "the index of a loss that it sustains, that it visually operates."[78] To shift away from the distant, abstract comfort the horizon line offers to the ineluctable proximity of the art object is to deny the possibility of reassurance and to face the failure of self-referentiality to account for the visual enigma *Physical Art* sets up.

There is one short story by Borges—Meireles's favorite author—that is illustrative in this respect, especially if we read it against the backdrop of Jameson's comment on the impossibility of determining important navigational coordinates such as longitude. In the story, the king of Babylonia imprisons the king of Arabia in his intricately built labyrinth. But he eventually finds his way out, captures his former captor, and takes revenge by imprisoning him in his own labyrinth. The latter, as the Arab king describes it, has "no stairways to climb, nor doors to force, nor wearying galleries to wander through, nor walls to impede thy passage."[79] It is a desert. In the *Physical Art* drawing, Meireles proposes that the rope could be alternatively placed at the "extremity of deserts," which adds a further layer of implausibility to the work, since this is a kind of reference that is hardly available—unlike the horizon line—to any particular viewpoint. What is more, if the desert is a deadlier labyrinth, it is not because it is more elaborate than the Babylonian maze. On the contrary, its power lies in changing the rules of the game. As the Arab king's description makes clear, the body meets no resistances—this labyrinth involves no climbing, forcing, or wearying oneself. Just like the *Snark* map is useless because it is not properly cartographic, the desert offers no visual landmarks or signs of difference that can be intuitively mobilized, so that without recourse to a third term—without cartography proper, that is—one cannot possibly find one's way out:

> Finally, with the first globe (1490) and the invention of the Mercator projection at about the same time, yet a third dimension of cartography emerges, which at once involves what we would today call the nature of representational codes, the intrinsic structures of the various media, the intervention, into more naïve mimetic conceptions of mapping, of the whole new fundamental question of the languages of representation itself, in particular the unresolvable (well-nigh Heisenbergian) dilemma of the transfer of curved space to flat charts. At this point it becomes clear that there can be no true maps.[80]

In Jameson's account, this historical process is analogous to the integration of the Symbolic register into a dialectical critique of visuality. What is interesting to note is how the very codes of mapmaking come to a point where they are constituted around the very impossibility of "true maps." Cartography thus becomes a sort of fundamentally disjunctive, negative hinge between perception, projection, and symbolization. And yet the works I have been discussing propose that this is nevertheless the way through which it may be possible to dialectically arrive at a more truthful mode of representation "in which we may again begin to grasp our positioning as individual and collective subjects and regain a capacity to act and struggle which is at present neutralized by our spatial as well as our social confusion."[81] It is the nature of this particular confusion that finally needs to be addressed.

DEMATERIALIZATION

There is one element in *Tiradentes* whose placement resembles that of the "conventional signs" surrounding the *Snark* map. On top of the pole to which the hens were tied, Meireles placed a single clinical thermometer. On the one hand, it introduces a standard, a reference to measurement and (dis)proportion, so recurrent in his oeuvre, following his striking interest in Marcel Duchamp's *Three Standard Stoppages* (1913–1914).[82] On the other hand, this reference is rendered visually useless, since the device (let alone its numbered scale) is virtually invisible in the photographs, echoing the fact that it obviously would have been impossible to read in the heat of the moment. The only thing that can be gauged by the thermometer is the ultimate powerlessness of the image to account for what was going on. What is more, the thermometer points to another drastic scale shift in that its conventional scale falls short of both actual and symbolic heat (how not to imagine it exploding, unable to contain the tremendous expansion of the mercury?). This suggests that to give an account of the work is not a matter of detecting details or providing precise results, thus reinforcing my earlier point about the role of orality—of recounting what has taken place—in evoking the work's traumatic affect.

Even when it came to the political charge of a work such as *Tiradentes*, it was not enough to *display* it. The work had to address the very disjunction, or even incommensurability, between how (and if) events could be grasped and the material reality underlying them. This is the same contradiction that prompted Carlos Zilio to make *For a Young Man with Brilliant Prospects* soon after he left prison: the general alienation that sustained a euphoric middle class during the height of military repression, owing to the economic boom that became known as the "Brazilian economic miracle." As a matter of fact, there is a coincidental link between the histories of repression and the economy and that of art in Brazil. In 1967, a meeting of the International Monetary Fund (IMF) took place in Rio de Janeiro, at the Museum of Modern Art. The left-wing opposition to the presence of the IMF was heightened by the demolition of the Calabouço restaurant, a traditional student hangout next to the museum, in order to create a new access to the meeting site. In one confrontation, a student was shot dead, leading to mass demonstrations and bringing political tensions to a new height. This turn of events ultimately provided the government with a pretext for officially revoking civil rights and instituting censorship under the Institutional Act no. 5 (AI-5) in December 1968—the beginning of the bleak period known in Brazil as the "Years of Lead."

Against the backdrop of such emblematic events, the actual content of the IMF meeting is usually overlooked—but it shouldn't be, for it touches on the political at a less evident but more fundamental level. The aim of the meeting was to devise international financial instruments that would lessen the burden of the fixed-rate gold convertibility of the US dollar, the main pillar of the Bretton Woods financial system, on the economy of the United States. However, despite all efforts, the system deteriorated and finally collapsed, in 1971, as the Nixon administration unilaterally closed the gold window, effectively cutting loose major currencies to float against each other. For the Marxist geographer David Harvey, the effects of the replacement of the Bretton Woods system for one of "floating exchange rates"—partly ascribed to the "shifting dimensionalities of space and time generated out of capital accumulation"—were far-reaching:

> The question of how value should now get represented, what form money should take, and the meaning that can be put upon the various forms of money available to us, has never been far from the surface of recent concerns. Since 1973, money has been "de-materialized" in the sense that it no longer has a formal or tangible link to precious metals ... or for that matter to any other tangible commodity.... The world has come to rely, for the first time in its history, upon immaterial forms of money—i.e. money of account assessed quantitatively in numbers of some designated currency.... The question of which currency I hold is directly linked to which place I put my faith in.[83]

As for the cultural consequences of such a dramatic shift, Harvey is equally adamant: "the breakdown of money as a secure means of representing value has itself created a crisis of representation in advanced capitalism."[84] Works like *Money Tree* (1969), *Zero Cruzeiro* (1974–1978), and *Zero Dollar* (1978–1984) are evidence of this particular "structure of feeling."[85] As a matter of fact, Meireles actively studied this topic—around 1970, for example, he spent one year investing in the stock market just so he could get "a better understanding" of how money worked.[86] As he would later put it, speaking of *Money Tree*: "The contradiction is that it really is worth nothing, which is a paradox; money declares a value but in fact you have no way of knowing what it is really worth.

Money depends on reserves, and today there is a great deal of money floating about without reserves."[87] The problem of setting up a tangible representation of value would extrapolate the specific problem of money and become a major structuring motif in Meireles's oeuvre, as in works like *Eureka/Blindhotland* (1970–1975), *Fontes* (1992–2008), *Red Shift* (1967–1984), and *Mission/Missions* (1987), among others.

Red Shift is divided in three rooms, respectively titled *Impregnation, Surrounding/Spill* [*Entorno*], and *Shift*.[88] Meireles conceived the first room not "as a metaphor, but as a symptom of some procedure of choice."[89] The simplest way to describe *Impregnation* is to say that it is a collection of objects, all of them red, arranged as in a regular living room or studio. But this is symptomatic not simply of the potential taste (or obsession) of an imagined collector, but also of the more fundamental condition of subjective displacement that subtends the broader crisis in the representation of value. Obviously, those collected objects are all commodities, articles that circulate in the market, ranging from the kind of paraphernalia one typically finds in thrift stores to exclusive luxury goods (red artworks included). The strict criterion of *Red Shift* is thus made possible by a culture of consumerism rather than aesthetic purism: the only reason one might be able to collect all of these items in red is because it is possible to buy most of them in virtually any color, so that it would be equally easy to come up with a "Green Shift," a "Yellow Shift," or a "Purple Shift."

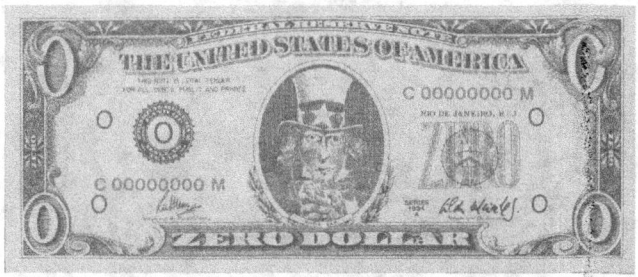

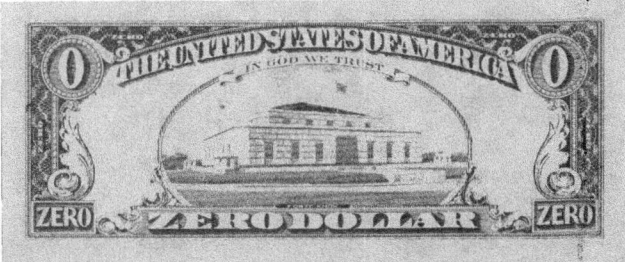

4.16
Cildo Meireles, *Zero Dollar*,
1978–1984. Offset print on
paper, unlimited edition,
6.5 × 15.5 cm. Photo: Pat
Kilgore. Courtesy of the artist.

4.17
Cildo Meireles, *Eureka / Blindhotland*, 1970–
1975. Rubber, fishing net, metal, cork, wood,
and audio, 400 × 700 × 700 cm. Photo: MAC-BA.
Courtesy of the artist.

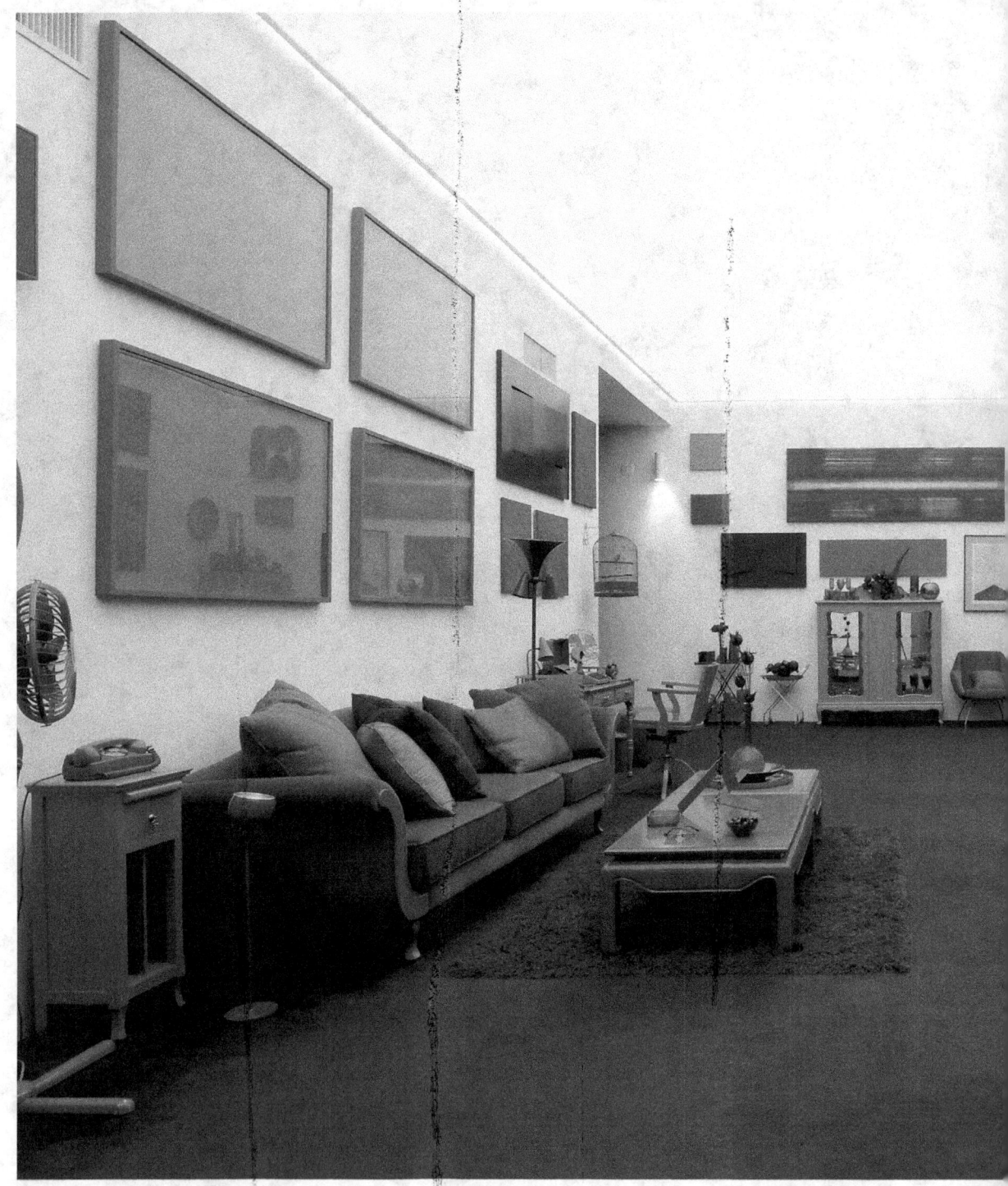

4.18
Cildo Meireles, *Red Shift: I. Impregnation*,
1967–1984. Mixed media installation, variable
dimensions. Photo: Eduardo Eckenfels.
Courtesy of the artist.

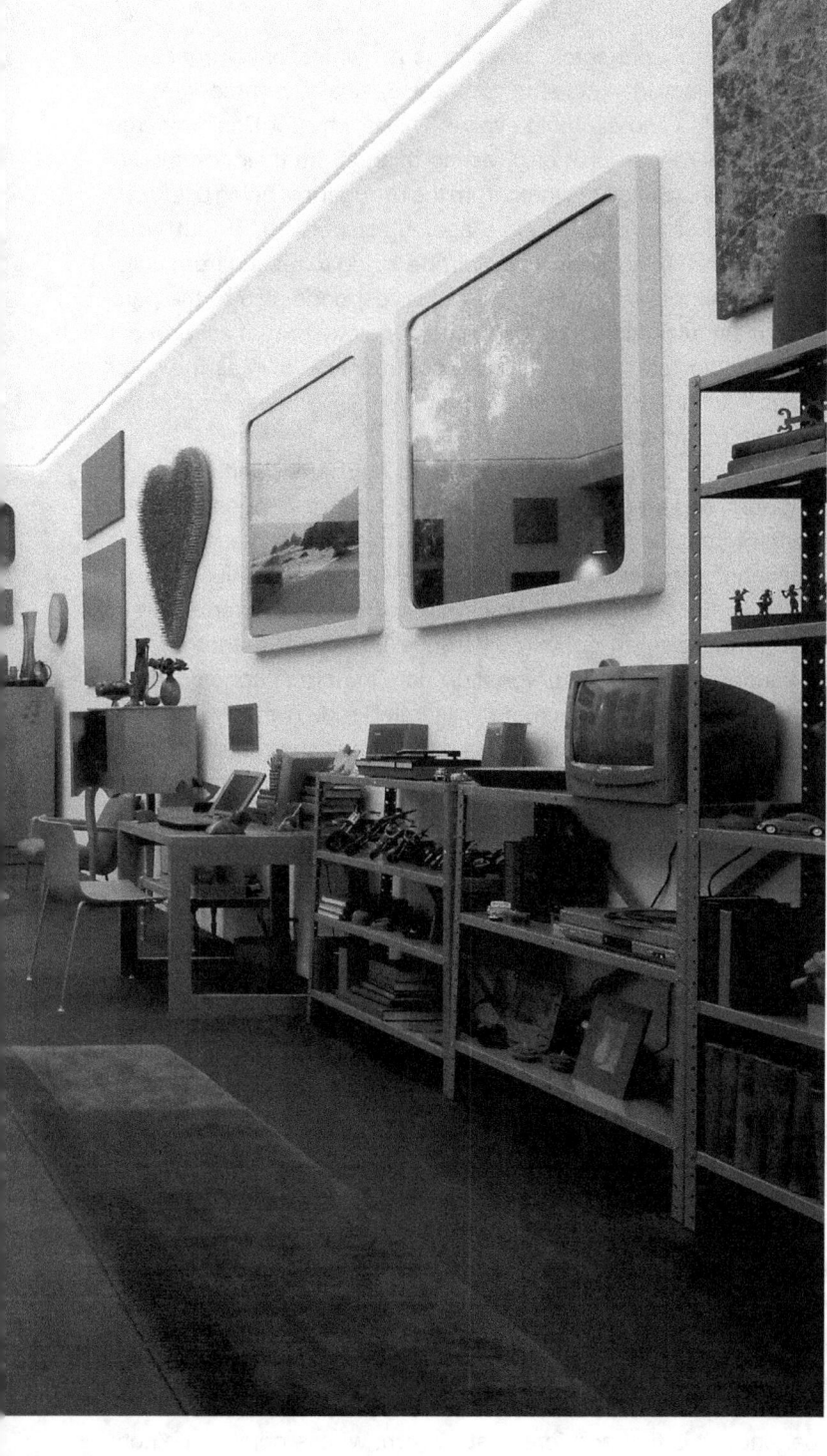

But this is not to say that this projected collector is a quintessential consumer (such as the contemporary art collector)—quite the contrary. Basically, commodities are staked on the coupling of use value and exchange value. This is why, for Benjamin, the true collector undertakes the "Sisyphean task of divesting things from their commodity character," because, in a collection, "things are freed from the drudgery of being useful."[90] What is more, "the collector takes up the struggle against dispersion."[91] But what exactly would the drive behind the collection in *Red Shift* be trying to rescue from utility and dispersion? The answer is simple: color. *Red Shift* thus responds also to the paradigmatic shift that turned the singular "color" of the painter's palette to that assortment of equivalent, industrially available "colors" that is more commonly known as the *color chart*.[92] This is what the impregnation of color aims at: the overall "redness" that dominates the room, exceeding each and every single hue.

And yet to rescue color from its plural dispersion into equivalent units is not to regain access to a premodern experience of it. This simply cannot happen because the shift is, once again, paradigmatic—the modes of experiencing color in each regime are incommensurable, making it impossible to reconcile one with the other (just like, as Dias once wrote, "we must not forget that hard times are not simply the reduction of epochs of abundance. No reduction can contain difference").[93] To put it another way, the different hues of the various objects in *Impregnation* can, in normal conditions, be infinitely exchanged, but never referred to as a more "essential" red. The only common denominator they can have is exchange value. Redness is thus not a chromatic mediator but the result of those objects coming into "the closest conceivable relation to things of the same kind" that Benjamin views as "the diametric opposite of any utility."[94] As an irrational negation of utility, it is not simply in excess in relation to all the various "reds." In *Red* Shift, redness is above all *a mark of excess* (just as the term "redness" exceeds the color red).[95]

However, and paradoxically, red is also a kind of standard. As Meireles explains, the name *Red Shift* comes from physics, referring to the fact that red is the color that "shifts the least as it moves about space. You use it to measure distances, it functions as a pattern."[96] The oppressiveness of the room is thus not simply a phenomenological exercise or a way of drawing attention to political issues through the use of a culturally charged color. Nor is it, from this viewpoint, still exchangeable for, say, a "Blue Shift," even though virtually all items in it do have blue equivalents. This collection of red objects, made possible by commodity culture, is simultaneously at one remove from it. This is crucial: *Red Shift* is marked by a kind of "double distance" that is no less radical than the discrepant visual distances in *Physical Art*. For Didi-Huberman, once again, this kind of "double bind" is what makes minimalist objects phenomenologically contradict the tautological closure of minimalist discourse.[97] Contrary to tautology, *Red Shift* becomes, as Meireles describes it, "a linking together of false logics."[98] But it also counters the primacy of the empirical object, serial or discrete, in providing a blueprint for the openness of experience: it is first and foremost a *room*, whose objects are nothing but tokens of unhomeliness. One's phenomenological (dis)orientation is only one part in a larger equation (to recall Brito's description) that cannot be accounted for without taking into consideration the broader cognitive problems—both economic and geographic—that were at stake in the "shift" from the 1960s to the 1970s. In other words, it also points to precisely that which advanced capitalism was most crucially dropping at that time: its standards.

Meireles was not simply addressing the purported dematerialization of the art object. More importantly, the very objectification of social relations in advanced capitalism was becoming radically dematerialized itself, in keeping with the representational crisis Harvey describes. Value was not simply becoming difficult to represent, it was becoming entirely disconnected from material reality, even though—as global capitalism and the recent chain of financial crises have demonstrated—the effects of this process are unequivocally real. Uncomfortable and intense, *Impregnation* is a room no one can possibly inhabit, a sign of the unprecedented level of subjective disjunction late capitalism enforced. Roughly speaking, just as the free-floating exchange rates opened up new grounds for financial speculation, the post-1968 crisis in representation opened up a new ground for "speculative attacks" on the ideological construction of use values, further distancing it from any material basis while simultaneously recuperating virtually any sign and elevating it to the depoliticized level of lifestyle (as any SUV commercial will show). To say that the objectification of social relations has been dematerialized is by no means to imply a critical process. Paradoxically, the less objective the support, the more flexible objectification seems to become.

5

/SLIDEWISE:
one- coke
plus
of v

two- more
slid

White on White

Integrating Hélio Oiticica's 1970s work into the rest of his oeuvre remains a challenge. Unsurprisingly so: his prolific production at that time—mostly of scale models, verbal propositions, unrealized projects and films—hardly fits the familiar image of Oiticica as a rigorous geometric abstract painter (in the 1950s and early 1960s) or as a cutting-edge avant-garde leader (in the mid- to late 1960s). His writings, which became increasingly fragmented and were incorporated into a multilayered and ultimately unfinished publication project—initially entitled *Newyorkaises* and later *Conglomerado* (Conglomerate)—only add to this complexity. "If no more vanguard movements exist," Oiticica wrote in 1978, back in Rio de Janeiro after spending eight years in New York, "it's because each one must be the VANGUARD."[1] It is clear that Oiticica had not forsaken the avant-gardism he so much prized in his chosen predecessors such as Mondrian and Malevich, but that, as he eventually moved away from a collective to a more individual (though still collaborative) sense of avant-gardism, his way of engaging with them also underwent a profound transformation. If we read signs that link the 1970s Oiticica back to his earlier concerns, then these must be understood not as stable references, but nodal points that signal significant relays and shifts in his trajectory.

I will focus on Malevich's historical importance here, but not because his presence in Oiticica's concerns is constant. It is rather because I see it as marking a hiatus in Oiticica's trajectory. There are two periods when Malevich's presence, in the guise of his famous "white on white" paintings of 1917–1918, is particularly noticeable in Oiticica's work. The first occurs in Oiticica's *White Series* of 1958–1959. These paintings coincide with the beginning of neoconcretism and form a highly experimental ensemble. Some display subtly nuanced planes either in contrast or separated by fine lines. Others rely on directional brushstrokes to produce different whites through the reflection of light. Oiticica was then avidly pursuing color as a privileged means of addressing the duration of experience, and white occupied, for a while, a privileged position in that pursuit; it was, for the artist, "the synthesis-light of all colors."[2]

Malevich appears again and at greater length during Oiticica's New York period, most notably after 1973, in a variety of works and writings. In between these two periods, his references to the Russian artist are generally scant or nonspecific.[3] Oiticica's way of engaging with the name of Malevich in each period is also distinct, but one thing

5.1
Hélio Oiticica, *Untitled (White Series)*, 1959.
Oil-case in emulsion on wood fiberboard,
100 × 60 cm. César and Claudio Oiticica
Collection. Photo: César Oiticica Filho.
Courtesy Projeto Hélio Oiticica.

remained constant: his interest in *white*. In order to understand how Oiticica articulated this in each moment, this chapter will introduce other crucial references and concepts that appeared in Oiticica's works and writings, so that the hiatus—and its configuration of a *return* to Malevich—becomes visible as a bridging movement in Oiticica's historiography. My aim is not to survey the vast range of references that ultimately informed Oiticica's investment in Malevich and in white. It is rather to single out some crucial threads in the latter—most especially its relation to Nietzsche—that will show how *white on white* becomes the emblem of a powerful logic of reclamation. Or, to put it another way, Oiticica's insistence on *white on white* as a trope is what motivates the singling out of a particular set of references.

Oiticica's constellation of references, especially in his New York writings, is notoriously vast. They include authors he read, friends he corresponded with, musicians he listened to, people who frequented his loft, films he watched, artists he worked with—all of these were quickly absorbed by the vertiginous speed and restlessness of his writing process so that they were mingled with one another and with his concepts and propositions. The list is eclectic, for sure, but not indiscriminate. For these references were also meant to define a certain discursive and communicative field where Oiticica's ideas could circulate, be received, and generate dialogue. This explains why he virtually ignored the mainstream New York art world: Oiticica was not much interested in discussing art, but rather in constituting a shared (and somewhat intimate) space for the circulation and development of ideas, a space where each new "invention" would feed a next one.[4] To find one's ground in this writerly web is a challenging task. In attempting to do so, I expect to demonstrate not only that there are powerful conceptual and historiographical formulations at play in there, but also how Oiticica's reading of some of these references is, in fact, a *re*invention of them.

SCREEN MALEVICH

The first reference I want to bring in is to John Cage. Cage was more than a passing interest for Oiticica, who shared with the composer a concern for what he called the "environmental" aspect of art—how art related to the world surrounding it. As was usual with the artist, his interest took the form of homages and quotations. One of the exemplary instances in this respect occurs in the series of works entitled *COSMOCOCA— programa in progress*, which Oiticica started to devise in 1973, alongside Brazilian filmmaker Neville D'Almeida. The *Cosmococas* were conceived as a series of environments with multiple slide projections of images, usually of posters, book covers, and other photographs, on top of which the artist had made drawings with cocaine. The slide photographs were taken by Oiticica and meant to be projected in conjunction with distinctive soundtracks that ranged from *forró*, a Brazilian regional music genre, to rock.[5] Each environment was to provide a distinct kind of accommodation for the spectators: hammocks, cushions, and even a swimming pool. In some cases, objects such as balloons and nail buffers were to be made available. The spectators were expected to engage in some other activity in addition to watching the projections, be it swimming, nail polishing, or resting. Oiticica and Almeida targeted the perceived seamlessness of film with a slide sequence that denied the projection any continuum. The latter was ascribed in contrast to the soundtrack and to the activities of a spectator immersed in a shifting architecture.[6] In short, what was at stake was the reality of experience, rather than representation, as flux.

Cage is the main reference in the *Cosmococa* entitled *CC4 Nocagions*—meant to include a swimming pool and music by the North American composer.[7] The title merges Cage's own name and his *Notations*, and the projected photographs include the closed white book cover with lines of coke traced over it. But the book was not simply a visual quotation: "not merely a punning allusion to CAGE's book—it demands consideration as experiment or as a moment within a program."[8] Oiticica formally conceptualizes Cage's involvement in his work through the whiteness of the book's cover. He thus brings Cage and Malevich together in his writings on *CC4 Nocagions* by speaking of "white coke-tracks on a white cover" and paying explicit homage to the Russian master.[9]

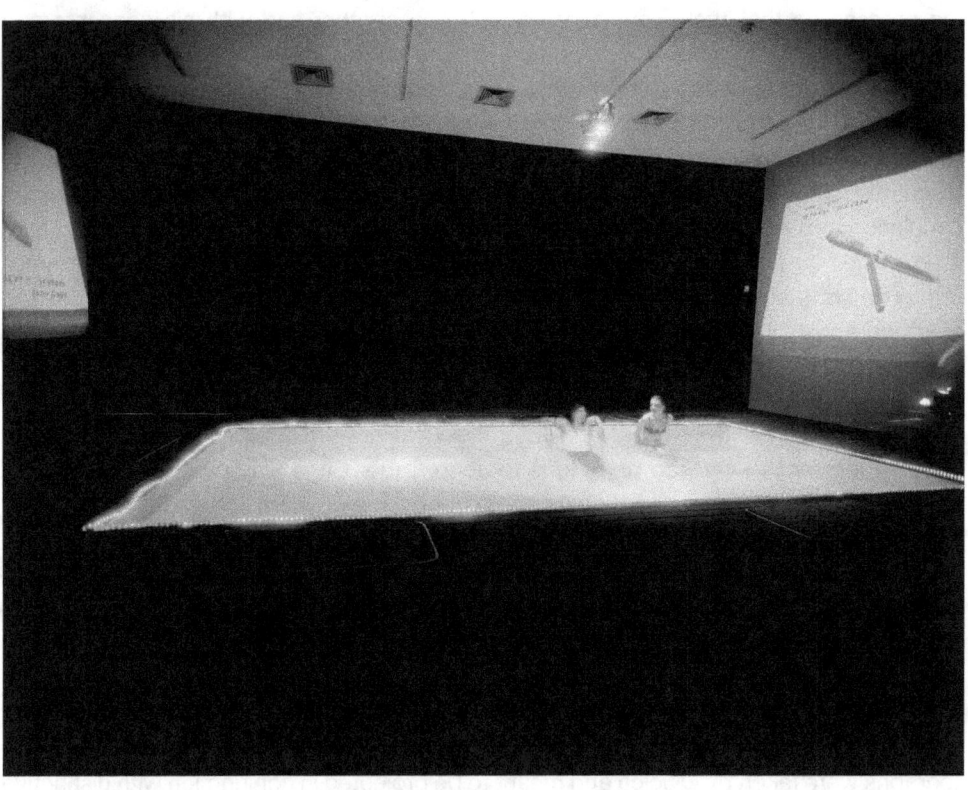

5.2
Hélio Oiticica and Neville D'Almeida, *CC4 Nocagions—Block Experiments in Cosmococa*, 1973. Installation photograph. Photo: César Oiticica Filho. Courtesy Projeto Hélio Oiticica.

Malevich and Cage may seem an arbitrary pair, but in fact their pairing is not restricted to Oiticica's writings. It is well known that Cage composed his famous silent piece, 4′33″, as a response to Robert Rauschenberg's *White Paintings.* In fact, as Branden Joseph has argued, Rauschenberg's own understanding of his *White Paintings* shifted as he became aware of Cage's now-famous reading of them as "airports for the lights, shadows and particles." Joseph also demonstrates how Cage partially derived this notion from Lázsló Moholy-Nagy's (mis)reading of Malevich's *Suprematist Composition: White on White* (1918) as a "plain white surface, which constituted an ideal plane for kinetic light and shadow effects which, originating in the surroundings, would fall upon it" and as "a miniature cinema screen."[10] While such a notion led Cage to equate whiteness with silence, I would argue that this very same notion renders the analogy ultimately flawed.

Crucial here, I believe, is that the hinge that brought silence and whiteness together was *transparency.* Joseph argues that for Cage "it is this idea of transparency, of a space or emptiness that allowed the artwork to open up to the environment."[11] If, as Cage famously proposes, "there is no such thing as silence," then silence cannot be posited as a sort of "background" for the experience of music, thus making music transparent, in the sense of it being completely fused with external incident.[12] It follows that there would be no point in distinguishing environmental sounds from music as such. The supposed "emptiness" of the white canvas would also be transparent in this sense, and the canvas would be always-already (once illuminated, that is) a screen. Moholy-Nagy's description of what happens to a white house in the sunshine is eloquent in this respect: "The white walls act as projection screens on which shadows multiply the trees, and the glass plates become mirrors in which the trees are repeated. A perfect transparency is the result; the house becomes a part of nature."[13] The concept of the screen—and, most importantly, of its *disappearance* in becoming "a part of nature"—reveals some of the problems in the whiteness-silence parallel. For such understanding of "the screen as mirror"—to return to a formulation by Joan Copjec that I have already considered in relation to Oiticica's work—is tantamount to an act of imaginary identification; that is, to the idea that the viewing subject is seamlessly sutured to the screen and that there is no remainder or interference to make this illusion somehow palpable as such.[14] This is evident not only in Moholy-Nagy's use of both figures (screen and mirror) but more particularly in his idea of a merger with nature. The Lacanian view on this problem, which informs Copjec, offers a useful counterpoint, for it holds the screen as anything but transparent: it is the opaque support of visuality as such and the subject itself is a spot on it, a mark of its opacity.[15] In this view, if and when transparency occurs, the result is not a redemptive merger with nature but the traumatic erasure of the subject in the blinding light of the gaze. Unlike the shadows in Moholy-Nagy's narrative, which are already a cinematic effect *on* the screen (which is, in its turn, cast into some sort of oblivion), the spot in Lacan's theory points to an irreducible persistence *of* the screen. Imaginary identification can only follow from a failure in perceiving such condition. The problem can also be approached in another, closely related way. The white canvas only captures reality as an index would—as an "airport of lights, shadows and particles." As such, it signifies reality, and is thus rendered irreducibly different from reality itself. Imaginary identification—the "plain surface" become nature—precisely overlooks this fundamental difference.

BODILY MALEVICH

Let us put these considerations to one side for the moment and return to Oiticica. His own interest in white and in Malevich emerged, quite surprisingly, as two distinct paths. Suprematism was a major reference for the geometric abstraction groups in 1950s Brazil, and Malevich was constantly mentioned in Oiticica's writings, but rarely as thoroughly discussed as, say, Mondrian and Kandinsky—until the *Cosmococas*, that is. More striking yet was Malevich's near absence from Oiticica's discussions of his *White Series*. In most of these paintings, as I mentioned, two or more planes rendered in different qualities of white were aligned or pitted against each other. Oiticica certainly knew Malevich's white paintings, as the plane clashing depicted in the *White Series* attests, but it is to Mondrian and even more to Lygia Clark that Oiticica turns when it comes to discussing the temporality of the "color-light" concept he was trying to formalize in these works.[16] In a note from 1960, "Malevich and the Russian avant-garde artists" are mentioned only in passing (and in brackets) as another example (after Mondrian) of representation in painting arriving "at its limit."[17] In other words, the name of Malevich was invoked simply to denote a general artistic framework and a break from the past (further allowing Oiticica to pose himself and his peers as the ones who would truly explore the consequences opened up by such a rupture), but is largely absent in a specific discussion of the *White Series* per se. Given how formally eloquent Oiticica's dialogue with Mondrian was, it is odd that in his *White Series* he bypassed much of the formal specificity of Malevich's work in favor of an overall understanding of it.

Neoconcretism, like Cage and Moholy-Nagy, had given rise to its own partial reading of Malevich. And it stemmed, as critic Paula Braga has skillfully detected, from a subtlety in translation: a 1959 Portuguese version of Malevich's essay "Suprematism" employed the Portuguese word for "sensibility" (*sensibilidade*), whereas the English version, for instance, preferred the more abstract, less *bodily* term "feeling."[18] The implications become clear as we consider the shift in meaning in the actual text. This is the English version: "Under Suprematism I understand the supremacy of pure *feeling* in creative art. To the Suprematist the visual phenomena of the objective world are, in themselves, meaningless; the significant thing is *feeling*, as such, quite apart from the environment in which it is called forth."[19] And this is a somewhat literal English version of a Portuguese translation (probably by Ferreira Gullar) that was published in 1959 at the Sunday supplement of the *Jornal do Brasil* (SDJB): "Under suprematism I understand the supremacy of pure *sensibility* [*sensibilidade*] in art. From the viewpoint of the suprematists, the external appearances of nature are of no interest: [what is] essential is *sensibility* [*sensibilidade*] as such, independently of the milieu it originates from."[20] More importantly, Braga notes, this version was published in the *SDJB* (which was edited by Gullar) at the height of the concrete-neoconcrete polemical schism within the Brazilian constructive avant-garde. As I have already discussed, this intense debate was fought through manifestos, articles, essays, and translations, mostly voiced by poets. Whether it was deliberate or not, then, such subtlety of translation is hard to dissociate from the cultural atmosphere that informed publications in this context. It is worth remembering, once again, how neoconcretism opposed the more dogmatic and rationalist approach of the São Paulo concretists, embracing a more experimental and subjectivist stance. Considering the influence of Merleau-Ponty in neoconcrete theory and the profound historicism that marked Gullar at that time, it may be perhaps unsurprising that a retro-spective gaze at Malevich would take the form of such formulation.[21]

Hence this "bodily" Malevich was freshly born as a discursive entity while Oiticica was working on his *White Series*. This could explain how such a generic allusion to Malevich as one of the artists who reached the "limits of representation" without going beyond them may have been enough for Oiticica at that moment. This was the height of neoconcretism and Oiticica was trying to incorporate the temporality of experience as a driving force rather than an aspect of painting to be more or less emphasized. The problem, he complained, was that Malevich (and others) "succeeded in finding time" without giving "priority to the concept of temporality."[22] What might that mean? Simply put, that Malevich had both unequivocally destroyed the temporality of representation and employed formal devices that implied the perceptual process belonging to the spectator in front of the paintings, but that he remained unable to reformulate painting as a whole in those new terms. After all, this was exactly Oiticica's ongoing project and on this point his dialogue with Mondrian is equally crucial.[23] So it becomes less surprising that he could at one and the same time relate it to a generalized and partial notion of supre-matism, while keeping the novelty of his formal achievements more or less detached from it (defining it more in terms of the ongoing, experimental practice of fellow neocon-cretist Lygia Clark). More broadly, it was not enough for the neoconcrete movement to recognize the precedence and the example of suprematism as a historical moment of rupture. Rupture had to be defined as an operation containing some overlooked speci-ficity (namely, the "bodily" Malevich). This would allow the neoconcretists to differentiate themselves and so to pose themselves as the *true* followers of Malevich, even though they were not fully aware of the historicizing nature of their move. Fifteen years later, Oiticica would retrospectively cast a light on this move in the *White on White* bloc (as he named the sections of his *Newyorkaises*) by stating that Malevich's *White on White* signaled the "premonition of the discovery of the body," thus introducing "something strange into the western creative process."[24]

But the Malevich of Oiticica's writings in the early 1970s no longer represented an abstract if congruent stance. It was more than that, just as Cage was more than simply a pun. Malevich was now treated as inextricable from his (and also from Cage's and from Oiticica's own) treatment of *white on white*. This shift requires that we account for a series of developments in Oiticica's work throughout these fifteen years. First, much of the sense of rupture in Brazilian avant-gardism would become a sense of *reclama-tion*. This process is adamant in the development of Oiticica's notion of the constructive, which sought to endow his work with the power to actualize the meaning of the earlier constructive avant-garde, a power the artist came to see as an urgent cultural task of the time. In short, from being just a new stage in a chronologically linear constructive development, Oiticica would reverse things and make himself the very historical point from which speaking of a "constructive will" made sense. This reversal became radical as a number of historical precedents were to be recast as "constructors" (the semantic charge Oiticica lent to this term would migrate to another term—"inventors"—which he borrowed from Ezra Pound and began to favor in his 1970s writings).

Second, and interconnected, was Oiticica's encounter with Oswald de Andrade's notion of anthropophagy. As we have seen, the concept defined a cultural operation regarding Brazilian identity, whereby foreign influences should be not so much opposed as *devoured*, that is, internalized and redeployed (or, to keep the metaphor, regurgitated).[25] Anthropophagy crystallized the notion of reclamation without the need for justification — a potential source of Oiticica's hesitations over Malevich during the making of the *White Series*. This was different from an artist torn between revering his predecessors and breaking away from them, and was most explicitly formulated by Oiticica in 1972: *"the experimental can reclaim never relive."*[26] So, by the time the artist moved to New York, Malevich was no longer simply a harbinger of rupture to be surpassed, but an "inventor" to be reclaimed. This may explain why Oiticica was less interested in Malevich's *Black Square on a White Background* than in his *White on White* — the former was too charged with rupture in too definitive a sense, while the latter provided a subtler reference point for Oiticica's formal and historical constitution of his own work.

Third, and most important, this new artistic and theoretical framework in which Oiticica started to operate allowed him to heal the wounds of the concrete-neoconcrete schism and become closer to the São Paulo poets Augusto and Haroldo de Campos.[27] Oiticica had already met them very briefly in 1968, but their friendship would grow after the poets visited him in New York. Their contact must have confirmed Oiticica's intuitions about the shape of history; that is, about the radical present implied in his notion of the constructive, which is very similar to the way the poets employed the Poundian notion of *paideuma* in order to account for their own predecessors (indeed, Oiticica borrowed the term "inventors" directly from Ezra Pound, to whose work he was introduced by the Campos brothers). As literary scholar Gonzalo Aguilar explains: "The concept of *paideuma* ... opposes ... that of the 'spirit of the age.' In Pound, in his *Guide to Kulchur*, or in the manifestos of the São Paulo poets, the difference between those traditions which are alive and the depleted or exhausted ones is established *in the present*."[28]

This reconnection between Oiticica and the São Paulo poets may still sound odd, considering how fierce the 1950s debates had been.[29] However, the fact is that the work of the poets had also suffered profound changes throughout the 1960s, to the point that their previous and radical commitment to mathematically derived forms had given way, for example, to the incorporation of newspaper cuttings and detritus in the case of Augusto de Campos's *Popcretos*. And even to declarations of bodily primacy: these are evident, as Aguilar demonstrates, in the opening lines of Haroldo de Campos's *Galaxies*, which can thus be read "as the death sentence for concrete poetry": "e começo aqui e meço aqui este começo" (I begin here and I hereby measure this beginning).[30] And as far as the figure of white on white is concerned, the most resonant point of contact between Oiticica and Haroldo de Campos is the latter's translation to Portuguese of the Japanese Noh theater play *Hagoromo* (The Feather Mantle), which the poet likened to the *Parangolé*. As he puts it, the play

> is a dance-poem. It tells of a divine feather-mantle which an angel, a female angel, during her descent to earth leaves behind on the branch of a tree. The mantle is found by a fisherman, who later demands the celestial creature to dance the dances of the moon ... an obligatory condition for him to give back the mantle so that she may return to her heavenly abode.... The play ends with the mantle dissolving into the heaven of heaven, the white of white, the ether of ether. A "suprematist" ending.... This impressed Hélio enormously.[31]

Based on this analysis, Campos further describes the *Parangolé* as "a hang glider to ecstasy, thus accounting not only for a sort of transformation of space-time … but also for this body element, this element of exultation."[32] Campos's highly evocative characterization of a "dance-poem" with suprematist overtones was bound to strike a chord with Oiticica, confirming and further informing his own unorthodox view of Malevich. The very first syllable, *no*, of the title *Nocagions* is telling in this respect—and it is worth recalling that this *Cosmococa* was dedicated to the Campos brothers, hailed by Oiticica as "INNOVENTORS" (the term obviously conflating, by adding the same syllable *no*, the words "innovator" and "inventor").[33]

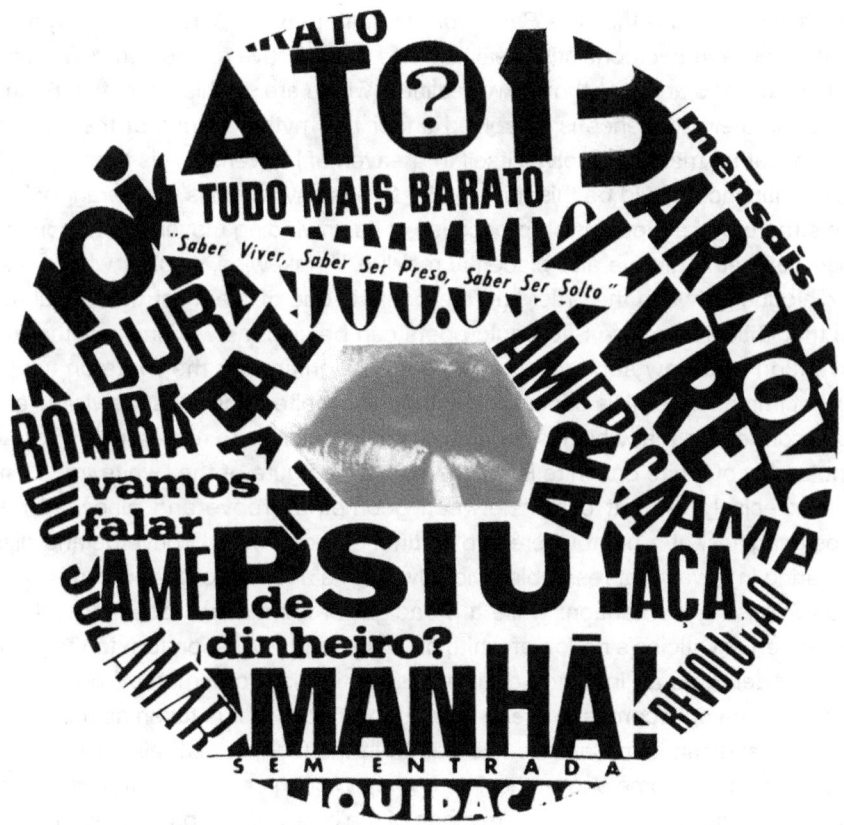

5.3
Augusto de Campos, *Psiu!*, 1965.

Before we move to an analysis of *CC4 Nocagions*, however, it is necessary to pay attention to the problem of the body in Oiticica's exchanges with the São Paulo poets. Haroldo de Campos argues that the *Parangolé* brings together two mythical moments in Oiticica's trajectory: on the one hand, his "intellectual" side, identified with his home education (Oiticica did not frequent schools, being taught by his family instead) and with his great appetite for philosophy and literature; on the other, his "bodily" side, supposed to correspond with his experience at Mangueira. Campos's distinction in this respect is reminiscent of the way Lygia Pape described Oiticica as alternately "Apollonian" and "Dyonisian." The poet first admits that the polarization he proposes is valid only for "didactic" purposes, cautioning that it does not correspond to the actuality of experience. But it is this polarization which is ultimately taken to supply the poetic core of the *Parangolé* and which is praised precisely for bringing the bodily insights Oiticica experienced firsthand at Mangueira—in his own experience as a *passista* (a proficient samba dancer)—into the formulation of an aesthetic program. But, then again, isn't that precisely what the *Parangolé* is supposed to do?

One might argue that the *Parangolé* initially plays a part in the staging of an encounter between two conflicting realities, as I myself have suggested.[34] The problem is that in Campos's account those two realities (which are, in this case, two myths) are conflated, as their difference is dissolved under the mythic mantle of the *Parangolés*, just as the feather mantle dissolves itself in "heaven of heaven." In his terminology, "the point of confluence would be this hang glider to ecstasy which is the *Parangolé*, which has the structure of a Moebius strip because of its unwinding movement … somewhere between geometric groove and placental residue."[35] Likewise, Aguilar, whose account of the dialogue between the artist and the poets is one of the most thoughtful to date, argues that Oiticica and the São Paulo poets can be seen as working together toward "the invention of a new sublime" that would be signified by the *white on white* qua "ecstasy of immanence." His conclusion is that "the white trace joins the visible and the invisible, condenses that which is separated and impossible to represent."[36] For Aguilar, the whole idea of white on white is mainly about the figure of the "white trace," meant to stand precisely on that cusp "between geometric groove and placental residue" Campos imagines, at a point where two distinct stances would converge and dissolve, disappearing in a way that resembles Moholy-Nagy's account of the screen.

So this is my contention: while a paradigm of immanence does indeed play an important part in Oiticica's notion of white on white (and I will soon turn to that), the fact that it is rendered as an instance of utter dissolution is problematic.[37] As a matter of fact, immanence only comes to mean dissolution because it is taken as the resolution of the mythical distinction Campos had set up in the first place. It allows the "intellect" and the "body" to become one (in the *Parangolé*). We can detect here traces of the theoretical move Copjec has termed "the revenge of the body."[38] The problem with this move lies in its acceptance (intentional or not) of the Cartesian mind/body dualism as a historical fact to be *rectified* rather than a philosophical problem to be *criticized*. For Copjec, this distortion leads to the assumption that the body has been historically wronged in a process that culminated in the emergence of structuralism. In turn, this led to theoretical overcompensation in the proliferation of discourses on the body. The irony is that the greatest problem of this overcompensation (this movement of "simply stating that 'bodies matter'—as though one need only revenge or answer their neglect") is that it fails to put the body in question, overlooking the full radicality of the subject's grounding in it.[39] Instead of rethinking the body as such, it simply accepts received wisdom regarding it and tries to raise its profile in current debates—a kind of theoretical affirmative action.

In short, this excessive emphasis on dissolution turns Oiticica into a great avenger of the body. It is reasonably clear in Campos's interview how the supposed convergence of intellect and body is carried on in the name of the latter (thus as a revenge); what is more, Oiticica becomes a mythical figure precisely in that he is supposedly able to have it both ways. The corollary is that no matter how much supremacy one appears to ascribe to the body, it is kept structurally in thrall of its originary schematism, remaining, ironically enough, a representation to be opposed to its pair, the intellect.[40] My point is that a proper account of the "bodily" in Oiticica's trajectory should not repress it from his earlier work and introduce it only after his contact with the favelas, but rather trace it back to the 1950s and consider the way it permeated his work at that time.[41] This is not to say that Oiticica's dialogue with Campos or their interest in white on white are dead ends. But, if we are to understand the radicality opened up by this interest, it is necessary to resist this celebratory narrative of joyous fulfillment and explore how Oiticica's affirmative ethos at this time is actually strengthened, in an important way, by a sense of internal disjunction.

SUN-MALEVICH

Oiticica's interest in Cage is sparked by the composer's books *Notations* and *Silence*, which were recommended to him by Augusto de Campos. It is in this context, then, that he engages once again with Malevich and whiteness. Take, for instance, some observations attached to the instructions for assembling *CC4 Nocagions*.[42] There is a hint here of how forceful Oiticica's mode of reclaiming his designated references had become as his homage to Malevich is played out as nothing less than an "assertion" of suprematism (and suprematist space). This is strikingly different from Oiticica's writings back in 1960, when he recognized his predecessors, but was also at pains to single out the importance of his own contribution. In contrast, Malevich was now fully "acknowledged," and, what is more, fully associated with and defined by his *White on White*—a painting that becomes, for Oiticica, an emblem of "suprematist space."

In the *CC4* notes, Oiticica defines this space through nonlinearity and chance, and he views this condition as structurally echoed (and temporally translated) in the randomness of the slide order. I want to draw attention to the way his writing at this point is immersed in the very logic it describes. This is most evident in Oiticica's agglutinations, juxtapositions, and amalgams of words, and in his abundant use of slashes and, especially, hyphens. All of this randomness and juxtaposition in his writing gives rise to a peculiar logic of free association, which becomes not simply illustrative, but also constitutive of Oiticica's own mode of thought. The signifier "white" becomes a privileged locus in this respect, a point from which different associations shoot out in a number of directions, as in the following 1974 fragment:

OBSERVATIONS/SLIDEWISE:

one- coke-tracking across the cover of NOTATIONS
plus the cocaccessories combine into a kind
of visual-transformable-NOTATION/MUSICWISE:

two- moreover is the sequence-NOTATION of the
slides themselves:each slide IMAGE-ined
(by means of camera placement/manipulation/
mobility through 360 :EVERYWHICHWAY- a filmic
space) with reference (HOMMAGEWISE) to
MALEVICH's WHITE ON WHITE (white coke-tracks
on white cover) and to SUPREMATIST space:
not as a SUPREMATIST revival - more as an
assertion of its very existence carried out
in a play-chance and candid (PURE-WHITE) way:

three- CHANCE as PLAY
in the shooting of the slides:
in the box-order from the lab:
in the carrousel-order (which may/maynot be
                                 box-order):

CHANCE-NOTATIONS

CHANCE-RELATIONS within performance-project

DEDICATION: this 4th block-experiment in COSMOCOCA
is dedicated in recognition of ABOVE-GROUND
INVENTION/ATTAINMENTS to TWO BRAZILIAN
                          CONCRETE-POETS and
                          PROSE-WRITERS and
                          THEORIZERS and
                  above all INNOVENTORS:
                      to the SAŌ PAULO brothers
                          the CAMPOS brothers

AUGUSTO and HAROLDO DE CAMPOS

PROPOSITION/GIVEWISE   - CC4 COPY I (each COPY is an exact duplicate-set
of-/and made by HÉLIO OITICICA from the ORIGIN-
AL) will be presented to DE CAMPOS brothers
along with INSTRUCTIONS for PERFORMANCE and
a PROPOSAL inviting them to contribute - INVENT
and/or TRANSFORM the INSTRUCTIONS for a PERFOR-
ANCE to take place in SAŌ PAULO or RIO.

OBSERVATIONS/BLOCKWISE - my work/relationship with NEVILLE may be
compared to that of film director and camera-
man: the difference being that there are just
two of us in the whole project: just
two of us INVENTING/EXTRAPOLATING/etc.   just
two of us in a multi-structural
                    multi-valent EXPERIMENTATION
which is not cinema nor photography nor narrative:

5.4
Hélio Oiticica, instructions for *CC4 Nocagions*,
1973. Courtesy Projeto Hélio Oiticica.

I want SNOW-COKE
SUN NIETZSCHE MIDDAY
GROUND-RIMBAUD
SUN-SNOW
WHITE ON WHITE
SUN-MALEVICH[43]

Let us disentangle and elucidate some of these references. It all starts with another translation incident, now a deliberate one. Oiticica became interested in a line by Rimbaud which reads "la neige éternelle du sol" (the eternal snow of the ground), but which he translated in a different order: "chão de neve eterna" (ground of eternal snow).[44] As Braga has noted, the order was changed so that the idea of "ground" could mean not only the ground on which we stand, but also ground as Earth, as something literally "planetary."[45] The artist further corroborates that association with another linguistic maneuver: "but I want SOL [as in French for 'ground'] to be SOL [as in Portuguese for 'sun']."[46] This splitting process—first between ground/planet/sun and then within the very same signifier: sol (ground) / sol (sun)—initiated in Rimbaud's line led Oiticica to associate with the sun the image of a white, snow-clad, luminous celestial body. All of these terms—sun, snow, coke—act as surrogates of "white," marking a series of circular slippages into and out of it.

Oiticica deploys Malevich's *White on White* as the emblem of "white" as a signifier enabling such associations and a signifier of slippage itself. It is the visual correlate of the hyphen, a major structuring principle of Oiticica's writing at that period (when writing was the core of his artistic activity). Malevich's painting was not considered a "plain surface," then, but a split.[47] A suggestive rendering of this split can be found in some of the *CC4* slides, in the tilted rectangular absence of the coke lines on the center of the cover of Cage's *Notations*. It also alludes to *White on White*, and does so not by pitching different hues, or by presenting an unbroken screen that disappears as environmental duration unravels upon it (as in Moholy-Nagy's account), but by fully collapsing figure and ground. This marks the *White on White* as a minimum, self-differentiating (note the reflexive role of the hyphen in this very term) split, whose generative potential was central both to Oiticica's word associations and to the conflictive temporalities at play in *CC4*.

But isn't silence in Cage's understanding already a mark of pure difference between two positive (musical) states, something that doesn't exist as such?[48] Granted, but this isn't exactly the same as saying that silence is a split. Joseph argues that following Cage's Bergsonism, Rauschenberg's *White Paintings* are "situated at the beginning of an aesthetic paradigm in which difference is conceived not in terms of negation at all, but rather as an ontological first principle, the positive and productive motor force behind the dynamic conception of nature."[49] However, if it is true that Rauschenberg endeavored "to show matter in its own duration,"[50] then Joseph is more accurate in saying that, in Bergson, "duration's irreversibility ultimately guaranteed that all of creation would incessantly differ from itself."[51] If we take Cage's "there is no such thing as silence" to mean that silence doesn't exist, then silence will be no more than a sign of the intellect's inability to grasp flux. Difference will then be a mere description of the continuous becoming of different states rather than an actual "ontological first principle." In other words, its ontological role remains more claimed than defined.

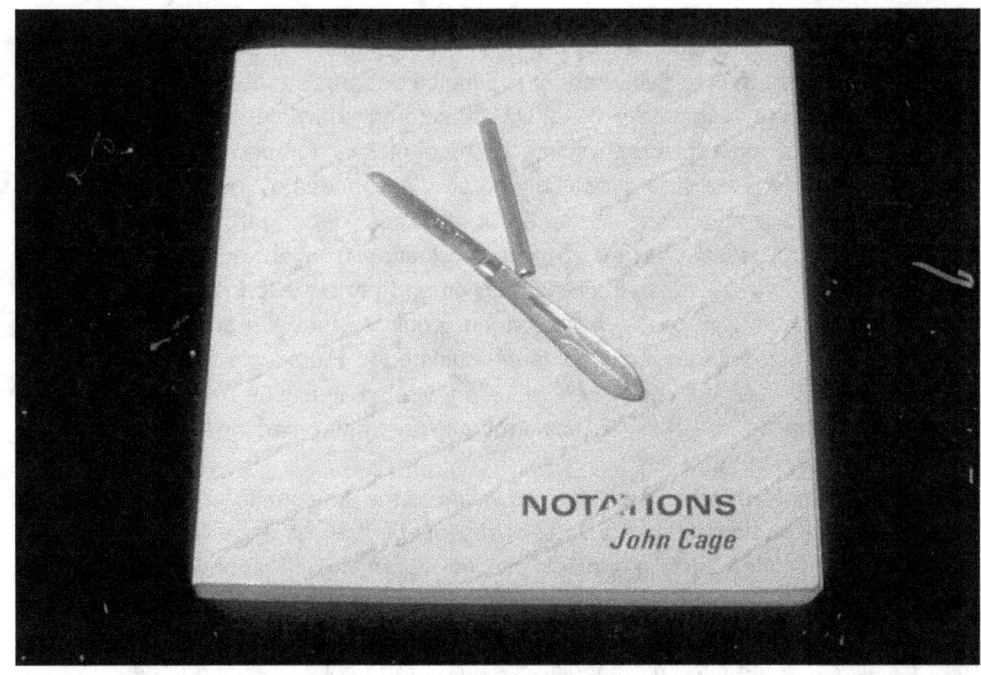

5.5
Hélio Oiticica and Neville D'Almeida, *CC4
Nocagions—Block Experiments in Cosmococa,*
1973. Slide photograph. Photo: Hélio Oiticica.
Courtesy Projeto Hélio Oiticica.

So both Oiticica and Cage (along with Rauschenberg) derived notions of differ-ence that were meaningful to their practices from their understanding of whiteness. However, I think, each gives rise to a dramatically different political paradigm. It is enlightening, in this respect, to address Nietzsche's appearance in the "sun" fragment I quoted, which raises the question of the philosopher's role in Oiticica's trajectory as a whole. This long-standing interest in Nietzsche may appear to sit uneasily with Oiticica's constructivist-oriented artistic beginnings. Thinking about this peculiar conjunction in an alternate manner (e.g., overemphasizing, as Pape and Haroldo de Campos did, his "dyonisian" or "bodily" turn while discovering dance and the favelas) is, as we have seen, a problematic way out. Bearing in mind Michael Asbury's warning that Oiticica's "radical leap" in the 1960s was somehow prefigured in his earlier work, it would seem unwarrant-ed to regard Oiticica's Nietzschean references as a sign of a postmodernist mentality on the artist's part; as his own juxtaposition of Nietzsche and Malevich should attest to, his understanding of the philosopher goes hand in hand with his modernist affiliation.[52]

If the "sun" in the passage I quoted from Oiticica earlier comes from Rimbaud, it also points to Nietzsche, especially in its association with the concept of "midday." Both terms are recurrent in Nietzsche's writings, as Oiticica certainly knew, but one particular passage from *Thus Spoke Zarathustra* can be read as indicating the kind of generative split I have referred to. Nietzsche writes of the "Great Midday" as "the middle of its [the human's] path between beast and Overhuman.... Then will the one who goes under bless himself, that he may be one who goes over; and the sun of his understanding will stand at midday for him."[53]

This line describes a well-known narrative of passage in Nietzsche's writing, but not by simply celebrating its final realization in the "Overhuman." Instead, the passage itself becomes a moment of truth ("the sun of his understanding") to the extent that before and after are brought together in it as simultaneously beast and Overhuman. In fact, "before" and "after" are terms that lose their sense in this process, for the impor-tance of these two stages lies first and foremost in the passage they articulate from one to another. Nietzsche insists, in the beginning of *Thus Spoke Zarathustra*, that "the human is a rope, fastened between beast and Overhuman—a rope over an abyss," praising it in that "it is a bridge and not a goal: what can be loved in the human is that it is a *going-over* and a *going-under*."[54]

If for Nietzsche the human "is a bridge," for Oiticica, then, these two—beast and Overhuman—could be said to be "hyphenated." And since this paradoxical, hyphenated entity is actually made of different, though conjoined stages of the same—the same "human"—it is defined by sheer self-difference. In Deleuze's reading (in a book Oiticica was later to acquire and admire), this is a crucial definition of the Nietzschean "eternal return": a return of the different, a temporally defined logic of becoming self-different.[55]

This is not a simple convergence. Slovenian theoretician Alenka Zupančič equates this logic to the very "becoming" of the subject in the formula *subject-event-subject*.[56] The end point inaugurates its own conditions of possibility. The subject is split, and this split becomes contained, as self-difference, in this nonidentical "second" subject. Zupančič visualizes this structure through Chris Marker's filmic photo-novel *La Jetée*. She points out that the hero's realization, in the end, that the image driving him through the whole film was the image of his own death is not simply the "end"; that is, the film mustn't be read in a linear manner. This realization is rather the moment when the hero actually becomes a subject—a subject constituted by the film's trajectory as an edge between the two moments on the jetty, constituting this "same" moment as split (and thus "hyphenated"). Furthermore, it is as the subject emerges in the event (of its split) that the whole film (the hero's life) becomes structured.[57] In other words, event and subject must emerge together, or emerge not at all.

The formal logic of La Jetée is similar to that of Oiticica's Cosmococas. As a sequence of stills, it interrupts cinematic continuum and suggests nonlinearity. This is what Oiticica termed "EVERYWHICHWAY—a filmic space with reference (HOMMAGE-WISE) to MALEVITCH's [sic] WHITE ON WHITE."[58] White on White translates nonlinearity into the absence of inherent representational hierarchies (such as figure-ground). This also suggests the complex temporality I have been describing: as one white is "split" into two, the very split generates an event of self-difference, enabling a logic of conflicting forces that pervaded most of Oiticica's career.[59] Instead of the passive, screenlike whiteness of Rauschenberg or Moholy-Nagy, displaying image after image, what Oiticica had in mind was the nonlinear and confrontational Malevich of the split, of self-differentiating whiteness. In cinematic terms, each new image was an active interruption of the last. Cage's "no silence" ultimately can be read (against Cage, perhaps) in this way. The impossibility of positively experiencing silence doesn't mean that it has vanished. It is more like a decentering whereby silence is split into two: the materially impossible, though logically definable silence of nonmusic, and the unattainable silence of a sound-filled reality. Silence then opens up music to environmental sounds by incorporating the shifts from one of these modes to another, by becoming self-different. Logically, at least, silence is there—but as nothing other than a constitutive split.

By taking difference for granted, or as inevitable (even if not apprehendable), Rauschenberg is able to state: "Every minute everything is different, everywhere. It's all flowing. Where is the basis for criticism, for being right or wrong, without blindly or deliberately assuming or affecting a stop?"[60] This question may seem to warrant comparison with the Nietzschean theme of perspectivism (or multiplicity). But it is not quite that: the point here is not a free-for-all, where one forsakes any political position at all because of the supposed impossibility of critically relating different stances. Nietzschean perspectivism, Zupančič argues, leads to a certain "perspective of truth" rather than to the relativism of absolute multiplicity: "Skeptical truth pretends to exist 'outside life,' and constitute a point of view on life. Perspectival truth, on the other hand, is never a point of view on life; it is, rather, truth engaged in life."[61] The point is to break the dichotomy between absolute, unchanging truths and the utter, relativist absence of truth. Truth is to be found in the very possibility of perspective, emerging from the gap between different perspectives; it is what produces perspectives as different. This is why Deleuze speaks of the affirmation of unity through multiplicity, because truth is necessarily implicated in the rise of the subject as a subject engaged in (and through) an event, in the subject's perspective upon the event.[62] Affirmation, in this regard, means a radical immanence that leaves no place for a disengaged (skeptical) subject. To affirm is first and foremost to assume a perspective on things (therefore a perspectivity), defined by itself, and not by any specific perspective. The object of affirmation in the Eternal Return is nothing but one's singular and (actually) inescapable immersion in one's life. This "as-suchness" of perspectivism differs from a relativist position within which different perspectives are incommensurable. The latter is implicit in Cage and Rauschenberg's model of difference, which raises dubious political consequences. Joseph concludes that "the positive conception of difference that the *White Paintings* had rather passively opened up" would be part of "the goal of the neo-avant-garde paradigm opened up by Cage and Rauschenberg."[63] This deferral of political import in Joseph's account, alongside a vague allusion to a "politics of difference" (what would that amount to? multiculturalism? postmodernism?) is sharply at odds with Oiticica's sense of urgency.[64]

The problem is indeed one of passivity, of difference taken for granted. Paulo Herkenhoff has argued that the emergence of white monochromes in various artistic contexts in the 1950s and 1960s "points to the dispersal of the idea of center in art history."[65] One should add that the political effect of this dispersal was not the same to artists in different places. With hindsight, the historical overtones of the equation "decentering plus passivity" in postwar New York are clear enough, and they remind one of the expression "The King is dead. Long live the King!" In that context, to announce the death of European modernism was to implicitly state that artistic hegemony had crossed the (North) Atlantic in the footsteps of cultural and geopolitical hegemony—it was all flowing, for sure, but it was very clear where to. However, from Oiticica's position (as for neoconcretism before him), history could not be assumed to be coming one's way. Decentering had to be accompanied by a theory of historical intervention. Thus the avant-gardist forceful reclaiming of anthropophagy, for example, in Oiticica's characterization of the "general constructive will" as a "Super-Anthropophagy."[66] Modernism could not be simply denied; it had to be hijacked.

This is where Zupančič provides a fortuitous link between Nietzsche and Malevich, one that counters the logic of passivity by posing truth as *declarative*. The break signaled by Malevich is not simply a break with the past. It is completely dependent on a refusal of any metaposition of enunciation. The position inaugurated by this break is that of the "I" in the manifesto form, a position corresponding to art itself, and not to the artist. It is as Zupančič argues: "Manifestos constitute and introduce a singular point of enunciation. In them, art speaks in the first person; their form of enunciation is always something like 'I, the (new) art, am speaking.'"[67] In order for truth to be true, it must be a double affirmation. It must affirm the truth, and it must affirm the affirmation itself (as the manifesto does) in its declarative mode.[68]

Sure enough, Oiticica's role in the 1960s avant-garde was underscored by a number of manifestos he authored or coauthored. But the significance of Zupančič's description here lies beyond that, in the idea that the *writing of manifestos* gives way to a kind of *manifesto writing* (here understood as a way of conceiving of writing), one that was not actually restricted solely to writings intended to perform the public role of manifestos. The turning point can be located, I think, in 1969, during Oiticica's season in London. This was the moment when his writing became more autonomous—that is, independent from considerations of any particular artwork, artist, or artistic event—and when he started to title them according to—or more precisely *against*—literary genres.[69] His most innovative writing in London took the form of the pieces he chose to name *autos* and *contos* (tales). Oiticica describes the *autos* as "poetized memories (the facts are little lived-through experiences [*vivências*] that now become great things for me)."[70]

Again, here is a motif that recurs in his trajectory: the retrospective reclaiming of earlier experiences in a way that not only reevaluates their meaning but also decisively inflects his ongoing activity. The *autos* make explicit the way he conceives of his very subjective position as inflected—as an *auto*biography that is not simply a recording of past events, but an active invention of one's present stance.[71] And, as cultural critic Frederico Coelho puts it in his perceptive analysis, the *contos* "were short, no more than three pages long, and written without recourse to clear punctuation, in a flux of ideas, and generally based in facts in which the plot's diffuse narrator was involved. This narrator can often be read as being Hélio himself. The poetic prose of the *contos*, however, gives no space for the reader to comfortably pinpoint the biographical element in their lines."[72]

Briefly, if the *autos* represent another aspect of Oiticica's critical relation with the past, the *contos* effectively distill his present awareness into a writing form. Displacement (both geographic and linguistic) may have been the crucial element that added a transformative dimension to the restless demolition of a fixed identity in his work. My suggestion is that the same drive that pitted the *Metaesquemas* against the egomorphism of abstract painting and that sought to implode the "obviousness" of national identity in *Tropicália* is at work in this move toward writing (and against literary genres), especially in Oiticica's systematic avoidance of a comfortable position of enunciation. Again, one must consider the weight of Oiticica's playful title: the very word *conto*, after all, besides being the Portuguese word for "tale" or "short story," also means "I tell," just like this, in the first person of the present tense. "The texts allow us to think these titles as the enunciation of an action rather than the presentation of a genre," Coelho argues. "The literary genre is folded into the action that follows from its denomination: I don't write a 'tale' [*um 'conto'*], I proceed straight to the act and 'tell it' [*e 'conto'*]."[73]

This "fold" is precisely what makes affirmation twofold or double (i.e., declarative). To affirm is to proceed "straight to the act"—in fact, it *is* the act. This logic is subjectively immanent, thus erasing the possibility of a metalevel that would underscore both the absolute positing of metaphysical truths and the relativist ironic distance. By the same token, no metalevel is admitted in relation to the body as well, so that it could be externally posed as a representation that is distinct from and equivalent to intellect. This is the radical sense of bodily immanence in Oiticica's trajectory: not the junction of two distinct terms in a single whole (as Haroldo de Campos's narrative implied), but the realization that immanence itself involves a self-differential split.[74] The body should thus be located as an internal limit of the subject's unavoidable immersion in language rather than as a substantial, external limit. With this in mind, it is possible to suggest, as Vladimir Safatle does, that the point of subjective destitution is "to recognize the necessity of thinking a subject capable of formalizing experiences of non-identity."[75] To affirm is an act of subjective destitution in this sense; that is, in the sense that affirmation supposes a radical experience of immanence where difference is an internal split rather than the positing of an external and equivalent other against whom the subject's identity could be asserted.

Oiticica's manifesto form must not be understood, then, as an emulation of past forms, but as a structural necessity. No wonder it became more dominant in his writing over the years, instead of fading away. There is no contradiction in the fact that his manifesto-writing sits alongside an unequivocal sense of subjective destitution—that is, insofar as one doesn't interpret the latter as subjective erasure, but as the necessary divorce of subject from the identity principle (which is yet another way of envisioning self-difference). In contrast to the disowned subject of Rauschenberg's statement on the impossibility of criticism, Oiticica's subject is an effect of the formalization (to use Safatle's term) in his work and writings of an intense engagement with truth. And what crucially distinguishes both concepts of the subject here—what prevents subjective destitution from assuming an ethically problematic state of passivity—are the different, implicit understandings of difference I have discussed.

One could object that once truth is rendered "impersonal" it could simply become either an instrument of oppression or a bearer of ideology. But this contention is valid only insofar as truth is not only rendered "impersonal" but also "unsubjectivized"—that is to say, if we mistake perspectivity in itself (that self-reflective mode inherent to the engaged subject able to read politically the multiplicity of perspectives in the world) for any particular perspective. Multiple particular perspectives remain incommensurable to one another only insofar as the metalevel of "skeptical truth" is preserved; the subjectiv-izing event forecloses this metalevel. If self-difference is temporally posed as a product of the Eternal Return, then subjectivizing truth means to reaffirm it again and again, not as a return of the same, but as an actualization of difference. This is what makes Oiti-cica's initial distance from and subsequent "return" to Malevich so important: Malevich could become actual, in Oiticica's eyes, through someone like John Cage (although not necessarily in a strictly Cagean manner), and also through another musician, Jimi Hendrix (who became the focus of the following *Cosmococa, CC5 Hendrix-War*):

> everything starts in MONTEREY POP (or better, everything changes) JIMI HENDRIX ecstasiates all old references: guitar-amplifier-way of playing: body-hands-microphone: his performance-peak was not only ecstatic but dividing-limit-of an age secular water-shed as important as the MALEVICHian white on white as MALLARMÉ coup of dice, etc: that audience was there to live its end as audience of that kind it was unwillingly wit-nessing the beginning of something that RECOGNISES itself in the total-act peformance sacralised-sacrifice: all the naughty and intricately sophisticated and intentional orgasm-gimmick of JIMI was a MANIFESTO that said: I BURN THE PRODIGY'S GUITAR (THAT WAS BEFORE A DEMONSTRATIVE INSTRUMENT OF HIS SPECIALISED TALENT-GIFT) WITH AS MUCH LEVITY AND GIMMICK AS THE GIMMICK-INVENTIONS OF THE OLD SPECTACLE MEANT TO "BE WATCHED" as if the fire-orgasm was consuming all the linear-visual-specialized forms of performance-notation-relations music-writing/music-improvisation, etc.[76]

There is a strikingly Zarathustrian ring to this fragment in a number of the senses I have been describing. Hendrix himself, in Oiticica's eyes, assumes a role very close to Zara-thustra's own. Just as Nietzsche took Zarathustra as a moralist undoing morals, an emblem of "the *self-overcoming* of morality out of truthfulness," Oiticica takes Hendrix as a performer undoing performance as it were.[77] Oiticica also emphasizes that, for the audience, this overcoming is a moment of recognition (of itself as a self-differentiating entity) much as it was for the human passing from beast into Overhuman. And last, but not least, Oiticica reads Hendrix's performance as a manifesto, and collapses this description into his own manifesto mode of writing.

As far as Oiticica's own retrieval of Malevich goes, this logic of splitting and hyphen-ating, of self-differentiation and recognition, points to a demand for actualization. In the same 1978 text I quoted at the beginning of this article, Oiticica declares *White on White* "no longer only a phase or a work of MALEVICH's, but a sine qua non state for the *arrival of the new*."[78] Within a narrative of passage, this means a demand that we return to truth wherever we identify its past emergence and affirm it anew, in an act that both stems from and constitutes a properly engaged subject. There is something in this logic that cannot be reduced to the historical limits of avant-gardism. Indeed, Oiticica's work in the 1970s can be read as an effort at reconstructing engagement—at both the subjective and the collective dimensions—in ways that surpass those limits (thus his exhortation that "each one must be VANGUARD"). In this respect, this not only is what makes Hélio Oiticica still relevant, but also is the ethics that gives ongoing validity and urgency to the very practices of art and art history alike.

180

6

Coda: Radical Present

Historicism presents the eternal image of the past whereas historical materialism presents a given experience with the past—an experience that is unique. The replacement of the epic element by the constructive element proves to be the condition for this experience. The immense forces bound up in historicism's "once upon a time" are liberated in this experience. To put to work an experience with history—a history that is original for every present— is the task of historical materialism. The latter is directed toward a consciousness of the present which explodes the continuum of history.[1]

WALTER BENJAMIN

Chronological brackets such as that of this book—1949 to 1979—are always to some extent arbitrary. The precision of those dates can be questioned, just as I could have arguably picked other artists or have given more emphasis to works and events I have mentioned only in passing. On occasions art historians justify their object of study by briskly asserting that this or that artist, critic, movement, or group of works have been little or never studied. This strikes me as a misguided way of framing an intellectual project. First, it implicitly subjects the art historian to the imperative of filling gaps in the current structure of knowledge, which, as I have argued in relation to the problem of "fielding" Brazilian art, is at odds with the more urgent perspective of truth. The latter has nothing to do with the positive accumulation of empirical data or with the mastery of a specific subject. It is rather a problem of how the subject positions itself in relation to the narration of history. In fact, it is this perspective alone that gives rise to urgency proper. Second, and more specifically, there is simply too much art that has never been seriously examined in Brazil for this imperative to make sense as a valid criterion. To follow this path is tantamount to dooming the art historian to the Sisyphean task of excavating an ever-growing archaeological site. If echoes of Benjamin's angel of history can be heard here, it is because this metaphor is also intended as a critique of a positivist conception of history (indeed, one piece of evidence of how close Benjamin's position is to that of psychoanalysis is their common countering of the historicist stance).

If Oiticica's motto "from adversity we live," by now also a cliché in Brazilian debates, can still be critically mobilized, then it must be understood not as an apology for precariousness, but as the demand for a different way of positioning oneself vis-à-vis the contradictions of one's reality. Like color, Oiticica had earlier claimed, "man needs to structure himself."[2] The artist would later return to "white on white" in order to conceive a radically immanent mode of affirmation. No wonder then that Oiticica considered his "adversity" motto the synthesis of an ethical position. From our current historical perspective, this can now be related back to my initial discussion of a "point of view of the leftover." If we keep in mind Benjamin's allegory, then it becomes clear that the position of the leftover is nothing but the recognition of the leftover as such, in its repressed radicality, as opposed to a stash of not-yet-knowledge (whose projected and progressive organization into art history proper cannot but take the temporal form of the "continuum

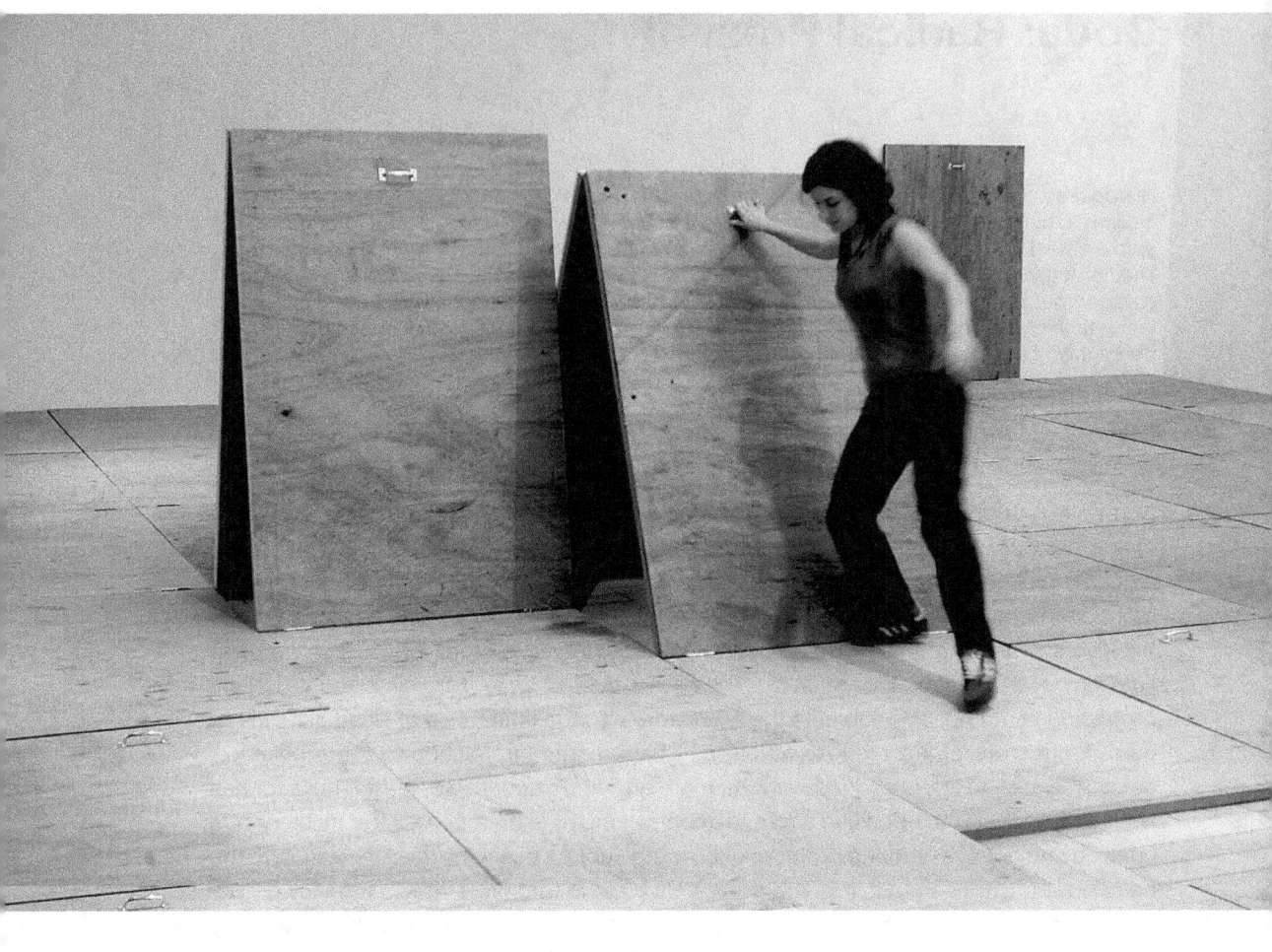

6.1
Renata Lucas, *Falha*, 2003. Plywood, hinges
and handles, variable dimensions. Photo: Kiko
Ferrite. Courtesy of the artist.

CHAPTER 6

of history").[3] My point is not, of course, to make an apology for the institutional precariousness of museums and art institutions in Brazil, which take part in a more general and formative precariousness that informed the Brazilian avant-garde as a whole.[4] It is rather that the present cannot be fully determined by the need to make up for lost time. Past failures need to be reclaimed *in*, rather than redeemed for, their inadequacy, thus reconfiguring the relationship between present and past as one of openness and shock. Only then can we speak of a radical present.

And yet I closed chapter 5 arguing for the ongoing validity and urgency of the very practices of *art and art history alike.* So one question remains: what about the status of the art practices of our lived present vis-à-vis this historical model I propose for approaching the Brazilian avant-garde?

In the interview for the catalog of her 2007 show in Los Angeles, contemporary Brazilian artist Renata Lucas remarked how curious it was that her first exhibition on North American soil should force her to carry her "own walking ground."[5] She was referring to the institutional constraints that prevented the realization of the initial projects she had planned and that ultimately led her to reprise her 2003 work *Falha* (Failure/Fault). In this work visitors manipulated wooden plaques that doubled the original floor area of the exhibition space, and chose whether to spread out the plaques and walk on them or leave segments stacked or folded. But there is a double valence to Lucas's statement. As she goes on to explain, in her view the experience of the Brazilian artist is "to have to construct the floor that you will step on; to construct the room where you will exhibit; to install the window you will open, because this country is like soft clay that you have to mold every day."[6] This metaphor is "constructive" in a way that cannot fail to recall Oiticica's terms in "Brazil Diarrhea," in which he advocated that a constructive attitude involved "plunging into the shit."[7] Thus he acknowledged the Brazilian setting's contradictions and adjusted to them instead of simply applying readymade solutions or preconceived intellectual frameworks. That the valences of the term "constructive" in Oiticica's and Lucas's vocabulary also recall Benjamin's countering of the "constructive" with the "epic" may be a fortuitous coincidence, but it is by no means insignificant, since in all cases what is at stake is indeed an "experience *with* the past."

In the same catalog, critic and curator Lynn Zelevansky rightly draws attention to Lucas's metaphorical description of Brazil as "soft clay." Zelevansky develops her argument as an intertwined survey of Lucas's career and of postwar Brazilian art in order to single out procedural affinities between the younger artist and works by Oiticica, Lygia Clark, Lygia Pape, and Cildo Meireles. She also attempts to relativize the problem of direct artistic influence by noting how Lucas also draws on North American artists such as Bruce Nauman and Gordon Matta-Clark. However, Zelevansky's account ultimately places Lucas's relationship with "Brazil's artistic legacy" in terms that make this legacy seem a somewhat self-enclosed and alternative line of development. As Zelevansky's epigraph, then, the soft clay metaphor risks suggesting that Brazil is a sort of curious place where things are very malleable in an almost exotic manner, making the fact that it produced "some of the world's best music and art" over the last fifty years or so yet another fascinating curiosity. The fact that Lucas draws on Nauman and Matta-Clark in addition to the Brazilian avant-gardists becomes little more than a token of eclecticism or contemporary cosmopolitanism. In any case, it thinly veils the strict historical and geographic framework that categorizes artists such as Oiticica and Meireles. At one point, Zelevansky likens *Falha* to Lygia Clark's *Bichos*, stating that it "functions similarly but on a grander scale."[8] Participation, of course, becomes the key word that brings the two together, dispensing with a more careful evaluation of their differences in favor of smooth identification.

By restricting the work of Meireles to matters of political commentary and phenomenological investigation, Zelevansky fails to register perhaps the most fruitful link between him and Lucas—the inclusion of fiction and myth within the coordinates of cognitive experience. This is no minor point of contention, for to claim that 1970s conceptualism in Latin America was thematically "political" is also to imply that it was deviant in the sense that it concerned itself with mundane commentary rather than with "hard" cognitive problems of language and representation. This would ultimately mean, in turn, that this "political" conceptualism was bound to miss the deeper political dimension of representation and its shifts—which, as I have argued, is a crucial dimension of both Meireles's and Antonio Dias's sophisticated linguistic displacements and scale shifts. In his "humiliminimalist" work *Southern Cross* (1969–1970), Meireles affirms phenomenological primacy only to subvert it with an affective take on myth. Certainly the empty setting (the cube is meant to be the sole piece on display in a very large room) prompts viewers' awareness of their gargantuan presence in relation to the tiny cube, which contrasts with the anthropomorphic size of so many minimalist sculptures. But, most importantly, this sense of self-presence is ultimately displaced as the work's narrative fills the empty room with a virtual presence of an incommensurable kind that, as the artist explains, has to do with the encounter between Jesuit missionaries and Tupi natives: "The 'white' culture reduced an indigenous divinity to the god of thunder when in reality their system of belief was a much more complex, poetic and concrete matter, emerging through the mediation of their sacred trees, oak and pine. Through the [rubbing together of] these two timbers [which are also the materials of the cube] the divinity would manifest its presence. The fire created was a form of evocation of the divinity."[9]

Crucially, then, the actual objectivity of the cube lies not so much in its actual size and materiality, but in the way it hinges perception and imagination—or, more suggestively, in the way it puts them in friction. Meireles's statement on *Southern Cross* in the "Information" catalog projects this friction between two different modes of presence onto a mythic and geographic split.[10] The latter corresponds, in turn, to the ideological pervasiveness of rationalism (enacted through its representational devices: "post cards, pictures, descriptions and books" and also "earth-works, think-works, nihil-works, water-works, conceptual-works and so on") and to entropic disruption of myth as it arises in the midst of this Symbolic mesh ("For a people who can transform its History into fantastic legends and fables and allegories, that people has a real existence").[11]

Curator Chus Martínez has stressed Lucas's vacillations "between the concrete and the allegorical," thus bringing her work tentatively close to my description of *Southern Cross*.[12] However, Martínez herself prefers to stick with the precedent of Oiticica's 1969 *Area Bolides*, a part of the *Eden* environment that, for the curator, amounted to "a predetermined space in which spectators can take off their shoes, lie down, dance, or do whatever they desire."[13] She departs from this particular openness of Oiticica's propositions in order to argue that Lucas's works evoke a "Habermasian conception of communicative action and its arena, the lifeworld: the space of mutually maintained assumptions, ideas and values."[14] In the end, Martínez concludes that the works "force reflection on the assumptions, ideas, and values that govern a situation, on the systems that pervade them, on what maintains them—not just architecture but language, image, habits—and, finally, on how they might be modified and even, perhaps, decolonized."[15]

Leaving aside the question of whether *Eden* can be properly read in a Habermasian key (which is a big if), the fact is that Martínez's comparison is more sophisticated, but not necessarily more pertinent than Zelevansky's rendering of *Falha* as large-scale successor of the *Bichos*. Participation, either actual or virtual (for example, Martínez's view that the works have the power of staging communicative exchanges), is the main idea that drives both authors as they attempt to connect Lucas with her Brazilian precedents. This choice makes the works readily intelligible not only within the context of current curatorial trends, but also in relation to the imperative of an immediate political pertinence. It is also symptomatic of the difficulty critics often have with placing participation, and its role in Brazilian art, in a historical perspective—its immediacy is often taken for granted. However, if we turn to the similarity I have suggested between *Falha* and *Southern Cross*, then we may grasp, or so I wish to argue, a different way of approaching this legacy.

For Lucas, *Falha* was an earlier work that seemed "to make sense in this new context." Her point is not only about the failure of her original project, for "failure" is just one possible translation for the work's original title. In Portuguese, the word *falha* also means "fault," as in—not coincidentally—the San Andreas Fault. This double meaning, which gained resonance in the 2007 version, actually opens up the work to an abrupt scale shift that is not unlike the displacement of phenomenological self-awareness by the mythical horizon of *Southern Cross*. For the rigid and powerful institutional structure Lucas dealt with in Los Angeles is shown to be incommensurably frail in relation to the geological forces that lie directly underneath it. Therefore, to bring a metaphor of Brazilian malleability into this context is not simply to compare two distinct realities, but also to shed a light on the contradictions of the new situation in its own terms. If *Falha* does indeed reclaim participation, it is in a starkly ironic mode: in a context where viewers increasingly go to museums in the expectation of interactive experiences, they are inadvertently invited to play with a metaphor of the uncertainty of what they ultimately take for granted—their own walking ground.

I want to go one step further and suggest that *Falha* is more than an apocalyptic symbol or an allegory of the ultimate fragility of a cultural and economic superpower. More importantly, it points to a crucial ideological deadlock, namely the role of disavowal in the structuring of everyday life. For it is indeed startling that California, the richest state in the world's richest country, lies on some of the world's most geologically unstable ground. Everyday life happens normally, even with the possibility that a potentially devastating earthquake—informally nicknamed "the big one"—can happen at any time (or not happen in a lifetime). The case is even more extreme: it is in this scenario that one of the most powerful lifestyle factories of the twentieth century—Hollywood—has thrived. As a matter of fact, Hollywood itself has devoted a whole genre, the disaster film, precisely to that which everyday life in its surroundings disavows. The contradiction here

6.2
Cildo Meireles, *Southern Cross*, 1969–1970.
Wooden cube, one section pine, one section
oak. 0.9 × 0.9 × 0.9 cm. Photo: Pat Kilgore.
Courtesy of the artist.

is apparent: as Slavoj Žižek has remarked (following Fredric Jameson), the fact that it is easier to represent the end of the world (and harder to take action against impending ecological catastrophe) than to imagine the end of capitalism is a symptom that capital "is the Real of our lives."[16] Paradoxically, then, the disaster film joins ranks with a series of everyday rituals in the ideological disavowal of a Real catastrophe.

Of course, capitalism has not yet managed to cause earthquakes. My point is simply to note how Los Angeles is a paradigmatic example of how tied the structural power of ideology is to everyday life and to the ritual disavowal of its potential end, both in the cataclysmic sense and in that of replacing it with a fairer form of collective organization. As Žižek puts it, "Ideology is not constituted by abstract propositions in themselves, rather, ideology is itself this very texture of the lifeworld which 'schematizes' the propositions, rendering them 'livable.'"[17] This goes against Martínez's understanding of the lifeworld as the Habermasian arena for "communicative action." Lucas does not set the stage for the positive constitution of an alternative social paradigm. Instead, what her work addresses is precisely the fact that the lifeworld itself is a fantasy, a set of fictions that dictates the consistence of the everyday. The works are political, for sure, but not in the sense of offering the blueprint for a new society. They operate instead against the background of a deep crisis in political imagination. And they do so by embedding at the heart of those fictions the uncanny dimension of experience. As Mladen Dolar argues, in a passage that elucidates this rather oblique instance of site specificity I have been describing:

> The uncanny is always at stake in ideology—ideology perhaps basically consists of a social attempt to integrate the uncanny, to make it bearable, to assign it a place, and the criticism of ideology is caught in the same framework if it tries to reduce it to another kind of content or to make the content conscious and explicit. This criticism is always on the brink of a naïve effort to fix things with their proper names, to make the unconscious conscious, to restore the sense of what is repressed and thus be rid of the uncanny.[18]

The most radical attitude toward the uncanny is, according to Dolar, to sustain it "as a *limit to interpretation*" by insisting on its "formal level," that of "the dimension of the object" at "the point that can never be successfully recuperated by the signifying chain."[19] On the one hand, this explanation clarifies the extent to which Lucas's allusion to the San Andreas Fault differs from that of disaster films, in which the catastrophes in question are disavowed precisely by being nominally and narratively integrated into the signifying chain. On the other hand, and more crucially, it exposes the problems of Martínez's communicative model: "The 'object,'" Dolar argues, "cannot become a part of accepted intersubjective space."[20] Meireles has recently praised what he regarded as Lucas's "explicit discretion."[21] As a matter of fact, it is this temporality of slowly revealing the complex layers that the works mobilize that brings both artists together. Zelevansky remarks that both also rely on "danger" and "discomfort," emphasizing the "threatening title" of certain works by Lucas.[22] This description initially seems to contradict the more hopeful, democratic view of Martínez. To evoke the uncanny is thus to advance both a critique and a synthesis of these accounts, for the uncanny provides a model in which danger and consensus are not a polar pair, but in which the latter actually produces the former as its internal excess.

This uncanny dimension emerges in various works by Lucas. In *Barulho de fundo* (*Background Noise*, 2004), for example, a barrier of five closed-circuit TV monitors stood in front of the escalators that lead from the hall of the Centro Cultural Tomie Ohtake, in São Paulo, to the office tower right above it. The whole complex, called Ohtake Cultural, was advertised as "a contemporary conception of the city, where culture, work and leisure are integrated."[23] However, four years after its completion, the overwhelming majority of the offices remained unsold, leaving the tower virtually empty (apart from two floors, it seems). Intended to be an effective but seamlessly integrated emblem of corporate power, especially in the way its colorful postmodernist architecture stood in the midst of a low-rise neighborhood, the building became, in Lucas's words, a "ghost-ship."[24]

The installation resembled a barrier that paradoxically allowed the visitors' *vision* to enter, as long as they voyeuristically identified with the surveillance cameras. This is not to claim, however, that the work was actually *about* surveillance. For not only was the emptiness of the building shown by the CCTV—already in opposition to a fully functional, codified, and controlled space—but its signifying lapses were further explored by the digital insertion of previously shot footage of wild animals, like panthers and hippos. Some of them were often shown leaving a scene, prompting viewers to scrutinize the neighboring monitors in search of their next step, in search of narrative sequentiality. But, since new images came up only according to CCTV's strictly cyclical logic, the scrutinizing power of the viewers was often eluded. The animals thus seemed to inhabit the space in between the shifting scenes, becoming fleeting presences glimpsed out of the corner of one's eyes—not unlike other works, such as *The Visitor* (2007) and *Venice Suitcase* (2009), in which the artist respectively transplanted a small portion of wild forest into the Tate Modern gardens and half-buried a section of asphalt road under the gravel surface of one of the Giardini della Biennale's many paths. These works are almost unnoticeable and, once perceived, give the impression that they were already there with us before we noticed them, thus acquiring a haunting aura. Furthermore, since one of *Barulho de fundo*'s monitors was linked to the actual gallery CCTV, viewers themselves became uncannily implicated in their muted scene, in an example of the all-encompassing subject of surveillance giving way to the object of the gaze.

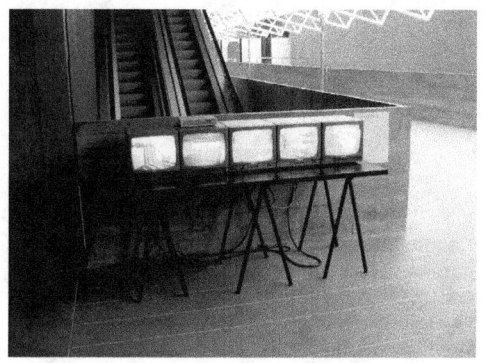

6.3
Renata Lucas, *Barulho de fundo*, 2005. Video installation (in collaboration with Daniel Steegmann and Dionis Escorça). Photo: Renata Lucas. Courtesy of the artist.

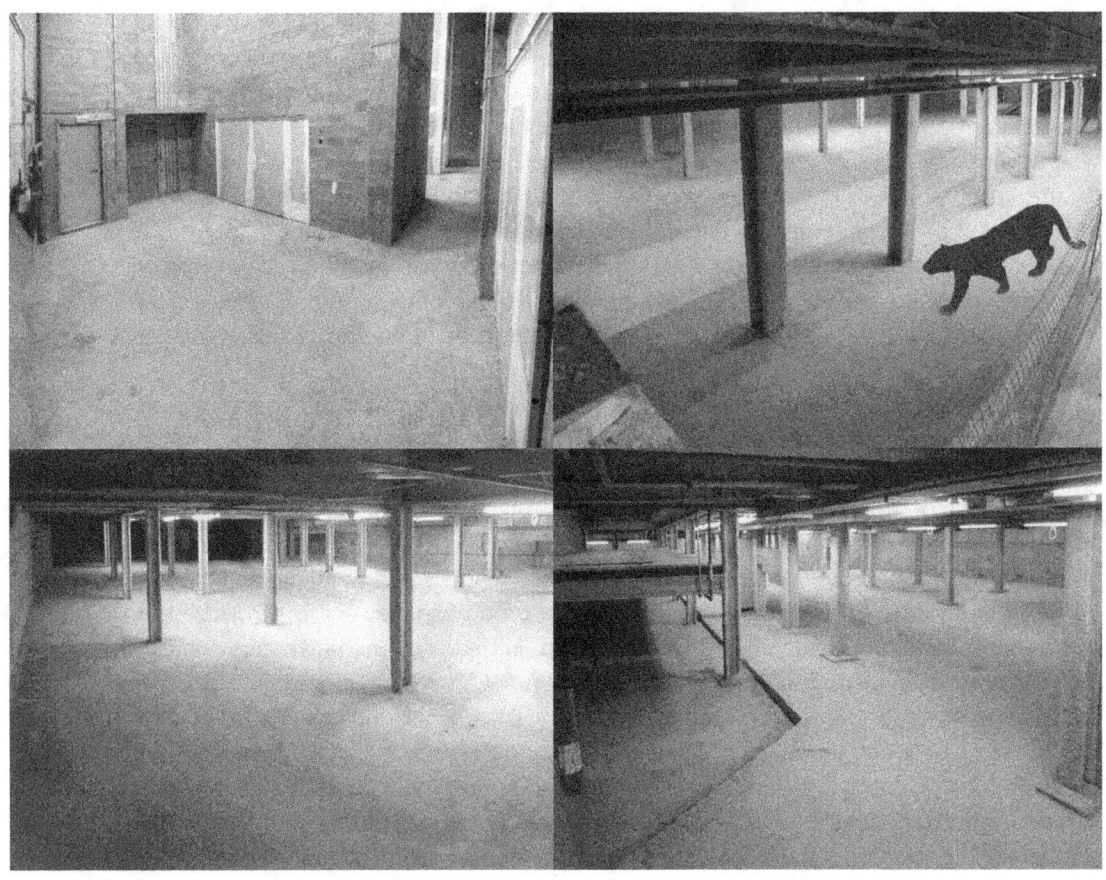

6.4
Renata Lucas, *Barulho de fundo*, 2005.
Video stills from monitor 4.

6.5
Renata Lucas, *The Visitor*, 2007 (Tate Modern
garden before and after the artist's intervention).
Northern England native trees and undergrowth,
variable dimensions. Photos: Renata Lucas.
Courtesy of the artist.

What I want to stress is how the second version of *Falha*, by virtue of its geographic displacement and the significance the work acquires in the Californian context, deals with the same problem as *Barulho de fundo*: the smooth functioning of ideology in the guise of the comfortable inexorability of everyday life in late-capitalist societies. If many of Meireles's works still communicate the perplexity of ever-growing abstractions such as money, Lucas intervenes in a scenario of full-fledged ideological efficacy. Furthermore, my aim in questioning Zelevansky's and Martínez's readings was to open the way for a different conception of the role of contemporary artists vis-à-vis the reception of the Brazilian avant-garde. In Zelevansky's model, Lucas simply inherits certain traits from her predecessors; despite the critic's warning, it ultimately boils down to a matter of influence. Martínez, in turn, formulates an interpretation that is based on the imperative of claiming immediate political efficacy for art. While I claim that Lucas is indeed responding to predecessors such as Oiticica and Meireles, I want to avoid pseudomorphic comparisons and try to understand instead how she transforms by bringing into the present their own concerns and mobilizes the legacy of Brazilian modernism, and more specifically its position as a leftover, in order to address a distinct ideological scenario. The principle of nonidentity, which I have continuously stressed, is turned into a subtle but unsettling device in the guise of the uncanny. Considering how central this notion—in its structural form, in opposition to more hackneyed renderings of it—is to the ideological scenario of late capitalist culture, Lucas's work can also be described as a critical hinge between present urgency and historical reclamation.

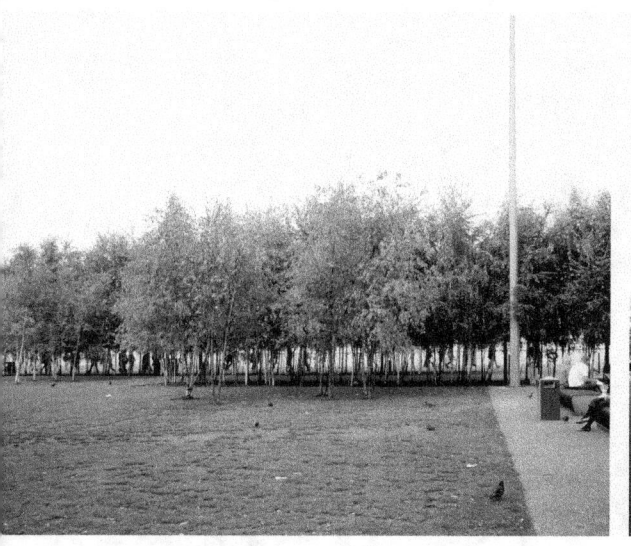
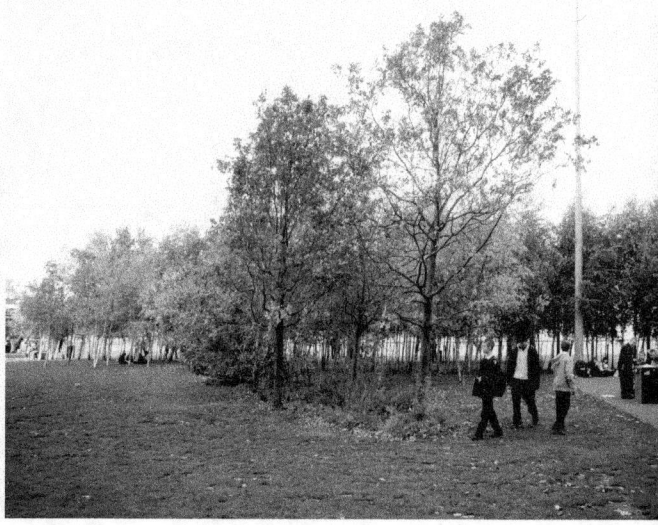

I want to conclude with one last observation: from an international perspective, contemporary art is *literally* contemporary to the Brazilian avant-garde. The work of Castro, Clark, Dias, Meireles, Pape, Oiticica, and of so many others remains relatively unknown, but its reception has been gaining impetus, mostly due to the changing position of Brazil in the broader cultural and geopolitical map. If, as I have insisted, the late reception of the Brazilian avant-garde has often led to misrepresentations of it, contemporary artists have the potential to reaffirm its actuality by addressing its original contribution in ways that critically bypass the mediation of curatorial trends and the codes of art history and other academic disciplines. From the perspective of the art historian, to remain alert to some of those artists may serve as an antidote against certain vices. By virtue of being indebted both to a critical reworking of the constructive tradition and to an uncanny sensibility that stems in great part from the complex lineage of the notion of the object in Brazil, Lucas's work reclaims the former while simultaneously problematizing the "antimodernist" label of certain key procedures that come from the surrealist tradition.

This odd vantage point that turns precariousness and late reception into a critical position also sets my account apart from Hal Foster's (which I have discussed in the introduction) on one more count, namely his excessive reliance on the 1960s as a surrogate for present stances. For to engage in the critique of those misrepresentations cannot be a matter of imagining or longing for an ideal scene of reception that would transmit or dictate the "authentic" meaning of those practices. One has to depart instead from their potential actuality. An interesting consequence in this regard is that, theoretically at least, the Brazilian legacy is not available only to contemporary Brazilian artists. To reclaim it, after all, depends on a certain act of structurally positioning one's practice in relation to it. Contemporary art thus has the double role of reformulating these terms and, of course, of opening up this legacy to a whole new set of urgent questions. It follows that the construction of the Brazilian avant-garde—in Oiticica's and Lucas's sense of construction, but also in Benjamin's—is an open process that speaks to us in the present, and radically so.

194

Notes

INTRODUCTION

1. Paulo Venâncio Filho, "Situações limite," in *Arte contemporânea brasileira: texturas, dicções, ficções, estratégias*, ed. Ricardo Basbaum (Rio de Janeiro: Rios Ambiciosos, 2001), 318. All translations from Portuguese originals in this book are mine, unless stated otherwise.

2. Guy Brett, *Transcontinental: Nine Latin-American Artists*, exh. cat. (London: Verso, 1990), 5.

3. Ibid.

4. Ibid., 5–6.

5. Venâncio Filho, "Situações limite," 319.

6. This has been a major critical concern in speculative historiographies of Brazilian art in the last decades. In his influential book *A forma difícil*, critic Rodrigo Naves tries to face this dilemma by suggesting that the lack of an established artistic milieu in which artists could confidently maneuver gave rise to a certain common aesthetic he terms—in a hardly translatable formulation—the "reluctance of form" (*dificuldade de forma*). This would in turn be incorporated as a positive formal value by certain works, prompting the critic to propose that they thus articulate a "difficult form" (*forma difícil*), that is, a certain ostensive opaqueness that could also be described as an antipositivist trait, an incorporation of negativity in the heart of modernist aesthetics. See Rodrigo Naves, *A forma difícil: ensaios sobre arte brasileira* (São Paulo: Ática, 1996), 9–39. Critic Sônia Salzstein approaches the same problem by suggesting that, in the recent history of Brazilian art, artworks have valued "the emancipatory aspect of a subjectivity that is not completely embedded in the public (cultural) and social sphere, something like a private sphere in continuous expansion, without prescriptions or well-defined limits." See Sônia Salzstein, "Uma dinâmica da arte brasileira: modernidade, instituições, instância pública," in Basbaum, *Arte contemporânea brasileira*, 393–394.

7. Paulo Sergio Duarte, "Modernity on the Fringes," in *Arte construtiva no Brasil: coleção Adolpho Leirner*, ed. Aracy A. Amaral, trans. Izabel Burbridge (São Paulo: DBA Melhoramentos, 1998), 184–186.

8. Venâncio Filho, "Situações limite," 320.

9. See Peter Bürger, *Theory of the Avant-Garde*, trans. M. Shaw (Manchester, UK: University of Manchester Press, 1984); and Hal Foster, *The Return of the Real: Art and Theory at the End of the Century* (Cambridge, MA: MIT Press, 1996), 1–34.

10. Foster, *The Return of the Real*, 56.

11. See Benjamin Buchloh, "The Primary Colors for a Second Time: A Paradigm Repetition of the Neo-Avant-Garde," *October* 37 (Summer 1986): 41–52.

12. Michael Asbury, "Neoconcretism and Minimalism: Cosmopolitanism at a Local Level and Canonical Provincialism," in *Cosmopolitan Modernisms*, ed. Kobena Mercer (London: Institute of International Visual Arts; Cambridge, MA: MIT Press, 2005), 179–180.

13. Ibid., 180.

14. Foster, *The Return of the Real*, 29.

15. In chapter 5, I will compare this paradigm with the rather different way in which Oiticica related to the white monochrome.

16. Foster, *The Return of the Real*, 25.

17. In a seminal study, critic Ronaldo Brito defines neoconcretism as a laboratory environment. See Ronaldo Brito, *Neoconcretismo: vértice e ruptura do projeto construtivo brasileiro* (Rio de Janeiro: FUNARTE/Instituto Nacional de Artes Plásticas, 1985), 107. One exception in the United States to the picture I describe is Black Mountain College where Josef Albers (one of the heroes of the neoconcretist generation) taught.

18. Asbury, "Neoconcretism and Minimalism," 185.

19. Foster, *The Return of the Real*, xiii.

20. In her essay for the catalog of curator Paulo Herkenhoff's groundbreaking twenty-fourth São Paulo Biennial (1998), Dawn Ades notes how references to anthropophagy, so central to the Brazilian avant-garde, also circulated among Dada and surrealist circles. Ades stresses, however, that these affinities cannot be discussed in terms of direct influence. Dawn Ades, "The Anthropophagic Dimensions of Dada and Surrealism," in *XXIV Bienal de São Paulo—Núcleo histórico: antropofagia e histórias de canibalismos*, exh. cat. (São Paulo: Fundação Bienal de São Paulo, 1998), 241–245.

21. Alenka Zupančič, *Why Psychoanalysis? Three Interventions* (Copenhagen: Aarhus University Press, 2008), 39.

22. Ibid., 40.

23. Rosalind Krauss, *The Optical Unconscious* (Cambridge, MA: MIT Press, 1994), 21.

24. As Georges Didi-Huberman (who probably did more than any other writer to put the psychoanalytic notion of work in a productive relation to art history) argues, also emphasizing the change in perspective that literally constitutes the unconscious: "The work of the Freudian unconscious is not envisaged through a consciousness that sharpens itself or looks for a priori principles—it requires another position vis-à-vis consciousness and knowledge, the always unstable *position* that psychoanalytic technique broaches during sessions in the guise of the play of the transference." Georges Didi-Huberman, *Confronting Images: Questioning the Ends of a Certain History of Art*, trans. John Goodman (University Park: Pennsylvania State University Press, 2005), 169.

25. This is precisely what Krauss aims at, in her own critique of the repressive status of "modernism and its visualist logic," when employing structuralist graphs not as a "static picture" but as the snapshot of a relation: "The relation between the L Schema and the Klein Group could configure this repression. Not because the L Schema shows an elsewhere, an 'outside' of the system. But because it shows the repressive logic of the system, its genius at repression. It can, that is, figure forth the 'beneath' of the system, although the figure of the beneath is peculiar of course." Krauss, *The Optical Unconscious*, 24–27.

26. Lygia Clark, "Letter to Mondrian," in *Lygia Clark*, exh. cat. (Barcelona: Fundació Antoni Tàpies, 1998), 116.

27. Taina Caragol and Isobel Whitelegg, "The Archival Avant-Garde: Latin American Art and the UK," paper given at the conference "Latin-America: The Last Avant-Garde," New York, April 4–5, 2008.

28. Ibid.

29. This show has indeed elevated curator Mari Carmen Ramirez to an unprecedented status of authority on Latin American art in the United States. One interesting confirmation of this that has even exceeded the traditional borders of the art world is a laudatory article on Ramirez in the Movers & Shakers section of the *New York Times Magazine*. See Arthur Lublow, "After Frida," *New York Times*, March 23, 2008.

30. Caragol and Whitelegg, "The Archival Avant-Garde."

31. Zupančič departs from the Lacanian formulation "Il n'y a de cause que de ce qui cloche." In her translation: "There is but the cause of that which does not work, or which does not add up." See Zupančič, *Why Psychoanalysis*, 36. Duarte's original title is "Modernos fora dos eixos," which literally means "modern[ism] out of order." It is curious that the very translation of the notion of a "leftover" modernism is so hard to convey—it is a modernism *qui cloche*.

32. It is very important to note that, while the Brazilian avant-garde holds a singular position in relation to modernism, this is not the only standpoint from which one may formulate a critique of the Western canon that goes beyond efforts to include the excluded. As some of my theoretical references symptomatically indicate, there are very interesting projects in this respect coming from the Eastern European cultural and artistic scene, such as the Slovenian group IRWIN's East Art Map—indeed, the title of my own project resonates strongly with IRWIN's motto: "History is not a given. It has to be constructed." See *East Art Map: Contemporary Art and Eastern Europe*, ed. IRWIN (London: Afterall, 2006); and also the website of the East Art Map project, http://www.eastartmap.org/. See also Piotr

Piotrowski, "How to Write a History of Central-East European Art?," *Third Text* 23, no. 1 (2009): 5–14. I thank Milena Tomic for bringing my attention to this topic.

33.   Zupančič, *Why Psychoanalysis*, 42.

34.   Ibid., 40.

35.   On the Platonic origins of the notion, see José Ferrater Mora, *Dicionário de filosofia: tomo IV (Q–Z)*, trans. (to Portuguese) Maria Stela Gonçalves et al. (São Paulo: Edições Loyola, 2001), 2509–2510.

36.   Jacques Lacan, *Écrits: A Selection*, trans. Bruce Fink (New York: Norton, 2002), 48.

37.   Beatriz Colomina, *Privacy and Publicity: Modern Architecture as Mass Media* (Cambridge, MA: MIT Press, 1996), ix.

38.   Once again, the terms here are borrowed from Didi-Huberman. See note 24.

39.   This is in no way to diminish the existing Brazilian art literature, but simply to state that the expectations of a structured field come from outside, as a projection (and indeed as an academic project).

40.   Rosalind Krauss, *Passages in Modern Sculpture* (Cambridge, MA: MIT Press, 1981), 6.

41.   See Felipe Scovino, "Corpoobjeto: o campo experimental de Hélio Oiticica (1954–1961)," in *Hélio Oiticica: museu é o mundo*, exh. cat. (São Paulo: Itaú Cultural, 2010), 86.

42.   The limitations of addressing Brazilian culture through the lenses of the zeitgeist are not restricted to the question of 1950s national-developmentalism. For a critique of how such historiographical maneuvers tend to subsume 1960s and 1970s marginal culture in Brazil under the sign of tropicalism and post-tropicalism, see Frederico Coelho, *Sou brasileiro, confesso minha culpa e meu pecado: cultura marginal no Brasil nas décadas de 1960 e 1970* (Rio de Janeiro: Civilização Brasileira, 2010), especially 15–32.

43.   The decision to restrict the 2006 "Hélio Oiticica: The Body of Color" retrospective to his earlier, abstract production (with the addition of an awkward display of *Parangolés* in the end), leaving his post-1964 works for a second show (which never happened due to disagreements between the Projeto Hélio Oiticica and the Museum of Fine Arts in Houston) further reinforces this distinction. For a critique of the tendency to overemphasize Oiticica's discovery of the favelas and its implications, see Michael Asbury, "Hélio Couldn't Dance," in *Fios soltos: a arte de Hélio Oiticica*, ed. Paula Braga (São Paulo: Perspectiva, 2008), 52–65.

44.   Vladimir Safatle, "Uma clínica do sensível: a respeito da relação entre destituição subjetiva e primado do objeto," *Interações* 10, no. 19 (January-June 2005): 144.

45.   See Cildo Meireles, "Untitled," in *Information*, ed. Kynaston McShine (New York: Museum of Modern Art, 1970), 85; and Hélio Oiticica, *Hélio Oiticica: Painting beyond the Frame*, ed. Luciano Figueiredo, trans. Stephen Berg (Rio de Janeiro: Silvia Roesler Edições de Arte, 2008), 212.

46.   Brett, *Transcontinental*, 9.

47.   The recent availability of Hélio Oiticica's writings and notebooks has indeed opened a new stage in his reception. The growing importance ascribed to his writings, especially in the 1970s, is attested by at least three recent doctoral dissertations: Lisette Lagnado, "Hélio Oiticica: o mapa do programa ambiental (Ph.D. thesis, Universidade de São Paulo, 2003); Paula Braga, "A trama da terra que treme: multiplicidade em Hélio Oiticica" (Ph.D. thesis, Universidade de São Paulo, 2007); and Frederico Coelho, *Livro ou livro-me: os escritos babilônicos de Hélio Oiticica* (Rio de Janeiro: Editora Uerj, 2010). Lagnados's thesis includes a remarkable annex entitled "Glossary of the Environmental Program [Glossário do programa ambiental]," a dictionary of terms and concepts by the artist; and Coelho's research (undertaken in a literature department) has recently become the first published book specifically devoted to Oiticica's own book project.

48.   Tânia Rivera, "Ethics, Psychoanalysis and Post-Modern Art in Brazil: Mário Pedrosa, Hélio Oiticica and Lygia Clark," *Third Text*, no. 114 (January 2012): 53–63. Rivera also discusses the broader relevance of a psychoanalytical model of subjectivity in the work of Lygia Clark and Hélio Oiticica. Her argument opposes art historian Otília Arantes's view that Pedrosa was "always reticent in relation to psychoanalysis." See Otília Arantes, *Mário Pedrosa: Itinerário crítico* (São Paulo: Cosac Naify, 2004), 58.

49.   Safatle, "Uma clínica do sensível," 126.

199

50. For an example of this kind of misreading performed on a work by Antonio Dias, see Antonio Quinet, *Um olhar a mais: ver e ser visto na psicanálise* (Rio de Janeiro: Jorge Zahar Editor, 2002), 123–124. While this kind of reading does no harm to the psychoanalytical argument it furthers, it does hinder a more productive dialogue between art and psychoanalysis.

51. Fredric Jameson, *The Political Unconscious* (London: Routledge, 1981), 2.

1 (NON-)OBJECTS

1. Ferreira Gullar, "Theory of the Non-object," trans. Michael Asbury, in *Cosmopolitan Modernisms*, ed. Kobena Mercer (London: Institute of International Visual Arts; Cambridge, MA: MIT Press, 2005), 170.

2. Carlos Zilio, "Da antropofagia à tropicália," in *O nacional e o popular na cultura brasileira*, ed. Carlos Zilio, João Luiz Lafetá, and Lígia Chiappini Moraes Leite (São Paulo: Brasiliense, 1982), 52.

3. See Michael Asbury, "Neoconcretism and Minimalism: Cosmopolitanism at a Local Level and Canonical Provincialism," in Mercer, *Cosmopolitan Modernisms*, 174.

4. Asbury's case aims to question "the high modernist canon, and in particular its obligatory passage via Clement Greenberg's highly influential views." Ibid., 178. In chapter 2, I make a specific case for the continuity of a modernist drive in Oiticica's ongoing obsession with what he terms "the constructive" throughout the 1960s.

5. In fact, one of the merits of Ronaldo Brito's groundbreaking study of neoconcretism was precisely to question Pedrosa's simplistic reading of the opposition between the Rio and São Paulo groups, although he fails to consider other important interventions by Pedrosa, as we will see shortly. See Ronaldo Brito, *Neoconcretismo: vértice e ruptura do projeto construtivo brasileiro*, trans. Lia Alvarenga Wyler and Florence Eleanor (Rio de Janeiro: FUNARTE/Instituto Nacional de Artes Plásticas, 1985).

6. Clark alludes to that episode in a note from early 1960, where she mentions a further meeting with Pedrosa where they would have discussed Gullar's conclusions. See Lygia Clark, *Lygia Clark* (Barcelona: Fundació Antoni Tàpies, 1998), 141–143. As for the date, it was most probably between mid and late 1959, as it must have been after Pedrosa's return from his long trip to Japan.

7. Gullar's enthusiasm for the way Lygia Clark's work exemplified the non-object was actually met with skepticism by the artist herself. In her writings, she reveals having further conversations with Pedrosa (whose opinion she held in higher regard than Gullar's) after the dinner episode, where both would question the suitability of the term. According to Clark, Pedrosa would have even proposed an alternative term: *trans-object* (which is exactly how Hélio Oiticica later described his *Bólides*). See ibid.

8. See Ferreira Gullar, "A trégua—entrevista com Ferreira Gullar," interview with Antonio Fernando de Franceschi, Rinaldo Gama, Leandro Konder, Alfredo Bosi, Armando Freitas Filho, Esther Góes, and Zuenir Ventura, in *Cadernos da literatura brasileira—Ferreira Gullar* (São Paulo: Instituto Moreira Salles, 1998), 38.

9. Lygia Pape reportedly recognized that Gullar's personal stakes played a large part in his theoretical dedication to neoconcretism. See Paula Terra Cabo, "Resignifying Modernity: Clark, Oiticica and Categories of the Modern in Brazil" (Ph.D. dissertation, University of Essex, 1996), 191. The São Paulo concretist poet Augusto de Campos, for his part, repeatedly accused Gullar of forging an exaggerated antagonism for personal reasons, arguing that in reality neoconcretism was not crucially different from concretism. See Augusto de Campos, "Não adianta ser 'Neo.' É preciso ser novo," *Folha de São Paulo* (September 5, 1984); and also Augusto de Campos, "Recordando Cordeiro," in *Waldemar Cordeiro, 1925–1973* (São Paulo: Centro Cultural São Paulo, 1983), 17–18.

10. Clark states that the *Bichos* were born out of an accidental manipulation of a *Counter-Relief* rather than from the *Cocoons*, mentioning that she suddenly noticed "two free parts [of the work] in the space." One hypothesis is that this "broken" *Counter-Relief* was the particular work she discussed with Gullar and Pedrosa. See Clark, *Lygia Clark*, 106.

11. In fact, while Gullar usually finds reason to explain why most of the non-object predecessors in modern art were not quite yet non-object in the full sense of the term, he often mentions Tatlin counter-reliefs without making this proviso.

12. See Brito, *Neoconcretismo*, 105.

13. Brito's book was written around 1975, initially as a series of articles for the journal *Malasartes*, of which he was one of the coeditors, and was only published as a book in 1985. In an introductory note to this edition, he states that he refrained from making any changes to the original writings. As for Pedrosa, he only returned to Brazil from his second period of political exile in 1977, when he was no longer actively interested in Gestalt theory. It is noteworthy that in another article from 1975, Brito enthusiastically praises Pedrosa but, once again, fails to mention the latter's involvement with Gestalt. See Ronaldo Brito, *Experiência crítica*, ed. Sueli de Lima (São Paulo: Cosac Naify, 2005), 48–52. The fact that Pedrosa's interest in Gestalt theory gradually vanished was revealed by Pedrosa to Otília Arantes when they first met in 1979. See Otília Arantes, *Mário Pedrosa: itinerário crítico* (São Paulo: Cosac Naify, 2004), 9.

14. Artist Almir Mavignier recalls sessions in Pedrosa's home when the critic read parts of his thesis to Mavignier, Abraham Palatnik, and Ivan Serpa—artists who shared Pedrosa's interest in the work of the mentally ill—so as to test their reactions to it. See Almir Mavignier in *Formas do afeto: um filme sobre Mário Pedrosa*, HDV, directed by Nina Galanternik (Rio de Janeiro: Gala Filmes, 2010).

15. See Gullar, "A trégua," 38.

16. Otília Arantes dates Pedrosa's engagement with abstraction from 1944 to 1945, with his return to Brazil and the publication of a series of articles on Alexander Calder. See Arantes, *Mário Pedrosa*, 55.

17. Ibid., 68–69.

18. Emiliano Di Cavalcanti, "Realismo e abstracionismo," in *Arte concreta paulista: documentos*, ed. João Bandeira (São Paulo: Cosac Naify; Centro Universitário Maria Antônia da USP, 2002), 17.

19. Mário Pedrosa, *Arte, forma e personalidade: 3 estudos* (São Paulo: Kairós Livraria e Editora, 1979), 14.

20. Ibid., 16.

21. Ibid.

22. Ibid., 64.

23. Di Cavalcanti, "Realismo e abstracionismo," 17.

24. Campofiorito, as quoted in Gláucia Villas Boas, "A estética da conversão: o ateliê do Engenho de Dentro e a arte concreta carioca (1946–1951)," *Tempo Social, Revista de Sociologia da USP* 20, no. 2 (2008): 206.

25. For a thorough account on the role of the workshop as one of the catalysts of concrete art in Brazil, see ibid.

26. As Villas Boas puts it, "the polemic of Quirino Campofiorito versus Mário Pedrosa became a reference for respectively conservative and progressive positions in the field of arts." Ibid., 208.

27. Waldemar Cordeiro, "Ainda o abstracionismo," in Bandeira, *Arte concreta paulista: documentos*,17.

28. Ibid.

29. Pedrosa, *Arte, forma e personalidade*, 56.

30. Ibid., 64, my emphasis.

31. Maurice Merleau-Ponty, *The Structure of Behavior* (Boston: Beacon Press, 1963), 150.

32. Pedrosa, *Arte, forma e personalidade*, 64.

33. Ibid., 57.

34. Arantes, *Mário Pedrosa*, 53.

35. In one of his first references to Trotsky, in a 1925 letter to his friend Lívio Xavier, Pedrosa compares the revolutionary leader to "a poet": "He dreams with the life of the future: Thomas More, Marxist Campanella. La refundicion de l'home." Pedrosa, as quoted in Jose Castilho Marques Neto, *Solidão revolucionária: Mário Pedrosa e as origens do trotskismo no Brasil* (São Paulo: Paz e Terra, 1993), 193. Trotskyism would bring Pedrosa closer to the French surrealists (he eventually married Benjamin Péret's sister-in-law Mary Houston)—in fact, in a 1967 article he would recall the subversive potential of the surrealist object and poetry in terms of its "messing up of the everyday." Mário Pedrosa, *Mundo, homem, arte em crise* (São Paulo: Perspectiva, 1975), 159–162.

201

36. Waldemar Cordeiro, "O objeto," in *Abstracionismo, geométrico e informal: a vanguarda brasileira nos anos cinquenta*, ed. Fernando Cocchiarale and Anna Bella Geiger (Rio de Janeiro: FUNARTE, 1987), 223.

37. See Brito, *Neoconcretismo,* 102–104.

38. Cordeiro, "O objeto," 223.

39. Brito, *Neoconcretismo*, 61.

40. Waldemar Cordeiro et al., "Ruptura," in Cocchiarale and Geiger, *Abstracionismo, geométrico e informal*, 219.

41. The Museums of Modern Art in Rio de Janeiro and São Paulo were created in 1947.

42. Waldemar Cordeiro, "Ruptura," in Cocchiarale and Geiger, *Abstracionismo, geométrico e informal*, 222 (a different text from the one cited in note 40).

43. Lorenzo Mammì, "Concret '56: The Root of Form," in *Concreta '56: a raiz da forma*, trans. Mariana Attiê and Noemi Jaffe (São Paulo: Museu de Arte Moderna de São Paulo, 2006), 36.

44. Ibid., 38.

45. Brito, *Neoconcretismo*, 102.

46. See Boris Fausto, *História geral do Brasil* (São Paulo: Edusp, 2004), 428.

47. Gonzalo Aguilar, *Poesia concreta brasileira: as vanguardas na encruzilhada modernista* (São Paulo: Edusp, 2005), 251.

48. See for example Cabo, "Resignifying Modernity," 28: "In the 1950s a whole project on *developmentalist nationalism* took place and at this time writers, academics, politicians, economists, the artists, the bourgeoisie, the left wing politicians, everybody, was involved with it." As Jameson explains, the periodizing dimension of the Althusserian notion of "expressive causality" tends to give "the impression of a facile totalization, a seamless web of phenomena each of which, in its own way, 'expresses' some unified inner truth—a world-view or a period style or a set of structural categories which marks the whole length or breadth of the 'period' in question." See Fredric Jameson, *The Political Unconscious* (London: Routledge, 1981), 12.

49. For Thomas Skidmore, the president managed to implement his ambitious developmentalist process by playing on widespread enthusiasm, and the construction of Brasília acted as a symbol of this: "Work proceeded at a break-neck pace, generating a sense of excitement among all classes of Brazilians, who looked upon the construction of a new capital in the neglected interior as the sign of Brazil's coming to age." Thomas E. Skidmore, *Politics in Brazil, 1930–1964: An Experiment in Democracy* (Oxford: Oxford University Press, 1967), 167–168.

50. I will address this issue in greater length in chapter 3.

51. Ana Maria Belluzzo, "Rupture and Concrete Art," in *Arte construtiva no Brasil: coleção Adolpho Leirner*, ed. Aracy A. Amaral, trans. Izabel Burbridge (São Paulo: DBA Melhoramentos, 1998), 123.

52. It is crucial to understand the meaning of "inventiveness," then, as the expansion of a repertoire that is meant not to challenge its overall predetermination, but on the contrary, to continuously confirm the validity and reach of the generative principle. In Brito's account, this kind of inventiveness is placed in opposition to neoconcrete *imagination*. See Brito, *Neoconcretismo*, 112.

53. Belluzzo, "Rupture and Concrete Art," 128.

54. Ibid., 118.

55. Merleau-Ponty, *The Structure of Behavior*, 160.

56. It is worth contrasting Merleau-Ponty's description to this passage by the Ulm School theoretician Max Bense: "We consider an absolutely constructive object that which can be methodically produced in a finite and exact series of conscious steps of decision and manipulation. And we consider a non-absolutely constructive object that which cannot be methodically produced in a finite and exact series of securely executable steps; an object whose existence does not originate from an act that can be subjected to decomposition and recomposition." Max Bense, *Inteligência brasileira: uma reflexão cartesiana*, trans. Tercio Redondo (São Paulo: Cosac Naify, 2009), 63–64.

57. Ferreira Gullar, Oliveira Bastos, and Reynaldo Jardim, "Poesia concreta: Experiência intuitiva," in Cocchiarale and Geiger, *Abstracionismo, geométrico e informal*, 229.

58. For critic João Bandeira, "The interaction between the arts and poetry distinguishes the Brazilian concrete art from other European or American constructivist movements, in which the dialog wasn't so remarkable, and results in an intense exchange of theoretical questionings and, with the necessary adaptations, of formal solutions." See João Bandeira, "Words in Space—Poetry at the National Exhibition of Concrete Art," in Attiê and Jaffe, *Concreta '56*, 120.

59. Waldemar Cordeiro, "Teoria e prática do concretismo carioca," in Cocchiarale and Geiger, *Abstracionismo, geométrico e informal*, 226.

60. Mário Pedrosa, "Paulistas e cariocas," in *Projeto construtivo brasileiro na arte (1950–1962)*, ed. Aracy Amaral (Rio de Janeiro: Museu de Arte Moderna; São Paulo: Pinacoteca do Estado, 1977), 136–138; and Mário Pedrosa, "Poeta e pintor concretista," in ibid., 145–146.

61. Pedrosa, "Poeta e pintor concretista," 145.

62. Ibid., 145–146.

63. Ibid., 145.

64. Haroldo de Campos, "Da fenomenologia da composição à matemática da composição," in Augusto de Campos, Haroldo de Campos, and Décio Pignatari, *Teoria da poesia concreta: textos críticas e manifestos, 1950–1960* (São Paulo: Atelie Editorial, 2006), 134.

65. Décio Pignatari, "Poesia concreta: Organização," in Campos, Campos, and Pignatari, *Teoria da poesia concreta*, 128.

66. Aguilar, *Poesia concreta brasileira*, 196. Aguilar's is the most thorough published study on Brazilian concrete poetry. However, despite the author's claims that he wants to examine concrete poetry without taking sides, he inexplicably fails to consider Ferreira Gullar's poetry in his discussion.

67. Both Cordeiro's and Gullar's texts were first published in the *SDJB* on June 23, 1957.

68. Although the terms of Gullar's rebuttal bring him closer to Cordeiro's manifesto, it should be noted that the São Paulo poets also displayed a didactic concept of the object, which they termed the "useful object."

69. The verbal tense *lembra* can thus be used to say both "this *reminds* me of that song" and "do you *remember* that song?"

70. Interestingly, Gullar has recently recalled the impact that the discovery of Artaud had on his poetry, claiming that it prompted his "disintegration of visual syntax" and led "to the implosion of language." See Kaira M. Cabañas, "Whither Artaud?," and Ferreira Gullar, "The Innumerable States of Being," in *Specters of Artaud: Language and Arts in the 1950s*, exh. cat., ed. Kaira M. Cabañas (Madrid: Museo Nacional Centro de Arte Reina Sofía, 2012), 37–41 and 187–190.

71. Merleau-Ponty's philosophy has indeed been discussed in terms of transubstantiation. For Hugh J. Silverman, in Merleau-Ponty's 1961 essay *Eye and Mind* (which Gullar obviously wouldn't have read), the philosopher argues that, through the painter's work, the "mountain or the bowl of fruit is no longer visible there; it has been replaced by the painting of a mountain or a bowl of fruit as what is visible there. The substance of visibility has been radically transformed: transubstantiated." See Hugh J. Silverman, "Cézanne's Mirror Stage,'" in *The Merleau-Ponty Aesthetics Reader: Philosophy and Painting*, ed. Galen A. Johnson (Evanston: Northwestern University Press, 1994), 267.

72. Ferreira Gullar, "A Dialogue on the Non-object," in *Neoconcrete Experience*, ed. Michael Asbury, Caroline Menezes, and Laura Barbi, trans. Michael Asbury, Luciana Dumphreys, Nadia Kerecuk, and Michael Marsden (London: Gallery 32, 2009).

73. Ferreira Gullar, "Brancusi e o problema da base na escultura," *Suplemento Dominical do Jornal do Brasil* (April 9, 1960).

74. Gullar's conclusions are strikingly close to those of Rosalind Krauss in her immensely famous article "Sculpture in the Expanded Field," by stating that Brancusi's sculpture "absorbs the pedestal into itself and away from actual place." She also states that, in the *Endless Column*, "the sculpture is all base." Rosalind Krauss, *The Originality of the Avant-garde and Other Modernist Myths* (Cambridge, MA: MIT Press, 1985), 280. However, the striking difference between art circulation conditions in the

203

United States (with a developed market and institutional framework) and in Brazil (where there was virtually no market) at that time promotes a crucial distinction here: Krauss is understandably more interested in drawing consequences that relate to the issue of the *site* in postminimalist sculpture than in the reconfiguration of experiential space apropos of the perceived object itself.

75. Gullar, "Brancusi."

76. Brito asserts that neoconcretism constituted itself in the terrain of history understood as *knowledge*: "The historical setting in which neoconcretism found itself was that of a knowledge, practically isolated from its political relations with the rest of Society: the exclusive reference points were art, science and philosophy. It called for a program consistent with this context." Brito, *Neoconcretismo*, 107.

77. There was some ambiguity as to whether the threshold between poetry and visual arts was also targeted. Gullar later revealed doubts about whether his work was still one of poetry: "Was such a drastic participation of verbal language in the spatial poems ... not diminishing my potentialities as a poet?" Ferreira Gullar, *Experiência neoconcreta: momento-limite da arte* (São Paulo: Cosac Naify, 2007), 129.

78. Gullar states his aim in the preface to the later collection of these articles. See Ferreira Gullar, *Etapas da arte contemporânea: do cubismo ao neoconcretismo* (Rio de Janeiro: Revan, 1998), 10. The articles were published during Gullar's second run at the *SDJB*, after a brief period of absence.

79. Gullar, "Theory of the Non-object," 173.

80. In 1960, Lygia Clark already would question whether the suppression of the base in sculpture was really equivalent to that of the frame in painting, and further argue that the whole thing would be more accurately posed as a problematic of the destruction of the *plane* (to be discussed presently). See Clark, *Lygia Clark*, 139–141.

81. Asbury, "Neoconcretism and Minimalism," 176.

82. In 1967, Pedrosa would write a retrospective article on the object in art, stressing the role of the surrealist operation of estrangement. Pedrosa, *Mundo, homem*, 160.

83. Gullar, "Theory of the Non-object," 172.

84. Ferreira Gullar et al., "Neoconcrete Manifesto," in Asbury, Menezes, and Barbi, *Neoconcrete Experience*.

85. It is telling in that respect that São Paulo concretists often "accused" Gullar of being in thrall to surrealism. See, for example, Haroldo de Campos, "Arte construtiva no Brasil," *Revista USP*, no. 30 (1996): 251–261.

86. The *Stages* series began one week after the publication of the "Neoconcrete Manifesto" and changed its title roughly two months later; that is, several months before the publication of the "Theory." See Elizabeth Varela, "Suplemento dominical do Jornal do Brasil e neoconcretismo: relações e manifestações" (M.Phil. dissertation, Universidade Federal do Rio de Janeiro, 2009), 24–25.

87. Castro had other, short-lived lines of work, but this particular procedure, which he first adopted in the mid-1950s (first by cutting and then welding together the iron/steel pieces and soon after folding the plaque or slab rather than welding it), accompanied him throughout his career. For a compilation of statements that insist on the 2D-3D account, drawn from the critical literature on Castro, see João Francisco Alves, *Amilcar de Castro: uma retrospectiva*, trans. Roberto Cataldo Costa (Porto Alegre: Fundação Bienal de Artes Visuais do Mercosul, 2005), 236–237. Alves himself is no exception: "Therefore, the operation of *cutting* and *folding* the plane into elementary geometrical forms (circular and quadrangular) is what makes the third dimension emerge." Even Gullar himself—who, in the neoconcrete period, refrained from describing such a passage—is later quoted marveling at how "the two-dimensional plate had become three-dimensional—volume!" Likewise, for critic Tadeu Chiarelli, "the incision in these sculptures is a means to configure the final form, which the work assumes the moment it shifts from two-dimensionality to tridimensionality [sic]." Tadeu Chiarelli, *Amilcar de Castro: corte e dobra*, trans. Izabel Murat Burbridge (São Paulo: Cosac Naify, 2003), 25.

88. For Naves, this schematism overlooks the fact that "the experience offered by Amilcar's pieces are in a rigorously inverse relation to the simplicity and clearness of his method." Rodrigo Naves, *O vento e o moinho: ensaios sobre arte moderna e contemporânea* (São Paulo: Companhia das Letras, 2007), 108. He clearly states elsewhere that "we face objects that repel the idea of procedures that can be

perceptually reconstituted." Rodrigo Naves, *A forma difícil: ensaios sobre arte brasileira* (São Paulo: Ática, 1996), 241.

89. Hélio Oiticica, "The Transition of Color from the Painting into Space and the Meaning of Construction," in *Hélio Oiticica: The Body of Color*, ed. Mari Carmen Ramirez, trans. Stephen Berg and Héctor Olea (London: Tate, 2007), 222–227.

90. In a way, Castro was very involved in the discursive space of neoconcretism: he was the graphic designer of the *SDJB* and responsible for its complete and revolutionary reconfiguration.

91. Amilcar de Castro, "Untitled," in Amaral, *Projeto construtivo brasileiro na arte*, 243.

92. Alves, *Amilcar de Castro*, 236.

93. Gullar, "A Dialogue on the Non-object."

94. For a discussion about the neoconcrete rejection of production, see Brito, *Neoconcretismo*, 108–109.

95. Haroldo de Campos, "Arte construtiva no Brasil," 254.

96. For critic Sônia Salzstein, Castro's sculptures create "a state of ambiguity, always referring back to the original unity, which, however must never be fully there." Although Salzstein does speak of a "primordial plane," she also (and somewhat contradictorily) perceives the works "carrying [an] original fracture"—my point is precisely that it is possible to think an "original fracture" without recourse to an "original plane." Sônia Salzstein, "Amílcar de Castro," *Guia das Artes Plásticas*, no. 8/9 (1988): 78.

97. Salzstein casts this insistence of the plane as "the memory of the primordial plane that generated [the sculpture]." (See ibid.) In my argument, as we will see shortly, the plane asserts itself more as *the repetition of a missed encounter* than as a positive memory. Likewise, Rodrigo Naves argues, "we know how to reconstitute the iron slabs that lie at the origin of the pieces, but a thick layer of work blocks this movement. This is why knowledge of the steps involved in the construction of the works is insufficient to apprehend or tame them." The apparently odd idea of a "layer of work" is indeed suggestive, for it points precisely to a transversal cut into a more conventional temporality of experience. See Naves, *A forma difícil*, 238.

98. Castro eventually adopted Cor-Ten steel—thick slabs of steel that allow rust on the surface but do not decay entirely.

99. Gullar, "A Dialogue on the Non-object" (translation altered by the author). Gullar is clear, however, that this does not mean that a non-object must have actual movement (like Clark's *Bichos*). In the original, the passage goes "uma imobilidade aberta a uma mobilidade aberta a uma imobilidade aberta." The translation renders the passage as "an immobility that is open to mobility that is open to an open immobility." I used brackets in order to account for the fact that the term "open" appears only once in relation to each noun (thus three times in total) and that, in Portuguese, the order of the words allows for a double meaning: the word "open" operates simultaneously as an adjective applying to the noun that precedes it (an open immobility) and as a verb in the past participle, thus linking one noun to the other (an immobility *open to* a mobility).

100. Joan Copjec, "Sex and the Euthanasia of Reason," in *Supposing the Subject*, ed. Joan Copjec (London: Verso, 1994), 39.

101. Ibid.

102. Ibid., 40.

103. Again, Brito's groundbreaking account is definitive in this respect.

104. Ricardo Fabbrini, "Constructivism Pulsions," in *Preto no branco: a arte gráfica de Amilcar de Castro*, ed. Yanet Aguilera, trans. Natália Giossa Fujita (São Paulo: Discurso Editorial; Belo Horizonte: Editora UFMG, 2005), 160.

105. "What is special in [Castro's] operational *demarche* is that he doesn't depart from an a priori, but from a vague drawing on paper so that later, in face of a plane circle, square or rectangle, he will open it, unfold it. He doesn't construct violently, or in fact he doesn't really construct. He follows a mysterious totality that lies for him in no a priori." Pedrosa, *Mundo, homem*, 166. Pedrosa will suggestively, but not fully question the plane as a starting point, and will still subscribe to the 2D-3D account, but it is clear in his writings that he is nevertheless struck (as Salzstein and Naves would later be as well) by the challenge Castro's sculptures pose to an origin-oriented narrative.

106. Krauss, *The Originality of the Avant-Garde*, 160.

107. From a strictly phenomenological perspective, indeed, both the lost object and the generating axis can be said to perform the similar role of unsettling the fixed identity of the perceived form. This is Merleau-Ponty: "as Klee said, the line no longer imitates the visible; it 'renders visible'; it is the blue-print of a genesis of things…. The beginning of the line's path establishes or installs a certain level or mode of the linear, a certain manner for the line to be and to make itself a line, 'to go line.' Relative to it, every subsequent inflection will have a diacritical value, will be another aspect of the line's relationship to itself, will form an adventure, a history, a meaning of the line…. Making its way in space, it neverthe-less corrodes prosaic space and its *partes extra partes*; it develops a way of extending itself actively into that space which subtends the spatiality of a thing quite as much as that of a man or an apple tree." Maurice Merleau-Ponty, "Eye and Mind," in Johnson, *The Merleau-Ponty Aesthetics Reader*, 143. I thank Ed Krcma for bringing this notion to my attention.

2 THE CONSTRUCTIVE

1. Hélio Oiticica, "Tropicália," in *Hélio Oiticica*, exh. cat., trans. Stephen Berg et al. (Rio de Janeiro: Centro de Arte Hélio Oiticica, 1992), 124–125.

2. It is conventional within Brazilian debates to refer to Oswald de Andrade as "Oswald" rather than "de Andrade," especially because of the need to differentiate between him and his close friend and ally, the poet and writer Mário de Andrade.

3. Oswald de Andrade, "Anthropophagite Manifesto," in *Readings in Latin American Modern Art*, ed. Patrick Frank (New Haven: Yale University Press, 2004), 24.

4. Mondrian is not mentioned in the "General Scheme of the New Objectivity," but there is a manuscript written soon after Oiticica drafted that text where he picks on the "contructive will" and discusses that precisely in relation to Mondrian's practice and ideas, in order to assert that a "constructive will" pos-sesses both a constructive and a "demolishing" aspect to it. I take this text to reinforce the transition from his 1962 ideas to the more socially oriented take on construction. As the final passage goes: "The constructive will, by virtue of possessing this ambivalence in its core, is thus transformative and also demolishing by itself, an ethical-social phenomenon characteristic in its specific way of manifest-ing itself." Hélio Oiticica, "Texto de HO sobre criação e vontade construtiva," unpublished manuscript (Archive of the Projeto Hélio Oiticica, document 0109/67, 1967).

5. Michael Asbury, "Hélio Couldn't Dance," in *Fios soltos: a arte de Hélio Oiticica*, ed. Paula Braga (São Paulo: Perspectiva, 2008), 52–65. The term "radical leap" was coined by Guy Brett to account for the radical change undergone by works of artists such as Oiticica, Lygia Clark, and Lygia Pape after the breakdown of neoconcretism toward more experimental and formally heterodox propositions. See Guy Brett, "A Radical Leap," in *Art in Latin America: The Modern Era, 1820–1980*, ed. Dawn Ades (New Haven: Yale University Press, 1989), 255–283.

6. My focus on Mondrian is neither exhaustive nor arbitrary, and a strong case could certainly be made for tracking other dialogues, as I shall do with Malevich in chapter 5.

7. Hélio Oiticica, *Aspiro ao grande labirinto*, ed. Luciano Figueiredo, Lygia Pape, and Waly Salo-mão (Rio de Janeiro: Rocco, 1986), 17. Originally written in English. Oiticica took this passage from the end of the text "Plastic Art and Pure Plastic Art," written in 1936 by Mondrian. This text can be found in Piet Mondrian, *The New Art—The New Life: The Collected Writings of Piet Mondrian* (London: Thames and Hudson, 1987), 288–300.

8. Hélio Oiticica, "Texto sobre estética e criação artística," unpublished manuscript (Archive of the Projeto Hélio Oiticica, document 2089/64, 1964).

9. See Yve-Alain Bois, "The Iconoclast," in *Piet Mondrian: 1872–1944*, ed. Angelica Zander Rudenstine (Boston: Little Brown, 1994), 357.

10. "I don't want paintings, I just want to find things out," Mondrian is famously said to have answered his friend Carl Holty when asked why he kept repainting *Victory Boogie-Woogie*. See Yve-Alain Bois, *Painting as Model* (Cambridge, MA: MIT Press, 1990), 183; and also Bois, "The Iconoclast," 316. In 1972 Oiticica would confirm that when he writes: "*the experimental exercitation of liberty* evoked by MARIO PEDROSA consists not in the 'creation of works' but in *the initiative of taking over the*

experimental" (his emphasis). In the same text, Oiticica would make a veiled reference to the same Mondrian passage he quoted in 1959 talking about his painterly experiments "in the limits of the frame-canvas mural spatial-environmental aspirations." Hélio Oiticica, "Attempt / Try / To Experiment the Experimental," in Braga, *Fios soltos*, 348. This is Oiticica's own translation from his earlier Portuguese original. His translation is idiosyncratic and sometimes results in seemingly unintended changes in the original meaning, as I will discuss at the end of this chapter. See note 106.

11. In 1968, Oiticica would write on the back of the work: "today I consider this work important, and for me, at the time, it was disconcerting for its sense of 'structural dilution' beyond the merely pictorial space." See Hélio Oiticica, "Note," in *Hélio Oiticica*, exh. cat., 30.

12. See Bois, "The Iconoclast," 315.

13. Briony Fer, untitled paper given at the symposium "Hélio Oiticica: The Body of Color" (Tate Modern, London, June 2, 2007).

14. As quoted in Bois, "The Iconoclast," 356. The "Neoconcrete Manifesto" already emphasized both poles of Mondrian's activity: "There would be no point in seeing Mondrian as the destroyer of surface, the plane and line, if we are not aware of the new space which this destruction creates." Ferreira Gullar et al., "Neoconcrete Manifesto," in *Neoconcrete Experience*, ed. Michael Asbury, Caroline Menezes, and Laura Barbi, trans. Michael Asbury, Luciana Dumphreys, Nadia Kerecuk, and Michael Marsden. Also, as Carel Blotkamp argues, it is important to bear in mind that for Mondrian "evolution was closely bound up with destruction," to the point that the latter affected not only his formal maneuvers, but also his earlier choice of "flowers in states of decay" as a subject matter. Carel Blotkamp, *Mondrian: The Art of Destruction* (London: Reaktion Books, 1994), 15.

15. Bois, *Painting as Model*, 162.

16. Hélio Oiticica, "Metaesquemas 57/58," in *Hélio Oiticica*, exh. cat., 27. We should ponder here the differences between two translations of the term *reinsistência* in Oiticica's original document. The version in the recent *Body of Color* catalog translates it as "insistence back and forth." Keeping both in mind is useful: there is indeed a sense of repetition and of temporal oscillation in Oiticica's text (and in the works). For the 1992 translation, see *Hélio Oiticica: The Body of Color*, ed. Mari Carmen Ramirez, trans. Stephen Berg and Héctor Olea (London: Tate Publishing, 2007), 147.

17. See Jacques Lacan, *The Four Fundamental Concepts of Psychoanalysis (The Seminar of Jacques Lacan, Book 11)*, trans. Alan Sheridan (New York: Norton, 1998), 184.

18. Ibid.

19. See Vladimir Safatle, "A teoria lacaniana da pulsão como ontologia negativa," *Discurso* 36 (2007): 149–190.

20. As Brazilian psychoanalyst and cultural critic Tania Rivera argues, the term "'body of color' signals that Oiticica goes beyond [the alternation between subject and object], by means of a notion of form that includes the spectator and thus *transforms* itself." See Tania Rivera, "O reviramento do sujeito e da cultura em Hélio Oiticica," *Arte & Ensaio* 19 (2009): 110. See also Oiticica, "The Transition of Color from the Painting into Space," in Ramirez, *Hélio Oiticica: The Body of Color*, 226. I will discuss this particular text at length below.

21. On the egomorphism of empirical objects, Lacan states that "all the objects of [man's] world are always structured around the wandering shadow of his own ego. They will have a fundamentally anthropomorphic character, even egomorphic, we could say." Jacques Lacan, *The Seminar of Jacques Lacan, Book II: The Ego in Freud's Theory and in the Technique of Psychoanalysis 1954–1955*, trans. Sylvana Tomaselli (New York: Norton, 1991), 166. See also Vladimir Safatle, "Uma clínica do sensível: a respeito da relação entre destituição subjetiva e primado do objeto," *Interações* 10, no. 19 (January–June 2005): 130–131.

22. The word "insistence" is thus extraordinarily precise. It is also useful in this regard to recall a definition by Slavoj Žižek: "In contrast to desire, which can be characterized as an intentional attitude, drive is something in which the subject is caught, a kind of acephalous force which persists in its repetitive movement." Slavoj Žižek, *The Ticklish Subject: The Absent Centre of Political Anthology* (London: Verso, 1999), 297.

207

23. In this context, this mythic painting would be, of course, the fully achieved non-object. This is Gullar in "Theory of the Non-object," 171: "the destruction of these lines begins, leading to his last two paintings: *Broadway Boogie Woogie* and *Victory Boogie Woogie*. But the contradiction in fact was not resolved, and if Mondrian had lived a few more years, perhaps he would have returned once more to the white canvas from which he began. Or, he would have left it favoring construction into space, as did Malevich at the end of his parallel development."

24. Oiticica, "Metaesquemas 57/58," 27.

25. Lygia Clark, "1960," unpublished manuscript.

26. Clark herself speaks of their "oblique tension." Lygia Clark, "Light Line," in *Lygia Clark*, exh. cat. (Barcelona: Fundació Antoni Tàpies, 1998), 102.

27. This is Bois: "[Clark] helped me completely get away [from] this very 'stiff' and fraudulent interpretation of abstraction ... and in particular Mondrian, who was prevalent at that time in France, and in Europe. She was the one who put me on track of a Mondrian which has nothing to do with that Neo-platonic Monk but was more of some kind of antiformalist destructor." Yve-Alain Bois in Jane de Almeida, "Ideologias da forma: Entrevista com Yve Alain Bois," *Novos Estudos CEBRAP*, no. 76 (November 2006): 242. English original available at http://www.janedealmeida.com/yve_alainbois .pdf, last accessed March 19, 2013.

28. Oiticica's *Inventions* were actually known until recently as *Monochromes*. New research associated with the restoration undertaken by Wynne H. Phelan at the Museum of Fine Arts, Houston, has revealed their layered complexity and suggested that the artist himself referred to them by the new name, which I here accept. Sadly, these virtually irreproducible works were mostly lost in the fire that struck the Projeto Hélio Oiticica in October 2009. See Wynne H. Phelan, "To Bestow a Sense of Light: Hélio Oiticica's Experimental Process," in Ramirez, *Hélio Oiticica: The Body of Color*, 94–97.

29. "Mondrian adopted a strategy rigorously opposed to the one Strezminsky had earlier adopted in his monochromes. (The monochrome settles nothing. No limit stops it from optically opening onto infinity.) Instead of suppressing all contrast, Mondrian multiplied contrasts, just as Seurat had done." Bois, *Painting as Model*, 172–173.

30. Hélio Oiticica, "Color, Time and Structure," in *Hélio Oiticica*, exh. cat., 34.

31. Oiticica, "The Transition of Color," 222.

32. Ibid., 224.

33. It is interesting in this respect, as the text shows, that by accepting this denomination from Mário Pedrosa and thus having to qualify its validity, Oiticica ends up conceptualizing such a distinct approach.

34. Celso Favaretto, *A invenção de Hélio Oiticica* (São Paulo: Edusp, 1992), 34.

35. Oiticica, "The Transition of Color," 55.

36. Sônia Salzstein, "Helio Oiticica: Autonomy and the Limits of Subjectivity," *Third Text* 8, no. 28 (1994): 123.

37. Ibid., 122.

38. Hélio Oiticica, "Carta para Pinedo," unpublished correspondence (Archive of the Projeto Hélio Oiticica, document 0036/60, 1960).

39. Mário Pedrosa, *Dos murais de Portinari aos espaços de Brasília* (São Paulo: Perspectiva, 1981), 347.

40. In 1961, the *SDJB* was terminated and Gullar was invited to be the director of the Fundação Cultural de Brasília (Brasília Cultural Foundation), distancing himself from the neoconcrete avant-garde. In 1962 he joined the Centro Popular de Cultura (Popular Culture Centre), or CPC, of the National Student Union.

41. Ferreira Gullar, interview with Fernando Cocchiarale and Anna Bella Geiger, in *Abstracionismo, geométrico e informal: a vanguarda brasileira nos anos cinquenta*, ed. Fernando Cocchiarale and Anna Bella Geiger (Rio de Janeiro: FUNARTE, 1987), 100.

42. I will address this point and other aspects of Gullar's shift more extensively in chapter 3, alongside a more extended argument on the problem of artistic stances in the Brazilian avant-garde.

43. Michael Asbury recalls Oiticica's negative reception of Gullar's defection and how the artist himself traced back the origin of *Tropicália* to this event. See Michael Asbury, "This Other Eden: Hélio Oiticica and Subterranean London," in *Oiticica in London*, ed. Guy Brett and Luciano Figueiredo (London: Tate Publishing, 2007), 35.

44. This does not mean that he was automatically elevated to the role of leading figure in an organized avant-garde (which did not really exist in the early 1960s), only that, at this point, he started to operate as an intellectual as much as an artist.

45. Oiticica conceives the fourth item of his New Objectivity proposal, "Position-taking in relation to political, social and ethical problems," in agreement with Gullar's new position, though an uninitiated reader might bypass the strong disagreement in both proposals as to *how* this position taking was supposed to operate. See Hélio Oiticica, "General Scheme of the New Objectivity," in *Hélio Oiticica*, exh. cat., 116–117. Art historian Paulo Reis argues that Oiticica paid attention to Gullar's new ideas, even if those ran counter the "formal experimentation of the avant-gardes," but formulated the poet's aims in a radically different manner by equating social commitment and the avant-garde attitude. See Paulo Reis, *Arte de vanguarda no Brasil* (Rio de Janeiro: Jorge Zahar Editor, 2006), 47–55.

46. For a brief but focused discussion that includes other exhibitions, see also Reis, *Arte de vanguarda no Brasil*. For a general account of the Brazilian art world in the 1960s, see Paulo Sergio Duarte, *Anos 60: Transformações na arte brasileira* (Rio de Janeiro: Campos Gerais, 1999).

47. According to artist Antonio Manuel, *Tropicália* was opened one week later than the rest of the show. Antonio Manuel, email conversation with the author, July 30, 2012.

48. Oiticica, "General Scheme of the New Objectivity," 110. It should be noted that Pedrosa referred to "post-modern art" as the negotiation of modernist, formal values with the demands of environmental—and social—insertion. This sense of negotiation renders this concept quite different from more well-known definitions of postmodern*ist* art.

49. Ibid., 111.

50. Ibid., 110–111.

51. Andrade, "Anthropophagite Manifesto," 24.

52. Ibid., 25. I have here altered the translation, which reads "From the equation—me as part of the Cosmos—to the axiom—the Cosmos as part of me. Subsistence. Knowledge. Anthropophagy." In the original: "*Da equação eu parte do Cosmos ao axioma Cosmos parte do eu. Subsistência. Conhecimento. Antropofagia.*" This change seeks to reinstate Andrade's original emphases and, most importantly, to restore the subject pronoun *I*, which had been changed for the object pronoun *me*. Andrade clearly had a point in employing an objectified form of the subject pronoun, especially in the second part of the sentence, where he writes "do *eu*" (of the *I*), for it would have sounded smoother for him to write "de mim" (of me/myself"). Considering the presence of Freudian ideas in the manifesto, this is no minor correction.

53. Benedito Nunes, "Antropofagia ao alcance de todos," in Oswald de Andrade, *Do pau-Brasil à antropofagia e às utopias* (Rio de Janeiro: Editora Civilização Brasileira, 1972), xxx–xxxi.

54. Andrade, "Anthropophagite Manifesto," 24.

55. Nunes, "Antropofagia ao alcance de todos," xxvi.

56. For a nuanced and brilliant discussion of the work of Clark and Oiticica as a new myth of origin of Brazilian contemporary art, see Rodrigo Naves's article "Um azar histórico: sobre a recepção das obras de Hélio Oiticica e Lygia Clark" in Rodrigo Naves, *O vento e o moinho: ensaios sobre arte moderna e contemporânea* (São Paulo: Companhia das Letras, 2007), 192–223.

57. Luciano Figueiredo, "Tropicália," in Brett and Figueiredo, *Oiticica in London*, 21.

58. Carlos Zilio, "Da antropofagia à tropicália," in *O nacional e o popular na cultura brasileira*, ed. Carlos Zilio, João Luiz Lafetá, and Lígia Chiappini Moraes Leite (São Paulo: Brasiliense, 1982), 30.

59. In Celso Favaretto's formulation, *Tropicália* "challenged the notion of 'formalism' and 'engagement' as polar opposites, terms that were in circulation at that time as a way of talking about the social significance of the avant-garde." See Celso Favaretto, "Tropicália: The Explosion of the Obvious," in *Tropicália: A Revolution in Brazilian Culture*, ed. Carlos Basualdo, trans. Aaron Lorenz, Renata Nascimento, and Christopher Dunn (São Paulo: Cosac Naify, 2005), 82.

60. See Mari Carmen Ramirez, "The Embodiment of Color—'From the Inside Out,'" in Ramirez, *Hélio Oiticica: The Body of Color*, 27–73.

61. Hélio Oiticica, "August 7, 1961," in Ramirez, *Hélio Oiticica: The Body of Color*, 250.

62. In media scholar Muniz Sodré's words, it was but "one of the many equipments and novelties that were feverishly imported in the postwar period"—not unlike geometric abstraction, one might argue. Muniz Sodré, *A máquina de Narciso: televisão, indivíduo e poder no Brasil* (Rio de Janeiro: Achiame, 1984), 101.

63. Sergio Caparelli, *Televisão e capitalismo no Brasil* (Porto Alegre: LP&M, 1982), 21–22.

64. Regina Mota, "A terceira margem da televisão," paper given at the Workshop de Programação para TV Pública (Salvador, August 22, 2007). A version of this paper was published as Regina Mota, "A terceira margem da televisão," *Contemporânea* Edition 9, 5, no. 2 (2007).

65. Ibid. It is also worth recalling David Harvey's insight that the late-modernist spectacle was not necessarily a conservative phenomenon from the outset; quite the contrary (and Harvey's main example—rock concerts—do indeed strike a chord both in the context of the tropicalist movement and Oiticica's later experience in New York). The case of TV and the role it played in the beginnings of tropicalism may well be a Brazilian analog in this respect. See David Harvey, *The Condition of Postmodernity: An Enquiry into the Origins of Cultural Change* (Malden, MA, and Oxford, UK: Wiley-Blackwell, 1990), 88.

66. If, as David Joselit argues in relation to television, "the fetish may be liberated by breaking open its closed circuit," then Oiticica's anthropophagic redeeming of its procedures may well be exemplary. See David Joselit, *Feedback: Television against Democracy* (Cambridge, MA: MIT Press, 2007), 29–30.

67. Hélio Oiticica, "Brazil Diarrhea," in *Hélio Oiticica*, exh. cat., 18.

68. A flong (or *flan*, as it is known in France and in Brazil) was an element in the process of stereotype printing still common in newspapers at the time.

69. See Paulo Venâncio Filho, "Act and Fact," in *Fatos: Antonio Manuel*, exh. cat., trans. Renato Rezende (São Paulo: Centro Cultural Banco do Brasil, 2007), 127–134.

70. As Michael Asbury argues, "Antonio Manuel would have been aware [of the graphic reform of the *SDJB*] since he considered the newspaper as a graphically constructed site. His procedure involved the act of concealing and uncovering sections of the page, and thus emphasizing its layout." Michael Asbury, "Antonio Manuel: Occupations/Discoveries," in *Antonio Manuel*, ed. Michael Asbury and Garo Keheyan (Nicosia: Pharos Centre for Contemporary Art, 2006), 34.

71. Hélio Oiticica, "Block-Experiments" in *Hélio Oiticica*, exh. cat., 179. Manuel confirms that he was not invited to take part in "New Brazilian Objectivity" and that his work was shown as a part of *Tropicália*. Antonio Manuel, email conversation with the author, July 30, 2012.

72. Antonio Manuel, conversation with the author, April 24, 2010.

73. Oiticica, "Tropicália," 124.

74. The terms are Joan Copjec's, from her critique of film theory's presupposed, Foucauldian subject. The mirror would not represent imaginary completeness, but the sheer fact that there is something always unknowable in the field of vision. See Joan Copjec, *Read My Desire: Lacan against the Historicists* (Cambridge, MA: MIT Press, 1996), 16–38.

75. Waly Salomão, *Hélio Oiticica: qual é o Parangolé? E outros escritos* (Rio de Janeiro: Rocco, 2003), 89–90.

76. As Brazilian psychoanalyst Tania Rivera puts it, "the water barrel/mirror doesn't only reflect the I, but becomes an open object." Rivera, "O reviramento do sujeito," 114.

77. Salomão grants the barrel/mirror a certain redemptive capacity, suggesting that by "reflecting" as an "original and renewable source of pleasure," it ends up undoing repression and reunifying "body and soul, body and language." My agreement with him doesn't go so far, as I prefer to stress how the splitting tension of his initial description is sustained in this and other works by Oiticica.

78. Oiticica, "Tropicália," 125. I will return to the issue of the Brazilian avant-garde's relation to pop in chapter 4.

79. Oiticica, "Brazil Diarrhea," 19.

80. Figueiredo, "Tropicália," 21.

81. Guy Brett, "Recollection," in Brett and Figueiredo, *Oiticica in London*, 14. In a text on *Tropicália* written in English in 1969, Oiticica strongly suggests the complexity of his dialectical operation regarding myth elements: "Folcklore [sic] is completely put down: *folcklore* [sic] for all Tropicalia creators *is reaction*—but, that doesn't mean that *all* folckloric [sic] elements are reaction: it depends *why* or *by whom* or *what for* this element is recalled. The elements I put on in Parangolé ideas, that Glauber Rocha puts on his films, that José Celso Correa in the 'King of the Candles,' that Gilberto Gil in his music, etc., that can relate to Brazilian popular roots, they relate in a *reinforming* way, because it is the way of *informing* a creative idea that *reinforms* the general scene. This is just the opposite of static reactionary folckloric [sic] conformism … it is, thus, reactionary, as far as it is *desinformatory*." Hélio Oiticica, "Tropicália," unpublished manuscript (Archive of the Projeto Hélio Oiticica, document number 0350/69, 1969), 2.

82. Those were the adjectives employed by Lygia Pape in her account to Paola Berenstein Jacques. See Paola Berenstein Jacques, *Estética da ginga: a arquitetura das favelas através da obra de Hélio Oiticica* (Rio de Janeiro: Casa da Palavra, 2001), 27.

83. Paulo Venâncio Filho, "Tropicália, Its Time and Place," in Brett and Figueiredo, *Oiticica in London*, 29.

84. Hélio Oiticica, "Hélio Oiticica Retrospective at the Whitechapel Gallery, until April 6: Oiticica Talks to Guy Brett," *Studio International* 177, no. 90 (March 1969): 134.

85. Jacques, *Estética da ginga*, 82.

86. Maria Cecília França Lourenço, *Museus acolhem o moderno* (São Paulo: Edusp, 1999), 153. For a historical documentation of the construction of MAM-Rio, see Frederico Coelho, org., *Museu de Arte Moderna: arquitetura e construção* (Rio de Janeiro: Cobogó, 2010).

87. Near the end of his life, Oiticica recalled having noticed, back in 1964, an ephemeral "kind of construction" made by a homeless person with improvised materials and the word *parangolé* written on it. Hélio Oiticica, "A última entrevista," interview with Jorge Guinle Filho, in *Hélio Oiticica: encontros*, ed. Cesar Oiticica Filho and Ingrid Vieira (Rio de Janeiro: Azougue, 2009), 269.

88. The northeastern state of Maranhão, where Gullar is from, is one of the poorest regions of Brazil. Gullar, interview with Cocchiarale and Geiger, 100.

89. I will return to Brasília and to Gullar's relationship with it in chapter 3.

90. As Gullar himself puts it, in a rather judgmental remark, "Oiticica lives the contradiction, neither following Lygia's path [he alludes here to Lygia Clark abandoning art in favor of a therapeutic practice], nor the political path, and ends up destroying himself." Gullar, interview with Cocchiarale and Geiger, 98.

91. Jorge Luis Borges, *Collected Fictions*, trans. Andrew Hurley (London: Penguin, 1999), 325.

92. Oiticica, "Brazil Diarrhea," 20.

93. In an article from 1968, Oiticica opposes "a really universal, profoundly revolutionary critical position" to "attempts to impose universalist cultural colonialism, undeniably an instrument of repression," arguing that the former would "demystify" the latter. Hélio Oiticica, "The Plot of the Earth that Trembles: The Avant-garde Meaning of the Bahian Group," in Basualdo, *Tropicália: A Revolution in Brazilian Culture*, 245–253.

94. Describing *Tropicália* in this way brings it close to the ideological framework as described by Slavoj Žižek. For Žižek, "the function of ideology is not to offer us a point of escape from our reality but to offer us the social reality itself as an escape from some traumatic, real kernel." As distinct from Louis Althusser, Žižek envisages ideology as structurally faulted, as long as one realizes that this fault cannot be explored within the Symbolic, but as a traumatic breakdown that gives way for reconfigurations (maintenance of the political, then, would presuppose the possibility of precipitating such a breakdown)—a breakdown tied to the recognition of the subject's desire. A productive mapping, in this sense, would further undo coordinates rather than fix them, but would do so with a sort of meta-coordinate in mind: that is the ethical dimension of Oiticica's avant-gardist formulation. Slavoj Žižek, *The Sublime Object of Ideology* (London: Verso, 1989), 45.

95. Reis, *Arte de vanguarda no Brasil*, 54.

211

96. Very few commentators actually take the discussion of works such as the *Parangolés* beyond participation, even though Guy Brett had already and presciently warned about this cliché as early as 1969.
One exception is Tania Rivera, who recently emphasized that Oiticica's work "is not about inviting the
spectator to take some action in front of a work, maintaining its status and the places of its creator and
its receiver unquestioned," but about a "subject [that] appears in the other, in the object, in culture."
See Guy Brett, untitled, in *Whitechapel Experiment*, exh. cat. (London: Whitechapel Catalogue, 1969);
and Rivera, "O reviramento do sujeito," 107 and 116.

97. In an opposite direction, art historian Anna Dezeuze recognizes the historical specificity of the
Parangolés but nevertheless claims that a 1967 Mangueira dancer is "no more 'authentic' or 'sincere'
a wearer of the *Parangolé*" than she is. Though I do find it important to downplay notions of authenticity and the generative role usually ascribed to Oiticica's encounter with Mangueira, it is also essential
to retain the specificity of this encounter precisely as a set of historical coordinates, so that we read
participation as leading to a more fundamental level of meaning; Dezeuze's argument is focused instead on reaffirming the present validity of an immediate (and somewhat unmediated) experience of
the *Parangolé*. Anna Dezeuze, "Tactile Materialization, Sensory Politics: Hélio Oiticica's *Parangolés*,"
Art Journal 63, no. 2 (Summer 2004): 65–67.

98. For Salomão, the dancers "were fully enjoying the mess they were making, that unexpected and unin-
vited people, with no suit or tie ... with their wide-opened and joyful eyes, crashing into the MAM. An
evident activity of subversion of values and behaviors." Significantly, Salomão notes that the samba
school environment has long ceased to represent subversion, since it has become (like the favela itself,
in fact) part of the official tourism industry. See Salomão, *Hélio Oiticica: qual é o Parangolé?*, 52–55
and 59.

99. This asymmetry—very rarely acknowledged by Oiticica scholars—is incipient in Rivera's suggestive
likening of the structure of participation in the *Parangolés* to the topology of a Moebius strip, in the
sense that "it annuls the distinction between inside and outside—not because both are united in
a gapless conjunction, but because something happens between subject and object, in a torsion,
displacing them from the position of masters of space, of the visual field and of the object." Rivera,
"O reviramento do sujeito," 115.

100. Hélio Oiticica, "Cara de Cavalo," in *Hélio Oiticica*, exh. cat., 25. I will discuss this particular *Bolide* at
more length in chapter 3.

101. The tendency to portray Oiticica as such is dramatically evident in the fact that his works were recently
exhibited along with Liam Gillick's at the Whitechapel Gallery, of all places. According to its website,
the gallery even organized joint "Gillick & Oiticica Community Group Workshops" in 2002; see http://
white.cyberporte.net/content.php?page_id=4038 (accessed February 18, 2011). Critic Claire Bishop
analyses relational aesthetics as an equivalent of service-oriented capitalism and ultimately opposed
to a really disruptive notion of antagonism (as in Laclau and Mouffe). It is telling in this regard that
Žižek's formulation of ideology is explicitly indebted to Laclau and Mouffe's antagonism, and I certainly
do include my reading of Oiticica in this genealogy, so his propositions become all the more distant
from the likes of relational aesthetics (as opposed to what the recent Whitechapel show would suggest). See Claire Bishop, "Antagonism and Relational Aesthetics," *October*, no. 110 (Fall 2004): 51–79.

102. See chapter 1.

103. Žižek, *The Sublime Object of Ideology*, 140. This idea of a radical present can be finally grasped by
recourse to Walter Benjamin's "Theses on the Philosophy of History": "Thinking involves not only the
flow of thoughts, but their arrest as well. When thinking suddenly stops in a configuration pregnant
with tensions, it gives that configuration a shock, by which it crystallizes into a monad. A historical
materialist approaches a historical subject only where he encounters it as a monad." Walter Benjamin,
Illuminations, trans. Harry Zohn (New York: Schocken), 262–263.

104. Žižek stresses that the Benjaminian historical present is based on the conception of history as the
repetition of past, failed events. By the same token, Oiticica seems to be recasting his historical
position by means of repetition: first of the constructive itself, as appearing in different artists (the
so-called constructors), and secondly, and in perfect analogy with the Benjaminian procedure, of
anthropophagy.

105. For a critique of the problematic contemporary success of the anthropophagic metaphor in the context of the international reception of Brazilian art, see Michael Asbury, "The Uroborus Effect: Brazilian Contemporary Art as Self-Consuming," *Third Text*, no. 114 (January 2012): 141–147.

106. Oiticica, "Attempt / Try / To Experiment the Experimental," 350. In Portuguese: "*o experimental* pode retomar nunca *reviver.*" Oiticica translated the verbs as "retake" and "revive," but considering the Portuguese original this is probably a mistranslation on his part, as he is obviously interested in criticizing the idea of something being *lived again*—as in, for example, a pastiche.

3 TAKING POSITIONS

1. *Ver ouvir*, 35mm film, directed by Antonio Carlos da Fontoura (Rio de Janeiro: Canto Claro Produções Artísticas, 1966).

2. Ibid.

3. Ibid.

4. Hélio Oiticica, "General Scheme of the New Objectivity," in *Hélio Oiticica*, exh. cat., trans. Stephen Berg et al. (Rio de Janeiro: Centro de Arte Hélio Oiticica, 1992), 116–117.

5. As Ferreira Gullar puts it, "Painters are once more giving their opinion [*voltaram a opinar*]! This is fundamental." Ferreira Gullar, "Opinião 65," *Arte em revista*, no. 2 (May-August 1979): 22.

6. See Antonio Dias and Rubens Gerchman, "Entrevista de Antônio Dias e Rubens Gerchman a Ferreira Gullar," *Revista da Civilização Brasileira*, no. 11–12 (1966–1967): 170–171.

7. I will address this change in Dias's production in chapter 4. Very briefly, what is most striking is that his somewhat informal, comic-like, and visceral works gave way to a sober, seemingly conceptual aesthetics.

8. See *Ver ouvir*.

9. Gullar, "Opinião 65," 22.

10. For Gullar's emphases on communication, see ibid.; also Dias and Gerchman, "Entrevista," 170.

11. Significantly enough, the Teatro de Arena was one of the origins of the Popular Centers of Culture (CPC). See Carlos Estevam Martins, "História do CPC," *Arte em Revista*, no. 3 (1980): 77–82.

12. Boris Fausto, *História geral do Brasil* (São Paulo: Edusp, 2004), 426–427.

13. Thomas E. Skidmore, *Politics in Brazil, 1930–1964: An Experiment in Democracy* (Oxford: Oxford University Press, 1967), 169.

14. For an account of the dialogue between modernist and vernacular aesthetics in modern Brazilian architecture, see Guilherme Wisnik, "Doomed to Modernity," in *Brazil's Modern Architecture*, ed. Elisabetta Andreolli and Adrian Forty (London: Phaidon, 2004), 20–55, especially 25–26.

15. Adrián Gorelik, *Das vanguardas a Brasília: cultura urbana e arquitetura na América Latina*, trans. from Spanish to Portuguese by Maria Antonieta Pereira (Belo Horizonte: Editora UFMG, 2005), 164.

16. Ibid., 157–158 and 179. As Gorelik explains, the categories are Colin Rowe's.

17. Ibid., 176.

18. Ibid., 157.

19. Mário Pedrosa, *Dos murais de Portinari aos espaços de Brasília* (São Paulo: Perspectiva, 1981), 339. For a full discussion of Pedrosa's shifting viewpoints on Brasília, see Otília Arantes, *Mário Pedrosa: itinerário crítico* (São Paulo: Cosac Naify, 2004), 107–156.

20. Pedrosa, *Dos murais de Portinari aos espaços de Brasília*, 310.

21. Ibid., 310 and 352–353. I will return to this point, but it is worth noticing that, as Guilherme Wisnik argues, there were two competing paradigms of artistic integration that informed constructive tendencies in Brazil: one, of Bauhausian inspiration, and ultimately indebted to the Wagnerian *Gesamtkunstwerk*, that ran through concretism and privileged the cooperation at equal footing between the various arts (including the applied arts); and the other, the French *synthèse des arts*, whose major representative was Le Corbusier, which posited architecture as the ultimate art that would synthetically assimilate the plasticity of sculpture and painting (the other "major" arts). Lúcio Costa and Oscar

Niemeyer obviously favored the latter conception, but the fact is that this primacy of architecture was somewhat at odds with the more cooperative synthesis Pedrosa envisaged. See Guilherme Wisnik, "Brasília: The City as Sculpture," in *Das Verlagen nach Form—O desejo da forma*, ed. Robert Kudielka, Angela Lammert, and Luiz Camillo Osório (Berlin: Akademie der Künste, 2009), 276–299.

22. Max Bill cited in Flávio de Aquino, "A nossa moderna arquitetura," in *Arte concreta paulista: documentos*, ed. João Bandeira (São Paulo: Cosac Naify; Centro Universitário Maria Antonia da USP, 2002), 32.

23. Gorelik, *Das vanguardas a Brasília*, 176–177. Considering the staunch opposition to Costa's project of the architecture review *Habitat*—a publication familiar to the concretists—their omission becomes all the more telling.

24. Ibid., 177.

25. See chapter 1.

26. See chapter 1.

27. Lorenzo Mammì, "A construção da sombra," in *As construções de Brasília*, ed. Heloísa Espada and Sergio Burgi (São Paulo: Instituto Moreira Salles, 2010), 97–105.

28. According to Mammì, the German painter Johann-Moritz Rugendas is said to have complained that nature in the Amazon region was contrary "to the laws of art." Ibid., 101.

29. Ibid., 103; Lorenzo Mammì, untitled presentation at the roundtable "Brasília sol e sombra" (Insituto Moreira Salles, Rio de Janeiro, May 27, 2010).

30. See Ferreira Gullar, interview with Fernando Cocchiarale and Anna Bella Geiger, in *Abstracionismo, geométrico e informal: a vanguarda brasileira nos anos cinquenta*, ed. Fernando Cocchiarale and Anna Bella Geiger (Rio de Janeiro: FUNARTE, 1987), 100.

31. For a full discussion of *Tropicália*, see chapter 2.

32. *Brasília: contradições de uma cidade nova*, 35mm, directed by Joaquim Pedro de Andrade (Brasília, 1967), my translation.

33. Ibid.

34. Ibid.

35. According to the poet, most of the voiceover was written by Joaquim Pedro de Andrade and by the screenwriter and film theorist Jean Claude Bernadet. Nevertheless, Gullar acknowledges having given "a few contributions." Ferreira Gullar, interview with the author, December 18, 2010.

36. Pedrosa, *Dos murais de Portinari aos espaços de Brasília*, 356 and 361.

37. Ferreira Gullar, *Cultura posta em questão* (Rio de Janeiro: Editora Civilização Brasileira, 1965), 40–41.

38. Gullar, interview with Cocchiaralle and Geiger, 97. The city in this case was Rio de Janeiro.

39. Sônia Salzstein, "Uma dinâmica da arte brasileira: modernidade, instituições, instância pública," in *Arte contemporânea brasileira: texturas, dicções, ficções, estratégias*, ed. Ricardo Basbaum (Rio de Janeiro: Rios Ambiciosos, 2001), 397.

40. Antonio Dias recalls that many young artists didn't even attend exhibition openings (before the "Opinião 65" show, that is), alienated by the strict dress code (i.e., by the lack of means to buy a suit). To a certain extent, then, the two sides of the museum—personal and institutional—corresponded to segregation within the museum itself. Antonio Dias, interview with Sergio Martins, Michael Asbury, Isobel Whitelegg, and Felipe Scovino, unpublished (April 23, 2010).

41. For Salzstein, "the emancipatory impulse of Brazilian art in this period [the 1950s] is not *directly* linked to then-emergent institutional initiatives, so much so that the articulation of the concrete and neoconcrete movements irradiated 'from inside out,' in the intimate contexts of *personal* relations, and thanks to an affinity of ideas that encouraged, in a precise moment, the formation of a circle of artistic and intellectual relations, only contingentially professional or institutional." Salzstein, "Uma dinâmica da arte brasileira," 396.

42. Gullar, *Cultura posta em questão*, 57.

214

43. Martins, "História do CPC," 80. Gullar also recalls how affected he was by the movement that guaranteed Goulart's inauguration. See Ferreira Gullar, interview with Carla Siqueira, in *Memória do movimento estudantil* (2004), previously available at http://www.mme.org.br/ (last accessed February 16, 2011).

44. Martins, "História do CPC," 80.

45. For Marxist literary critic Roberto Schwarz, the most crucial mistake by the left-wing sector was to assume that the national bourgeoisie (whose majority firmly supported the coup) was on its side, thus mistaking the real problem (class struggle) for a fight against imperialism. See Roberto Schwarz, *Misplaced Ideas*, trans. Peter Anti (London: Verso, 1992), 130–131. This point is particularly well portrayed in Glauber Rocha's 1967 film *Entranced Land*, when a left-wing bourgeois media mogul is bluntly warned: "Class struggle is real. Which class is yours?"

46. Gullar himself uses the term "conversion" in this regard. Gullar, interview with Siqueira, 7.

47. Slavoj Žižek, *The Sublime Object of Ideology* (London: Verso, 1989), 47.

48. In a suggestive article, Irene Small has reached similar conclusions by a different route, revealing the similarity between the narrative mode employed by Gullar and that of the left-wing intellectuals associated with the Instituto Superior de Estudos Brasileiros (ISEB), an important 1950s national-developmentalist think tank. Irene Small, "Exit and Impasse: Ferreira Gullar and the 'New History' of the Last Avant-Garde," *Third Text*, no. 114 (January 2012): 91–101.

49. Hélio Oiticica, "Brazil Diarrhea," in *Hélio Oiticica*, exh. cat., 17.

50. Gullar, interview with Siqueira, 8.

51. Carlos Estevam Martins, "Anteprojeto do manifesto do CPC," *Arte em Revista*, no. 1 (January-March 1979): 70–71.

52. Gullar, *Cultura posta em questão*, 2.

53. My account of *Five Times Favela* and of *cinema novo* in general is greatly indebted to philosopher and film scholar Rodrigo Nunes. See Rodrigo Nunes, "Do You See What the People Is?," lecture (Chelsea College of Art & Design, London, November 18, 2009); Rodrigo Nunes, "Stronger Are the Powers of the People: Politics, Poetics and Popular Education in Brazilian Cinema, 1962–1979," lecture (no.w.here, London, December 4, 2009); and Rodrigo Nunes, email communication with the author, June 3 and 4, 2010.

54. Nunes, "Stronger Are the Powers of the People." Andrade's episode focuses on the ill-fated relationship between a favela boy and a cat he abducts from an upper-class house in order to sell it for skinning. Without dialogue, the film shows the boy emotionally bonding with the cat but ultimately resigning himself to his economic needs and selling it anyway.

55. Cid Vasconcelos de Carvalho, "Aspectos do nacionalismo no cinema brasileiro," *Ciberlegenda*, no. 13 (2004).

56. See Ismail Xavier, *Cinema brasileiro moderno* (São Paulo: Paz e Terra, 2001), 63–65; and Rodrigo Nunes, "*Terra em transe*, cinema e política: 45 anos," in Luciano Gatti, Rodrigo Nunes, and Carlos Shimote, *Prêmio Serrote de ensaísmo* (São Paulo: IMS, 2012), 29–48. Other films that question the role of the intellectual in that period are Paulo César Saraceni's *O desafio* (*The Challenge*, 1965), Nelson Pereira dos Santos's *Fome de amor* (*Hunger for Love*, 1968), Carlos Diegues's *Os herdeiros* (*The Heirs*, 1970), and Gustavo Dahl's *O bravo guerreiro* (*The Brave Warrior*, 1969).

57. Émile Benveniste, *Problems in General Linguistics*, trans. Mary Elizabeth Meek (Coral Gables, FL: University of Miami Press, 1971), 226.

58. The effect is to evidence, as Slavoj Žižek puts it, that "everything that I positively am, every enunciated content I can point at and say 'that's me,' is not 'I'; I am only the void that remains, the empty distance toward every content." Slavoj Žižek, *Tarrying with the Negative: Kant, Hegel, and the Critique of Ideology* (Durham: Duke University Press, 1993), 40. For a further discussion of the effects of such illegitimate conflation in terms of ego formation, see Slavoj Žižek, *The Parallax View* (Cambridge, MA: MIT Press, 2009), 219–220.

59. Antonio Dias cited in Paulo Herkenhoff, "Antonio Dias: nexo entre diferenças," trans. José Gabriel Flores, in *Antonio Dias*, exh. cat. (São Paulo: Cosac Naify, 1999), 51–52.

60. Georges Bataille, *Visions of Excess: Selected Writings, 1927–1939*, ed. Allan Stoekl, trans. Allan Stoekl with Carl R. Lovitt and Donald M. Leslie Jr. (Minneapolis: University of Minnesota Press, 1985), 57.

61. As I have argued in the preceding chapters, this was a driving force at the core of some of the most original readings of modern art performed in Brazil during the 1950s and 1960s.

62. I briefly introduced this work, hereafter referred to simply as *Box Bolide 18*, in the previous chapter.

63. In the original: "*AQUI ESTÁ E FICARÁ! CONTEMPLAI SEU SILÊNCIO HERÓICO.*"

64. "I knew Cara de Cavalo personally, and I can say he was my friend," Oiticica explains, "but for society he was public enemy number one." Hélio Oiticica, "Cara de Cavalo," in *Hélio Oiticica*, exh. cat., 25.

65. See chapter 2.

66. Oiticica was not actually allowed to remain inside the museum with the *Parangolés*, and the performance happened outside.

67. Jean Bohici cited in Vera Pacheco Jordão, "Ainda o Parangolé," *O Globo* (August 23, 1965). In the original: "O que é o Parangolé? / Parangolé é o que é / É o mito / Hélio Oiticica, Flash Gordon nacional, / Não voa nos espaços siderais / voa através das camadas sociais."

68. Vera Pacheco Jordão, "Parangolé no MAM," *O Globo* (August 16, 1965).

69. See Guy Brett, "The Experimental Exercise of Freedom," in *Hélio Oiticica*, exh. cat., 229.

70. Michael Asbury, "Hélio Couldn't Dance," in *Fios soltos: a arte de Hélio Oiticica*, ed. Paula Braga (São Paulo: Perspectiva, 2008), 53.

71. Herkenhoff, "Antonio Dias," 38.

72. Especially considering the prominence of strikes in political and cultural life (for example, in the play *They Don't Wear Black Tie*) in the preceding decade.

73. Oiticica, "General Scheme of the New Objectivity," 110–111 and 116.

74. Dias and Gerchman, "Entrevista," 177.

75. Ibid., 170.

76. Ibid.

77. Antonio Dias, interview with the author, May 8, 2009.

78. Benjamin H. D. Buchloh, "Residual Resemblance: Three Notes on the Ends of Portraiture," in *Face-Off: The Portrait in Recent Art*, ed. Melissa E. Feldman (Philadelphia: Institute of Contemporary Art, 1994), 62.

79. Hal Foster, *The Return of the Real: Art and Theory at the End of the Century* (Cambridge, MA: MIT Press, 1996), 132–134.

80. In a classic and (and skeptical) diagnosis written not long after the tropicalist heyday, Schwarz implies how tropicalism in general relied heavily on the fragility of public cultural mediation for its shock effect: "The stock of images and emotions belonging to the patriarchal country, rural and urban, is exposed to the most advanced or fashionable forms and techniques in the world.... It's in the internal contrast that the peculiar attraction, the trade mark of the tropicalist image lies. The result of the combination is strident, like a family secret dragged out to the middle of the street, like treachery to one's own class." Schwarz, *Misplaced Ideas*, 140.

81. See chapter 2.

82. Gerchman responded to Dias's criticism of this imagery suggesting that they consisted in the "expression of a class." See Dias and Gerchman, "Entrevista," 177.

83. Paulo Sergio Duarte, *Anos 60: Transformações na Arte Brasileira* (Rio de Janeiro: Campos Gerais, 1999), 42.

84. Ibid.

85. Oiticica, "General Scheme of the New Objectivity," 111. For the notion of "transobject," see Hélio Oiticica, "Bolides," in *Hélio Oiticica*, exh. cat., 66–67.

86. Hélio Oiticica, "Life-Experience at the Morro do Quieto," in *Tropicália: A Revolution in Brazilian Culture*, ed. Carlos Basualdo, trans. Aaron Lorenz, Renata Nascimento, and Christopher Dunn (São Paulo: Cosac Naify, 2005), 218.

87. As a matter of fact, Gullar's reasoning in *Culture in Question* is extensively addressed in the "General Scheme of the New Objectivity." See Oiticica, "General Scheme of the New Objectivity," 116–118.

88. Oiticica, "Life-Experience at the Morro do Quieto," 219.

89. For another discussion of Oiticica's reading of *Note on an Unforeseen Death*, see Gustavo Motta, "Uma fratura na participação. Hélio Oiticica lê a 'Nota sobre a morte imprevista,'" in *Prêmio Estudos e Pesquisas sobre Arte e Economia da Arte, Programa Brasil Arte Contemporânea*, online publication (São Paulo: Programa Brasil Arte Contemporânea—Ministério da Cultura (Minc) / Fundação Bienal de São Paulo, 2010), http://www.bienal.org.br/FBSP/pt/ProjetosEspeciais/Documents/Gustavo_Motta.pdf (accessed December 19, 2012).

90. I owe this suggestive remark to Ana Wambier.

91. Pedrosa, *Dos murais de Portinari aos espaços de Brasília*, 217–221. The word *sertanejo* designates those who come from the semiarid northeastern backcountry—the *sertão*. It also connotes a quality of uncultivated rudeness.

92. What's more, a series of paintings by the Brazilian artist Quissak Jr. entitled *Meditations upon the National Flag* was removed on the grounds that any use of the flag, with the exception of patriotic or official ceremonies, was constitutionally illegal in Brazil. See *Bienal 50 anos*, ed. Agnaldo Farias (São Paulo: Fundação Bienal de São Paulo, 2001), 138.

93. Pedrosa, *Dos murais de Portinari aos espaços de Brasília*, 221.

94. Ibid., 218.

95. Ibid.

96. Ibid., 221.

97. In this regard, one should bear in mind the importance of political and experimental theater in the 1960s avant-garde. Particularly important to Oiticica (and to the reclaiming of anthropophagy as a whole) were the shocking performances of the Oficina Theater group, including their groundbreaking adaptation of Oswald de Andrade's *The King of Candles*.

98. There may be also a wry remark on reactionary collective formations (such as the conservative, middle-class support of the military coup) in Oiticica's *Bolide*: Cara de Cavalo was tracked down and murdered by a death squad named "Scuderie LeCoq" after the detective Milton LeCoq, whom the outlaw had killed in an earlier confrontation. Death squads are evidence of social hypocrisy, as they tend to be publicly condemned but informally tolerated and accepted as a method of "social cleansing"; the inscription in the *Bolide* saying that Cara de Cavalo's body would *remain* there, in sight, despite the fact that he was actually eliminated, can be thus read as a confrontation in this respect as well. In short, Oiticica's comment about violence being justified as a means of "individual revolt" but not of "oppression" is meant to ethically differentiate both murders, and it points to the death squad as the violent arm of an illegitimate collective formation. See Oiticica, "Cara de Cavalo," 25.

99. It is telling in this respect that, in their interview, Gullar quickly interrupts Dias when the artist starts to discuss his initial ventures into informal abstraction, mentioning Antoni Tàpies: "Yes, but then you got fed up. Let us return to [Dias's interest in] comics." See Dias and Gerchman, "Entrevista," 171.

100. Gullar, *Cultura posta em questão*, 50–51.

101. In December of that year the military government issued the Institutional Act number 5 (AI-5), dissolving the parliament and revoking many civil rights, including those of speech and assembly.

102. See Carlos Zilio, interview with Fernando Cocchiaralle, Paulo Sérgio Duarte, Vanda Mangia Klabin, and Maria Del Carmen Zilio, in *Carlos Zilio*, ed. Paulo Venâncio Filho, trans. Carolyn Brissett (São Paulo: Cosac Naify, 2006), 203.

103. Ibid.

104. Milton Machado, "Power to the Imagination: Art in the 1970s and Other Brazilian Miracles," in *Arara*, no. 3 (2000).

217

105. Zilio explains that pop "had a great impact" on him in the 1960s, but that he ultimately had a CPC-oriented reading of it as "alienated." See Zilio, interview with Cocchiarale et al., 205.

106. Ibid., 204.

4 ENIGMAGES

1. Gerardo Mosquera, "Gerardo Mosquera in Conversation with Cildo Meireles," in Dan Cameron, Paulo Herkenhoff, and Gerardo Mosquera, *Cildo Meireles* (London: Phaidon, 1999), 15.

2. Ibid.

3. Paulo Herkenhoff, "A Labyrinthine Ghetto: The Work of Cildo Meireles," in Cameron, Herkenhoff, and Mosquera, *Cildo Meireles*, 65. The critic refers to the fact that Tiradentes is symptomatic of Brazilian political conditions, having been all but nonexistent in cultural representations before the beginning of the Republic, since the Brazilian empire occupied an ambivalent position between representing a new, independent country and a continuation of a European monarchy against which Tiradentes had rebelled.

4. Carmen Maia, *Cildo Meireles* (Rio de Janeiro: Funarte, 2009), 26.

5. Frederico Morais, *Frederico Morais*, ed. Silvana Seffrin (Rio de Janeiro: Funarte, 2004), 120.

6. Cildo Meireles, "Um sutil ato de malabarismo," interview with Ronaldo Brito, in *Cildo Meireles: Encontros*, ed. Felipe Scovino (Rio de Janeiro: Azougue Editorial, 2009), 29.

7. As Thierry de Duve puts it, "it is the sudden vanishing of the present tense [in photography], splitting into the contradiction of being simultaneously too late and too early, that is properly unbearable." Thierry de Duve, "Time Exposure and Snapshot: The Photograph as Paradox," *October* 5 (Summer 1978): 121.

8. Meireles continues: "I was looking for something that had nothing to do with *Tropicália*. I was involved in a construction process that led me to *Virtual Spaces: Corners*." Cildo Meireles, interview with Felipe Scovino, in *Arquivo contemporâneo*, ed. Felipe Scovino (Rio de Janeiro: Sette Letras, 2010), 112.

9. Ibid., 131.

10. Hélio Oiticica, "Tropicália," in *Hélio Oiticica*, exh. cat., trans. Stephen Berg et al. (Rio de Janeiro: Centro de Arte Hélio Oiticica, 1992), 125.

11. Hélio Oiticica, "Tropicália, the New Image," unpublished manuscript (Archive of the Projeto Hélio Oiticica, document 0535/69, 1969).

12. Oiticica, "Tropicália" (1992), 125.

13. Critic Vera Pedrosa, for example, employed this very expression: "Although it is a logical continuation of his earlier work, all has changed when it comes to the so-called Antonio Dias 'style.'" Vera Pedrosa, "Conversa puxa conversa," *Correio da Manhã* (August 13, 1968).

14. Hélio Oiticica, "Special for Antonio Dias Project-Book," unpublished manuscript (Archive of the Projeto Hélio Oiticica, document 0306/69, 1969).

15. Ibid.

16. Antonio Dias, "Carta de Antonio Dias para HO," unpublished correspondence (Archive of the Projeto Hélio Oiticica, document 1535/69, May 4, 1969).

17. Hélio Oiticica, "Appearance of the Supra-Sensorial," in *Hélio Oiticica*, exh. cat., 127.

18. The term was originally coined by the Brazilian designer and countercultural agitator Rogério Duarte. See Oiticica, "Special for Antonio Dias Project-Book."

19. Hélio Oiticica, "O objeto," unpublished manuscript (Archive of the Projeto Hélio Oiticica PHO 0152/68, 1968).

20. Hélio Oiticica, "The Possibilities of Creleisure," in *Hélio Oiticica*, exh. cat., 136.

21. Ibid.

22. Ibid., 137.

23. Oiticica, "Special for Antonio Dias Project-Book."

24. Oiticica already referred to Pedrosa's dictum as early as 1968. See Hélio Oiticica, "The Plot of the Earth That Trembles: The Avant-Garde Meaning of the Bahian Group," in *Tropicália: A Revolution in Brazilian Culture*, ed. Carlos Basualdo, trans. Aaron Lorenz, Renata Nascimento, and Christopher Dunn (São Paulo: Cosac Naify, 2005), 245–254.

25. Antonio Dias, "'O lugar que vejo:' entrevista com Antonio Dias," *Arte & Ensaios* 9, no. 9 (2002): 15.

26. Antonio Dias in conversation with the author, May 8, 2009.

27. Cildo Meireles, "Cruzeiro do sul, 1969–70," in *Cildo Meireles*, ed. Guy Brett (London: Tate Publishing, 2008), 58.

28. As Rosalind Krauss has argued, conceptual art in its defense of "art-as-theory" assimilates itself to a kind of purity that is not specific (like that of modernist medium specificity), but rather is *general*—i.e., pure exchange value. Meireles, whose work can be read as an insistent and incredibly varied effort to implode equivalence, was clearly sensitive to this issue and tackled it most forcefully, as we will see, via the notion of the standard. See Rosalind Krauss, *"A Voyage on the North Sea": Art in the Age of the Post-Medium Condition* (London: Thames & Hudson, 1999), 10–15. I am grateful to Kaira Cabañas for bringing this point to my attention.

29. For a discussion on the relation between language and visuality in the context of North American postwar art and of Fluxus, see Liz Kotz, *Words to Be Looked At: Language in 1960s Art* (Cambridge, MA: MIT Press, 2007).

30. Mário Barata, "Antonio Dias em Milão," *Jornal do Commercio*, December 30, 1969.

31. Paulo Sergio Duarte, *Antonio Dias* (Rio de Janeiro: FUNARTE, 1979), 21.

32. Ronaldo Brito, *Experiência crítica*, ed. Sueli de Lima (São Paulo: Cosac Naify, 2005), 194.

33. Paulo Herkenhoff, "Antonio Dias: nexo entre diferenças," trans. José Gabriel Flores, in *Antonio Dias*, exh. cat. (São Paulo: Cosac Naify, 1999), 49. Translation modified by the author.

34. Dias recounts an anecdote, of how he explained the picture to a disbelieving critic at the Guggenheim Museum: "It is a picture of a man taking his dog for a walk ... the man is GOD and the dog is DOG, but between the two there is a kind of connection created by the leash." Antonio Dias cited in Nadja von Tilinsky, "Antonio Dias in Conversation," in *Antonio Dias: Trabalhos, 1967–1994*, exh. cat. (Ostfildern: Hatje Cantz Verlag, 1994), 53.

35. Ibid.

36. What's more, this is a distinction within Dias's oeuvre. In *Project for an Artistic Attitude* the word "reality" is fully flipped—meaning that not only is the word written in reverse with regular letters (as in *The Hardest Way*), but also each individual letter is flipped as well (unlike what happens in *The Hardest Way*).

37. For a brief but clear consideration of the meanings of the words *cão* and *cachorro* in Portuguese, see translator José Gabriel Flores's note in Tilinsky, "Antonio Dias in Conversation," 59.

38. Dias, "O lugar que eu vejo," 14.

39. This is why, in Lacan's famous mirror stage, the child's dealings with its mirror image are exemplary of the construction of its "I"; bluntly put, the mirror image allows the child to apprehend itself from the outside, to synthesize its fragmentary consciousness of itself into a unified image. See Jacques Lacan, "The Mirror Stage as Formative of *I* Function, as Revealed in Psychoanalytic Experience," in *Écrits: A Selection*, trans. Bruce Fink (New York: W. W. Norton, 2002), 3–7.

40. Mladen Dolar, *A Voice and Nothing More* (Cambridge, MA: MIT Press, 2006), 17.

41. As Dolar puts it: "Even at the most banal level of daily experience, when we listen to someone speak, we may at first be very much aware of his or her voice and its particular qualities, its color and accent, but soon we accommodate to it and concentrate only on the meaning to be conveyed. The voice itself is like the Wittgensteinian ladder to be discarded when we have successfully climbed to the top—that is, when we have made our ascent to the peak of meaning." Ibid., 15.

42. Herkenhoff notes that the gap between GOD and DOG has a circular quality, although he doesn't link that to the sonic quality of the words. Herkenhoff, "Antonio Dias," 56.

43. As Dolar explains, Derrida has criticized the assumption of the vocal basis of language on the basis of

its intended authenticity vis-à-vis the self—i.e., the hypothesis that its "essence lies in auto-affection and self-transparency, as opposed to the trace, the rest, the alterity and so on," thus leading to a metaphysical scheme of things (which Herkenhoff at this point seems to embrace). I follow Dolar here in his attempt not to defend the supposed authenticity of the voice against the charge levied on it by deconstruction, but to see it instilled with a remainder that acts as "an interior obstacle to (self-) presence." See Dolar, *A Voice and Nothing More*, 42.

44. Elisabeth Roudinesco and Michel Plon stress that the Lacanian notion of fantasy is distinct (for instance, from the Kleinian one) in that it is already a "signifying structure" and thus "irreducible to the imaginary." So while Herkenhoff's argument seems to imply that Dias's use of language surely builds upon specularity in a disruptive manner, I would argue that the relation is not so straightforward: there is always the risk that the symbolic is simply supplementing imaginary identification with the register of fantasy. My own effort in this session can thus be read as introducing vocalization as the true nodal point that forces us to reconfigure this relationship by critically hinging (i.e., short-circuiting) ego and fantasy into a consideration of the subject proper (therefore the relevance of this particular picture vis-à-vis Dias's engagement with self-portraiture). See Elisabeth Roudinesco and Michel Plon, *Dicionário de psicanálise*, translated into Portuguese by Vera Ribeiro and Lucy Magalhães (Rio de Janeiro: Jorge Zahar Editor, 1998), 225.

220 45. Dolar continues: "The time of fantasy is situated in the time for understanding ... it is a defense against the excessive nature of the initial moment, it frames the voice and underpins it with a fiction, it emerges in the place of understanding, instead of understanding, as a stand-in for understanding before the concluding moment when the true sense will finally be revealed, and there will no longer be any need for fantasy." He quickly adds, however, that this final moment never actually arrives, so the point is not simply, in this case, to dislodge a "wrong" interpretation of GOD DOG with a "right" one (which would simply provide a new fantasy for the subject). In other words, though I want to use vocalization in an effort of positioning a subject—this is what I mean by a subject of vocalization—it would be wrong to conceive of the voice per se as the location of the subject, as a positive sign of its presence. See Dolar, *A Voice and Nothing More*, 136–139.

46. For Žižek "it is a condition of the experience of (linguistic) meaning that the (language) medium should be transparent (this transparency collapses when we suddenly become aware of the obscene material presence of the sound of words): in order to experience meaning, we have to 'see through' words." Slavoj Žižek, *The Parallax View* (Cambridge, MA: MIT Press, 2009), 220–221.

47. Ibid., 161.

48. Sônia Salzstein, "The Many Masquerades of Antonio Dias," in *Antonio Dias: Anywhere Is My Land*, exh. cat. (Ostfildern: Hatje Cantz Verlag, 2009), 60–62.

49. Rosalind Krauss, *The Optical Unconscious* (Cambridge, MA: MIT Press, 1994), especially 15–19.

50. Vladimir Safatle, "Uma clínica do sensível: a respeito da relação entre destituição subjetiva e primado do objeto," *Interações* 10, no. 19 (January-June 2005): 144. For a lengthier discussion of Safatle's argument, see the introduction.

51. Oiticica writes: "i am not here representing brazil; or representing anythingelse: the idea of representing-representation-etc. are over;" further adding that "tropicália was a tentative to create a synthetic face-brazil: the image taken to a dimension 'more than that of representation': but i am not interested in that anymore." Likewise, Meireles begins by stating, "I am here, in this exhibition, to defend neither a career nor any nationality." See *Information*, ed. Kynaston McShine (New York: Museum of Modern Art, 1970), 12 and 85.

52. Robert Smithson, *Robert Smithson: The Collected Writings*, ed. Jack Flam (Berkeley: University of California Press, 1996), 90.

53. Ibid.

54. Ibid., 88.

55. Antonio Dias in conversation with the author, May 8, 2009.

56. *Robert Smithson: The Collected Writings*, 91.

57. Interestingly, it is after the proclamation of the Brazilian Republic that both the idea of building a new capital and the promotion of *Tiradentes* as a national hero gain impetus, as part of the symbolic refoundation of the country after the Imperial period.

58. One need only remember here the international boycott of the 1969 São Paulo Biennial, which counted not only on Brazilian artists, but also on the active support of others like Gordon Matta-Clark.

59. McShine, *Information*, 85.

60. Ibid.

61. Antonio Dias in conversation with Roberto Conduru, "Entrevista com Antonio Dias," in *Antonio Dias: Depoimento*, ed. Roberto Conduru and Marília Andrés Ribeiro (Belo Horizonte: C/Arte, 2010), 11.

62. Lewis Carroll, *The Complete Illustrated Lewis Carroll* (Ware, Hertsfordshire, UK: Wordsworth Editions, 1996), 683. Smithson's essay reproduces the first four lines of this passage.

63. Jean-Jacques Lecercle, *The Philosophy of Nonsense: The Intuitions of Victorian Nonsense Literature* (London: Routledge, 1994), 231–232.

64. *Robert Smithson: The Collected Writings*, 83–84.

65. Lecercle, *The Philosophy of Nonsense*, 231.

66. Walter Benjamin, *Selected Writings, 1938–1940*, trans. Edmund Jephcott (Cambridge, MA: Belknap Press of Harvard University Press, 2006), 392.

67. Cildo Meireles, "Para ser curvada com os olhos, 1970/5," in Brett, *Cildo Meireles*, 104. As the artist puts it: "The idea of this work is that, no matter what exhibition I prepared, it would always be there, until one day, slowly, the second bar would also become curved by the sum total force of the gaze of the spectators." As Guy Brett puts it, "what Meireles is placing at issue here is seeing, looking, as a determinant in the real world." Guy Brett, *Transcontinental: Nine Latin-American Artists*, exh. cat. (London: Verso, 1990), 46.

68. Fredric Jameson, *Postmodernism, or, the Cultural Logic of Late Capitalism* (Durham: Duke University Press, 1991), 53–54.

69. Ibid., 54.

70. Ibid., 53–54.

71. Ibid., 52.

72. Ibid.

73. Cildo Meireles, "Arte física, 1969," in Brett, *Cildo Meireles*, 40.

74. Piero Manzoni cited in Briony Fer, *The Infinite Line: Remaking Art after Modernism* (New Haven: Yale University Press, 2004), 29.

75. As Briony Fer has pointed out, in Manzoni the "move from the small and banal to the huge utopian gesture slips by without a breath, only the inevitability of one thing leading to another." This description almost fits Meireles as well, but only almost, for the latter is at odds with Manzoni's showmanship (which was in any case impracticable in the repressive conditions of 1970s Brazil) and with what Fer describes as his "touch of the magician." Fer, *The Infinite Line*, 29.

76. Norman Bryson, "A Walk for a Walk's Sake," in Catherine de Zegher and Avis Newman, *The Stage of Drawing: Gesture and Art* (London: Tate Publishing, 2003), 149. As Bryson puts it, a line in Klee's sense continuously emerges "from an initial state, blank paper, to the state we eventually see."

77. Cildo Meireles, interview with the author, November 23, 2010.

78. Georges Didi-Huberman, *O que vemos, o que nos olha*, Portuguese trans. Paulo Neves (São Paulo: Editora 34, 1998), 148. This is Meireles, in a statement that strongly resonates with Didi-Huberman's argument: "The most beautiful word I know is *lejos* [Spanish for "far-off"] because it presupposes that your being is here and there at the same time. *Lá* [Portuguese for "over there"] is a confirmation of being." Cildo Meireles, "Textos de Cildo Meireles," in *Cildo Meireles, geografia do Brasil*, ed. Paulo Herkenhoff, trans. Peter Lenny and Owen Beith (Rio de Janeiro: Artviva Produção Cultural, 2001), 20 and 86, translation altered by the author.

79. Jorge Luis Borges, *Collected Fictions*, trans. Andrew Hurley (London: Penguin, 1999), 263.

80. Jameson, *Postmodernism*, 52.

81. Ibid., 54.

82. Meireles, interview with the author. Another relevant reference in this respect would be, of course, Marcel Duchamp's readymade *Why Not Sneeze, Rose Sélavy* (1921).

221

83. David Harvey, *The Condition of Postmodernity: An Enquiry into the Origins of Cultural Change* (Malden, MA, and Oxford, UK: Wiley-Blackwell, 1990), 295–296.

84. Ibid., 298.

85. Jameson shares Harvey's view on the significance of those major economic events: "It is my sense that both levels in question, infrastructures and superstructures—the economic system and the cultural 'structures of feeling'—somehow crystallized in the great shock of the crises of 1973 (the oil crisis, the end of the international gold standard, for all intents and purposes the end of the great wave of 'wars of national liberation' and the beginning of the end of traditional communism), which, now that the dust clouds have rolled away, disclose the existence, already in place, of a strange new landscape." Jameson, *Postmodernism*, xx–xxi.

86. Meireles, interview with the author.

87. Meireles in "Gerardo Mosquera in Conversation with Cildo Meireles," 21.

88. The Portuguese word *entorno* can have both senses depending on whether it is read as a noun or as a verbal tense.

89. Cildo Meireles, "Desvio para o vermelho, 1967–84," in Brett, *Cildo Meireles*, 222.

90. Walter Benjamin, *The Arcades Project*, trans. Howard Eiland and Kevin McLaughlin (Cambridge, MA: Belknap Press of Harvard University Press, 2002), 9.

91. Ibid., 211.

92. See David Batchelor, *Chromophobia* (London: Reaktion Books, 2000), 104–105.

93. Antonio Dias, *Antonio Dias*, exh. cat. (Rio de Janeiro: Galeria Saramenha, 1979), front cover.

94. Benjamin, *The Arcades Project*, 205.

95. Krauss similarly mobilizes the Benjaminian collector as an explanatory model for Marcel Broodthaers, and further argues that the emblematic label of his collections—the "Fig." notation—also grounds his work in fiction, which becomes, in turn, a kind of self-differing medium—as opposed to the ultimate lack of valid standards for judging installation art. *Red Shift* takes another direction: it also contains the problematic dispersal Krauss detects in installation art, but via a kind of phenomenological shock that suddenly (and paradoxically) coalesces out of dispersal itself. In other words, and in keeping with the dual aspect of the commodity, "redness" is both a mark of (quantitative) dispersal and (qualitative) wholeness. See Krauss, *"A Voyage on the North Sea,"* 38–56.

96. Meireles, "Desvio para o vermelho," 122.

97. For Didi-Huberman's critique of the tautological discourse of minimalism, see Didi-Huberman, *O que vemos*, 61–77.

98. Meireles, interview with the author.

5 WHITE ON WHITE

1. Hélio Oiticica, "Drop by Drop Notes," in *Fios soltos: a Arte de Hélio Oiticica*, ed. Paulo Braga, trans. Ben Kohn (São Paulo: Perspectiva, 2008), 361.

2. Hélio Oiticica, "Color, Time and Structure," in *Hélio Oiticica*, exh. cat., trans. Stephen Berg et al. (Rio de Janeiro: Centro de Arte Hélio Oiticica, 1992), 34.

3. A notable exception is a 1965 *Bolide* subtitled "Homage to Malevich Gemini."

4. Frederico Coelho's *Livro ou livro-me: os escritos babilônicos de Hélio Oiticica* (Rio de Janeiro: Editora Uerj, 2010) is the best study available in any language on Oiticica's 1970s book project and on his relationship with literature, poetry, and marginal culture. Other recent works that have been exploring Oiticica's manifold interests in that decade include my own and Michael Asbury's concomitant and yet unpublished works on his engagement with rock and roll music; Luke Skrebowski's "Revolution in the Aesthetic Revolution," *Third Text*, no. 114 (January 2012): 65–78, which addresses Oiticica's references to the Brazilian guerrilla leader Carlos Marighella and to the philosopher Herbert Marcuse; and Max Jorge Hinderer Cruz's "TROPICAMP: PRE- and POST-TROPICÁLIA at Once: Some Contextual Notes on Hélio Oiticica's 1971 Text," *Afterall: A Journal of Art, Context, and Enquiry* 28, no. 1 (Autumn/Winter 2011): 4–15, which discusses Oiticica's interest in the New York underground film culture, and especially in the work of Jack Smith.

5.   COSMOCOCA—programa in progress names both the series of works and the conceptual place it occupies in Oiticica's writings. I refer to Cosmococa(s), with initial capital only, for one or more of the environments conceived by Oiticica and Almeida, which gave rise to the series. The distinction is also important because the environments were not built before Oiticica's death. Other Cosmococas projected in partnership with Neville D'Almeida include CC1 Trashiscapes (with a photograph of Luis Buñuel), CC2 Onobject (a reference to Yoko Ono), CC3 Maileryn (an amalgamation of the names of Normal Mailer and Marilyn Monroe, with photographs of the latter), and CC5 Hendrix-War (an homage to Jimi Hendrix). Oiticica planned to make four additional CCs, either on his own or to be proposed to friends like Guy Brett and Carlos Vergara.

6.   As Katia Maciel argues, "On the one hand, projection is multiplied and expanded like a construction; and, on the other, the use of fixed images is a return to a photographic quality that precedes and forms the cinema experience." See Kátia Maciel, "The Quasi-cinema Experiences of Hélio Oiticica and Neville D'Almeida," in COSMOCOCA—programa in progress, exh. cat., trans. Ricardo Quintana and Steve Berg (Buenos Aires: MALBA, 2005), 295.

7.   Like all other Cosmococas, CC4 Nocagions was only posthumously assembled, following the detailed instructions left by the artist. See figure 5.5.

8.   Hélio Oiticica, "Hélio Oiticica's Instructions for Cosmococa," in COSMOCOCA—programa in progress, 225.

9.   Ibid., 224. See figure 5.4.

10. Moholy-Nagy, as cited in Branden W. Joseph, "White on White," Critical Inquiry 27, no. 1 (Autumn 2000), 98.

11. Ibid., 103.

12. John Cage, Silence (Middletown, CT: Wesleyan University Press, 1961), 191. Cited in Joseph, "White on White," 107.

13. László Moholy-Nagy, The New Vision (New York: Wittenborn and Company, 1946), 64. Cited in Joseph, "White on White," 98.

14. Joan Copjec, Read My Desire: Lacan against the Historicists (Cambridge, MA: MIT Press, 1996), 16–38. For the pertinence of Copjec's formula to Oiticica's work, see chapter 2.

15. Jacques Lacan, The Four Fundamental Concepts of Psychoanalysis (The Seminar of Jacques Lacan, Book 11), trans. Alan Sheridan (New York: Norton, 1998), 96–97.

16. A close analysis of Oiticica's painting technique became possible after the superb work of restoration led by Wynne H. Phelan at the Museum of Fine Arts Houston. See Wynne H. Phelan, "To Bestow a Sense of Light: Hélio Oiticica's Experimental Process," in Hélio Oiticica: The Body of Color, ed. Mari Carmen Ramirez, trans. Stephen Berg and Héctor Olea (London: Tate Publishing, 2007), 76–81. On the parallelism between Clark's and Oiticica's painterly investigations at this moment, see chapter 2.

17. Hélio Oiticica, Hélio Oiticica: Painting beyond the Frame, ed. Luciano Figueiredo, trans. Stephen Berg (Rio de Janeiro: Silvia Roesler Edições de Arte, 2008), 78.

18. Paula Braga, "A trama da terra que treme: multiplicidade em Hélio Oiticica," Ph.D. dissertation (Universidade de São Paulo, 2007), 44–46. Braga notes that Malevich actually strove to distinguish "feeling" from "senses."

19. Kasimir Malevich, "Suprematism," in Theories of Modern Art: A Source Book by Artists and Critics, ed. Herschel B. Chipp (Berkeley: University of California Press, 1984), 341, my emphasis.

20. Kasimir Malevich, "Suprematismo," in Projeto construtivo brasileiro na arte (1950–1962), ed. Aracy A. Amaral (Rio de Janeiro and São Paulo: Museu de Arte Moderna and Pinacoteca do Estado, 1977), 32.

21. For an in-depth account of the concrete-neoconcrete polemic and of Gullar's theoretical formulations, see chapter 1.

22. Oiticica, Hélio Oiticica: Painting beyond the Frame, 78.

23. For an in-depth discussion of this topic, see chapter 2.

24. Hélio Oiticica, "Anotações para bloco branco no branco," unpublished manuscript (Archive of the Projeto Hélio, document 095/74, 1974). Also, the very fact that Oiticica named the sections of his book "blocs" and that one of its provisional titles was "conglomerate" gives a sense of how present constructive metaphors remained in his work.

25. For a fuller account of the constructive and of anthropophagy, see chapter 2.

26. Hélio Oiticica, "Attempt / Try / To Experiment the Experimental," in Braga, *Fios soltos*, 345. On the translation of this passage, see note 106 in chapter 2.

27. This move was also probably made easier by the fact that Ferreira Gullar, whose rivalry with São Paulo concretists has never really faded even to this day, grew personally distant from Oiticica's avant-gardist moves (despite remaining an important artistic and theoretical reference for the latter). An initial sign of renewed proximity between Rio and São Paulo artists was Waldemar Cordeiro's inclusion in the 1967 "New Brazilian Objectivity" show.

28. Gonzalo Aguilar, *Poesia concreta brasileira: as vanguardas na encruzilhada modernista* (São Paulo: Edusp, 2005), 66.

29. For a discussion of the concrete-neoconcrete schism, see chapter 1.

30. Gonzalo Aguilar, "In the White Forest: The Veiled Dialogue between Hélio Oiticica and Haroldo de Campos," trans. Martín Gaspar, in Braga, *Fios soltos*, 251.

31. Haroldo de Campos, "Asa delta para o êxtase," in *Hélio Oiticica*, exh. cat., 217.

32. Ibid.

33. Oiticica, "Hélio Oiticica's Instructions for Cosmococa," 224. In Portuguese, Noh is written *Nô*.

34. See chapters 2 and 3.

35. Haroldo de Campos, "Asa delta para o êxtase," 219.

36. Aguilar, "In the White Forest," 253–356.

37. It is true that Malevich titled one of his paintings *White Planes in Dissolution* (1917–1918). However, it is equally true that Oiticica insistently retained operative tensions and splitting lines in his work, rather than make them simply disappear—the two antagonistic modes of participation of the *Parangolés* (see chapter 3) are a good example of that.

38. Joan Copjec, *Imagine There Is No Woman: Ethics and Sublimation* (Cambridge, MA: MIT Press, 2002), 179.

39. Ibid.

40. Ibid., 190.

41. This was the aim of my discussion, in chapter 2, of the anti-egormorphic thrust of Oiticica's *Meta-esquemas*.

42. Oiticica, "Hélio Oiticica's Instructions for Cosmococa," 224.

43. Hélio Oiticica, "Carta a Waly," unpublished correspondence (Archive of the Projeto Hélio Oiticica, document 0896/74, 1974), 4. It is tempting to think here of Malevich's involvement in *Victory over the Sun*, but, to the best of my knowledge, there is no evidence that Oiticica had any knowledge of this episode.

44. For a further discussion of this line, see Braga, "A trama da terra que treme," 64–67.

45. Ibid., 65.

46. Oiticica, "Carta a Waly," 3.

47. In keeping with Aguilar, Braga prefers to read it instead as a "pause that covers and reveals, simultaneous existence of two intensities." See Braga, "A trama da terra que treme," 65.

48. Joseph, "White on White," 113–117.

49. Ibid., 113.

50. Ibid., 115.

51. Ibid., 109.

52. Michael Asbury, "Hélio Couldn't Dance," in Braga, *Fios soltos*, 52–65.

53. Friederich Nietzsche, *Thus Spoke Zarathustra: A Book for Everyone and Nobody*, trans. Graham Parkes (Oxford: Oxford University Press, 2005), 68.

54. Ibid., 13.

55. As Deleuze emphasizes, "The eternal return is thus an answer to the problem of *passage*.... We misinterpret the expression 'eternal return' if we understand it as 'return of the same.'" See Gilles Deleuze, *Nietzsche and Philosophy*, trans. Hugh Tomlinson (New York: Columbia University Press, 1983), 48.

56. Alenka Zupančič, *The Shortest Shadow: Nietzsche's Philosophy of the Two* (Cambridge, MA: MIT Press, 2003), 19.

57. "The 'end' is not conclusive, but inaugural; it inaugurates the very split that leads to it." Ibid., 19–25.

58. Oiticica, "Hélio Oiticica's Instructions for Cosmococa," 224. See figure 5.4.

59. Even given white understood as synthesis, Oiticica had earlier stressed that different whites "confront each other, unlike 'gray neutrality'" (a rejection that underlines how distant Oiticica was from any idea of mediation). Oiticica, "Color, Time and Structure," 34.

60. Robert Rauschenberg in "The Art of Assemblage: A Symposium," as quoted in Joseph, "White on White," 113. Cage made similar statements regarding the impossibility of criticism.

61. Zupančič, *The Shortest Shadow*, 98.

62. Deleuze, *Nietzsche and Philosophy*, 26.

63. Joseph, "White on White," 121.

64. Joseph notes elsewhere that Rauschenberg's silkscreens shift this conception and introduce negativity as an internal split in the image. It is important, then, that the silkscreens would offer a correction to the political problem I describe. See Branden W. Joseph, "A Duplication Containing Duplications," in *Robert Rauschenberg*, ed. Branden W. Joseph (Cambridge, MA: MIT Press, 2002), 133–160.

65. Paulo Herkenhoff, "Monochromes, the Autonomy of Color and the Centerless World," in *XXIV Bienal de São Paulo—núcleo histórico: antropofagia e histórias de canibalismos*, exh. cat., trans. Veronica Cordeiro (São Paulo: Fundação Bienal de São Paulo, 1998), 201.

66. Hélio Oiticica, "General Scheme of the New Objectivity," in *Hélio Oiticica*, exh. cat., 111. For Herkenhoff, in the Latin American context the "knowledge of art history is imperative for choosing the points of insertion and rupture in the common ground of western culture." Herkenhoff, "Monochromes," 200.

67. Zupančič, *The Shortest Shadow*, 10.

68. Ibid., 133–147; see also Deleuze, *Nietzsche and Philosophy*, 72.

69. For a brief, specific approach of Oiticica's London writings, see Stephen Berg, "On the Bridge, Looking down from Olympus: Notes on the Prose Poems of Hélio Oiticica," in *Oiticica in London*, ed. Guy Brett and Luciano Figueiredo (London: Tate Publishing, 2007), 74.

70. Hélio Oiticica, "Carta para Nelson Motta," unpublished correspondence (Archive of the Projeto Hélio Oiticica, document 0994/69, 1969), 3.

71. Stephen Berg informs that, according to the *Princeton Encyclopedia of Poetry and Poetics*, an *auto* is originally a medieval genre of drama that became eventually associated with "religious plays that recorded the miracle of transubstantiation." The word is indeed recurrent in the history of theater in colonial Brazil, as Oiticica certainly knew. Considering that soon after explaining the *autos* Oiticica states that he liked to write them with "ambivalent" language, it is quite likely that the very title was a first case in point here and that he had an ironic reference to that "miraculous" universe in mind while simultaneously speaking of the self-construction of his artistic position. See Berg, "On the Bridge," 74.

72. Coelho, *Livro ou livro-me*, 125, my translation.

73. Ibid., 125–126.

74. Or, to put it in Zupančič's terms, it is a matter of "one becoming two" (not one plus another, but one split by self-difference).

75. Vladimir Safatle, "Uma clínica do sensível: a respeito da relação entre destituição subjetiva e primado do objeto," *Interações* 10, no. 19 (January-June 2005): 144.

225

76. Hélio Oiticica, "NTBK 2/73," unpublished manuscript (Archive of the Projeto Hélio Oiticica, document 0189/73, 1973), 6.

77. Friederich Nietzsche, *On the Genealogy of Morals and Ecce Homo*, trans. Walter Kaufman (New York: Vintage, 1989), 328, my emphasis.

78. Oiticica, "Drop by Drop Notes," 361.

6 CODA: RADICAL PRESENT

1. Walter Benjamin, *Selected Writings*, vol. 3, ed. Howard Eiland and Michael W. Jennings, trans. Edmund Jephcott, Howard Eiland, et al. (Cambridge, MA: Harvard University Press, 2002), 262.

2. Hélio Oiticica, *Aspiro ao grande labirinto*, ed. Luciano Figueiredo, Lygia Pape, and Waly Salomão (Rio de Janeiro: Rocco, 1986), 18. In the original: "É preciso que o homem se estruture." This passage has been translated recently as "Man must find a sense of structure." However, I think this translation loses the sense of self-reflexivity that informs Oiticica's text. See Hélio Oiticica, *Hélio Oiticica: Painting beyond the Frame*, ed. Luciano Figueiredo, trans. Stephen Berg (Rio de Janeiro: Silvia Roesler Edições de Arte, 2008), 78.

3. In a similar vein, Georges Didi-Huberman states that the dominance of iconology over the discipline of art history has "delivered up all images to the tyranny of the concept, of definition, and, ultimately, of the nameable and the legible: the legible understood as a synthetic, iconological operation, whereby invisible 'themes,' invisible 'general and essential tendencies of the human mind' — invisible concepts or Ideas—are 'translated' into the realm of the visible." Georges Didi-Huberman, *Confronting Images: Questioning the Ends of a Certain History of Art*, trans. John Goodman (University Park: Pennsylvania State University Press, 2005), 122.

4. See note 6 of the introduction and also chapter 3.

5. Renata Lucas in conversation with Adriano Pedrosa, "Interview with Renata Lucas," trans. Alberto Dwek, in *Renata Lucas*, exh. cat. (Los Angeles: California Institute of the Arts/REDCAT, 2007), 72.

6. Renatas Lucas, as quoted in Lynn Zelevansky, "Soft Clay: Renata Lucas and Brazil's Artistic Legacy," in *Renata Lucas*, exh. cat., 34.

7. Hélio Oiticica, "Brazil Diarrhea," in *Hélio Oiticica*, exh. cat., trans. Stephen Berg et al. (Rio de Janeiro: Centro de Arte Hélio Oiticica, 1992), 18.

8. Zelevansky, "Soft Clay," 34.

9. Cildo Meireles, "Cruzeiro do sul, 1969–70," in *Cildo Meireles*, ed. Guy Brett (London: Tate Publishing, 2008), 58.

10. While this statement, which I discussed in chapter 4, speaks of a mythic land named "Southern Cross," the homonymous work was not shown in "Information."

11. Cildo Meireles, "Untitled," in *Information*, ed. Kynaston McShine (New York: Museum of Modern Art, 1970), 85.

12. Chus Martínez, "Renata Lucas," *Artforum* 47, no. 10 (Summer 2009): 313.

13. Ibid., 315.

14. Ibid.

15. Ibid.

16. Slavoj Žižek, *Living in the End Times* (London: Verso, 2010), 334. Elsewhere, Žižek further pursues this insight by arguing, "One can thus categorically assert the existence of ideology *qua* generative matrix that regulates the relationship between visible and non-visible, between imaginable and non-imaginable, as well as the changes in this relationship." See Slavoj Žižek, "The Spectre of Ideology," in *Mapping Ideology*, ed. Slavoj Žižek (London: Verso, 1994), 94.

17. Žižek, *Living in the End Times*, 1.

18. Mladen Dolar, "'I Shall Be with You on Your Wedding-Night': Lacan and the Uncanny," *October* 58 (Autumn 1991): 19.

19. Ibid., 19–20.

20. Ibid., 14.

21. Cildo Meireles, "Renata Lucas," *Época*, no. 603 (December 5, 2009), 110.

22. Zelevansky, "Soft Clay," 46.

23. This description can be found at the website of Instituto Tomie Ohtake, http://www.institutoto mieohtake.org.br/inicio/teinicio.htm (last accessed July 31, 2012).

24. Renata Lucas, portfolio of the artist, unpublished.

227

Index

Page numbers in italics represent illustrations.

Aguilar, Gonzalo, 34, 168, 170
AI-5. *See* Institutional Act no. 5
AICA (International Association of Art Critics)
    congress, 89
Albers, Josef, 61
Althusser, Louis, 145
Alves, José Francisco, 43
Andrade, Joaquim Pedro de, 95, 98–99
Andrade, Oswald de, 51, 63–64, 167
    anthropophagy, 51, 63–64, 72, 76, 78, 168
Arantes, Otília, 23, 25
Art & Language, 128
Artaud, Antonin, 111
Asbury, Michael, 3–5, 17–18, 41, 54, 175

Barata, Mário, 128
Barr, Alfred H., Jr., 3–4
Barthes, Roland, 106
Bataille, Georges, 100
Belluzo, Ana Maria, 30
Benjamin, Walter, 76, 145, 158, 183, 185, 194
Bense, Max, 202n56
Benveniste, Émile, 99
Bergson, Henri, 173
Bill, Max, 61, 89
Boccioni, Umberto, 61
Boghici, Jean, 103
Bois, Yve-Alain, 54–55, 57, 208n27
Borges, Jorge Luis, 72, 150
Borges, Miguel, 98
Braga, Paula, 166, 173
Brancusi, Constantin, 40, 61
Brasília, 27, 62, 71–72, 82, 87–89, 91, 95–96, 119,
    122, 138
    Pilot Plan (Plano-Piloto), 89–91, 95
Brett, Guy, 1, 7, 70
Bretton Woods agreement, 152
Brito, Ronaldo, 12, 21–22, 26–27, 48, 128, 158,
    200n5, 201n13, 204n76
Buchloh, Benjamin H. D., 3, 5, 106–107
Bürger, Peter, 2–3, 5

Cage, John, 13, 163–167, 171, 173, 175–177, 179
Calder, Alexander, 61
Campofiorito, Quirino, 24
Campos, Augusto de, 31, 34, 48, 168, 171
    Ovonovelo (1956), 34, *36–37*
    Psiu! (1965), *169*
    Tensão (1956), 34, *37*
Campos, Haroldo de, 3, 31, 34–35, 45, 48, 90,
    168–171, 175, 178
Cara de Cavalo, 73, 100, 109, 111, 217n98
Caragol, Taina, 7–8
Carroll, Lewis, 139

"The Hunting of the Snark," 139, *143*, 145,
    149–150
Castro, Amilcar de, 12, 14, 43, 45–48, 67, 90, 194,
    204n87, 205n96, 205n105
    preparatory drawing, *44*
    Untitled (early 1960s), *42*
Centro Cultural Tomie Ohtake, 191
César (sculptor), 113
Cinema Novo, 98, 104
Clark, Lygia, 6, 12, 14, 17–21, 43, 57, 61, 122,
    166–167, 185–186, 194, 200n7
    Bichos, *20*, 21, 43, 186–187, 200n10
    Cocoons, 43
    Counter-Reliefs, 21, *22*, 43, 200n10
    Modulated Spaces (1958–1959), 57
    Unities (1958), 57, *58*
Coelho, Frederico, 178
Colomina, Beatriz, 9
Copjec, Joan, 46, 67, 165, 170
Cordeiro, Waldemar, 18–19, 24–27, 30–31, 35
    Untitled (1958), *18*
    Visible Idea, 27
Corman, Roger, 138
Costa, Lúcio, 71–72, 89–90
CPC. *See* Popular Center of Culture

D'Almeida, Neville, 163
Degand, Léon, 23
Deleuze, Gilles, 175–176
Dias, Antonio, 9–14, 82, 86–87, 99, 104, 106–107,
    109, 111, 113, 122–124, 129, 131–133, 135,
    138–139, 145, 158, 186, 194
    Anywhere Is My Land (1968), 9, *10*, 123–124,
        128, 133, 135
    The Art of Transference (1972), *99–101*
    The Desert: Let It Absorb (1970), *133–134*
    Do It Yourself: Freedom Territory (1968),
        124–127
    The Hardest Way (1970), 14, 129–*130*, 131–133,
        145
    History (1968), 145–*146*
    History/Story (1971), 139, *144*
    The Illustration of Art / One & Three /
        Stretchers / Model (1971), 135–*136*, *137*
    My Portrait (1967), 82, *85*, 99–100, 104, 107,
        109
    Notes on an Unforeseen Death (1965), 107,
        109–*110*, 111, 123
    The Occupied Country (1971), 138, *140–141*
    Self-Portrait for the Counterattack (1966),
        82–*83*, 139
    Sun Photo as Self-Portrait (1968), 99–*101*,
        123, 139
Di Cavalcanti, Emiliano, 23–24

Didi-Huberman, Georges, 150, 158, 198n24, 226n3
Doesburg, Theo van, 24
Dolar, Mladen, 132–133, 190, 219n41, 219–220n43, 220n45
Duarte, Paulo Sergio, 2, 8, 107, 128
Duchamp, Marcel, 2–5, 41, 151

Egomorphism, 55, 57, 82, 100, 207n21
Eisenstein, Sergei, 98
Engenho de Dentro psychiatric hospital, 14, 24
Enigmages. See Oiticica, Hélio
Estevam Martins, Carlos, 96–98

Fabbrini, Ricardo, 47
Favaretto, Celso, 61
Fédida, Pierre, 14
Fer, Briony, 55
Fiaminghi, Hermelindo, 19
    Circles with Alternated Movement (1956), 19, 28–29
Figueiredo, Luciano, 69, 78
Five Times Favela (film, 1962), 98
Fontana, Lucio, 61
Fontoura, Antônio Carlos, 82, 87
    Ver ouvir (1966), 81–82, 86–88
Foster, Hal, 2–7, 106, 194
Freud, Sigmund, 2, 14, 46, 63–64
    Nachträglichkeit, 2, 6
Fried, Michael, 19
"From Figurativism to Abstractionism" (exhibition), 23

Gabo, Naum, 61
Gautherot, Marcel, 75, 91, 92, 93, 94, 95
Gerchman, Rubens, 12, 82, 86, 104–107, 111
    Identity Card: Self Right Thumb (1965), 82–83
    Lindonéia—The Gioconda of the Suburbs (1966), 107–108, 109, 111
    Self-Portrait (1968), 82
    Viação Foguete (1965), 105
Gestalt, 12, 14–15, 19, 21–26, 30, 35, 40, 45
Gil, Gilberto, 107
Gorelik, Adrián, 88–90
Goulart, João, 88, 96–97
Gramsci, Antonio, 26
Greenberg, Clement, 3–6
Gris, Juan, 61
Grupo Frente, 18, 71, 96
Gullar, Ferreira, 3, 11–12, 14, 17–19, 21–22, 25, 30–31, 35, 40–41, 43, 45–48, 62–63, 72, 86–87, 90–91, 95–98, 104–107, 109, 111, 113, 166–167, 200n7
    Buried Poem, 35
    "Culture in Question," 96, 98
    "Neoconcrete Manifesto," 19, 41
    Spatial Poems, 35, 38–39, 40
    "Theory of the Non-Object," 12, 17–18, 21, 31, 41, 47–48, 97, 208n23

Habermas, Jürgen, 187, 190
Harvey, David, 152, 159
Hendrix, Jimi, 179
Herkenhoff, Paulo, 104, 119, 128–129, 131, 177
Hirzsman, Leon, 98
Husserl, Edmund, 3

Indiana, Robert, 109
"Information" (exhibition), 13, 138
Institutional Act no. 5 (AI-5), 152
International Monetary Fund (IMF), 152
"Inverted Utopias" (exhibition), 7

Jacques, Paola Berestein, 70
Jameson, Fredric, 145, 149, 150–151, 190, 222n85
Johns, Jasper, 109
Jornal do Brasil. See SDJB
Joseph, Branden W., 165, 173, 177

Kandinsky, Wassily, 61, 166
Klee, Paul, 150
Kosuth, Joseph, 128
Krauss, Rosalind E., 6, 11, 47, 135, 198n25, 219n28, 222n95
Kubitschek, Juscelino, 27, 88–89, 96–97

Lacan, Jacques, 9, 55, 145, 165, 207n21, 219n39
Lecercle, Jean-Jacques, 139, 145, 149
Le Corbusier, 71, 89
Lichtenstein, Roy, 106, 109
Lourenço, Maria Cecília França, 71
Lucas, Renata, 185–187, 190–191, 193–194
    Barulho de Fundo (2004), 191, 192, 193
    Falha (2003), 184, 185–187, 191
    Venice Suitcase (2009), 191
    The Visitor (2007), 191, 193

Machado, Milton, 113
Magalhães, Roberto, 82
Malevich, Kazimir, 13, 164–169, 171, 173, 175–177, 179, 180
    White on White (1917–1918), 161, 163, 165, 167, 171, 173, 176, 180
Mallarmé, Stéphane, 179
Mammì, Lorenzo, 26–27, 30, 91
Manuel, Antonio, 67, 68
Manzoni, Piero, 149
Marker, Chris, 175
Martínez, Chus, 186–187, 190, 193
Matta-Clark, Gordon, 185
Meireles, Cildo, 1, 13, 119, 122, 128, 135, 139, 145, 149–153, 158–159, 185–186, 190, 193–194
    Eureka/Blindhotland (1970–1975), 153, 154–155
    Fontes (1992–2008), 153
    Mission/Missions (1987), 153
    Money Tree (1969), 152
    Physical Art (1969), 148–150
    Red Shift (1967–1984), 128, 153, 156–157, 158–159

230

Southern Cross (1969–1970), 186–*188*, *189*
Tiradentes: Totem-Monument to the Political Prisoner (1970), 119–*120*, *121*–122, 138, 151–152
To Be Curved with the Eyes (1970/1975), 145, *147*
Zero Cruzeiro (1974–1978), 152
Zero Dollar (1978–1984), 152, *153*
Merleau-Ponty, Maurice, 3, 21, 25, 30–31, 35, 46–47, 166, 206n107
Ministry of Education and Health building, 4, 71, 89
Moholy-Nagy, László, 165–166, 170, 173, 176
Mondrian, Piet, 4, 6, 12, 41, 54–55, 57, 60–61, 69, 76, 161, 166–167
Morais, Frederico, 119
Museum of Modern Art, New York (MoMA), 4, 13, 135
Museum of Modern Art, Rio de Janeiro (MAM-RJ), 4, 26, 71, 73, 96, 100, 122, 152
Museum of Modern Art, São Paulo (MAM-SP), 4, 23, 26

"National Exhibition of Concrete Art," 19, 31, 71, 90
Nauman, Bruce, 185
Naves, Rodrigo, 197n6, 205n97
Neoconcretism, 11, 17–19, 21, 30–31, 87, 90–91, 95–97, 166 –168
"New Brazilian Objectivity" (exhibition), 63–64, 71, 73, 106
Niemeyer, Oscar, 71–72, 89, 91
Nietzsche, Friedrich, 63–64, 163, 173, 176–177, 179
Nouveau Réalisme, 106, 111, 123
Nunes, Benedito, 63–64

Oiticica, Hélio, 3, 8, 11–13, 17–18, 43, 48, 51–73, 76–78, 82, 97, 100, 103–104, 106–107, 109, 111, 122–124, 135, 161, 163–171, 173, 175, 177–180, 183, 185–186, 193–194
Bilaterals, 60, 64
Bolides, 67, *68*, 73, 77, 100, 103–104, 107, 109, 111, *124*, 186
"Brazil Diarrhea," 69, 72–73, 78, 97, 185
B33 Box Bolide 18—Poem Box 2 "Homage to Cara de Cavalo" (1966), 73, 77, 100, 104, 107, 109, 111
Cosmococas, 163–*164*, 166, 169, 176, 179, 223n5
CC4 Nocagions (1973), *163*, 169–*174*
CC5 Hendrix-War, 179
Creleisure (Crelazer), 124
Eden (1969), 124, 186–187
enigmages, 13, 123, 131
"General Scheme of the New Objectivity," 51, 63, 82
Inventions, 57, *59*, 60, 64, 208n28
Metaesquemas, 19, 55, *56*, 69, 178
Nuclei, 65, *66*
Parangolés, 3, 54, 70–71, 73, *74*, 78, 100, 103,
109, 168–170
Sêco 27 (1957), 55, *56*, 59
Spatial Reliefs, 57, 60, 64–65
Suprasensorial, 123–124
"The Transition of Color from the Painting into Space and the Meaning of Constructivity," 60–61, 64
Tropicália, 51, *52–53*, 54, 63–65, 67, 69–73, 76, 78, 95, 107, 122–124, 178
White Series (1958–1959), 161–*162*, 166–168
Oldenburg, Claes, 109
Olitski, Jules, 133
"Opinião 65," 71, 103
"Opinião 66," 71

Pacheco Jordão, Vera, 103
Palatnik, Abraham, 24
Pape, Lygia, 82, 170, 175, 185, 194
Pedrosa, Mário, 11, 12, 14–15, 18–19, 21–26, 31, 34, 35, 40–41, 45, 47, 62, 63, 76, 89, 95, 106, 109, 111–*112*, 124, 200n7, 201n35, 205n105
On the Affective Nature of Form (1949/1979), 23–25
Péret, Benjamin, 14
Pevsner, Antoine, 61
Picasso, Pablo, 5, 61
Pignatari, Décio, 31, 34, 48
Pollock, Jackson, 5, 61, 63, 106, 133, 135
Popular Center of Culture (CPC), 96–98, 111, 113
Portinari, Candido, 26
Pound, Ezra, 167–168

Quadros, Jânio, 96

Rauschenberg, Robert, 4, 13, 109, 165, 173, 175–177, 179
Reidy, Affonso Eduardo, 71
Reinhardt, Ad, 138, 139
Ribeiro, Jackson, 70
Rimbaud, Arthur, 173, 175
Rivera, Tânia, 14
Rocha, Glauber, 98
Entranced Land (1967), 98, 100
Rosenquist, James, 109
Ruptura (group), 26
Ruscha, Ed, 109

Sacilotto, Luís, 30, 45–46
Concretion 5942 (1959), 30, *32–33*
Concretion 6045 (1960), 30, *32*
Safatle, Vladimir, 13–14, 178–179
Salomão, Waly, 67, 103
Salzstein, Sônia, 61, 63, 96, 106, 133, 197n6, 205n96, 205n97, 214n41
São Paulo Biennial, 26, 96, 106, 109
Schwarz, Roberto, 215n45, 216n80
Schwitters, Kurt, 61
SDJB (Sunday supplement, Jornal do Brasil), 18, 35, 40, 67, 72, 96, 166

231

Segal, George, 109
Segall, Lasar, 26
Serpa, Ivan, 4, 31, 71
Smithson, Robert, 135, 138–139, 145
  "A Museum of Language in the Vicinity of Art,"
      138–139

Tate Modern, 191
Tatlin, Vladimir, 21
Teatro de Arena, 88
"Transcontinental," 1, 7
Trini, Tommaso, 128
Tropicalism, 51, 54, 104, 106
Tunga (artist), 1

Valéry, Paul, 47
Veloso, Caetano, 107
Venâncio Filho, Paulo, 1–2, 8, 9, 70
Villas Boas, Glaucia, 24

Warhol, Andy, 106–107, 109
Wesselman, Tom, 109, 111
Whitelegg, Isobel, 7–8
Winnicott, Donald, 14
Wisnik, Guilherme, 213n21
Wols (artist), 61

Zelevansky, Lynn, 185–187, 190, 193
Zilio, Carlos, 17, 64, 113–114, 151
    For a Young Man of Brilliant Prospects (1974),
        113–115, 151
    Pieces of Mine (1971), 114, 117
    Self-Portrait Aged 26 (1970), 114, 116
    Unknown Identity (1973), 113–115
Žižek, Slavoj, 76, 97, 190, 211n94, 215n58, 220n46
Zupančič, Alenka, 5–6, 8–9, 175–177, 198n31

232